The WRITING ARC

From Discovery to Presentation

Steve Sansom | Brian H. Kyser
Bruce Martin | Robert Miller

D1517513

FOUNTAINHEAD
PRESS

Fountainhead Press's green initiatives include:

Electronic Products and Samples. Products are delivered in non-paper form whenever possible via Xample, an electronic sampling system. Instructor samples are sent via a personalized web page that links to PDF downloads.

FSC-Certified Printers and Recycled Paper. All of our printers are certified by the Forest Service Council, which promotes environmentally and socially responsible management of the world's forests. This program allows consumer groups, individual consumers, and businesses to work together hand in hand to promote responsible use of the world's forests as a renewable and sustainable resource. Most of our products are printed on a minimum of 30 percent post-consumer waste recycled paper.

Acknowledgments

We wish to thank the publishers and staff of Fountainhead Press for their patience in guiding and assembling this text. Without their assistance, the rationale and design of its contents would not have reached its completion. We wish, too, to thank those students who kindly permitted us to include their works. We also wish to express our gratitude to Michael McFarland for his insightful contributions to this project and to our staff and colleagues for their support and suggestions. Whatever success this text enjoys, we share with these kind folks. Whatever shortcomings it contains are ours alone.

Contents

Student Examples

Appendices

Preface

The construction of any book is fraught with pitfalls. Like any composition or creative work, the writers of this textbook set out to address a very specific audience—freshman college writing students. Our purpose was to ground the student writer in the functional, core principles of writing, even as the assumptions of writing within the academy—whether composition should be taught as an academic, professional, or personal enterprise—have continued to evolve. To decide upon an effective strategy, we surveyed the multitude of pedagogical directions the field has taken, from recent pedagogical theory and the Framework for Success in Post-Secondary Writing of the National Council of Teachers of English to the various permutations our own textbook has experienced over the last several decades. Needless to say, there is a wide variety in the forms and functions of textbooks created for the first-year college writing classroom. After exploring a number of approaches, we determined that student writers would benefit most from a close examination of the writing process itself, learning how to create, structure, and present their own ideas. As a group of authors—rather than a single, authoritative voice—our purpose was to provide a flexible handbook that student writers could mine and apply toward any application.

Changes to the state learning outcomes (Texas Higher Education Coordinating Board) for the first-year writing course drove this change in strategy. Although argument is no longer required, writing arguments is fundamental to many disciplines, so we have included a chapter on both argument and analysis. The focus throughout has shifted to reading in addition to writing because the ability to read professionally written prose essays is necessary to be able to write them. We have also avoided limiting the textbook to the so-called modalities, or to writing the five-paragraph theme, though we refer to these strategies in Chapter 6. At a time when students are emerging from public schools with reduced confidence in their academic abilities, particularly with regard to their ability to express themselves on paper, the focus on process over product strikes us as both necessary and appropriate.

Finally, students are often asked to transfer what they have created into an oral format, so we have included a chapter on presentation, as this fits into state mandates stressing oral and visual communication and merges well into a textbook devoted to the process of crafting effective communication. Presentation skills are in growing demand, both as a component of co-curriculum programs and among institutions that stress writing across the curriculum, so we believe it valuable to address specifically how writers might adapt their work to the oral medium, rather than simply producing a presentation or speech from scratch.

While we created this text partly to address the changes happening in the state of Texas, we also envisioned a much broader applicability nationally, as other colleges and universities across the country face similar issues within their states. We sincerely hope, whether student or instructor, you find this book both useful and comprehensible.

SS
BK
BM
RM

CHAPTER 1

Why Write?

Deciding how to write a composition often misses the point. The how is important, as we will soon discuss, but it should come only after you have answered a more pertinent question: Why should you write in the first place? Whom are you addressing? What is your purpose in addressing that audience? If we think about this problem logically, or even intuitively, we arrive at a fairly obvious conclusion: when we speak to someone, we typically know to whom we are speaking. There is always the assumption of an *audience*. Even when you talk to yourself in the mirror, you have an audience. You are addressing an alter ego, an invisible friend, a projection of a friend or boss you might need to interact with later that day—or perhaps just talking aloud to yourself, trying to convince yourself of a particular course of action, working out an opinion, pulling yourself out of repeated procrastination, or making yourself feel better about a particular relationship.

While the analogy of talking to yourself in the mirror might strike you as awkward, the truth is we spend a great deal of time conversing with ourselves, and we almost always have a purpose when doing so. Knowing the purpose often dictates how we talk, whether we are soft-voiced or firm, impassioned or scolding, informative or analytical. This assumption of an audience when speaking, even to the face in the mirror, is not that different from the assumption of an audience when writing. Like the mirror analogy, our persuasiveness will largely depend on how well we address our audience.

Key differences exist between verbal and written communication. When you speak aloud, you cannot take the words back. While you can rehearse and rehearse and shape the message exactly that you wish to convey, when the time comes to speak to your audience, there are no "take backs" or "redos" unless your audience is particularly understanding—and even then, the effectiveness of your message and the audience's impression of you as a speaker may be affected by your inability to express your intentions in a clear and competent manner. Writing lacks some of the communication possibilities of conversation: we can't use nonverbal methods, such as hand gestures, facial expressions, or body language, and we are not able to raise or lower our voices. Yet writing encompasses many attributes of the spoken word while also providing the benefits of careful and conscious planning and pruning.

Because written communication is often a slow, meticulous process rather than a one-shot performance, writing also serves as a form of exploration. Once you begin to see writing as a method for finding and conveying ideas and developing solutions to complex problems, then you begin to see your compositions as part of a greater process of creation, re-creation, and fine-tuning an idea or message. Instead of talking to the face in the mirror, you might instead prepare a written explanation in the form of an email, blog post, or essay. When doing so, you are engaging in a *recursive* process—a process you can repeat many times over—a process that, practiced enough times, helps you to discover how best to communicate (Figure 1.1).

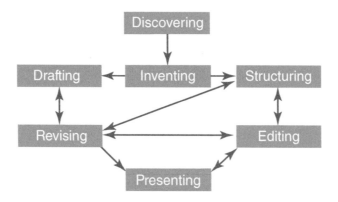

Figure 1.1: The Writing Process

Purpose

There is no such thing as writing (or communicating) without a purpose. Ask yourself: what would communicating without purpose even look or sound like? Perhaps an appropriate analogy would be to travel without knowing your destination. Even when you walk out the door with no specific destination in mind, your goal is to wander—which is itself a purpose.

Consider how this translates to writing. Many beginning writers think they can tell stories about themselves or their friends, but they are at a loss when it comes to crafting the elements necessary to shape an essay or an informative article. Yet even if your purpose is simply to entertain through a narrative or a blog posting, there is a good chance your intention is also to inform via the same story. Thus, understanding your writing objective, your purpose, will help you shape your message.

The concept of "academic writing" is often misunderstood. Many student writers have ill-formed preconceptions about what makes a good essay. Whether these notions spill over from high school or are a result of our standardized test-taking culture, often the result is that the student spends an excessive amount of time trying to express *the* right answer. For the student, the audience is often that single intellect, the instructor, who enforces the right answer, the grammatically correct answer, ignoring the multitude of other possible answers. Sadly, this expectation crushes the idea that writing should be an exploration—that through description and analysis we can create new interpretations, new insights, and thus new knowledge. This concept of writing for the right answer greatly oversimplifies what writing is all about.

Academic writing is, and should be, an exploration, a reinvention of experience into fresh knowledge; it is an organized method for writing about ideas and sharing them with an audience in a clear and concise manner. Your purpose should always be intrinsic to the writing itself, whether you are seeking to inform, compare, or analyze an issue of interest to yourself or to the world at large.

Consider the following example: Two of your classmates have asked you to read their papers. The first paper is a perfectly executed five-paragraph essay on a trivial topic while the second is a multiparagraph article analyzing a relevant dilemma in your community. Assuming both of your classmates' compositions are clearly written and concise, which paper would you prefer to read?

Just as it is dangerous to use the words "never" or "always," it is not a good practice to consider writing as content-free. You are always writing about something, and a writer always endeavors to inform her reader about that something—that is the writer's purpose. While finding your purpose, what some call a topic, is not always easy, you know about and are interested in a lot of things that can become subjects for writing assignments. For example, starting with yourself, consider the following connections you make with the world around you.

> Local. The persons, places, and issues affecting you every day within your family, community, school, city, county, and state.

Global. The persons, places, and issues that may not affect you every day but that have profound implications for you as you grow up in an increasingly connected global village.

Cultural. The persons, places, and issues that involve you in the densely packed, modern, technologically driven worlds of music, art, sports, religion, and social networks.

Furthermore, what you write about will, to a great extent, dictate the way you write—the way you will structure and develop your topic. Consider the following three most common purposes for writing about a topic in a college composition classroom (Figure 1.2).

To describe or inform. Strong writing, first and foremost, attempts to inform, either through description, illustration and example, narration, or classification.

To compare and contrast. We use comparison and contrast every day as we make decisions about all sorts of things, such as which phone to buy, which instructor to take, or who the greatest soccer star is. It is also a powerful writing method that allows us to express in sharp detail the similarities and differences between any two objects or ideas and thus help our audience to understand both with greater clarity.

To analyze. To really understand anything, whether it is how to set up our new iPad, how to solve an equation in algebra, or how to get along with the opposite sex, we must study it in detail; we must analyze it. Through critically evaluating a topic, writers can draw inferences and meaning from events, speeches, texts, other forms of communication, such as television, books, and digital media, and even the language used by our peers.

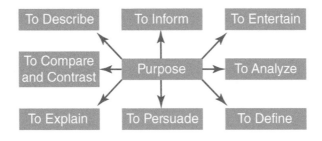

Figure 1.2: Purposes for Writing

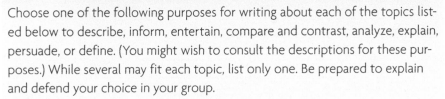

Activity 1.1

Choose one of the following purposes for writing about each of the topics listed below to describe, inform, entertain, compare and contrast, analyze, explain, persuade, or define. (You might wish to consult the descriptions for these purposes.) While several may fit each topic, list only one. Be prepared to explain and defend your choice in your group.

Pets	Vacations
Football	Phones
Bullying	Dreams
Mistakes	Jobs
Professors	Climate Change

Audience

Effective writing always presupposes an audience. To whom are you writing? There is no writing to the empty room or for posterity. Recalling our earlier example, even when rehearsing in front of the mirror, you are addressing a very specific someone, imagined or real. Whether writing an assignment for your instructor, composing a blog post, or an article for broad consumption, you should imagine your audience as an intelligent, open-minded group of people interested in the world, curious and respectful of a certain decorum and precision, moral in substance, and willing to learn about new ideas and experiences. Given these qualities, a writer needs to write competently, convincingly, and without error or distraction.

Obviously, this general audience description should serve only as a starting point. Should you choose to compose for a more specific audience, say a readership composed of diehard comic book fans, a conference of musicians, or a mainstream magazine for software engineers, you would need to adjust your tone and use of jargon (technical terminology) so these readers will accept your credibility and will be able to relate to you.

Activity 1.2

Write a short paragraph describing the intended audience for each of the following topics. Discuss these in your group.

Taylor Swift	Sexual Assault on College Campuses
Panera Bread	Animal Liberation
Apple Watch	Homelessness
Recycling	Freshman English

Voice

Every speaker embodies a voice she uses when speaking with others. Many factors central to the speaker can influence her voice—gender, ethnic background, upbringing, and education, for example. Also, the situation we are in and our mood affect our voice; we sound different when we are happy, sad, angry, or being reprimanded by a parent or a boss. Finally, we can consciously assume different attitudes and tones of voice. Thus, we have many different methods, or registers, available to us when we speak. The same is true when we write. We can assume an objective, lawyer-like tone; we can write derisively, humorously, ironically, or angrily; we can write eloquently or bluntly.

The truth is, when we speak or write, we generally assume the voice to which we feel our audience will best respond. When you speak to your employer, for instance, you might focus on a respectful, contained tone so as not to break employer-employee etiquette. When speaking with a group of friends your own age, however, you will probably incorporate more intimate colloquial terms and even slang phrases. When telling a story or sharing a personal experience, you might evoke a more familiar, casual tone.

The English language, for all of its grammatical rules and definitions, is an elastic language, capable of great reconfiguration and adjustment. It can handle the incorporation of words from other languages as well as new words. The idea that only one voice should be used for all of your writing runs contrary to logic and creative practice. Take a look at these two examples.

Family structure and interaction assume cardinal functions in the social control theories and delinquency. However, myriad factors are assimilated with family configuration and criminal behavior and consequently folk's relations and felony. Akers R.L. (1998). Family interface dynamics include: management and control, character prop up, compassionate and dependence cherished communiqué, influential communication, parental condemnation of peers and variance; these factors have the equivalent upshots on crime in both-parents. Akers, R. L. (1998). "Family Social Control." *Sociology*. UK Essays. Web. 9 Dec. 2014.

¿ Comó empezo everything? How did I stumble upon it? Walking the streets of El Barrio in New York City, at least initially. Wandering around, as the Mexican expression puts it, con la oreja al vuelo, with ears wide open. Later on, of course, my appreciation for Spanglish evolved dramatically as I traveled around los Unaited Esteits. But at the beginning was New York. It always is, isn't it? *Spanglish: The Making of a New American Language*. Ilan Stavans. 2003.

The first example is typical of what we might expect from an academic essay, but is the second example any less valuable because it incorporates Spanish words? Consider how both of these essays seek to inform the reader about similar issues. Is one more or less effective than the other? Do these voices address different audiences?

This concept of changing our voice to match a given audience has many names— code-switching, variation, using different registers—but in the end, it is an important feature of all written communication. Once you have chosen your purpose and your audience, you must choose the voice you think will be the most appropriate for that situation.

Activity 1.3

Read the following paragraphs, and then write a short description of the voice you hear in each. Discuss with your group. You might first want to look at Understanding Voice and Tone in Writing, by Julie Wildhaber, on the Grammar Girl site, Quick and Dirty Tips. (Google it.) Paragraph A below is taken from Gloria E. Anzaldúa's "How to Tame a Wild Tongue" (see page 299 for the complete essay). Paragraph B is taken from E. O. Wilson's "Why Humans, Like Ants, Need a Tribe" (see page 181 for the complete essay).

A. As a culture, we call ourselves Spanish when referring to ourselves as a linguistic group. It is then that we forget our predominant Indian genes. We are 70-80 percent Indian. We call ourselves Hispanic or Spanish-American or Latin American or Latin when linking ourselves to other Spanish-speaking peoples of the Western hemisphere and when copping out. We call ourselves Mexican-American to signify we are neither Mexican nor American, but more the noun "American" than the adjective "Mexican."

B.   Any excuse for a real war will do, so long as it is seen as necessary to protect the tribe. The remembrance of past horrors has no effect. It should not be thought that war, often accompanied by genocide, is a cultural artifact of a few societies. Nor has it been an aberration of history, a result of the growing pains of our species' maturation. Wars and genocide have been universal and eternal, respecting no particular time or culture. Overall, big wars have been replaced around the world by small wars of the kind and magnitude more typical of hunter-gatherer and agricultural societies. Some societies have tried to eliminate torture, execution, and the murder of civilians, but those fighting smaller wars do not comply.

Structure

Finally, once you have found the purpose for your writing project and directed it, with the right voice, to the chosen audience, you can engage in the process of finding the proper form for your words. Because the structure of your writing comes directly from the process of discovery and exploration, the majority of this textbook seeks to create a walk-through of this process, examining as best as we can the variety of shapes and delivery methods for your own ideas. Even if you feel you are writing the "same old thing" others have written about before, by engaging in this process and by permitting yourself—empowering yourself—to have a say, you are leaving the door open for a fresh exploration of the idea from which you may potentially draw conclusions in a profoundly new way.

Final Word

Before crossing the threshold into the chapters that follow, envision yourself as a professional writer. What do professional writers look like? More importantly, how do they behave? As you read this textbook, embrace this opportunity of exploring your own world and the various worlds around you through writing. Your job in this class is to embrace the craft of writing, to take it seriously, and to learn strategies other successful writers have employed before you. Consider the examples on the next page.

Write in a journal. Obtain a small notebook, and write in it every day, or, alternatively, write on your laptop, or tablet, or even a small pad of paper you keep in your backpack. Pour ideas into it. You may at first start putting formless thoughts or feelings into this journal, or you might choose to focus on issues concerning you, such as observations (written sketches) about your community, friends, family, or work setting. These ideas may eventually provide the foundation for serious writing projects. Movies abound with images of writers, thinkers, or inventors scribbling onto scraps of paper, fearful of losing the momentary magic of their thoughts. As chaotic as this might seem, it is sound practice.

Schedule time to write. Make a point to schedule periods of time each day when you do nothing but write. It is important to practice your new craft every day. There is no such thing, after all, as the gifted savant who does not need to work hard at his profession. Do not attempt to be "the natural" who is not concerned with process, only the final product. Start with a structured journal-writing time. While you can jot down an idea that creeps unexpectedly upon you in your notepad, that moment cannot take the place of the time you need to develop it in a more disciplined way.

Find an appropriate place to write. At first, you might practice writing in different places and environments, and take note of how the place affects your productivity. Some writers must have complete silence when they write and retreat to the seclusion of their study. Others cannot stand complete silence, so they choose a place to write where they can listen to music. Still others need a sense of community and so go to libraries or coffee shops to write. Find the place most conducive to your own inner writer.

Be alert and interested. It is far too easy to become lost in your own mind, cycling over the week's events or some random triviality. Flip the lens outward. Take pleasure in the larger world—whether through people-watching, direct interaction with others, or by simply keeping up to date on the news with what is happening locally and globally. It is hard to write when you are self-contained. Curiosity is a key ingredient of the best writing.

Turn off the perfectionist. Many writers never succeed at blossoming because their inner editor emerges to stifle creativity. The perfectionist is often never satisfied with what he sees on the page and, as a result, never develops it. If this textbook attempts to achieve one thing, it is to impress upon you the notion that communication, writing in particular, is a process of discovery and exploration. At times, as with all processes—such as baking a cake—it will be messy.

When you write, you subscribe to the idea that new knowledge can be created and that you can play a role in its discovery. More importantly, by writing you also suggest these ideas are worth sharing with the world, and through the power of language you may convey these ideas to others in unique and hitherto unimagined ways. Finally, through the act of writing you can transform yourself, expanding the possibilities of what you can become.

Why I Write

George Orwell

George Orwell (1903-1950) was the pen name of Eric Arthur Blair. He was born in British-controlled India and served as an imperial policeman in Burma between 1924 and 1927. After returning to England because of an illness, he decided to abandon his position and become a writer. He described his experiences in *Burmese Days* (1934) and the essay "Shooting an Elephant" (1936), which explains his growing disgust with the injustice of the British imperial system. He is known today for his novels and satires, primarily the political allegory *Animal Farm* (1945) and the dystopian novel *1984* (1949). He was also keenly aware of the connections between language manipulation and authoritarian rule, which he analyzed in his essay "Politics and the English Language" (1946).

In this essay, Orwell explores his own urge to write, to put his experiences on paper and create meaning out of them. He discusses his early desire to be a writer and how he was influenced by the ambience of his age and position and the literature popular at the time. As he grew and developed, his purpose and audience changed, from his rather flippant satires as a student and his later desire to record the reality of his life to his growing concern with injustice and politics. He describes how he found his voice as a writer and why, while continuing to be concerned with language and the artistry of writing, he could not conceive of writing, at least in the time he lived, without a political purpose.

From a very early age, perhaps the age of five or six, I knew that when I grew up I should be a writer. Between the ages of about seventeen and twenty-four I tried to abandon this idea, but I did so with the consciousness that I was outraging my true nature and that sooner or later I should have to settle down and write books.

I was the middle child of three, but there was a gap of five years on either side, and I barely saw my father before I was eight. For this and other reasons I was somewhat lonely, and I soon developed disagreeable mannerisms which made me unpopular throughout my schooldays. I had the lonely child's habit of making up stories and holding conversations with imaginary persons, and I think from the very start my literary ambitions were mixed up with the feeling of being isolated and undervalued. I knew that I had a facility with words and a power of facing unpleasant facts, and I felt that this created a sort of private world in which I could get my own back for my failure in everyday life. Nevertheless the volume of serious—i.e. seriously intended—writing which I produced all through my childhood and boyhood would not amount to half a dozen pages. I wrote my first poem at the age of four or five, my mother taking it down to dictation. I cannot remember anything about it except that it was about a tiger and the tiger had "chair-like teeth"—a good enough phrase, but I fancy the poem was a plagiarism of Blake's "Tiger, Tiger." At eleven, when the war of 1914-18 broke out, I wrote a patriotic poem which was printed in the local newspaper, as was another, two years later, on the death of Kitchener. From time to time, when I was a bit older, I wrote bad and usually unfinished "nature poems" in the Georgian style. I also, about twice, attempted a short story which was a ghastly failure. That was the total of the would-be serious work that I actually set down on paper during all those years.

However, throughout this time I did in a sense engage in literary activities. To begin with there was the made-to-order stuff which I produced quickly, easily and without much pleasure to myself. Apart from school work, I wrote *vers d'occasion*, semi-comic poems which I could turn out at what now seems to me astonishing speed—at fourteen I wrote a whole rhyming play, in imitation of Aristophanes, in about a week—and helped to edit school magazines, both printed and in manuscript. These magazines were the most pitiful burlesque stuff that you could imagine, and I took far less trouble with them than I now would with the cheapest journalism. But side by side with all this, for fifteen years or more, I was carrying out a literary exercise of a quite different kind: this was the making up of a continuous "story" about myself, a sort of diary existing only in the mind. I believe this is a common habit of children and adolescents. As a very small child I used to imagine that I was, say, Robin Hood, and picture myself as the hero of thrilling adventures, but quite soon my "story" ceased to be narcissistic in a crude way and became more and more a mere description of what I was doing and the things I saw. For minutes at a time this kind of thing would be running through my head: "He pushed the door open and entered the room. A yellow beam of sunlight, filtering through the muslin curtains, slanted on to the table, where a match-box, half open, lay beside the inkpot. With his right hand in his pocket he moved across to the window. Down in the street a tortoiseshell cat was chasing a dead leaf," etc. etc. This habit continued till I was about twenty-five, right through my non-literary years. Although I had to search, and did search, for the right words, I seemed to be making this descriptive effort almost against my will, under a kind of compulsion from outside. The "story" must, I suppose, have reflected the styles of the various writers I admired at different ages, but so far as I remember it always had the same meticulous descriptive quality.

When I was about sixteen I suddenly discovered the joy of mere words, i.e. the sounds and associations of words. The lines from *Paradise Lost*,

> *So hee with difficulty and labour hard*
> *Moved on: with difficulty and labour hee.*

which do not now seem to me so very wonderful, sent shivers down my back-bone; and the spelling "hee" for "he" was an added pleasure. As for the need to describe things, I knew all about it already. So it is clear what kind of books I wanted to write, in so far as I could be said to want to write books at that time. I wanted to write enormous naturalistic novels with unhappy endings, full of detailed descriptions and arresting similes, and also full of purple passages in which words were used partly for the sake of their sound. And in fact my first completed novel, *Burmese Days*, which I wrote when I was thirty but projected much earlier, is rather that kind of book.

I give all this background information because I do not think one can assess a writer's motives without knowing something of his early development. His subject matter will be determined by the age he lives in—at least this is true in tumultuous, revolutionary ages like our own—but before he ever begins to write he will have acquired an emotional attitude from which he will never completely escape. It is his job, no doubt, to discipline his temperament and avoid getting stuck at some immature stage, or in some perverse mood; but if he escapes from his early influences altogether, he will have killed his impulse to write. Putting aside the need to earn a living, I think there are four great motives for writing, at any rate for writing prose. They exist in different degrees in every writer, and in any one writer the proportions will vary from time to time, according to the atmosphere in which he is living. They are:

1. Sheer egoism. Desire to seem clever, to be talked about, to be remembered after death, to get your own back on the grown-ups who snubbed you in childhood, etc., etc. It is humbug to pretend this is not a motive, and a strong one. Writers share this characteristic with scientists, artists, politicians, lawyers, soldiers, successful businessmen—in short, with the whole top crust of humanity. The great mass of human beings are not acutely selfish. After the age of about thirty they abandon individual ambitions, in many cases, indeed, they almost abandon the sense of being individuals at all—and live chiefly for others, or are simply smothered under drudgery. But there is also the minority of gifted, witful people who are determined to live their own lives to the end, and writers belong in this class. Serious writers, I should say, are on the whole more vain and self-centered than journalists, though less interested in money.

2. Aesthetic enthusiasm. Perception of beauty in the external world, or, on the other hand, in words and their right arrangement. Pleasure in the impact of one sound on another, in the firmness of good prose or the rhythm of a good story. Desire to share an experience which one feels is valuable and ought not to be missed. The aesthetic motive is very feeble in a lot of writers, but even a pamphleteer or writer of textbooks will have pet words and phrases which appeal to him for non-utilitarian reasons; or he may feel strongly about typography, width of margins, etc. Above the level of a railway guide, no book is quite free from aesthetic considerations.

3. Historical impulse. Desire to see things as they are, to find out true facts and store them up for the use of posterity.

4. Political purpose. Using the word "political" in the widest possible sense. Desire to push the world in a certain direction, to alter other people's idea of the kind of society that they should strive after. Once again, no book is genuinely free from political bias. The opinion that art should have nothing to do with politics is itself a political attitude.

It can be seen how these various impulses must war against one another, and how they must fluctuate from person to person and from time to time. By nature—taking your "nature" to be the state you have attained when you are first adult—I am a person in whom the first three motives would outweigh the fourth. In a peaceful age I might have written ornate or merely descriptive books, and might have remained almost unaware of my political loyalties. As it is I have been forced into becoming a sort of pamphleteer. First I spent five years in an unsuitable profession (the Indian Imperial Police, in Burma), and then I underwent poverty and the sense of failure. This increased my natural hatred of authority and made me for the first time fully aware of the existence of the working classes, and the job in Burma had given me some understanding of the nature of imperialism: but these experiences were not enough to give me an accurate political orientation. Then came Hitler, the Spanish civil war, etc. By the end of 1935 I had still failed to reach a firm decision. I remember a little poem that I wrote at that date, expressing my dilemma:

A happy vicar I might have been
Two hundred years ago,
To preach upon eternal doom
And watch my walnuts grow;

But born, alas, in an evil time,
I missed that pleasant haven,
For the hair has grown on my upper lip
And the clergy are all clean-shaven.

And later still the times were good,
We were so easy to please,
We rocked our troubled thoughts to sleep
On the bosoms of the trees.
All ignorant we dared to own
The joys we now dissemble;
The greenfinch on the apple bough
Could make my enemies tremble.

But girls' bellies and apricots,
Roach in a shaded stream.
Horses, ducks in flight at dawn,
All these are a dream.

It is forbidden to dream again;
We maim our joys or hide them;
Horses are made of chromium steel
And little fat men shall ride them.

I am the worm who never turned,
The eunuch without a harem;
Between the priest and the commissar
I walk like Eugene Aram;

And the commissar is telling my fortune
While the radio plays,
But the priest has promised an Austin Seven,
For Duggie always pays.

I dreamt I dwelt in marble halls,
And woke to find it true;
I wasn't born for an age like this;
Was Smith? Was Jones? Were you?

The Spanish war and other events in 1936–37 turned the scale and thereafter I knew where I stood. Every line of serious work that I have written since 1936 has been written, directly or indirectly, *against* totalitarianism and *for* democratic Socialism, as I understand it. It seems to me nonsense in a period like our own, to think that one can avoid writing of such subjects. Everyone writes of them in one guise or another. It is simply a question of which side one takes and what approach one follows. And the more one is conscious of one's political bias, the more chance one has of acting politically without sacrificing one's aesthetic and intellectual integrity.

What I have most wanted to do throughout the past ten years is to make political writing into an art. My starting point is always a feeling of partisanship, a sense of injustice. When I sit down to write a book, I do not say to myself, "I am going to produce a work of art." I write it because there is some lie that I want to expose, some fact to which I want to draw attention, and my initial concern is to get a hearing. But I could not do the work of writing a book, or even a long magazine article, if it were not also an aesthetic experience. Anyone who cares to examine my work will see that even when it is downright propaganda it contains much that a full-time politician would consider irrelevant. I am not able, and I do not want, completely to abandon the world-view that I acquired in childhood. So long as I remain alive and well I shall continue to feel strongly about prose style, to love the surface of the earth, and to take pleasure in solid objects and scraps of useless information. It is no use trying to suppress that side of myself. The job is to reconcile my ingrained likes and dislikes with the essentially public, non-individual activities that this age forces on all of us.

It is not easy. It raises problems of construction and of language, and it raises in a new way the problem of truthfulness. Let me give just one example of the cruder kind of difficulty that arises. My book about the Spanish civil war, *Homage to Catalonia*, is, of course, a frankly political book, but in the main it is written with a certain detachment and regard for form. I did try very hard in it to tell the whole truth without violating my literary instincts. But among other things it contains a long chapter, full of newspaper quotations and the like, defending the Trotskyists who were accused of plotting with Franco. Clearly such a chapter, which after a year or two would lose its interest for any ordinary reader, must ruin the book. A critic whom I respect read me a lecture about it. "Why did you put in all that stuff?" he said. "You've turned what might have been a good book into journalism." What he said was true, but I could not have done otherwise. I happened to know, what very few people in England have been allowed to know, that innocent men were being falsely accused. If I had not been angry about that I should never have written the book.

In one form or another this problem comes up again. The problem of language is subtler and would take too long to discuss. I will only say that of late years I have tried to write less picturesquely and more exactly. In any case I find that by the time you have perfected any style of writing, you have always outgrown it. *Animal Farm* was the first book in which I tried, with full consciousness of what I was doing, to fuse political purpose and artistic purpose into one whole. I have not written a novel for seven years, but I hope to write another fairly soon. It is bound to be a failure, every book is a failure, but I do know with some clarity what kind of book I want to write.

Looking back through the last page or two, I see that I have made it appear as though my motives in writing were wholly public-spirited. I don't want to leave that as the final impression. All writers are vain, selfish and lazy, and at the very bottom of their motives there lies a mystery. Writing a book is a horrible, exhausting struggle, like a long bout of some painful illness. One would never undertake such a thing if one were not driven on by some demon whom one can neither resist nor understand. For all one knows that demon is simply the same instinct that makes a baby squall for attention. And yet it is also true that one can write nothing readable unless one constantly struggles to efface one's own personality. Good prose is like a windowpane. I cannot say with certainty which of my motives are the strongest, but I know which of them deserve to be followed. And looking back through my work, I see that it is invariably where I lacked a *political* purpose that I wrote lifeless books and was betrayed into purple passages, sentences without meaning, decorative adjectives and humbug generally.

Topics for Writing and Discussion

1. Orwell mentions writing as a child. Did you write as a child? Did you keep a diary or write poetry? Write a paragraph about what you remember about yourself as a child writer.

2. Orwell also mentions words and lines of verse that particularly caught his attention, such as the lines from *Paradise Lost* that he quotes. What passages or lines of poetry have stuck with you from your earlier reading? Write down what you can remember, and then share and discuss with your group.

3. Orwell lists four reasons for writing. Can you think of any others? Notice he does not mention writing as a skill that will help one get a good job.

4. Near the end of his essay, Orwell says, "And yet it is also true that one can write nothing readable unless one constantly struggles to efface one's own personality. Good prose is like a windowpane." Can you explain what he means here? If one gets rid of one's personality, does that not get rid of one's voice? Have you not been told in the past that writing is a vehicle for personal expression? Discuss with your group or the class, and come up with another metaphor for windowpane: "Good prose is like a ___."

CHAPTER 2

Discovering

We are a curious lot. Evolving over thousands of years in Africa, we moved north and east into what we now call the Middle East, through west and central Asia to China, into Europe—where we encountered Neanderthals around 44,000 years ago—down through Malaysia to Australia, and eventually, by boat and across the Bering Strait, to the Americas. Thousands of years later, we settled down and began farming in the fertile lands between the Tigres and Euphrates rivers, growing wheat and domesticating animals. But for thousands of years more, contact between the eastern and western hemispheres was cut off. A few hardy individuals did make it to the Americas, but most did not survive; their presence is seen in a handful of archeological sites. Then in 1492, Columbus, thinking he was blazing a new trail to the riches of the East for his Spanish patrons, stumbled upon an island and its indigenous people in the West Indies, and everything changed.

Discovery and change have been the watchwords of our species. We speculate, we travel, we learn. And because we do these things, because they excite us, we want to share what we have learned, what we have discovered, with others. So we developed language, art, and eventually writing. The very survival of our species, of our family, of ourselves, depends upon passing on to others, to the next generation, what we have discovered.

So what does all this have to do with you, a freshman in college taking your first college composition class? The answer is that in going to college you are setting out on a personal voyage of discovery. If you continue on, it will change you. You will learn many new things in college, and if you are persistent, you will want to share what you have learned with others. You will want to join in conversations with other students, with your teachers, and with others beyond your immediate circle of friends and family. You will even converse with writers and thinkers who, though long dead, still speak to us today—you will be joining the great conversation, one that has been going on for at least six thousand years.

To join this conversation, you must learn to express yourself in writing, and as a writer engaging in this conversation, you will need to develop a variety of skills. In order to further develop your personal tool kit, for example, you will need to do the following.

- ⊙ Develop certain mental habits.

- ⊙ Become an active reader.

- ⊙ Locate information.

- ⊙ Evaluate information.

- ⊙ Manage information.

Mental Habits

As writers, we create meaning from the knowledge we gain directly as well as from the knowledge we develop in collaboration with others. Yet, as writers, we do more than read and repeat what others have already said. We actively work to understand other writers, show our understanding of the ongoing conversation, and then add to the conversation with new information and new ways of interpreting that information.

Many students call this process "research," but it is much more than this. Writing is *meaning making*—coming to understand our world and our relationships in it. As a famous linguistic philosopher once said, "The limits of my language are the limits of my world." Thus, using strategies of inquiry, interpretation, and various structural and stylistic choices, we do more than just research; we contribute to the world's knowledge. To become a part of this conversation, therefore, you need to develop certain mental habits. (*Merriam-Webster's Collegiate Dictionary* describes *habit* as "an acquired mode of behavior that has become nearly or completely involuntary.") These habits include the following.

Curiosity. The desire to know more about the world.

Openness. The willingness to consider new ways of being and thinking in the world.

Engagement. The ability to invest yourself and your time in learning.

Creativity. The ability to develop novel approaches to generate, investigate, and represent ideas.

Persistence (Grit). The ability to maintain interest in and to complete projects to the best of your ability in the time you are given.

Responsibility. The mental and moral quality of taking ownership of your actions.

Flexibility. The ability to adapt to changing situations, expectations, and demands.

Reflection. The ability to challenge your own thinking as well as the "received wisdom" of your immediate culture.

*The above habits of mind were developed collaboratively among the Council of Writing Program Administrators, the National Council of Teachers of English, and the National Writing Project. The habits and their impacts on college success are described in their *Framework for Success in Postsecondary Writing*.

Active Reading

For millennia after the invention of writing, literacy—being able to read and write— was confined to special classes of scribes and scholars. For example, during the Middle Ages in the West, books were rare because every book had to be copied by hand, so they were kept chained to the walls of libraries. Today, however, we are inundated with words. We all have billions of words at our fingertips. Yet we are told that actual reading is in decline. Jordan Weissmann, writing for *The Atlantic*, cites a Pew Research Center study that reports, "The number of non-book-readers has nearly tripled since 1978." However, in order to become an educated and functional member of our increasingly knowledge-driven society, you must become an active reader and take an interest in the multiple worlds around you, particularly the scientific and political worlds, because they have a direct effect on your life. Move beyond Twitter, blogs, and Wikipedia articles to books, magazines, and newspapers. Read regularly and often, and keep a journal of new ideas and new words that you encounter. Expand your mental horizons—isn't that one of the reasons you are paying money to go to college?

You will be required to read a lot in college. Each class will have a (sometimes) hefty textbook. You will be required to assimilate a good bit of the information in the book—you will be tested on it. So how are you going to retain and remember all that information? If you have not done so already, you will need to develop a suite of reading strategies. But the first major hurdle is to not be afraid of marking up your textbook. If you have been through a public school system that owned the books and actively discouraged you from marking in them, you must overcome that phobia. These are your books; you paid for them. And don't be dissuaded by the thought that you want to sell them back to the bookstore at the end of the semester: a textbook is like a car—it depreciates once you buy it. Even if you keep it in pristine shape you will only receive about half of what you paid for it, so you might as well use it. It is a tool in your education, and tools are to be used, not set on the table to be admired.

As you read, practice the following reading strategies to strengthen your use and mastery of what you read.

Scan the material for headings, subheadings, and graphics.

Read at a normal pace.

Make annotations in the margins of your text (see below for suggested questions).

Summarize what you understand in your writing journal.

Mark what you do not understand in the margins.

Circle words you do not know, and look them up in a dictionary.

Reread the text, and summarize what you have learned in your second read-through in your writing journal. Use your own words and not the words of the author.

Ask questions. Write them out so you can raise them in class.

Make connections with what you know and what you are learning in other classes.

Read the text *at least twice*, look up unfamiliar words, and summarize their definitions in your writing journal. Contrast your original summary with your growing understanding of this new vocabulary.

Remember that as a reader you are not limited to words, so draw visual images of your own, use arrows to connect ideas, or use different colored pens to highlight different concepts. If your writing journal is electronic (as on Google Drive), link your ideas to images and mind maps from the Web.

Rest. Let your mind relax, physically change your surroundings, and let your mind wander. Take a walk and think about what you are learning without a text in front of you. When you return, maybe a few hours later or even the next day, write your questions in your writing journal.

Collaborate with other writers. Practice these reading strategies together, and build on each other's learning experiences and perceptions.

Use a graphic method, such as *KWL* (What we *KNOW*, What we *WANT* to learn, and what we've *LEARNED*— illustrated in Figure 2.1), to organize your growing knowledge.

K: What I Know	W: What I Want to Learn	L: What I Learned

Figure 2.1: KWL

*Based on a chart developed by Donna Ogle in 1986.

Like other learning strategies, *KWL* is one means of establishing what you already know about your topic; it then helps you see where you need to focus your inquiry. *KWL* asks you to first list what you *know*, then what you *want* to learn, and—after collaborative and individual inquiry—what you have *learned*. Using each of these categories will assist in your organization as well as planning for collaborative inquiry with your writing group.

Activity 2.1

Pick an essay from the *Additional Readings* section of this book. Read and annotate the essay according to the list on page 20. In your group, share your annotated essay with the other members and discuss the annotations.

Activity 2.2

Take the essay you have annotated, and Google the author, the subject of the essay, and any key terms you have listed. Again, share what you found, and where, with your group.

Now look up the author, subject, and key terms in several of your library's databases. What additional information did you find?

Finding Information

Besides learning directly through reading and taking classes, in college you will be expected to actively look for more information on specific topics and incorporate what you find into papers—and not only in English classes. Being able to locate and use information are skills you will need throughout your college career and beyond.

Like maintaining human relationships, learning takes planning and commitment. Finding and engaging with other writers doesn't "just happen," and finding the right information depends on your method of inquiry, your resources, and your intended publication medium, among other things. Though we are fortunate to have enormous sources of information available today via the internet, simply using a search engine to quickly find a paragraph to insert into your writing is not actually engaging in a conversation; it does not add to your personal growth as an informed individual, nor does it add to the overall amount of information in the world at large.

Because using information in writing is a multistep process, start from a broad perspective, and then narrow to a specific topic. To appreciate the larger perspective, the big worldview, as it were, writers read encompassing overviews of specific areas of knowledge before making their research more focused. To help us see this big picture, it is always advantageous to start with a reliable encyclopedia. The word encyclopedia comes from the Greek words *enkyklios*, meaning "circular, recurrent, required regularly, general" and *paideia*, meaning "education." Together, the phrase literally means "complete instruction" or "complete knowledge." Though we know of an encyclopedia written two thousand years ago by a Roman naturalist, Pliny the Elder, what we consider the modern encyclopedia was developed in eighteenth-century France between 1751 and 1772.

A good encyclopedia will give us not only a large *overview* of our inquiry, but it will also provide us additional *key words, history, context, interdisciplinary connections, and controversies*—in other words, different ways of seeing our topic. *Wikipedia*, the largest electronic encyclopedia, is available in hundreds of languages, and is available free on the Internet. Before jumping to this convenient source, however, understand the difference between a peer-reviewed encyclopedia, such as the *Gale Virtual Reference Library,* and a crowdsourced collection, such as *Wikipedia*. For the *Gale Virtual Reference Library*, the editors seek out experts in their fields, and each entry is checked and double-checked by other experts before being published. *Wikipedia*, however, relies on a crowdsourcing process where anyone—with or without academic credentials—can edit an entry. Though crowdsourcing assumes that the majority of editors will eventually settle on some sense of what the truth is, and though reading a *Wikipedia* article can, in fact, help us understand the big worldview on a topic, writers rarely use this for reliable information and rely instead on peer-reviewed publications. Besides

Wikipedia, however, there are many other online encyclopedias. You can find a listing of them at the *Wikipedia* site "List of online encyclopedias."

One of the advantages of encyclopedias and similar sources is to give us a better understanding of the *keywords* needed to pursue our inquiry. Keywords are those ideas that relate to our inquiry in both space and time, as in the following list of keywords associated with an article on "Athens" from the online *Ancient History Encyclopedia.*

- City
- Athens
- Greece
- Acropolis
- Greek
- Peloponnesian War

These keywords represent various important events and cultural institutions across history and the geography of Ancient Greece. With such keywords, you can focus your attention on more specific points relevant to your writing purpose, the limitations of available resources, and your publishing intentions. These keywords, in turn, can be used to find other, more precise sources to expand your view of the topic and to understand what other writers feel is important, what information is being ignored, and how the discipline uses writing to exchange information. Now, from your broad understanding and collection of key words, you can begin to develop precise questions to guide you toward more focused research.

Once you learn about your topic and create keywords, specify your research questions, and then gather your initial resources, it is time to focus your writing to answer a specific question. This question, of course, is addressed in your project's thesis statement. (See Chapter 4.) Your focus must be precise, assertive, and informed by the larger academic discussion as you have determined it from your research thus far. Now, with this focus, you are ready to find sources to support your inquiry and specific topic.

A good place to start your search is the college library. It has numerous places where information is stored and highly competent and dedicated professionals to help you find what you need. Consider the following.

   The catalog. A library's catalog is a comprehensive classification of its collections, including print and electronic books, print and electronic journals, and audio and video resources.

Databases. A library's databases will include electronic references and full-text articles for thousands of historical and contemporary serial publications, such as magazines and journals, as well as full-text books and videos. Abstracts (summaries) of most resources are provided so you can quickly review their relevance to your inquiry.

Interlibrary loans. Most college libraries have agreements with other libraries to loan their materials for short periods if the primary library doesn't carry that resource. In other words, if your library doesn't have a specific book or article you need, you can ask your library to find a copy from another college, and it will be sent to your library. The interlibrary loan is one of the most powerful sources of information in your college experience and is also one of the most underused. Because your library can request a loan from thousands of other college libraries, your resources now become nearly limitless. However, keep in mind that you must make a request and fill out a form; the library must locate the source and send out the request; the library that has the source must find it and then send it to your library, and, finally, the library must contact you and tell you the source is now available. All this takes time. This is yet another reason to get started on an assigned project as soon as you can.

In addition to your college library, there are other locations where you can locate sources for your research project.

Your community library. Your local community library can be an important resource. Community libraries include (mostly) free access to multiple literacy sources for entertainment, self-help, and personal edification. You will also find information on your local community here—its history, leaders, and controversies.

Community associations. State and local associations, such as history societies, ethnic groups, and genealogical societies, are valuable sources of information on your local community. Here, as you enter the realm of primary sources and local experts, your credibility as a writer increases significantly. Local resources are too often overlooked and are too rarely used and shared in the larger publishing world of academic research and writing. Depending on your writing project, using these local insights can significantly strengthen your writing and demonstrate the local application of larger national conversations. Using local voices in your writing will strengthen your arguments and help you appeal to your local audience. As always, all materials used in your writing must be referenced. (See Chapter 9.)

Public records and archives. All governments create records of some sort, and most of these records are available to the public in some form. Though not every public library has government records, usually you can find a regional library that acts as a depository for your area. Ask your college librarian where government records are located in your area. Local governments often maintain an archive of important records, such as land transactions, vital records (births, marriages, deaths), population shifts, administrative budgets, ordinances and laws, minutes of governmental meetings, and much more, and many of these records can be accessed via the internet. Work with your local public or college librarian to understand what records are available, how to access them, and when personal visits to governmental archives are permitted. Once there, you will be instructed how to access and handle original documents. Using local material strengthens your writing and demonstrates an important mastery of the local domain.

As a college student, you will be expected to use multiple resources—textbooks, magazine and journal articles, books, and the internet—to create new knowledge through interpretation and synthesis. You will present this new knowledge many times through your writing. As a student about to join an educated community through your learning and writing, keep in mind that (according to the Association of College & Research Libraries), the following are true.

- ⊙ Scholarship is a conversation.
- ⊙ Research is inquiry into our world.
- ⊙ Authority is contextual and constructed.
- ⊙ Formatting is the process of structuring information for our audience.
- ⊙ Searching is exploration of others' ideas and discoveries.
- ⊙ Information has value.

The fundamental purpose of expository writing is to use, create, and share information—to create knowledge. As we come to understand our part in the knowledge-making process of writing, we need to understand how information becomes knowledge, how information is organized, how we find information and integrate it into our own writing projects, and then how to share this new information with others.

Activity 2.3

As a class, or as a group, talk to a reference librarian, and set up a library tour. Make sure you know how to find books on the library's shelf, how to use several different databases, and what other resources your library has. After your tour, discuss what you have learned with your group and your class.

Evaluating Information

All information is not created equal. Neither is it formatted or disseminated or valued the same. Though ultimately all knowledge has some value to someone in some discipline, you should learn to discern which information is more credible, which is more likely to be true, and which information is more useful for your specific writing project. For example, which of the following statements are true, and how could you find out?

⊙ The Great Wall of China is the only man-made object visible from the Moon.

⊙ The average person swallows eight spiders a year in his sleep.

⊙ A light bulb manufactured in 1901 is still operational today.

⊙ Rubber tires on a car protect the passengers during a lightning storm.

⊙ In 2014, a Chinese coal miner was found alive in an abandoned mine seventeen years after he had been trapped inside it by an earthquake.

⊙ Caffeine-infused underwear can help the wearer lose weight.

Each of these claims is common in one community or another and shared through discussion, emails, social networks, and commercial advertisements. However, just because a claim is shared, even multiple times, does not make the claim true. The amount of knowledge is increasing, more than we can imagine, in every field, so determining the truth of claims becomes ever more complex.

As you evaluate the credibility of your information, you should keep in mind the distinction between what are called *primary* sources and *secondary* sources. Primary sources are the original work of individuals and groups, such as Martin Luther King Jr.'s "Letter from Birmingham Jail," *The Declaration of Independence*, or Isaac Newton's *Principia Mathematica*, for instance. Secondary sources are works derived from, based on, or developed from primary sources. Your history textbook is a secondary source based on earlier secondary sources and original historical documents. As you begin to evaluate the information you have collected, ask yourself the following questions.

What is the original source of the data? This may tell you about the creator's intention, resources, purpose, and possible biases.

How far is this information from the original data source? Your author may have used information filters and interpretations when presenting the information in your source. Filters (such as summaries) are sometimes used to simplify data, but they can also be used to obscure data (as in propaganda).

What are the author's credentials? For example, is the author well-known in her field? (Google her name.) Has she published other books or essays on this topic? Have others written reviews or evaluations of this source? What is the purpose?

What biases does the author demonstrate in the choice of information? What is the tone? Is it objective, combative, humorous?

Who is the source's intended audience? Just as we make rhetorical choices as we write, the authors of our information make choices and assumptions about their audiences as well, and those choices affect how they present their information and what they include or exclude.

How current is the information? Sometimes we want the most current information, but when doing historical analyses, for example, original and older sources might be more useful.

How accurate is the information? Sometimes we must rely upon the credibility of the author (He has a PhD in genetics, teaches at Harvard, and is writing about genetically modified crops, for example.) However, another way to check the accuracy of the information in a given source is to look for confirmation of the data presented in a second and even third source.

Information is the valuation and organization of various pieces of knowledge. In essence, as a writer you create information from multiple sources, both primary and secondary, through the invention, composition, revision, editing, and reflection stages of writing. Instead of simply repeating what others say, instead of stating the obvious about your own experiences that most members of your audience have also experienced, your privilege as a writer is to see your world in new ways and convey that vision through information.

Sharing your discoveries requires both access and skill. You must know how to access information through collaboration with information specialists, such as your instructors and librarians, as well as with other students. More importantly, you should practice creating new information through writing—repeatedly, regularly, and reflectively. One method to develop not only your writing skills but also your store of knowledge is to write in a journal daily, to add to your knowledge and to your skill at creating information. This practice will be immensely useful throughout your college experience and on through your professional and public life.

Activity 2.4

Take the challenge presented under "Evaluating Information," and see whether you can find out which of the statements is true. Each member of your group might take one or two of the items. When you are finished, share your answers—and where you found them—with the whole class.

Managing Information

Organization is a key to effective writing. As you proceed in your writing process, you will accumulate multiple forms of information at different times, from different sources, each answering different research questions. Learn early to create a reliable management system and to preserve your resources so you will always know where they are and where they came from. Here are some helpful hints.

Cloud storage. Data storage in the cloud, such as in Google Drive or Dropbox, is especially reliable, inexpensive (often free), and always available; it ensures your data are preserved in case of your own machine's failure. A good idea is to save material in multiple places. When you find an article in a database, for example, send it to yourself as an email, and also print it out or save it to a flash drive. Too often a student loses or breaks a device the day before a project is due. Don't be that student.

Bookmarking tools. As a means of both tracing your database and internet resources and sharing those resources with others, consider using bookmarking tools, such as Diigo or Google Bookmarks on your Web browser. These bookmarking applications offer multiple means of organizing your electronic resources, including file structures and keyword tagging. Importantly, you can also share your research history with other writers to collaborate in your writing process.

Annotated bibliographies. Annotated bibliographies are important means of collecting information about your sources as both a summary of their contents and a critique of the methods and usefulness of your inquiry. Keeping an annotated bibliography also provides you with a quick reference for research in years to come, so make your bibliographies count. The annotations to your bibliography should be useful in multiple ways, beyond just a summary. Thus, as your writing progresses you can quickly determine whether a source is essential to supplement your own learning or it can be put aside for another project. Your annotated bibliography should include the following.

1. The bibliographic entry appropriate to your discipline
2. A list of key terms in the article
3. A summary of the author's claims and procedures with interpretive comments
4. A commentary to relate the article to your investigative question as well as ask questions, pose arguments, and point out biases

5. Direct quotations stated so eloquently you will want to cite them completely in your research project, perhaps later in another paper, or simply because you find them appealing

The following is an example of an entry in an MLA-formatted annotated bibliography:

Johnson, Teddi Dineley. "Pedestrians: Take the Steps to Stay Safe." *The Nation's Health. American Public Health Association.* Apr. 2011. Web. 14 Dec. 2014.

Johnson talks about the importance of being safe while walking alongside a road. For example, she gives us statistics for the number of pedestrian deaths that occurred in 2009— 4,100. Deaths occur every two hours, while every nine minutes pedestrians are injured by automobiles. Since many young Americans want to go outside for physical activities, parents need to be concerned about the safety of the streets in their neighborhood. Senior citizens and children, particularly, are the ones most at risk of being hit, leading to injury or death. Johnson explains that alcohol-impaired motorists cause at least half of pedestrian deaths each year because of their mental and physical impairment. She then gives tips for being safe while walking near the streets. For example, one should wait until reaching an intersection to cross a street because drivers expect a pedestrian to cross there rather than in the middle of the block. It is always best to walk on sidewalks, and if they are unavailable, pedestrians should walk facing the traffic so they can see approaching cars. Walkers should always wear reflective gear while walking at night so they are visible to drivers. One should always be aware of one's environment, and Johnson recommends strongly not to use cell phones while walking. Last, Johnson suggests that, as drivers, we should especially be alert to pedestrians at all times.

This is an enlightening source to read and will be used in my essay to demonstrate how easy safety can be if both pedestrians and motorists are made more aware of safety rules. The author assumes, however, that pedestrians always have sidewalks available in their neighborhoods. She does not consider that some neighborhoods have no sidewalks, such as my own. I plan to use this source to suggest that if the city could provide sidewalks to my community, people's lives would be much safer when they have to travel by foot. The risk of injury or death would be drastically reduced.

If you are required to turn in an annotated bibliography, ask your instructor whether additional measures are required, such as citing quotable passages, identifying unfamiliar vocabulary words, or arguing against the claims made by the source's author.

Activity 2.5

Take the material you gathered in activities 2.1-2.3, and prepare an annotated bibliography.

Plagiarism

Finally, a word of caution: When you begin to explore and use other people's ideas, other people's work, you must give credit to them. You cannot simply appropriate someone else's work and call it your own. That is cheating; it is a species of fraud called plagiarism. Just as you would not want to go to a doctor and later discover that he had received his MD fraudulently, your instructor does not want to read your paper only to discover that you stole it from the internet. Why do people cheat? More specifically, why do students cheat? Research shows that students cheat for many reasons.

- ⊙ The most common reason students plagiarize is because they feel insecure about their own writing abilities, and they do not realize the amount of time it takes to write a paper. It is that simple. Feeling insecure, students do not work through the writing process: they do not engage with the topic, develop the sources, make use of librarians, or work with groups. It all seems to take so much effort. As a first-year writer, you are not expected to have all the skills needed to write the "Great American Essay," but you are expected to write. So, like all skills, the more you practice, reflect, and practice again, the more secure you will become in your use of these strategies, including using other writers' voices in your projects.

- ⊙ Students may also plagiarize if they are not interested in the project, so they make no effort to activate those habits of mind—such as curiosity, engagement, and responsibility—to make the project their own. If you find yourself simply uninspired from the beginning of the writing process, then collaborate with your writing group for revision strategies, or consult with your instructor about possibly negotiating a new, more interesting project.

Even when beginning writers do not intend to plagiarize, however, sometimes they do so unintentionally because of their lack of knowledge of the correct procedures for incorporating the ideas and text of other writers into their own work. To avoid unintentional plagiarism, always let the reader know when you are borrowing ideas or text from someone else. Writers for newspapers and magazines do this all the time. For example, science writer Kate Wong, writing about what we have come to understand about Neandertals' mental abilities in a February 2015 article in *Scientific American*, says "the bigger, more connected membership of *H. sa-*

piens 'increasingly provided a more efficient ratchet effect to maintain and build on knowledge compared with earlier humans, including the Neandertals,' offers Chris Stringer of the Natural History Museum in London." Note that she uses a direct quotation, tells us who said it, and indicates his highly eminent position in the field. There are a number of conventions such as this for using information from sources that will be discussed in Chapter 9 on documenting and formatting.

Final Word

You have set out upon a great adventure; you have set out to explore "strange new worlds," to engage in new conversations, to learn and transform yourself, and, in the process, transform the world—as *H. sapiens* have been doing for thousands of years. Make use of this unique opportunity; make learning active, not passive; read, explore, think, and go "where no one has gone before."

Activity 2.6

Reflect on how your knowledge and literacy have expanded over time since you started school. Has your formal education ever conflicted with the knowledge you absorbed from your family and culture? For example, how has new information you acquired in classes, such as history, science, and literature, squared with what you were taught at home? Write a short account of your "intellectual odyssey," and share and compare it with other members of your group and the class.

I Type, Therefore I Am

Tom Chatfield

Tom Chatfield is a British writer and commentator on technology. He also works on apps, games (*The End*) and interactive media. His latest book is *Live This Book!* (2015). The following essay was written for the digital magazine *Aeon* in May of 2013.

In this essay, Chatfield discusses the development of our modern communication system, based today primarily on text, by which we type ourselves into existence via our cell phones and Twitter. We promote ourselves and discover ourselves and others in ever-widening circles that make us more connected than we have ever been. He says, "ours is the first epoch of the articulate crowd," and, quoting Jean-Paul Sartre, that we are "condemned to be free." So in a sense we use language, and even more today text, to discover the world around us and our own parameters. Without language and writing, how could we ever come to know other people and the world? Writing is literally an act of discovery.

At some point in the past two million years, give or take half a million, the genus of great apes that would become modern humans crossed a unique threshold. Across unknowable reaches of time, they developed a communication system able to describe not only the world, but the inner lives of its speakers. They ascended—or fell, depending on your preferred metaphor—into language.

The vast bulk of that story is silence. Indeed, darkness and silence are the defining norms of human history. The earliest known writing probably emerged in southern Mesopotamia around 5,000 years ago but, for most of recorded history, reading and writing remained among the most elite human activities: the province of monarchs, priests and nobles who reserved for themselves the privilege of lasting words.

Mass literacy is a phenomenon of the past few centuries, and one that has reached the majority of the world's adult population only within the past 75 years. In 1950, UNESCO estimated that 44 per cent of the people in the world aged 15 and over were illiterate; by 2012, that proportion had reduced to just 16 per cent, despite the trebling of the global population between those dates. However, while the full effects of this revolution continue to unfold, we find ourselves in the throes of another whose statistics are still more accelerated.

In the past few decades, more than six billion mobile phones and two billion internet-connected computers have come into the world. As a result of this, for the first time ever we live not only in an era of mass literacy, but also—thanks to the act of typing onto screens—in one of mass *participation* in written culture.

As a medium, electronic screens possess infinite capacities and instant interconnections, turning words into a new kind of active agent in the world. The

21st century is a truly hypertextual arena (*hyper* from ancient Greek meaning 'over, beyond, overmuch, above measure'). Digital words are interconnected by active links, as they never have and never could be on the physical page. They are, however, also above measure in their supply, their distribution, and in the stories that they tell.

Just look at the ways in which most of us, every day, use computers, mobile phones, websites, email and social networks. Vast volumes of mixed media surround us, from music to games and videos. Yet almost all of our online actions still begin and end with writing: text messages, status updates, typed search queries, comments and responses, screens packed with verbal exchanges and, underpinning it all, countless billions of words.

This sheer quantity is in itself something new. All future histories of modern language will be written from a position of explicit and overwhelming information—a story not of darkness and silence but of data, and of the verbal outpourings of billions of lives. Where once words were written by the literate few on behalf of the many, now every phone and computer user is an author of some kind. And—separated from human voices—the tasks to which typed language, or visual language, is being put are steadily multiplying.

Consider the story of one of the information age's minor icons, the emoticon. In 1982, at Carnegie Mellon University, a group of researchers were using an online bulletin board to discuss the hypothetical fate of a drop of mercury left on the floor of an elevator if its cable snapped. The scenario prompted a humorous response from one participant—'WARNING! Because of a recent physics experiment, the leftmost elevator has been contaminated with mercury. There is also some slight fire damage'—followed by a note from someone else that, to a casual reader who hadn't been following the thread, this comment might seem alarming ('yelling fire in a crowded theatre is bad news ... so are jokes on day-old comments').

Participants thus began to suggest symbols that could be added to a post intended as a joke, ranging from per cent signs to ampersands and hashtags. The clear winner came from the computer scientist Scott Fahlman, who proposed a smiley face drawn with three punctuation marks to denote a joke :-). Fahlman also typed a matching sad face :-(to suggest seriousness, accompanied by the prophetic note that 'it is probably more economical to mark things that are NOT jokes, given current trends.'

Within months, dozens of smiley variants were creeping across the early internet: a kind of proto-virality that has led some to label emoticons the 'first online meme.' What Fahlman and his colleagues had also enshrined was a central fact of online communication: in an interactive medium, consequences rebound and multiply in unforeseen ways, while miscommunication will often become the rule rather than the exception.

Three decades later, we're faced with the logical conclusion of this trend: an appeal at the High Court in London last year against the conviction of a man for a 'message of menacing character' on Twitter. In January 2010, Paul Chambers, 28, had tweeted his frustration at the closure of an airport near Doncaster due to snow: 'Crap! Robin Hood Airport is closed. You've got a week and a bit to get your shit together, otherwise I'm blowing the airport sky high!!'

Chambers had said he never thought anyone would take his 'silly joke' seriously. And in his judgment on the 'Twitter joke trial,' the Lord Chief Justice said that—despite the omission of a smiley emoticon—the tweet in question did not constitute a credible threat: 'although it purports to address "you," meaning those responsible for the airport, it was not sent to anyone at the airport or anyone responsible for airport security . . . the language and punctuation are inconsistent with the writer intending it to be or to be taken as a serious warning.'

The phrase a 'victory for common sense' was widely used by supporters of the charged man, such as the comedians Stephen Fry and Al Murray. As the judge also noted, Twitter itself represents 'no more and no less than conversation without speech': an interaction as spontaneous and layered with contingent meanings as face-to-face communication, but possessing the permanence of writing and the reach of broadcasting.

It's an observation that speaks to a central contemporary fact. Our screens are in increasingly direct competition with spoken words themselves—and with traditional conceptions of our relationship with language. Who would have thought, 30 years ago, that a text message of 160 characters or fewer, sent between mobile phones, would become one of the defining communications technologies of the early 21st century; or that one of its natural successors would be a tweet some 20 characters shorter?

Yet this bare textual minimum has proved to be the perfect match to an age of information suffusion: a manageable space that conceals as much as it reveals. Small wonder that the average American teenager now sends and receives around 3,000 text messages a month—or that, as the MIT professor Sherry Turkle reports in her book *Alone Together* (2011), crafting the perfect kind of flirtatious message is so serious a skill that some teens will outsource it to the most eloquent of their peers.

Almost without our noticing, we weave worlds from these snapshots, until an illusion of unbroken narrative emerges

It's not just texting, of course. In Asia, so-called 'chat apps' are re-enacting many millions of times each day the kind of exchanges that began on bulletin boards in the 1980s, complete not only with animated emoticons but with integrated access to games, online marketplaces, and even video calls. Phone calls, though, are a degree of self-exposure too much for most everyday communications. According to the article 'On the Death of the Phone Call' by Clive Thompson, published in *Wired* magazine in 2010, 'the average number of mobile phone calls we make is dropping every year . . . And our calls are getting shorter: in 2005 they averaged three minutes in length; now they're almost half that.' Safe behind our screens, we let type do our talking for us—and leave others to conjure our lives by reading between the lines.

Yet written communication doesn't necessarily mean safer communication. All interactions, be they spoken or written, are to some degree performative: a negotiation of roles and references. Onscreen words are a special species of self-presentation—a form of storytelling in which the very idea of 'us' is a fiction crafted letter by letter. Such are our linguistic gifts that a few sentences can conjure the story of a life: a status update, an email, a few text messages. Almost without our noticing, we weave worlds from these snapshots, until an illusion of unbroken narrative emerges from a handful of paragraphs.

Behind this illusion lurks another layer of belief: that we can control these second selves. Yet, ironically, control is one of the first things our eloquence sacrifices. As authors and politicians have long known, the afterlife of our words belongs to the world—and what it chooses to make of them has little to do with our own assumptions.

In many ways, mass articulacy is a crisis of originality. Something always implicit has become ever more starkly explicit: that words and ideas do not belong only to us, but play out within larger currents of human feeling. There is no such thing as a private language. We speak in order to be heard, we write in order to be read. But words also speak through us and, sometimes, are as much a dissolution as an assertion of our identity.

In his essay 'Writing: or, the Pattern Between People' (1932), W H Auden touched on the paradoxical relationship between the flow of written words and their ability to satisfy those using them:

> Since the underlying reason for writing is to bridge the gulf between one person and another, as the sense of loneliness increases, more and more books are written by more and more people, most of them with little or no talent. Forests are cut down, rivers of ink absorbed, but the lust to write is still unsatisfied.

Onscreen, today's torrents of pixels exceed anything Auden could have imagined. Yet the hyper-verbal loneliness he evoked feels peculiarly contemporary. Increasingly, we interweave our actions and our rolling digital accounts of ourselves: curators and narrators of our life stories, with a matching move from internal to external monologue. It's a realm of elaborate shows in which status is hugely significant—and one in which articulacy itself risks turning into a game, with attention and impact (retweets, likes) held up as the supreme virtues of self-expression.

Consider the particular phenomenon known as binary or 'reversible language' that now proliferates online. It might sound obscure, but the pairings it entails are central to most modern metrics of measured attention, influence and interconnection: to 'like' and to 'unlike,' to 'favourite' and to 'unfavourite'; to 'follow' and 'unfollow'; to 'friend' and 'unfriend'; or simply to 'click' or 'unclick' the onscreen boxes enabling all of the above.

Ours is the first epoch of the articulate crowd, the smart mob: of words and deeds fused into ceaseless feedback.

Like the systems of organization underpinning it, such language promises a clean and quantifiable recasting of self-expression and relationships. At every stage, both you and your audience have precise access to a measure of reception: the number of likes a link has received, the number of followers endorsing a tweeter, the items ticked or unticked to populate your profile with a galaxy of preferences.

What's on offer is a kind of perpetual present, in which everything can always be exactly the way you want it to be (provided you feel one of two ways). Everything can be undone instantly and effortlessly, then done again at will, while the machinery itself can be shut down, logged off or ignored. Like the author oscillating between Ctrl-Y (redo) and Ctrl-Z (undo) on a keyboard, a hundred indecisions, visions and revisions are permitted—if desired—and all will remain unseen. There is no need, ever, for any conversation to end.

Even the most ephemeral online act leaves its mark. Data only accumulates. Little that is online is ever forgotten or erased, while the business of search and social recommendation funnels our words into a perpetual popularity contest. Every act of selection and interconnection is another reinforcement. If you can't find something online, it's often because you lack the right words. And there's a deliciously circular logic to all this, whereby what's 'right' means only what displays the best search results—just as what you yourself are 'like' is defined by the boxes you've ticked. It's a grand game with the most glittering prizes of all at stake: connection, recognition, self-expression, discovery. The internet's countless servers and services are the perfect riposte to history: an eternally unfinished collaboration, pooling the words of many millions; a final refuge from darkness.

There's much to celebrate in this profligate democracy, and its overthrow of articulate monopolies. The self-dramatizing ingenuity behind even three letters such as 'LOL' is a testament to our capacity for making the most constricted verbal arenas our own, while to watch events unfold through the fractal lens of social media is a unique contemporary privilege. Ours is the first epoch of the articulate crowd, the smart mob: of words and deeds fused into ceaseless feedback.

Yet language is a bewitchment that can overturn itself—and can, like all our creations, convince us there is nothing beyond it. In an era when the gulf between words and world has never been easier to overlook, it's essential to keep alive a sense of ourselves as distinct from the cascade of self-expression; to push back against the torrents of articulacy flowing past and through us.

For the philosopher John Gray, writing in *The Silence of Animals* (2013), the struggle with words and meanings is sometimes simply a distraction:

> Philosophers will say that humans can never be silent because the mind is made of words. For these half-witted logicians, silence is no more than a word. To overcome language by means of language is obviously impossible. Turning within, you will find only words and images that are parts of yourself. But if you turn outside yourself—to the birds and animals and the quickly changing places where they live—you may hear something beyond words.

Gray's dismissal of 'half-witted logicians' might be a sober tonic, yet it's something I find extraordinarily hopeful—an exit from the despairing circularity that expects our creations either to damn or to save us. If we cannot speak ourselves into being, we cannot speak ourselves out of being either. We are, in another fine philosophical phrase, condemned to be free. And this freedom is not contingent on eloquence, no matter how desperately we might wish that words alone could negotiate the world on our behalf.

Topics for Writing and Discussion

1. Write a short paper comparing the advantages and disadvantages of talking on your phone versus texting. Which do you prefer and why?

2. Chatfield says that "our screens are in increasingly direct competition with spoken words themselves—and with traditional conceptions of our relationship with language." Do you think that the instantaneous and pervasive communication provided by texting and Twitter have degraded our ability to talk face to face? For example, can emoticons replace real emotional clues we get while talking with another person?

3. Chatfield speaks of "the particular phenomenon known as binary or 'reversible language' that now proliferates online." Write a short essay, using yourself and your friends as examples, in which you explain the effect on both the sender and the receiver of "likes" and "dislikes," or of being "friended" or "unfriended." Do such actions have an effect on an individual's self-image?

CHAPTER 3

Inventing

Deciding how to begin writing is always a daunting prospect. More often than not, the inexperienced writer will deal with the stress of "not knowing" what to write about by diving straight in, rushing to the blank page (or screen) under the assumption that somehow the finer details of the writing will take care of themselves. Doing so is problematic because you skip over several steps (outlined in this chapter, as well as Chapter 4) geared toward aiding writers in moving from *generality* toward *specificity*.

However, specificity is not the sole purpose of invention (even if it is perhaps the best indicator of whether you have succeeded at inventing a worthwhile project). As with the previous chapter, the invention stage of the writing process has several goals. At this stage you will do the following.

Create a starting point. By sorting through the information you have gathered on a particular subject, you are in fact internally processing that information, determining what is valuable and selecting what is important. In effect, you begin writing when you begin sorting through that material. You begin to explore ideas.

Generate insights. Sorting through this material, you begin to draw connections between specific details; you also have the opportunity to build correlations between the facts and observations you have found and your own ideas. At this stage, you probably will not know what, specifically, you want to write about, or what is important about your topic, but in the process of drawing conclusions from these connections you will have begun the process of narrowing down, of focusing.

Determine the writing situation. While you might not know when starting out what your purpose is—whether you are seeking to inform, compare, or analyze—these components will take shape from your arrangement of the material of your project.

By now, you will have decided on a starting point, something of interest, that will lead you down a path of familiarization and research (recall Chapter 2), using a wide range of credible sources. You should now be somewhat literate in the subject at hand and know a wide, perhaps disorganized, range of details related to and stemming from your initial point of interest. You might already have some notes with dates, facts, events, names, or even pictures to sort through.

What do you do with all of this information? Moreover, how do you move from your initial curiosity to a more specific focus, a *working thesis* or *unifying idea*? The process of invention is the creative step when you effectively "spill your ideas" down on paper in what might seem like a chaotic manner. This chapter outlines many of the strategies you might consider to accomplish this task, whether brainstorming, making a list, or even drawing maps and sketches. However, getting your ideas on paper is only the initial part of the process. Ultimately, invention is an analytical stage, an opportunity to organize these details once you have put them on paper and to interrogate your initial subject as you attempt to lend it greater depth and focus.

There is a creative concept known as the *bone pile*. You might imagine a figurative cave, the lair of an insatiable creature (a nice analogy for the human imagination) littered with discarded bones, representing the ideas you have chewed over, picked apart, and even discarded—but that may still prove useful at some future time. The invention stage is when you build your bone pile, without fear of outside scrutiny. The bone pile is your stack of supporting topics, key details, and connections. Just as the maid never visits the monster's cave to clean it out, you should never throw away your ideas, whether they are in your journals, freewriting, lists, or brainstorms; you might return to them. They can provide the basis for future revisions or even new projects.

In this act of invention, the goal is never to establish a final, accurate sense of what you wish to write about, but rather to allow your ideas to grow and evolve. Until you get your ideas onto the page (a metaphor for the writing canvas, whether you are writing with pen and paper, a computer screen, or a digital tablet) and select details that represent your interests and observations, you cannot know how your project will take shape or how your audience will interpret your writing. In effect, the invention stage is your first opportunity (one of many) to scrutinize your own ideas in a constructive manner, without fear of rules or grammar, playing with the ideas until the desired level of specificity or focus is achieved. Eventually, when you are ready to move on to the next stage (Chapter 4), you will further develop them into a working thesis and put together the rough skeleton of your project.

Find a Unifying Idea

Ultimately, the goal of invention is to help you find and flesh out a *unifying idea* for your project. What will this essay be about? What key details support this idea? Whom am I addressing with this project, and for what purpose? Again, this step can be extremely frustrating given the weight of such responsibility, especially when you have complete freedom to decide your own subject.

For now, you should have at the very least a rudimentary topic, even if it is a work in progress. For example, you begin with a general area of interest (think back to Chapter 2), let's say the Middle East conflict. The reasons for this could be varied, but assuming you took one of our starting points in Chapter 1, an interest of *global, local,* or *cultural* significance, you are probably already familiar with the subject. Whether you have read news feeds online, searched a database for articles, visited the library, or even talked to people with direct experience or knowledge of the region, you have been building a variety of ideas—many bits of information you can develop into a more specific topic to anchor your paper.

Through the processes outlined in this chapter, you might develop the vague "Middle East" into a more pertinent focus, such as "the current conflict in the Middle East," or even more specifically, "the current political climate in Palestine." Further examination of the facts you have gathered on this developing idea might spur you to ask why this is the most relevant direction to take and who your audience might be. The details unearthed by using the following invention strategies should help you refine this statement even further and determine the best strategy for the project (whether it will be a descriptive, comparative, or analytical paper).

You may find you need to repeat these steps many times. Chapter 1 introduced the idea that these strategies are recursive—meaning they are repeatable—so at any time you might return to the familiarization stage and gather more information, should some of these invention strategies result in the discovery of a new line of inquiry you feel is worth exploring or should you decide you need more specific details on a subject.

Remove the Inner Editor

The invention process is often messy. This should be seen as liberating, not restricting. You are able, and in fact encouraged, to disobey what you perceive to be the conventions of writing. This is a free-form stage. As such, it is imperative—and imperative for many of the writing stages discussed in early parts of this textbook—to turn off the inner editor, the perfectionist inside each of us that threatens to stifle creativity for the sake of that "ideal product."

First off, no such ideal product exists. We have tried to stress early and often that writing is a form of inquiry, of exploration, of discovery, and to build anything meaningful from this process requires you to open doors. Allow yourself not to worry about things such as grammar, correctness, and even, at the preinvention stage, who your audience is and what they might think about your idea—even if you develop a greater understanding of audience through the invention process. What matters most at this stage is that you allow yourself the freedom to get everything you can think of down on the page.

Interrogate Your Topic

The following are strategies you might employ to further test and develop your general area of interest and transform it into a functional topic or central statement. For the time being, consider only that your goal is to move from a general interest area (the turmoil in the Middle East, for example) to a more specific area that will help direct your paper, such as the current political climate in Palestine.

However, as you move from the general to the specific, also ask the following questions.

Who am I addressing? A general American audience? American Jews? Palestinian Americans?

How am I explaining this issue? Am I simply describing the issue, comparing it to another issue or concern, or analyzing it by using a significant concept or theory? What is my purpose?

What do I bring to the discussion? What insights am I adding by addressing this issue? What is the relevance?

The process of getting from a general idea to a more specific focus will largely evolve from the types and amount of information you accumulate, your personal interest in the topic, and the most important points of discussion.

Employ Multiple Strategies

The process of exploring your topic does not contain a set number of steps. You can employ multiple strategies multiple times to achieve your desired goal. Only when you think you have an operating idea capable of becoming the thesis for your paper should you consider this stage complete. Consider the following strategies.

- Brainstorming
- Mind Mapping
- Listing
- Drawing and Sketching
- Using Other Media
- Freewriting
- Collaborative Invention

Brainstorming. *Brainstorming* is the process by which you simply spill ideas or details about a chosen subject onto the page. The primary purpose of brainstorming is to get as many details as possible. The manner in which you organize these details is less important than getting it all down on paper so that you might see the breadth and scope of the ideas you are working with. You can jot them willy-nilly on a paper, or you might type them using phrases or single words. Again, the point of this exercise is to see the broadest shape of your ideas so you might sift through them later, identify further areas of interest, and establish connections between them.

Figure 3.1 is an image of a student brainstorm activity conducted in a first-year writing course. Note how the student, after writing the details down, went through an additional step, circling some items and crossing out others. The first step, writing everything down, was the creation step. The second, circling and crossing out, was a process of interrogating the topic. It helped the student determine what was most important, what was not, and what was worth digging into more deeply. The author could have connected certain ideas or even elaborated by spilling more ideas onto the paper once certain connections became apparent.

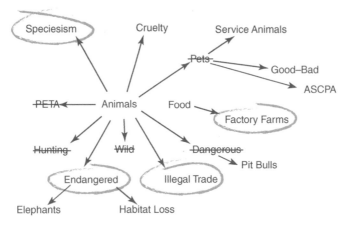

Figure 3.1: Brainstorming

This sounds messy, and it is. However, this process of creating threads and then choosing some, eliminating others, and making connections aids in sifting through material to find a more specific focus. This secondary step is also when you comment upon the importance of your own ideas.

Activity 3.1

Brainstorm two of the following topics, jotting down everything that comes to mind. Use the graphic above as a model. Compare your brainstorms with those of your group.

Topics: high school graduation night, family life, the anxieties of a first date, advantages of a community college, peer pressure, funny TV commercials, careers, sports, love, death.

Mind Mapping. Writers employ *mind mapping* as an early form of an outline to help draw connections between details or roughly shaped ideas. Whereas brainstorming is an indiscriminate jotting of ideas as they come to you, the mind map is a more controlled, conscious attempt to follow a common thread from one idea to another. Figure 3.2 is an example of a mind map.

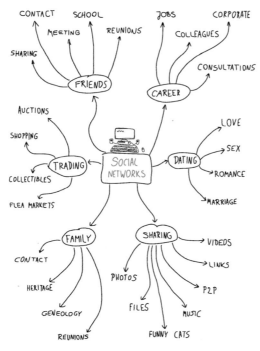

Figure 3.2: Mind Mapping

Listing. Another useful method, akin to brainstorming and mind mapping, is *listing.* Here you simply sort your material into categories to clarify connections and balance your main ideas. The following list started from the general topic, sports, moved to several different types of sports (soccer, football, baseball) the student had participated in, then narrowed to football.

- ⊙ Football
- ⊙ Offense
- ⊙ Defense
- ⊙ Quarterbacks
- ⊙ Passing Versus Running
- ⊙ Blitzing
- ⊙ Super Bowl
- ⊙ Penalties
- ⊙ Coaches

Activity 3.2

Choose one of the topics you brainstormed in the previous activity, and write out a list of details supporting that topic, following the example above. Share and compare with your group.

Now group the list of details, and compose three topic sentences. Next, write a thesis sentence for an essay about the topic you have chosen. Make sure your thesis sentence covers the three major headings you have just listed. Below the thesis sentence, write an outline for an essay on your topic. When you are finished, share your outline with your group.

Drawing and Sketching. Still another method is *drawing and sketching* (Figure 3.3). Students who think visually might consider drawing, using different-colored pens, or creating shapes to help organize their thoughts. As you conceptualize relationships through drawing and shapes, try to capture the dynamics of your topic—try to show, visually, the relationships of your facts and ideas. Because the ultimate goal of the invention stage is to filter through possible subtopics and key details, visual organization is helpful in culling and balancing your ideas.

Figure 3.3: Drawing and Sketching

Using Other Media. The first time through the invention process, you might consider speaking easier than writing so you might consider using *other media* to help. In fact, you might be speaking out loud or mumbling to yourself as you sort through your material. You might have several lists or brainstorms with bullet points or key facts, but you still cannot see how to connect the dots. So, try recording yourself or asking another person to perform an interview.(See collaborative invention below.) You might even turn on your webcam and create a video. Use the recording as an opportunity to cover as much ground as possible. See whether verbally summarizing key points or research helps you to a greater understanding of the material. Sometimes, when you talk through a subject, you may discover new ideas or ways of presenting those ideas. This method might also assist you to establish a sense of voice or help you determine your audience. Listen to your recording. Be prepared to transcribe this information onto the page in your journal or as another form of invention.

Freewriting. Yet another method of inventing is *freewriting*. It is quite literally a "freedom to write" exercise. You may have no idea where you are headed with the project, but you should still attempt to write your ideas in complete sentences (though at this point, do not be preoccupied with perfect grammar). Some writers prefer this mode because it is how they think—from one idea to the next, without transition, getting all of their thoughts down onto paper (or the screen).

Freewriting may be a good place to begin for those writers who fight the constant urge to "simply get started," to rush to the page because they feel they already have an idea of what they want to say. This practice allows you to write in a fairly conventional method and sample ideas without any restrictions. However, you should not confuse your freewrite with a completed composition.

Collaborative Invention. Finally, *collaborative invention* is one of the more dynamic forms of invention, because it involves working with at least one other person in a shared process. This process may take the shape of an interview with one person asking questions about an initial set of facts or ideas, or a discussion, in which one or more writers invent as a team, discussing a broad topic and producing a wider net of supporting details and connections. Either way, collaborative invention has a greater capacity than many other forms of invention to fuel interest in a project. Collaborative invention also offers added bonuses for the future, as the ability to collaborate is also one of employers' most sought-after qualities in new employees.

While there are no limits to how many can collaborate for a successful invention exercise—for example, you could create a video and send it to all your friends—the number chosen should be small enough to maintain a focused inquiry into a topic. Remember, the strength of a collaboration is in the questions that are raised.

Activity 3.3

Take one of the topics in Activity 3.1 (a different one from the one you worked on in Activity 3.2), and pair up with an individual in your group. Brainstorm this new topic together, list details, and compose three topic sentences for an essay. Was this collaborative invention easier than brainstorming alone? Discuss what you learned with your group, and share it with the whole class.

Balancing Your Ideas

A vibrant invention stage should produce a clear sense of your unifying idea. To use our example of the current situation in the Middle East, you might write, "The current political climate between Palestine and Israel may be used to help define the greater Middle East conflict." You could also have several key subpoints identified in your brainstorm or mind map.

- ⊙ Israel's expanding policy toward settlements
- ⊙ Looming water shortages
- ⊙ Growing religious intolerance on both sides

You might have reached these supporting topics from what was initially "settlements, water, and religion." Having spent the time balancing and exploring these topics until you feel they are now specific, relevant, and balanced in proportion, you can conceive of writing further about them. This is a key benchmark for deciding whether you have spent an adequate amount of time inventing.

Why are balance and specificity so important? Think back to the introduction to this chapter. Specificity is not the only desired characteristic of successful writing. You should be ready to answer the following questions.

- ⊙ Who does this writing address? Who is your audience?
- ⊙ Why is this writing relevant? What is your purpose?
- ⊙ How does this writing attempt to address the issue? What is your approach?

The balance of your supporting points and details is largely a consequence of the time and thought you spend on this stage and demonstrates your preparedness to move on to the next stage, which is structuring this project for a more thorough exploration through the actual writing of a draft.

A Reflection on This Chapter

In constructing this textbook, the authors used the same strategies we now present to you, the student writer. Invention is a challenging topic to fully flesh out, as it is unique to the writer and his or her personal preferences. In writing this chapter, it was necessary to explore the various topics (brainstormed and then listed at the beginning) and then explore them again, this time through the eyes of a first-year writing student. The initial idea was simply to focus on the move from generality to specificity because, quite frankly, this is a skill with which most writers struggle, however advanced they might feel at the craft of writing.

However, by re-envisioning the chapter through the eyes of a first-year writer, it became evident this challenge was only the first layer of concern. Focusing solely on specifics would render the chapter fairly mechanical, superficial almost. A reinvention of the ideas behind this chapter yielded a more important conclusion: most writers do not realize that it is here, in the invention stage, when the relevance of their work is discovered—the "why am I doing this," and "why will anyone care" moment. While striving to understand this relevance, you should see the key elements of the writing situation begin to take shape—the "who" (the audience) and the "how" (to compare, to determine causation, or to analyze).

Final Word

A final word of caution: Writers do not spend nearly enough time on invention, despite its being a stage without many rules and despite the fairly common agreement among them that they dislike the existence of rules. Why? Why ignore perhaps the most liberating stage of the writing process? Often the answer is time. Writing is seen as a task, something one needs to get on with. Because it needs to be done, writing often ends up lacking the necessary specifics to generate interest for both reader and writer. Might interest be generated by spending more time inventing before a single sentence is written? Instead of "Why read it?" perhaps we should revisit the more important question from Chapter 1, "Why write it?"

This Is the Life

Annie Dillard

Annie Dillard is an American author of fiction, nonfiction, and poetry. Her book *Pilgrim at Tinker Creek* won the 1975 Pulitzer Prize for nonfiction. She taught for many years in the English Department at Wesleyan University and is particularly recognized for her nature writing, being called a modern Henry David Thoreau. Her latest book is called *The Abundance: Narrative Essays Old & New* (2016). The following essay was published in *Image* in 2002.

Dillard raises a fundamental question in this essay: how should I live my life? This is not only a major question most of us face as we mature and leave high school, but it was also a major question posed by philosophers and thinkers in classical and medieval times. The Greek philosopher Socrates, for example, said that the *unexamined* life is not worth living. We should not simply follow the crowd and believe what everyone around us believes or do as everyone else does. For Socrates, the best life is that of Plato's presentation to him: one of the continual pursuit of truth, of learning. It is the highest attainment of what it means to be human. And knowledge helps us make better choices and so lead better lives. Therefore, at your age particularly, but also throughout your life, you can use the strategies mentioned in Chapter 3 not only to invent ideas for papers you must write for your classes but also to explore ways of being and relating to the world.

Any culture tells you how to live your one and only life: to wit as everyone else does. Probably most cultures prize, as ours rightly does, making a contribution by working hard at work that you love; being in the know, and intelligent; gathering a surplus; and loving your family above all, and your dog, your boat, bird-watching. Beyond those things our culture might specialize in money, and celebrity, and natural beauty. These are not universal. You enjoy work and will love your grandchildren, and somewhere in there you die.

Another contemporary consensus might be: You wear the best shoes you can afford, you seek to know Rome's best restaurants and their staffs, drive the best car, and vacation on Tenerife. And what a cook you are!

Or you take the next tribe's pigs in thrilling raids; you grill yams; you trade for televisions and hunt white-plumed birds. Everyone you know agrees: this is the life. Perhaps you burn captives. You set fire to a drunk. Yours is the human struggle, or the elite one, to achieve . . . whatever your own culture tells you: to publish the paper that proves the point; to progress in the firm and gain high title and salary, stock options, benefits; to get the loan to store the beans till their price rises; to elude capture, to feed your children or educate them to a feather edge; or to count coup or perfect your calligraphy; to eat the king's deer or catch the poacher; to spear the seal, intimidate the enemy, and be a big man or beloved woman and die respected for the pigs or the title or the shoes. Not a funeral. Forget funeral. A big birthday party. Since everyone around you agrees.

Since everyone around you agrees ever since there were people on earth that land is value, or labor is value, or learning is value, or title, necklaces, degree, murex shells, or ownership of slaves. Everyone knows bees sting and ghosts haunt and giving your robes away humiliates your rivals. That the enemies are barbarians. That wise men swim through the rock of the earth; that houses breed filth, airstrips attract airplanes, tornadoes punish, ancestors watch, and you can buy a shorter stay in purgatory. The black rock is holy, or the scroll; or the pangolin is holy, the quetzal is holy, this tree, water, rock, stone, cow, cross, or mountain and it's all true. The Red Sox. Or nothing at all is holy, as everyone intelligent knows.

Who is your "everyone"? Chess masters scarcely surround themselves with motocross racers. Do you want aborigines at your birthday party? Or are you serving yak-butter tea? Popular culture deals not in its distant past, or any other past, or any other culture. You know no one who longs to buy a mule or be named to court or thrown into a volcano.

So the illusion, like the visual field, is complete. It has no holes except books you read and soon forget. And death takes us by storm. What was that, that life? What else offered? If for him it was contract bridge, if for her it was copyright law, if for everyone it was and is an optimal mix of family and friends, learning, contribution, and joy of making and ameliorating what else is there, or was there, or will there ever be?

What else is a vision or fact of time and the peoples it bears issuing from the mouth of the cosmos, from the round mouth of eternity, in a wide and parti-colored utterance. In the complex weave of this utterance like fabric, in its infinite domestic interstices, the centuries and continents and classes dwell. Each people knows only its own squares in the weave, its wars and instruments and arts, and also the starry sky.

Okay, and then what? Say you scale your own weft and see time's breadth and the length of space. You see the way the fabric both passes among the stars and encloses them. You see in the weave nearby, and aslant farther off, the peoples variously scandalized or exalted in their squares. They work on their projects; they flake spear points, hoe, plant; they kill aurochs or one another; they prepare sacrifices as we here and now work on our projects. What, seeing this spread, multiply infinitely in every direction, would you do differently? No one could love your children more; would you love them less? Would you change your project? To what? Whatever you do, it has likely brought delight to fewer people than either contract bridge or the Red Sox.

However hypnotized you and your people are, you will be just as dead in their war, our war. However dead you are, more people will come. However many more people come, your time and its passions, and yourself and your passions, weigh equally in the balance with those of any dead who pulled waterwheel poles by the Nile or Yellow rivers, or painted their foreheads black, or starved in the wilderness, or wasted from disease then or now. Our lives and our deaths count equally, or we must abandon one-man-one-vote, dismantle democracy, and assign six billion people an importance-of-life ranking from one to six billion, a ranking whose number decreases, like gravity, with the square of the distance between us and them.

What would you do differently, you up on your beanstalk looking at scenes of all peoples at all times in all places? When you climb down, would you dance any less to the music you love, knowing that music to be as provisional as a bug? Somebody has to make jugs and shoes, to turn the soil, fish. If you descend the long rope-ladders back to your people and time in the fabric, if you tell them what you have seen, and even if someone cares to listen, then what? Everyone knows times and cultures are plural. If you come back a shrugging relativist or tongue-tied absolutist, then what? If you spend hours a day looking around, high astraddle the warp or woof of your people's wall, then what new wisdom can you take to your grave for worms to untangle? Well, maybe you will not go into advertising.

Then you would know your own death better but perhaps not dread it less. Try to bring people up the wall, carry children to see it to what end? Fewer golf courses? What is wrong with golf? Nothing at all. Equality of wealth? Sure; how?

The woman watching sheep over there, the man who carries embers in a pierced clay ball, the engineer, the girl who spins wool into yarn as she climbs, the smelter, the babies learning to recognize speech in their own languages, the man whipping a slave's flayed back, the man digging roots, the woman digging roots, the child digging roots—what would you tell them? And the future people, what are they doing? What excitements sweep peoples here and there from time to time? Into the muddy river they go, into the trenches, into the caves, into the mines, into the granary, into the sea in boats. Most humans who were ever alive lived inside one single culture that never changed for hundreds of thousands of years; archaeologists scratch their heads at so conservative and static a culture.

Over here, the rains fail; they are starving. There, the caribou fail; they are starving. Corrupt leaders take the wealth. Not only there but here. Rust and smut spoil the rye. When pigs and cattle starve or freeze, people die soon after. Disease empties a sector, a billion sectors.

People look at the sky and at the other animals. They make beautiful objects, beautiful sounds, beautiful motions of their bodies, beating drums in lines. They pray; they toss people in peat bogs; they help the sick and injured; they pierce their lips, their noses, ears; they make the same mistakes despite religion, written language, philosophy, and science; they build, they kill, they preserve, they count and figure, they boil the pot, they keep the embers alive; they tell their stories and gird themselves.

Will knowledge you experience directly make you a Buddhist? Must you forfeit excitement per se? To what end?

Say you have seen something. You have seen an ordinary bit of what is real, the infinite fabric of time that eternity shoots through, and time's soft-skinned people working and dying under slowly shifting stars. Then what?

Topics for Writing and Discussion

1. In a well-developed paragraph, summarize what you think is the point of Dillard's essay.

2. In a short paper, define what you think would be the "best life" you think a person today could live.

3. How do you see yourself living in twenty years? What will you be doing? Where will you be living? What will your society look like?

CHAPTER 4

Structuring

Too often, novice writers move from the invention to the drafting stage of their writing without interruption. After an exhaustive process of brainstorming or list making, the details of the project should be ready to be employed—yet many writers stall at precisely this point in the process, staring at a blank screen or embarking on a freewriting exercise. However, the writer has skipped an integral stage of the writing process—structuring the project. The structuring stage provides the map—the key elements of the project, such as the thesis statement and discussion points—which anchors the composition and eliminates the panic that often comes when trying to figure out how to proceed.

Think of a construction blueprint. Can you start a building without knowing where the supports or the plumbing will go? A related metaphor might be to consider the scaffolding surrounding a building under construction—visible while the building takes shape but easily removed after construction is completed. For writers, the structuring stage functions much the same way; whether you use an outline, a proposal, or some other form of "map," you are placing the key ideas you have invented into a logical order before proceeding with the actual draft.

It is important to remember that structural tools, such as outlines, are flexible and designed to adjust to the shape of your original ideas. There is no prescription to follow, no neat formula designed to replicate an "out-of-the-box" composition, such as an essay; rather, the structure should replicate your own thought process and provide logical places to reinforce your major points with supporting details (all products of your successful invention stage).

To begin structuring your paper, draw on your invention material to craft a *working thesis statement* and *main discussion points*. Once you have those, you can move onto two key structuring strategies: writing an *outline* and/or writing a *proposal*.

Elements of Structure

As you develop the structure of your paper, begin thinking in terms of two key structural elements: your *thesis*, which defines what you want to say, and your *discussion points*, which define the support of that thesis. By writing a good thesis and then arranging your ideas and research under your discussion points, you will find that the work of drafting your paper becomes much easier.

Pretend for a moment your writing is a human skeleton. Once your work is completed and you give it to the world, your writing needs to stand on its own. You might see the thesis statement as the head of your project, the guiding force behind your composition. The related discussion points might serve as the vertebrae or the spine of your skeleton—the backbone of your ideas. Moving forward with your project without these elements would be akin to animating a pool of jelly. The writing will have difficulty holding its shape, let alone standing on its own.

These analogies are intended to help you to see the key elements of writing in a different context. Many of us tend to have difficulty verbalizing our ideas; we prefer visual images. The structuring stage will help you see your ideas in an organized pattern.

The Working Thesis

Most college writers are familiar with the idea of a thesis statement as part of the introductory paragraph. It is a specific statement of what your writing project will discuss, argue, or accomplish, and it is an important part of preparing a reader for your finished paper. The thesis statement provides guidance for your readers, as it gives them a general overview of your paper and helps them notice the major points you are making. A good thesis helps your reader feel that everything fits together.

However, before you write your introduction and before you consider the thesis statement that will appear in your final paper, it is helpful to think in terms of a *working thesis*. A working thesis is still a road map, but it is a road map for your benefit that gives you a plan for moving forward with your paper. It is a road map that will likely be revised as your paper develops in order to better reflect the changing landscape of your essay, although it will rarely be the thesis statement that appears in your final paper.

From Topic to Thesis

In the invention stage of your writing, you have probably come up with many great ideas about your topic. In crafting a working thesis, you will in essence set boundaries within that topic that define what your specific paper will do. Such boundaries will help you know which information will take you down useful paths and which information will lead off to dead ends (or whole other maps). The process of defining a thesis is one of moving from the broad topic, with which you began your invention phase, toward a very specific statement of what you will actually do in your writing project. It is a process of moving from the general to the specific, and it will require you to ask a lot of important questions about what your writing project will accomplish.

For example, you might have begun your invention stage knowing that you were interested in writing about food—especially your favorite food, avocados. Through the process of inquiry and invention, you might have narrowed down your broad topic to a more specific idea about avocados and personal health and then ended up with a possible statement, such as the following: *Avocados are a healthy food, but many avoid them because of their high fat content.* Ideas you could use to develop this thought might include the following points.

- ⊙ Saturated Versus Unsaturated Fat
- ⊙ Vitamin Content
- ⊙ Fiber Content
- ⊙ Public Perceptions of Fat
- ⊙ Low-Fat Product Sales
- ⊙ The Impact of the Diet Industry on Food Sales
- ⊙ Avocado Farming
- ⊙ The Importance of Avocados in Mexican History
- ⊙ The Cost of Avocados

In order to turn your statement and the most related ideas into a working thesis, you will need to start by thinking about your audience and what you want to offer them. Are you interested in showing a *comparison* between avocados and a more commonly understood "healthy" food in order to demonstrate the health benefits of avocados? Are you more interested in *informing* your audience, through *description* of the situation, about the way perceptions of fat have changed? Or are you more interested in an *analysis* of why a food that has health benefits is considered unhealthy because of its fat content—what is it about fat content that makes people nervous?

Arriving at your working thesis will involve more invention and digging into the material you developed in your invention stage in order to notice connections and important details. For example, to develop an idea about the connections between a common healthy food—such as a low-fat granola bar—and avocados, we could do some further research on the similarities and differences between these products (Table 4.1).

Low-Fat Granola Bar	Half an Avocado
90 calories	160 calories
2 g fat	15 g fat
1 g fiber	7 g fiber
7 g sugar	0 g sugar
Preservatives and "nonfood" ingredients	No preservatives
Some versions with artificial sugar	Nothing artificial
Not a significant source of vitamins	Vitamins A, C, B-6, B-12, iron, magnesium
0.5 g trans fats	Unsaturated fat, shown to help aid absorption of vitamins

Table 4.1: Low-Fat Granola Bar Versus Avocado

See Chapter 3 ❯ Other intervention strategies might leave us with the following observations.

⊙ The association between "low fat" and "healthy" appears on the marketing/boxes for low-fat foods, so it seems to be something that probably helps their sales.

⊙ "Fat" (the macronutrient found in foods) sounds the same as "fat" (the subcutaneous adipose tissues in our bodies), which might confuse people worried about fat (the macronutrient).

⊙ Low-fat processed foods are particularly marketed toward women, so fear of fat might be tied to gender in particular. Ideals of healthy eating have vacillated between low sugar and low fat.

Armed with these further invention resources, you can move on to the work of crafting a working thesis.

Crafting Your Thesis

As you develop your ideas into a clear road map of your project, it is important to keep in mind some basic guidelines about what makes a good thesis statement. A thesis statement should:

- be narrow;
- join a conversation;
- describe what your essay will do; and
- be contestable.

Further, you must avoid fallacious reasoning (See Appendix 2: Common Informal Fallacies). Here are a few suggestions to make your thesis sentence work for you and not against you.

Avoid the obvious. While you want to make it clear to your audience what you intend to do, never say, "In this paper I will . . ." or "It is my opinion that . . ." Statements like this are dull, plodding, and unsubtle. Make your wording original and fresh.

Be direct and forceful in stating your opinion without alienating the reader.

Make it clear that you are taking a stand and are allied with a certain position. Do not, however, say, "It is my opinion that . . .". The reader will know the opinions in the essay are yours. Phrasing a sentence thus only makes for another dull and plodding sentence. If the ideas are not yours, they must be correctly documented.

Make sure your thesis sentence indicates your paper's organization.

If you have, for example, three characteristics of excellence in teachers to discuss, mention each briefly in the thesis sentence, and mention them in the order you wish to discuss them in the body of the paper. This method of organization creates confidence in the reader regarding your ability to be clear, logical, and organized from the outset.

Make certain the length of your sentence is appropriate for the length of your paper. A 45-word thesis statement is too long for a 600-word essay. Your introductory paragraph should not consist only of a thesis. This paragraph introduces your thesis as well as the entire essay.

The thesis statement should be ONE SENTENCE ONLY. A compound sentence is okay, but do not make it merely a string of independent clauses or a rambling sentence.

Finally, never hesitate to revise your thesis statement at any stage in drafting your essay if you feel you can improve it. Even though it may mean additional adjustments in the body of the essay, your extra effort will usually pay off. You should make at least two revisions.

Sample Thesis Statements

1. Although avocados are high in fat, their high fiber content, vitamin content, and the type of fat they contain make them a good part of a healthy diet.

2. While many people eat "low-fat" foods thinking they are healthful, many low-fat foods are high in sugar and low in vitamins, making them less healthy than a high-fat, whole-plant food such as avocados.

3. The public perception of avocados as unhealthy because of their high fat content is indicative of a general fear of fat in Western culture.

Activity 4.1

Pick one of the following topics, brainstorm it, narrow it, and write out a thesis statement.

High school versus college, siblings, first jobs, video games, social media sites, favorite teachers, bad drivers, sports heroes, belief, comedy.

Discussion Points

Discussion points are the main points you will make in your essay, and they will generally become your *topic sentences* as you move into the drafting stage. To develop your discussion points, you simply need to return to your thesis and your invention material. Developing your thesis should already have given you a good handle on the points you want to make, so this stage will involve laying out those points and deciding where you will give supporting description, evidence, and analysis. Developing your discussion points will, again, draw on some of the invention tools discussed in Chapter 3. Examples of potential strategies for developing your discussion points include the following.

⊙ Listing pieces of evidence/observations as they fit under the main points outlined in your thesis

⊙ Writing down important facts or quotations about your topic and then engaging in some analysis of why the points are important

⊙ Freewriting to see what connections and observations you can make

As you develop your discussion points, make sure you are very clear about how each point relates to your working thesis. If you find a point that you think needs development but that does not fit into the boundaries defined by your working thesis, then either drop that point or change your thesis to better reflect your new understanding. Finally, keep in mind that discussion points will be developed into topic sentences, so they should not be facts or specific details but generalizations and opinions that you will support and prove within your paragraphs.

Structuring Strategies

There are many different ways to think about structuring your paper, and you should experiment to see what works for you. Most beginning writers find the process of developing an outline to be very useful as a way to visualize their writing project. Again, an outline is like a map, showing a traveler where he is headed, or like a blueprint, showing a builder where everything will go in a project. Another structuring strategy, which many writers approach after completing an outline, is the proposal.

The Outline

While the word *outline* itself provokes scurrilous mutterings and utter contempt from most composition students, it need not be treated as an adversarial force to be conquered or endured. It must, however, be done *before you write the essay*, not after. Once you become familiar enough with the benefits of outlining, you might discover it is the most critical step in all the prewriting stages. The outline functions much like the blueprints of an architectural project. It is the framework on which to build your essay. You must overcome the tendency to resist this key step in the stage of writing, for, regardless of which rhetorical mode you select for your essay, good planning is essential. Likewise, poor planning is quickly evident. The value is endless for the writer as well as the reader. Consider the following advantages.

- ⊙ For the writer, the outline encourages brevity.

- ⊙ An outline can keep you from violating unity by indicating that an idea does not belong. At the same time, the outline will often suggest that some additional idea might be included.

- ⊙ The outline can ensure that important ideas are placed in the appropriate places according to relative value.

- ⊙ An outline's format allows you to check for stylistic consistency, continuity, and clarity.

- ⊙ Outlines keep you focused on the separate ideas and let you actually **visualize** the level of generality among your ideas. Your ideas in the outline format are simply easier to see.

- ⊙ Finally, the outline will provide you with a psychological boost. Having succeeded in organizing your ideas logically, you enjoy a sense of accomplishment that should allow you to move on to the next writing stage with increased confidence.

Consider again, despite the examples that follow, that the outline is *a flexible form*—which is to say it can adapt and change to your ideas, to the structure of your project—not the other way around.

There are two basic outline forms—the *topic outline* and the *sentence outline*. Regardless of the assignment, you will want to consider using both forms at strategic stages in the prewriting phase. You might use a topic outline when your grasp over your paper is still in its infancy and then move toward a sentence outline as your ideas necessitate further specificity. Now that your purpose is clear, your audience is designated, and you have a workable thesis clearly in mind, it is time to impose the standard outline system of organization on your thoughts. The following system is the universal format for outlining ideas (Figure 4.1).

Thesis

I.   [First discussion point related to thesis statement]

    (Note: The old adage "If you have a 1, you must have a 2" is a valid point. The same holds true of any subheading or level of development. A good rule to remember is that a pair is the required minimum.)

    A.

       1.

          a.

          b.

          c.

       2.

          a.

          b.

          c.

    B.

       1.

          a.

          b.

          c.

       2.

          a.

          b.

          c.

II. [Second discussion point related to thesis statement]

    A. [etc.]

Figure 4.1: Outlining Format

Each Roman numeral is a major division of the thesis of the essay, and each of the subheadings, capital letters, Arabic numerals, and lowercase letters hold more specific information that develops each division (paragraph). Again, the exact usage of letters and numbers is far less important than the shape the structure provides your writing project.

Topic Outline Versus Sentence Outline

The topic outline is helpful in the preliminary organization of the essay when you want to determine the main points of your discussion and the order in which you will discuss them. Each entry in a topic outline is just what the term implies: a topic heading, much like a title, not a complete sentence, but a "bare-bones" phrase. The topic outline delineates the areas to be discussed but does not yet deal with what specifically will be said about them. Even at the topic outline level, however, you should be grammatically consistent. If you want to use nouns, nouns plus a verb form, or prepositional phrases, make certain you use them at each letter or number level in order to create a *parallel structure*. This consistency will assist you later when transforming your topic outline to the body paragraphs of the essay. The following is a topic outline for a paper on what makes a good teacher (Figure 4.2).

Good Teachers

Thesis: A good teacher respects students, has a personal interest in them, and motivates them to do their best.

I. Respect for students
    A. Considerate
        1. Tactful
        2. Nonridiculing
        3. Patient
        4. Nonpatronizing
    B. Fair
        1. Flexible
        2. Fair in testing
        3. Objective in grading
        4. No favoritism
    C. Values students' contributions
        1. Compliments students' work
        2. Praises student involvement

Figure 4.2: Sample Outline—Good Teachers

Whether it is used initially or instead of the topic outline, the sentence outline requires more effort. You will still be required to list, categorize, and order your ideas by relative importance. This time, however, you must write your thoughts in *complete sentences*. The biggest advantage of a sentence outline is that you are, in fact, composing sentences that will find their way into your actual project or paper. (You are in fact writing part of it.) The first stage of a sentence outline might look like the sample in Figure 4.3.

I. Good teachers respect their students.
    A. They are considerate of their students.
        1. They criticize them tactfully.
        2. They do not ridicule them or embarrass them.
        3. They are patient with them.
        4. They never patronize their students.
    B. They treat their students fairly.
        1. They are flexible and open-minded.
        2. Their tests are fair.
        3. They grade objectively and consistently.
        4. They do not have favorites.
    C. They show that they value the contributions of everyone in the class.
        1. They compliment their students on their work.
        2. They praise students for their involvement even when they disagree with students' opinions.
II. (etc.)

Figure 4.3: Sentence Outline

A hint about outlining: regardless of which outline form you use, it is a good idea to write down all the headings/sentences for the first level of organization (i.e., the Roman numerals) before going on to the next level (i.e., the capital letters and all the capital letter headings). Doing so helps keep the levels of development, the subtopics, and details clear. With this systematic organizational plan behind you, you can now concentrate on the next phase, drafting.

Activity 4.2

Arrange the following sentences in order, putting the number of the sentence in the proper place in the outline. Remember to look specifically for levels of generality.

1. The staff greets each diner with the traditional "ma'am" or "sir" and treats her or him with the utmost respect and dignity.

2. They treat everyone as if they are life-long friends, greeting patrons with "Hey! How's it going?"

3. When dining at the classy Pappadeaux, each patron is greeted by an exquisitely dressed staff.

4. Although the service is impeccable at both Pappadeaux and Joe's Crab Shack, the manner in which one is served varies greatly.

5. In contrast, it is much more relaxed at Joe's Crab Shack.

6. The entire staff wears t-shirts and shorts or jeans.

7. The waitstaff is clad in black slacks, white tuxedo shirts, and classic bow ties.

   I.   Topic sentence: _____

      A. _____

          1._____

          2._____

      B. _____

          1._____

          2._____

Activity 4.3

Construct an appropriate topic sentence for a paragraph based on the evidence given in the following sentences.

1. Topic sentence:_____
    a. Kate's toys always seem to be misplaced.
    b. She is usually late for dinner.
    c. She sometimes forgets her homework assignments.
    d. Her room, despite her mother's pleadings, is a mess.

2. Topic sentence:_____
    a. Colleen is always available to talk to her friends about their problems.
    b. Colleen never judges anyone.
    c. She is dependable and reliable.
    d. Colleen is very trustworthy.

3. Topic sentence:_____
    a. I once forgot to feed my kids' parakeet, and it died.
    b. One rainy day I accidentally ran over my dog Fido.
    c. Even goldfish turn white and float on their backs at my house.
    d. My pet iguana jumped off the roof and impaled himself on a metal rod.

4. Topic sentence:_____
    a. Bubba dips snuff and wears boots and tight Wrangler jeans.
    b. He drives an extended-cab pickup truck.
    c. Bubba's belt buckle is larger than his truck's chrome rims.
    d. He has nothing but contempt for any kind of music other than country and western.

5. Topic sentence:_____
    a. Over 26 percent of all traffic accidents are linked to drivers' negligence while talking on their phones.
    b. A driver's attention is diverted from the road for a minimum of five seconds each time she sends or receives a text.
    c. Cell phones constantly ring at inappropriate times and disturb other people in public places.
    d. Accidents while texting and walking occur more often than texting and driving.

The Proposal

A *proposal* is a common tool for planning a larger project; it may be used in a business or academic setting in order to introduce and develop a plan for moving forward. Completing a proposal for a writing project might be a step that you take either before or after completing an outline, and it consists primarily of developing your thesis and further defining your project, your main discussion points,  and your plan for moving forward. Figure 4.4 on page 68 is a sample proposal. As you write a proposal, consider your thesis as the starting point—it defines your subject and gives a broad idea of your focus—and then further define your project with some of these questions.

What is your purpose in writing? (Are you attempting to change your readers' minds? Are you just informing them about your topic? What kind of audience response would be ideal?)

Why does it matter?

What are your most important points?

What sources, including your own experience, do you already have to make your points?

What kind of sources and research would be helpful for you to find?

How does your writing project fit into a larger conversation? How is what you are saying similar to what others have said? How is it different? What do you add?

What do you hope to learn through this writing project?

Thesis: The public perception of avocados as unhealthy because of their high fat content is indicative of a general fear of fat in Western culture.

This paper will analyze the reasons people avoid avocados, focusing on the fear of their fat content. So far, I think the main reason people avoid avocados is that the diet industry has placed a lot of focus on the danger of fat, leading people to think eating *any* fat is bad for you. I'll also talk  about ignorance among consumers who don't understand the difference between saturated fat and unsaturated fat. Finally, I think part of the problem is that "fat" can mean both the nutrient in food *and* the stuff on our body doctors say can be unhealthy. This could connect to nutrition discussions of what actually leads to obesity and increased fat deposits, but also to a discussion of body positivity in US culture.

I will need to do an analysis of some weight-loss advertisements in order to look at the way they talk about fat. I will also need to look for literature that talks about public perceptions of fat. If I can't find discussions of whether consumers know what saturated versus unsaturated fat means, I might need to do a survey. Journals that talk about nutrition and health will also be important for showing possible health benefits people miss out on by being afraid of good fats.

There is a larger conversation about whether fat or sugar is the bigger problem in public health, with many nutritionists focused more on sugar. So looking at the reasons why many people are still wary of avocados would be a good way to begin helping nutritionists understand how to reach Americans and get them to eat the healthiest possible diet.

Figure 4.4: Sample Proposal

Activity 4.4

Rewrite each of the following sentences, narrowing the subject and limiting the focus of each so they can serve as effective topic sentences for paragraphs. Compare and discuss with your group.

1. Ted is a fascinating man.

2. Houston drivers are bad.

3. My friend Juan is weird.

4. Teens today face many challenges.

5. My parents' taste in music sucks.

6. I need a new car.

7. Online classes are quite helpful.

8. High school, when compared to college, was a real drag.

9. A girlfriend/boyfriend is awfully expensive.

10. Living in an apartment is more fun than living at home.

Activity 4.5

Take one of the topic sentences you generated in the above activity and write a 200-300-word paragraph.

Final Word

When this text was first conceived, one of the most important steps was structuring the chapters. The decision to break the chapters down into discrete stages of the writing process was a conscious choice and needed to be made before any of the chapters were written. Beginning writers do not spend enough time on the steps needed to complete a writing project and, therefore, experience difficulties diagnosing what is wrong with a composition and how to fix it—perhaps because writing instruction has historically been wedded to the idea of the *finished product*.

Once structured as a "process manual," we then took further structural steps to outline the individual chapters so we might in greater detail expand from broad steps in the writing process to specific techniques and methods employed within each stage. Organizing our efforts this way enabled us to work as a team of authors—working collaboratively toward a common goal—with authors tackling topics best suited to their expertise.

Very few beginning writers employ a discrete "structuring" stage in their writing process. However, you should realize that by engaging in this stage, you have in fact already started the composition process—the actual writing of your project. The ideas taken from the invention stage become placeholders as topics in a topic outline. These, in turn, become sentences as part of a sentence outline and undergo a slow but identifiable transformation, moving from general concepts to more specific statements. Developing these specific points will help your project because it is a process of testing (or interrogating) your whole project. Ideas that survive this process will be worthy of keeping. You will also find that these ideas, such as your thesis and key discussion points, are also now the best sentences in your paper (having been tested and probably rewritten), and the further expansion of them will become much easier as a result.

With these key sentences in place, and with your roadmap charted out, you are now ready to explore your ideas further in the actual draft.

Our Vanishing Night

Verlyn Klinkenborg

Verlyn Klinkenborg is a writer of nonfiction who has taught creative writing at a number of colleges as well as Harvard University. In addition to many books, he has written articles for magazines such as *The New Yorker*, *Harper's Magazine*, and *The New York Times*, for which he contributed a regular column called The Rural Life from 1997 to 2013. He lives on a farm in upstate New York. The following essay was published in *National Geographic* in November of 2008.

Klinkenborg's essay, about light pollution and the loss to nocturnal creatures and to ourselves of darkness and the night sky, is clearly structured. Following an introductory paragraph, he states his thesis at the beginning of the second paragraph and then goes on to develop it in three sections: the first about how we humans have altered the night sky over the past several centuries (paragraphs 2, 3, 4, and 5), the second about the effects of light pollution on birds, insects, and turtles (paragraphs 6, 7, 8, and 9), and the third about the effects of light pollution on us, humans (paragraphs 10, 11, 12, and 13). In the concluding paragraph, he says "light pollution causes us to lose sight of our true place in the universe."

If humans were truly at home under the light of the moon and stars, we would go in darkness happily, the midnight world as visible to us as it is to the vast number of nocturnal species on this planet. Instead, we are diurnal creatures, with eyes adapted to living in the sun's light. This is a basic evolutionary fact, even though most of us don't think of ourselves as diurnal beings any more than we think of ourselves as primates or mammals or Earthlings. Yet it's the only way to explain what we've done to the night: We've engineered it to receive us by filling it with light.

This kind of engineering is no different than damming a river. Its benefits come with consequences—called light pollution—whose effects scientists are only now beginning to study. Light pollution is largely the result of bad lighting design, which allows artificial light to shine outward and upward into the sky, where it's not wanted, instead of focusing it downward, where it is. Ill-designed lighting washes out the darkness of night and radically alters the light levels—and light rhythms—to which many forms of life, including ourselves, have adapted. Wherever human light spills into the natural world, some aspect of life—migration, reproduction, feeding—is affected.

For most of human history, the phrase "light pollution" would have made no sense. Imagine walking toward London on a moonlit night around 1800, when it was Earth's most populous city. Nearly a million people lived there, making do, as they always had, with candles and rushlights and torches and lanterns. Only a few houses were lit by gas, and there would be no public gaslights in the streets or squares for another seven years. From a few miles away, you would have been as likely to *smell* London as to see its dim collective glow.

Now most of humanity lives under intersecting domes of reflected, refracted light, of scattering rays from overlit cities and suburbs, from light-flooded highways and factories. Nearly all of nighttime Europe is a nebula of light, as is most of the United States and all of Japan. In the south Atlantic the glow from a single fishing fleet—squid fishermen luring their prey with metal halide lamps—can be seen from space, burning brighter, in fact, than Buenos Aires or Rio de Janeiro.

In most cities the sky looks as though it has been emptied of stars, leaving behind a vacant haze that mirrors our fear of the dark and resembles the urban glow of dystopian science fiction. We've grown so used to this pervasive orange haze that the original glory of an unlit night—dark enough for the planet Venus to throw shadows on Earth—is wholly beyond our experience, beyond memory almost. And yet above the city's pale ceiling lies the rest of the universe, utterly undiminished by the light we waste—a bright shoal of stars and planets and galaxies, shining in seemingly infinite darkness.

We've lit up the night as if it were an unoccupied country, when nothing could be further from the truth. Among mammals alone, the number of nocturnal species is astonishing. Light is a powerful biological force, and on many species it acts as a magnet, a process being studied by researchers such as Travis Longcore and Catherine Rich, co-founders of the Los Angeles-based Urban Wildlands Group. The effect is so powerful that scientists speak of songbirds and seabirds being "captured" by searchlights on land or by the light from gas flares on marine oil platforms, circling and circling in the thousands until they drop. Migrating at night, birds are apt to collide with brightly lit tall buildings; immature birds on their first journey suffer disproportionately.

Insects, of course, cluster around streetlights, and feeding at those insect clusters is now ingrained in the lives of many bat species. In some Swiss valleys the European lesser horseshoe bat began to vanish after streetlights were installed, perhaps because those valleys were suddenly filled with light-feeding pipistrelle bats. Other nocturnal mammals—including desert rodents, fruit bats, opossums, and badgers—forage more cautiously under the permanent full moon of light pollution because they've become easier targets for predators.

Some birds—blackbirds and nightingales, among others—sing at unnatural hours in the presence of artificial light. Scientists have determined that long artificial days—and artificially short nights—induce early breeding in a wide range of birds. And because a longer day allows for longer feeding, it can also affect migration schedules. One population of Bewick's swans wintering in England put on fat more rapidly than usual, priming them to begin their Siberian migration early. The problem, of course, is that migration, like most other aspects of bird behavior, is a precisely timed biological behavior. Leaving early may mean arriving too soon for nesting conditions to be right.

Nesting sea turtles, which show a natural predisposition for dark beaches, find fewer and fewer of them to nest on. Their hatchlings, which gravitate toward the brighter, more reflective sea horizon, find themselves confused by artificial lighting behind the beach. In Florida alone, hatchling losses number in the hundreds of thousands every year. Frogs and toads living near brightly lit highways suffer nocturnal light levels that are as much as a million times brighter than normal, throwing nearly every aspect of their behavior out of joint, including their nighttime breeding choruses.

Of all the pollutions we face, light pollution is perhaps the most easily remedied. Simple changes in lighting design and installation yield immediate changes in the amount of light spilled into the atmosphere and, often, immediate energy savings.

It was once thought that light pollution only affected astronomers, who need to see the night sky in all its glorious clarity. And, in fact, some of the earliest civic efforts to control light pollution—in Flagstaff, Arizona, half a century ago—were made to protect the view from Lowell Observatory, which sits high above that city. Flagstaff has tightened its regulations since then, and in 2001 it was declared the first International Dark Sky City. By now the effort to control light pollution has spread around the globe. More and more cities and even entire countries, such as the Czech Republic, have committed themselves to reducing unwanted glare.

Unlike astronomers, most of us may not need an undiminished view of the night sky for our work, but like most other creatures we do need darkness. Darkness is as essential to our biological welfare, to our internal clockwork, as light itself. The regular oscillation of waking and sleep in our lives—one of our circadian rhythms—is nothing less than a biological expression of the regular oscillation of light on Earth. So fundamental are these rhythms to our being that altering them is like altering gravity.

For the past century or so, we've been performing an open-ended experiment on ourselves, extending the day, shortening the night, and short-circuiting the human body's sensitive response to light. The consequences of our bright new world are more readily perceptible in less adaptable creatures living in the peripheral glow of our prosperity. But for humans, too, light pollution may take a biological toll. At least one new study has suggested a direct correlation between higher rates of breast cancer in women and the nighttime brightness of their neighborhoods.

In the end, humans are no less trapped by light pollution than the frogs in a pond near a brightly lit highway. Living in a glare of our own making, we have cut ourselves off from our evolutionary and cultural patrimony—the light of the stars and the rhythms of day and night. In a very real sense, light pollution causes us to lose sight of our true place in the universe, to forget the scale of our being, which is best measured against the dimensions of a deep night with the Milky Way—the edge of our galaxy—arching overhead.

Topics for Writing and Discussion

1. This essay recounts a type of pollution we do not normally discuss, light pollution. It details the effects of this pollution on various life forms, particularly those adapted to darkness. For images of earth at night, go to the NASA site *Visible Earth*. The International Dark Sky Association's website lists "dark-sky" parks and places where one can go to experience the night sky. If you live in a large city, as most of us do, you almost never experience the night sky. Do you agree with Klinkenborg that we are "trapped by light pollution" and have lost "sight of our true place in the universe"? Explain.

2. Do a search of the internet for the effects of light pollution on humans, and write a report on your findings. Be sure to cite your sources and avoid plagiarism.

CHAPTER 5
Drafting

The next step after structuring is the drafting stage, which is the stage of the writing process that most of us imagine when we think about writing. Here is where we take all of our ideas and begin to record them in sentences and paragraphs in order to construct a paper. But it is important to understand drafting as a stage. Drafting builds on the structuring work you did in the last chapter; neither drafting nor structuring is a single entity, but each contains its own process.

Most writers draft in pieces, putting together paragraphs as they are ready to and revising paragraphs as they write more. For this reason, it can sometimes be especially helpful to do your drafting out of order. This chapter will suggest that you begin by developing your body paragraphs based on the thesis and discussion points that you have chosen. As you write, you might find that your ideas develop and change, so we recommend that you postpone writing your introduction and conclusion paragraphs until you have largely finished with the body of your essay.

Body Paragraphs

While student writers often begin their draft with the introduction, most experienced writers have an easier time when they begin their draft in the middle. Try beginning your draft somewhere in the middle by developing your first body paragraph based on the invention and planning you have already done.

One of the most difficult tasks you face as a writer is remembering that the reader is not inside your head. So ideas that seem clear to you probably need to be developed in much more detail in order to make sense to someone else. Everything you say, even something that seems obvious to you, needs to be supported and developed through the paragraphs in your writing project.

Remember that if your thesis alone were enough, there would be no need to engage in a larger writing project. The goal is to develop and elaborate on the discussion points brought up in your thesis statement so that your audience can understand and accept the validity of your ideas. For them to do that, your ideas need to be logically arranged and appropriately developed.

As you already know, we develop our ideas in blocks of prose called paragraphs. What you might not know is that the word *paragraph* is derived from two Greek words—*para*, meaning "beside" or "alongside of," and *graph*, from the Greek word for "to write." The word evolved from the practice of Greek scholars who, when confronted with early texts of the *Iliad*, wrote notes in the large margins of the original scrolls to indicate such things as shifts in speakers. Today, paragraphs help readers navigate long blocks of prose. Readers expect paragraphs to be unified, coherent, and sufficiently developed.

Paragraph Unity

Within a larger writing project, you can think of your paragraph as a basic unit of meaning. Each paragraph works to develop and articulate a specific idea and should be unified around that idea. As you draft a paragraph, think about the way that every sentence builds on the previous one in order to make the point you want to make. Similarly, think about the way that each paragraph builds on the previous one in order to develop your thesis.

Within your paragraph, your goal should be to show how every sentence builds on the one that came before to create new meaning. This focus will give your paragraphs unity, and it will also keep you on task in writing a paper that effectively develops and supports your thesis statement. To keep your ideas focused and on topic, start with topic sentences.

Topic sentences are the sentences that begin each paragraph and provide the unifying idea that holds your paragraph together. Your topic sentences should develop your discussion points and should always refer back to your thesis. As you progress through the sentences in your paragraph, your goal should always be to make sure that your sentences all work together to develop the main unifying idea expressed in your topic sentence.

Activity 5.1

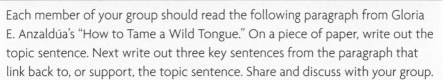

Each member of your group should read the following paragraph from Gloria E. Anzaldúa's "How to Tame a Wild Tongue." On a piece of paper, write out the topic sentence. Next write out three key sentences from the paragraph that link back to, or support, the topic sentence. Share and discuss with your group.

> Chicana feminists often skirt around each other with suspicion and hesitation. For the longest time I couldn't figure it out. Then it dawned on me. To be close to another Chicana is like looking into the mirror. We are afraid of what we'll see there. Pena. Shame. Low estimation of self. In childhood we are told that our language is wrong. Repeated attacks on our native tongue diminish our sense of self. The attacks continue throughout our lives. Chicanas feel uncomfortable talking in Spanish to Latinas, afraid of their censure. Their language was not outlawed in their countries. They had a whole lifetime of being immersed in their native tongue: generations, centuries in which Spanish was a first language, taught in school, heard on radio and TV, and read in the newspaper.

Paragraph Coherence

The sentences within each paragraph should cohere, stick together, so that the reader moves smoothly from one idea, one sentence, to another. To achieve this coherence, this smooth flow of ideas, writers use several techniques. One is the *repetition of key words and phrases* throughout the paragraph. This repetition, such as pronouns that refer back to nouns, keeps the reader focused on the main point of the paragraph. A second technique is to use *parallel sentence structures* for parallel points within the paragraph, again providing coherence and flow to the paragraph. A third technique often used by writers is to insert *transitional devices* (words or phrases) to help readers navigate the logical sequence of ideas within the paragraph.

For example, note the *repetition of key words and pronouns* in the following student paragraph.

> Since I've been working as a cashier at Wal-Mart, I've discovered there are several kinds of **customers** who drive me crazy. First are the openly rude **ones**. **They** frown and make loud, sarcastic remarks about how long the line is and how long **they**'ve been waiting. **They** throw their money on the counter and never say hello or acknowledge me as anything but human scum. I'm embarrassed for myself, but I'm also embarrassed for **them**. Second are the silent but obviously impatient

customers. They make faces, roll **their** eyes, and look at **their** watches every ten seconds. What do **they** expect? This is Wal-Mart; there are always lines. The third kind is really my least favorite: suspicious **customers** who watch my every move as if my goal in life is to overcharge **them. They** turn the monitor so **they** can see every price, but that's not enough. After looking at the price there, **they** lean over the counter toward me and look at what price comes up on the register. Then **their** heads snap back to look at the monitor. **They** clearly don't trust me and are just waiting for me to make a mistake, at which point **they** will jump all over me. This kind of **customer** makes me nervous and a lot more likely to mess up. If you are one of these three kinds of **customers**, remember me next time you're at Wal-Mart; I'm the one just trying to do my job, and you're driving me crazy!

—Joyce Kenneally

Putting parallel ideas in parallel grammatical forms is another way to achieve paragraph coherence. The following is perhaps the most famous use of *parallel structure* in American history—Abraham Lincoln's Gettysburg Address, delivered on November 19, 1863:

Four score and seven years ago our fathers brought forth on this continent, a new nation, conceived in Liberty, and dedicated to the proposition that all men are created equal. Now we are engaged in a great civil war, testing whether that nation, or any nation so conceived and so dedicated, can long endure. We are met on a great battle-field of that war. We have come to dedicate a portion of that field, as a final resting place for those who here gave their lives that that nation might live. It is altogether fitting and proper that we should do this. But, in a larger sense, we cannot dedicate—we cannot consecrate—we cannot hallow—this ground. The brave men, living and dead, who struggled here, have consecrated it, far above our poor power to add or detract. The world will little note, nor long remember what we say here, but it can never forget what they did here. It is for us the living, rather, to be dedicated here to the unfinished work which they who fought here have thus far so nobly advanced. It is rather for us to be here dedicated to the great task remaining before us—that from these honored dead we take increased devotion to that cause for which they gave the last full measure of devotion—that we here highly resolve that these dead shall not have died in vain—that this nation, under God, shall have a new birth of freedom—and that government of the people, by the people, for the people, shall not perish from the earth.

Next, using transitional words—such as *first, second, third, next, on the contrary,* and *in addition*—that signal additional or contrasting material within a paragraph is also a good way to help your reader follow your train of thought. They are like road signs pointing the reader in the right direction so he will not get lost while navigating the paragraph. In addition, transitions between paragraphs help readers stay focused on the main thesis of your paper. Table 5.1 (page 82) shows some of the most commonly used transitional devices.

The following paragraph illustrates the use of one method of using transitional devices.

> People marry the wrong people for the wrong reasons. **Of course**, they seem to be the right people and the right reasons at the time the decision is made, but the trouble really begins here. **First**, many couples are too young when they marry. They meet in high school or college, "fall in love," which is really just lust, and know that they have found the person they are going to marry. **Next**, many young girls think that they are ready to marry, but many times they simply want to get out of their parents' house. The situation may involve abuse in some form or another, or the girl simply may not be getting along with her folks and sees marriage as a way out. She believes that if she can just make a home of her own everything will be fine. She looks on the young man as her salvation, and he begins to see himself in that role. **In addition**, she may also be pregnant. This situation always makes things worse for the young couple. The coming baby takes many choices away from the pair and adds many responsibilities that they are just not prepared to take on. **Finally**, there are financial burdens to be dealt with, such as hospital and doctor bills, as well as the burdens of trying to be parents when they themselves are little more than children. The frustration and the stress of all these burdens can be devastating to everyone concerned, which makes the situation all the more tragic.
>
> —Debbie Born

Activity 5.2

Type or write out the following paragraph on a piece of paper. Circle all the words (repetitions, synonyms, pronouns, transition words) that help to tie the sentences and ideas together. Share and discuss with your group.

> Finally, there is the power of the extended mind. There is also a developed body of research on how much our very consciousness is shaped by the people around us. Let me simplify it with a classic observation: Each close friend you have brings out a version of yourself that you could not bring out on your own. When your close friend dies, you are not only losing the friend, you are losing the version of your personality that she elicited. Once we acknowledge that, in life, we are playing soccer, not baseball, a few things become clear. First, awareness of the landscape of reality is the highest form of wisdom. It's not raw computational power that matters most; it's having a sensitive attunement to the widest environment, feeling where the flow of events is going. Genius is in practice perceiving more than the conscious reasoning.

Paragraph Development

Paragraphs can be developed in many ways. The thesis and main points you have set up will generally dictate the method you will use to develop, or flesh out, the body of your paragraphs. But no matter how organized and unified your ideas are, if they are not fully developed, you will have failed to communicate to your audience. Supporting evidence or examples come from the following.

- Your own experiences
- Hypothetical examples
- Research material
- Authoritative evidence
- Facts
- Just about any sound, reliable source

Many students ask, "What is enough support?" The answer is arbitrary, but some general guidelines apply. You want enough support to convince your audience that your argument is sound. Whose opinion, for example, is more likely to be accepted in a court of law: a defense attorney's claim that her client is innocent because the defendant's family and friends know he is innocent or the prosecuting attorney's claim that the defendant is guilty because of fourteen eyewitnesses and extensive forensic evidence? Valid evidence is convincing and supports opinions and observation. The same is true of paragraph development. You must provide enough information to convince readers that your argument is sound.

As a rule, the average length of a paragraph in a college-level essay might run approximately three-fourths of a typed page. While striving arduously for quantity, however, NEVER forget that quality is more important. The fact that Aunt Zona Gail believes men make better teachers than women is not the strong evidence you want to support your contentions about good teachers. But surveying students or speaking with teachers who have won awards or recognition for excellence in teaching would serve as appropriate proof.

In moving from topic sentence to supporting evidence in a paragraph, you are moving from general to specific. The order and progression of this movement is essential to effective paragraphs, and the outline is the most efficient method of making certain this progression occurs logically. This order ranks and demonstrates the levels of generality in a paragraph (Figure 5.1).

Thesis: Igor often failed to live up to his expectations. LEVEL ONE

   I.   [topic sentence—general statement] Igor was a poor student. LEVEL TWO

      A.   [subtopic—less general] He was not conscientious. LEVEL THREE

         1. [example—specific] He never handed in assignments on time. LEVEL FOUR

            a. [more specific] He handed in his first English composition two weeks late. LEVEL FIVE

Figure 5.1: Levels of Generality

These levels constitute the arrangement of ideas in the paragraph, from general statement to specific examples. Always develop your ideas in the outline of your paragraph at least to level four. The logic behind this recommendation is that you most likely will have to reach level three before you can provide examples that are specific and concrete enough to persuade your readers of your general assertion (level one). In addition, the ideal number of level two or level three statements is three; that is, A, B, C and 1, 2, and 3. If you offer only two examples, you could risk sounding dogmatic and inflexible. Four or more examples under the same subtopic, however, suggest you wish to appeal emotionally to your readers. Some readers might cry out "Enough already!" There is such a thing as overkill, especially if your examples tend to be repetitive. You will not always be able to provide three examples, but the goal is a worthy one. Make sure you understand and can recognize the different levels so you can create good, effective outlines and, consequently, good paragraphs (Figure 5.2).

Thesis: Good teachers have certain qualities in common. LEVEL ONE

   I.   Good teachers respect their students. LEVEL TWO

      A.   They are considerate of their students. LEVEL THREE

         1. They criticize them tactfully. LEVEL FOUR

            a. They always tell them something positive about their work along with giving suggestions on how to improve it. LEVEL FIVE

Figure 5.2: Developing Ideas

Sequence or Addition		Narrowing of Focus	
And	Besides	Definitely	Explicitly
Again	Finally	After all	Specifically
Also	Furthermore	In fact	That is
Too	In addition	Indeed	In other words
Moreover	One . . . another	In particular	Expressly
Next	First… second…third	**Conclusions**	
Last	Still	In summary	Consequently
Additionally		In conclusion	In other words
Time Order		To conclude	Thus
At first	Afterword	Therefore	As a result
Soon	At length	**Concession**	
Earlier	At the same time	Granted	Certainly
Before	Now	Naturally	Of course
After	As soon as	Although it is true	Admittedly
Finally	· Meanwhile	Although you could say that	
Then	In the meantime	**Cause and Effect**	
Later	Until	Hence	Then
Next	Immediately	Since	Thus
During	Eventually	Therefore	As a result
Subsequently		Still	On the one hand
Comparison		Notwithstanding	So
Similarly	In comparison	On the other hand	Accordingly
Likewise	Also	Nonetheless	In contrast
By the same token	Additionally	On the contrary	Although
Furthermore	Moreover	Despite	Meanwhile
Contrast		Conversely	
However	Nevertheless	**Example**	
But	Instead	For example	Thus
Yet	Even though	To illustrate	Specifically
		Especially	Explicitly
		For instance	Namely

Table 5.1: Transitional Words

Finally, if your paragraph is a long one, you might consider including a summary sentence, a "clincher," to close your paragraph. The inclusion of such a sentence serves at least two purposes. First, it brings closure to the main idea of the paragraph, especially if you have provided extensive examples. Closure helps your audience by returning them to your central idea and reminding them of your specific intention in the paragraph. Second, the summary sentence is on the same level of generality as your topic sentence; therefore, it will make your task of bridging the connection between this paragraph and the next easier than it would be if you had to move from a very specific level of generality, a minor support statement, to a new topic sentence in a new paragraph. This final summary sentence "clinches" the discussion and emphasizes the main idea. Some writers prefer to provide in this final sentence some notion of what is to come in the next paragraph through some kind of transition device (Table 5.1).

There are many methods for developing your paragraphs. It all depends upon your purpose, your audience, and your topic. See Chapter 6 for many different ways to develop a paragraph—and a complete essay.

From Paragraph to Essay

When you understand the principles that constitute a good paragraph, you will understand the general organization of the essay. Remember that a paragraph is a miniature essay. Only the scope of a paragraph changes to meet the requirements of the essay. The system remains the same, but the form expands. Consider the diagram below, and note the simple changes that occur when the components of the paragraph are converted to the essay.

   I. Topic sentence *becomes* Thesis statement
      A. Subtopic *becomes* I. Topic sentence
         1. Example *becomes* A. Subtopic
         2. Example *becomes* B. Subtopic
      B. Subtopic *becomes* II. Topic sentence
         1. Example *becomes* A. Subtopic
         2. Example *becomes* B. Subtopic
      C. Subtopic *becomes* III. Topic sentence

What is needed now in the essay is an additional level of development. Under the subtopics in the above essay format, you would add specific, supporting examples to complete the essential skeleton of the essay (i.e., add 1., 2., 3. under A. and B., etc.).

In general, most of your writing will have an introductory paragraph, usually three or more body paragraphs, and a concluding paragraph. But regardless of the length of the essay, the principles of organization remain the same.

Now you are ready to conclude the writing process by putting the finishing touches on your essay. This stage of your writing actually includes several steps. Having completed the heart of your thoughts in your body paragraphs (the middle), you now need to introduce those thoughts in an opening paragraph that includes your thesis and to conclude your discussion by offering closure. Although the techniques vary considerably regarding these two paragraphs, the primary function is to provide the framework for the ideas you convincingly present to your audience. This stage completes the writing phase.

Introductions

Many students are confused by the idea that they should save their introduction for last, but it can be a very useful strategy for writing effective introductions. The introduction, after all, serves as a way to introduce your thesis statement, your road map, to your audience. Although you have been writing with a working thesis in mind, you need to step back and make sure that the final thesis you develop in your introductory paragraph *actually matches* the topography of your paper. Writing it last helps ensure that your introduction serves its purpose well. You can think of your introductory paragraph as having three main functions.

- ⊙ It sets the context by providing general information about your topic so that your reader will be able to understand how your thesis fits into a larger conversation.

- ⊙ It shows why your project is important by showing how your ideas will give your reader a new perspective or new ideas.

- ⊙ It states your thesis in a sentence that will help your readers understand the paper they are about to read and give them a guide to follow as you make your key points.

Your *hook*, or the way you begin your introductory paragraph, provides a way to draw your audience in and to show them that your paper will be compelling and important to read. Some good strategies for beginning an introductory paragraph include the following.

- ⊙ A brief, relevant quotation that sets up your subject matter. Use a quotation from a well-known source or a compelling statement from a community member or someone directly affected by the topic you will be discussing.

- An anecdote that sets up the situation you will be discussing and provides either context or a moving example. Remember that when you begin your essay with an anecdote or a quotation, it is important that you show your reader the connection between it and the rest of your essay.

- A question that drives your curiosity and might pique your readers' curiosity as well. You can begin an introductory paper with a question, or you can use a statement that introduces a question (with the intention of answering the question in the course of the essay).

- A common misconception that your paper will correct. This strategy can be very compelling, as long as the misconception you address is actually commonly held.

- Some interesting, general context that you can then build on as you develop your introduction.

The introductory paragraph for an average college-level essay usually will require no more than five or six sentences, depending upon how specific you are in your opening comments. The paragraph moves from a general statement introducing the subject to a specific thesis statement. The organization might be diagrammed as an inverted pyramid, as shown in Figure 5.3.

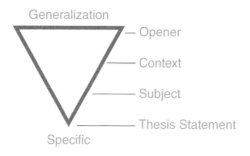

Figure 5.3: Inverted Pyramid

The thesis is the most specific statement in the paragraph and generally will appear as the last sentence of the paragraph. In the following introductory paragraph, notice how the writer moves from a general statement about the treatment of minor medical emergencies, to the independent emergency clinic, to her own experiences with such a clinic, to her thesis that the independent clinic will soon replace the hospital emergency ward.

In the past several years, a new concept in the treatment of minor medical emergencies has emerged. The independent emergency clinic is devoted to the patient with minor problems. In the past, I have had the misfortune of seeking minor emergency care in the hospital emergency ward. Even though I always received excellent medical care, I did encounter some disadvantages. But upon visiting this new type of facility as both observer and patient, I found the medical care equal to the hospital without many of the disadvantages. The independent clinic may very well replace the hospital emergency ward in the treatment of minor medical emergencies in the future.

Even though you will move in the paragraph from general to specific, you should avoid beginning with too broad a generalization. The more general you are at first, the longer it will take you to get around to your thesis and the more you risk losing your audience's attention. A first sentence about the quality of health care in the United States today would have been much too broad for the introductory paragraph on independent clinics.

Begin with a sentence that is not so general that it fails to get the readers' attention but that gets them involved in your discussion. There are several effective methods of achieving this goal.

Use a relevant anecdote or personal narrative. The writer of the paragraph on independent clinics could have had a much more compelling introduction if she had recounted one of the times when she had to go to an emergency ward. The anecdote might include the "attention-getter" sentence, or it can follow a separate "attention-getter" sentence.

Ask a question. "In this day of rising medical costs, what can the consumer do to get the best emergency health care at the best price?"

Offer a startling opening statement: "Medical technology has advanced as never before, yet more than 20 percent of Americans cannot afford even the most basic health care."

Use an analogy or comparison. "Many health care professionals scornfully refer to the independent clinic as 'Doc-in-the-Box' or 'Quack Shack.'"

Offer an informal definition. Without referring to the dictionary (denotative) definition, state your own meaning of a term that will allow you to introduce your subject and its discussion.

No matter which of these methods you select, make certain your beginning is interesting and says something important and relevant to your subject. Make sure your opening anecdote, analogy, or startling statistic fits smoothly into the rest of your introductory paragraph and leads logically to your thesis statement. Too many beginning writers come up with an attention-getting first sentence but then fail to tie it in smoothly to the rest of the opening paragraph; such a failure stops the reader cold.

The suggestions listed above certainly do not exhaust the possibilities. As you develop as a writer, you will discover other methods of introduction that might be even more suitable to your own taste, style, or technique. But never lose sight of the general purpose and function of the introductory paragraph.

Finally, as you choose introductory strategies, keep in mind that many common, overly general phrases have become cliché introductory lines: avoid them. For example, do not begin your paper with words and phrases such as *nowadays, in modern times, since the beginning of time, back in the day,* and *as we all know.* The following is an introductory paragraph written by a student for a paper about a major decision in his life.

> The choices we make have their consequences—some of them intended, some of them not; some of them good, some of them bad. It is what we make of those consequences that matters at the end of the day—our decision either to let the weight of our actions drag us down if they're negative, lift us up if they're positive, or turn the weight of negativity into a counterbalance in order to lift us anyway. During my high-school years, I decided to withdraw from public school and enroll in an online high-school program. At the time I thought nothing of it, but in retrospect this action led to a cascading series of effects. First it increased my self-motivation during school, but then it quickly deteriorated into my becoming so reliant only on myself that I subsequently pulled away from society as a whole when people failed to live up to my expectations. However, after realizing what I had done, I took the necessary measures required to begin reversing the course upon which I had set myself.
>
> —Alec Tyler

Conclusions

Your concluding paragraph is important in that it is your readers' last impression of your paper and will often be the thing that they remember the most. Too often, when students think about a conclusion, they think about a paragraph that restates the thesis or summarizes the points already made in the essay. Some very technical writing might work well with a conclusion that simply restates what has already been said, but in most of the writing in this course, you should think of the conclusion as a way to articulate not what you have already said but what you have *learned.* We write, after all, not simply to make points but to make points as part of a larger conversation. Your conclusion offers a way for you to invite others to join in that conversation as well.

Think of the conclusion not as something that just ends your paper but as a place to *draw conclusion(s)*. Of course, doing so will still mean calling your readers' attention back to your thesis and showing how you have developed this idea through your essay. However, by not simply *restating* your thesis, you open yourself up to saying much more interesting things as you conclude your writing project. The following are some concluding strategies.

- ⊙ Summarize what you (and your reader) have learned/discovered.

- ⊙ Connect your topic to larger issues in order to show its relevance beyond this single writing project.

- ⊙ Suggest furthering the conversation or taking action; give your readers an idea of what they might do to act on the information you have given them.

- ⊙ Point out unanswered questions or points you have not been able to develop.

- ⊙ Give an anecdote that shows how your topic is relevant to a current debate or problem. See Figure 5.4.

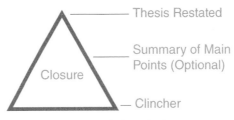

Figure 5.4: Conclusion

You should realize that much of what your readers will remember about your discussion is what you present in your concluding paragraph. You have kept their attention long enough to bring them to your closing remarks; don't lose them now! Offer something memorable. What you have said in the body paragraphs has surely taken your readers beyond the boundaries of your thesis statement. Now you must relate to your audience what your purpose and thesis imply. Do not, however, claim more than your presentation justifies or you can deliver. Make your point and close. Never give the impression you have simply stopped writing. The readers desire and expect a sense of closure—an end or conclusion. Never mention a new idea in your conclusion that could or should have been discussed earlier in the essay. Not much can be added at this point that might convince readers if it has not already been said in the body paragraphs.

Close while you still have the reader's attention, avoiding platitudes, overused generalities, or noble-sentiment endings. Sometimes the methods suggested earlier for opening your introductory paragraph can work for the closure of your final paragraph as well. Do not, however, merely repeat your opening sentence or your thesis. Make your closure interesting, provocative, informative, or inspiring. Whatever works for you, use it. The following is the conclusion to the student paper on a major life decision.

> Although the decision to switch from public school to home schooling was a simple, common one, it began a dark time in my life. Perhaps the entire emotional ordeal could have been prevented had I not made the choice to change schooling paths in the first place, but perhaps not: who's to say that this dark time wouldn't have happened after public high school anyway? What is done at the end of the day is done, and although this was a very craggy, uneven path in my life, I now have been walking it long enough that I can see a glimmer of light in the distance. I wouldn't go back and change a thing, even if I could.
>
> —Alec Tyler

Titles

Most writers prefer to consider a title after they have completed their entire draft. Now that your subject and focus, your tone, and your audience and purpose are all clearly determined, and you have the full picture of what you have said in the essay, you might try to capture the essence of this writing in a few words. After all, the title is the first thing your audience sees of your essay; therefore, why not establish an initial greeting that captures your whole discussion? Be accurate and specific in your title, and provide more than the mere subject of your essay. The title should let the reader see the link between what it promises and what the essay delivers. You might include a key word from the focus of your discussion, but never let a sentence be your title. Be consistent with the tone; a serious essay is undermined by a flippant title. In short, use your imagination and be creative; strive to get the attention of your audience. Instead of titling your essay "Good Teachers," why not "How Good Teachers Treat Their Students," or better yet, use a subtitle: "Good Teachers: Respect Begetting Respect."

Activity 5.3

Read the following student-written paragraphs. Next, write an appropriate introductory and concluding paragraph for them. Then, give the essay an appropriate title. Share and compare with the rest of your group.

To begin with, my father is of the Muslim faith while my mother is Catholic. One may wonder how Islam and Catholicism can be similar. Muslims, for instance, celebrate the month of Ramadan, during which they fast. They wake up before sunrise and feast. Throughout the day, however, there is absolutely no consumption of food or drink until sunset. The fasting usually continues for approximately forty days. At the end of the forty days there is a big celebration called Eid al-Fitr. This day is filled with monetary gifts, lots of food, and fancy dresses.

Likewise, Catholics have a similar practice. Lent is a time of fasting. During Lent, Catholics may choose to sacrifice a particular habit, and on Fridays they do not eat meat. Some Catholics choose to fast like the Muslims do. Many years ago, fasting was common among Catholics, but over the years the rules and customs have slightly changed. When Lent has come to an end, Easter is celebrated. Easter is usually a day filled with Easter egg hunts, barbecues, and family gatherings.

Both Muslim and Catholic practices are done in order to build tolerance and self-control. Often they are offered as sacrifices to show God appreciation. Both Catholics and Muslims share many of the same beliefs, only interpreted somewhat differently. Both religions believe in a supernatural being called God or Allah. Catholics read from the Bible; Muslims read from the Koran. Both accept Jesus. The difference is that Muslims do not accept the holy trinity. They do not believe Jesus was the son of God; they believe he was simply a prophet. Muslims do not eat pork because the Koran forbids this action. Although many Catholics do eat pork, the Jewish tradition also forbids this action.

Pakistani culture and Mexican culture may appear dissimilar, but if one were to dig a little into each culture, one would find surprising similarities. The role that men and women play in each society is surprisingly parallel. When it is time to eat, Pakistani women serve the men and allow them to eat first and socialize. After the men have filled their bellies, the women and children sit down and eat. Mexican families do the exact same thing. The only difference is that Pakistani families eat on the floor while Mexican families usually eat at tables. There is a strong sense of gender roles within both cultures. Men are the "breadwinners," and women must be submissive to their husbands, waiting on them hand and foot. Most Pakistani women feel this treatment is honorable. Marriage in both cultures is also similar. In most Pakistani marriages, the parents of the girl and boy to be engaged arrange the union of these two individuals. It is not uncommon for first cousins to join in marriage. In Mexico, many years ago parents suggested suitable lifelong partners for their children. Marriage between first cousins was also common. The biggest secret in my mother's family is that my grandparents were first cousins. My father's family openly accepts the union of my uncle and my aunt who are first cousins.

Since Pakistan is on the other side of the world from Mexico, one might wonder what values Pakistani and Mexican people could share. In reality, they share many of the same values. For example, both are extremely family oriented. Close contact between aunts, uncles, and cousins is common. There is usually a family function every week, whether it be a brunch or dinner. Both cultures have similar moral codes. For example, premarital sex is forbidden. Of course, there are those who choose not to accept this particular moral, but for the most part this is a moral shared by both cultures. In the past, if a woman became pregnant out of wedlock she would face extreme consequences. In Pakistan, she could be put to death. Today, family values usually outweigh this moral value. Most families tend to be understanding, especially when there is a child involved. Fidelity is also a moral value shared by both cultures. It is unheard of to be unfaithful in a relationship.

Final Word

Now that you've developed a draft, your next stage is to begin revising the content and organization of your paper. In doing so, you will likely revisit the drafting stage in order to improve the unity of some of your paragraphs, write new paragraphs that better fit your thesis, or look at transitions and the organization of your paragraphs.

Shitty First Drafts

Anne Lamott

Anne Lamott is a San-Francisco-based writer of fiction and nonfiction. Her works include *Hard Laughter* (1980), *Blue Shoe* (2002), *Traveling Mercies: Some Thoughts on Faith* (2000), and *Small Victories: Spotting Improbable Moments of Grace* (2014). The following essay is taken from *Bird by Bird: Some Instructions on Writing and Life* (1994).

Lamott's essay is about the process of drafting. Her method is to go through multiple drafts before being ready to let go of an essay. She starts with what she calls "the child's draft," where she spills everything she can think of down on paper. She also talks about the need during this process to get up from time to time and wander around to avoid writing. She then moves on to the revision stage, deleting and rearranging, and finally to writing a second draft, which she then edits. She begins her conclusion by saying, "Almost all good writing begins with terrible first efforts."

Now, practically even better news than that of short assignments is the idea of shitty first drafts. All good writers write them. This is how they end up with good second drafts and terrific third drafts. People tend to look at successful writers, writers who are getting their books published and maybe even doing well financially, and think that they sit down at their desks every morning feeling like a million dollars, feeling great about who they are and how much talent they have and what a great story they have to tell; that they take in a few deep breaths, push back their sleeves, roll their necks a few times to get all the cricks out, and dive in, typing fully formed passages as fast as a court reporter. But this is just the fantasy of the uninitiated. I know some very great writers, writers you love who write beautifully and have made a great deal of money, and not *one* of them sits down routinely feeling wildly enthusiastic and confident. Not one of them writes elegant first drafts. All right, one of them does, but we do not like her very much. We do not think that she has a rich inner life or that God likes her or can even stand her. (Although when I mentioned this to my priest friend Tom, he said you can safely assume you've created God in your own image when it turns out that God hates all the same people you do.)

Very few writers really know what they are doing until they've done it. Nor do they go about their business feeling dewy and thrilled. They do not type a few stiff warm-up sentences and then find themselves bounding along like huskies across the snow. One writer I know tells me that he sits down every morning and says to himself nicely, "It's not like you don't have a choice, because you do—you can either type or kill yourself." We all often feel like we are pulling teeth, even those writers whose prose ends up being the most natural and fluid. The right words and sentences just do not come pouring out like ticker tape most of the time. Now, Muriel Spark is said to have felt that she was taking dictation from God every morning—sitting there, one supposes, plugged into a Dictaphone, typing away, humming. But this is a very hostile and aggressive position. One might hope for bad things to rain down on a person like this.

For me and most of the other writers I know, writing is not rapturous. In fact, the only way I can get anything written at all is to write really, really shitty first drafts.

The first draft is the child's draft, where you let it all pour out and then let it romp all over the place, knowing that no one is going to see it and that you can shape it later. You just let this childlike part of you channel whatever voices and visions come through and onto the page. If one of the characters wants to say, "Well, so what, Mr. Poopy Pants?," you let her. No one is going to see it. If the kid wants to get into really sentimental, weepy, emotional territory, you let him. Just get it all down on paper because there may be something great in those six crazy pages that you would never have gotten to by more rational, grown-up means. There may be something in the very last line of the very last paragraph on page six that you just love, that is so beautiful or wild that you now know what you're supposed to be writing about, more or less, or in what direction you might go—but there was no way to get to this without first getting through the first five and a half pages.

I used to write food reviews for *California* magazine before it folded. (My writing food reviews had nothing to do with the magazine folding, although every single review did cause a couple of canceled subscriptions. Some readers took umbrage at my comparing mounds of vegetable puree with various ex-presidents' brains.) These reviews always took two days to write. First I'd go to a restaurant several times with a few opinionated, articulate friends in tow. I'd sit there writing down everything anyone said that was at all interesting or funny. Then on the following Monday I'd sit down at my desk with my notes and try to write the review. Even after I'd been doing this for years, panic would set in. I'd try to write a lead, but instead I'd write a couple of dreadful sentences, xx them out, try again, xx everything out, and then feel despair and worry settle on my chest like an x-ray apron. It's over, I'd think, calmly. I'm not going to be able to get the magic to work this time. I'm ruined. I'm through. I'm toast. Maybe, I'd think, I can get my old job back as a clerk-typist. But probably not. I'd get up and study my teeth in the mirror for a while. Then I'd stop, remember to breathe, make a few phone calls, hit the kitchen and chow down. Eventually I'd go back and sit down at my desk, and sigh for the next ten minutes. Finally I would pick up my one-inch picture frame, stare into it as if for the answer, and every time the answer would come: all I had to do was to write a really shitty first draft of, say, the opening paragraph. And no one was going to see it.

So I'd start writing without reining myself in. It was almost just typing, just making my fingers move. And the writing would be *terrible*. I'd write a lead paragraph that was a whole page, even though the entire review could only be three pages long, and then I'd start writing up descriptions of the food, one dish at a time, bird by bird, and the critics would be sitting on my shoulders, commenting like cartoon characters. They'd be pretending to snore, or rolling their eyes at my overwrought descriptions, no matter how hard I tried to tone those descriptions down, no matter how conscious I was of what a friend said to me gently in my early days of restaurant reviewing. "Annie," she said, "it is just a piece of *chicken*. It is just a bit of *cake*."

But because by then I had been writing for so long, I would eventually let myself trust the process—sort of, more or less. I'd write a first draft that was maybe twice as long as it should be, with a self-indulgent and boring beginning, stupefying descriptions of the meal, lots of quotes from my black-humored friends that made them sound more like the Manson girls than food lovers, and no ending to speak of. The whole thing would be so long and incoherent and hideous that for the rest of the day I'd obsess about getting creamed by a car before I could write a decent second draft. I'd worry that people would read what I'd written and believe that the accident had really been a suicide, that I had panicked because my talent was waning and my mind was shot.

The next day, though, I'd sit down, go through it all with a colored pen, take out everything I possibly could, find a new lead somewhere on the second page, figure out a kicky place to end it, and then write a second draft. It always turned out fine, sometimes even funny and weird and helpful. I'd go over it one more time and mail it in.

Then, a month later, when it was time for another review, the whole process would start again, complete with the fears that people would find my first draft before I could rewrite it.

Almost all good writing begins with terrible first efforts. You need to start somewhere. Start by getting something—anything—down on paper. A friend of mine says that the first draft is the down draft—you just get it down. The second draft is the up draft—you fix it up. You try to say what you have to say more accurately. And the third draft is the dental draft, where you check every tooth, to see if it's loose or cramped or decayed, or even, God help us, healthy.

Topics for Writing and Discussion

1. Near the beginning of this short essay, Lamott says that most writers she knows haven't planned what they are going to say when they sit down to write. "Very few writers really know what they are doing until they've done it," she says. However, they know the kind of thing they are going to write

(a review of a restaurant), how long it should be (say 600 words), and they have collected details beforehand (notes). In the same way, you have to know what kind of thing you are supposed to write (a comparison essay, for example), how long it should be (say 600 words), and have collected details beforehand (brainstorming, outline). At this point, how do you, as a writer, proceed? Write a short account of what you do at this point of the writing process.

2. Lamott mentions an important part of the writing process when she says: "The next day, I'd sit down, go through it all with a colored pen, take out everything I possibly could . . . and then write a second draft." Most writers find it difficult to cut words they have already written, but this is an essential step. Professional writers usually have editors, but one way you can cut out wordiness is to work in a group and allow others to make suggestions on what to cut. You can also find lists of words and phrases that can readily be cut out of most prose on the internet ("How to Cut Thousands of Words Without Shedding a Tear," for instance, by Rachelle Gardner).

CHAPTER **6**

Writing Exposition

In any writing you do, you must determine who your audience is, what your purpose is, what the situation is, and what tone you will adopt to fit those requirements. In order to communicate clearly, you will also need to consider the best possible organizational plan. Additionally, in expository essays there are different rhetorical strategies you can use, including description and narration, process analysis, definition, illustration/exemplification, comparison/contrast, classification/division, and causal analysis.

In this chapter these rhetorical strategies will be discussed as separate units. Each will be presented as a means to an end, but in actual writing situations, you will find that you must use multiple strategies. In almost any essay you write, your purpose will be served by paying attention to specific details in order to describe, by exemplifying and illustrating any generalizations you make, by keeping in mind that all writing is an ongoing process, and by keeping cause-effect relationships clear. You may need to develop each paragraph using one or the other of these rhetorical strategies while your overall purpose calls for a broader organizational plan.

You will find that your understanding of these rhetorical strategies, sometimes called modes, will assist you in developing your ideas clearly, whether for an essay, an essay exam, or some other purpose. Your thesis, in any case, will be determined by the situation, your audience, and your particular purpose.

Description

In nearly every essay-writing situation, we use description, especially in providing vivid examples. When we describe, we try to recreate for the audience the sensations we may have felt in a similar situation. The basis of any good description is, of course, close observation and a careful consideration of the audience and purpose. Remember the last time you were asked where you had parked your car and you had to rely on description to explain exactly what your car looked like and generally how to get there? Unless you observe the details, explaining anything clearly for your audience is difficult.

Description is used in almost any rhetorical mode. It is often not an end in itself. It clarifies your point in narration, explains in comparison and classification, makes definition interesting, and creates strong emotional appeals in persuasive writing.

Elements of Description

Diction. In addition to observing closely, choosing the right word is an essential feature of any writing experience. When we use any word in context, we must take several different things into consideration, including the degree of specificity and the nuances of the words. Beginning any discussion with a generalization or an abstraction is entirely possible. However, leaving the subject at that level does not create a very clear image or impression for the audience. In order to write evocatively, the writer must aim toward the specific rather than the general and the concrete rather than the abstract. Introducing an abstraction such as loyalty is a beginning; however, describing the black-and-white terrier named Scotty sleeping on his master's grave in the cemetery night after night becomes more specific. Certain techniques help create vivid writing.

For example, every writer understands the differences between denotation and connotation. Denotation is the dictionary definition of a particular word. If you look up *mother* in the dictionary, you find it means "female parent"—no real surprise. The connotation of a word, however, includes the associations our experience brings to that word. For some, the connotations of mother bring images of hot dogs, SUVs, and apple pies; for others, however, it connotes a busy, organized woman with a briefcase. Connotations can be positive, neutral, or negative as well. If we refer to a person as obstinate or principled, we mean that person has a tendency to stick tenaciously to convictions. A person with conviction might also be called stubborn or, in some contexts, pigheaded: in each case the connotations become progressively more negative.

Our choices of words indicate how we want the reader to understand what we mean. Using the wrong word in certain contexts communicates something to the reader that we never meant. Suppose you were writing about water pollution, for instance, and you found yourself repeating "pure" over and over again in the conclusion. You might open your thesaurus to find another word to vary the way you present your summation of evidence. Among the synonyms, you will find "chaste." Now, chaste does mean purity in some contexts, but it would give your reader an unusual perception of water. Diction—your choice of the right word in the right place—makes a major difference in how your audience understands your point.

Comparisons. Communicating means putting yourself in the place of the audience well enough for you to figure out what the audience knows and to fill the gaps so you can get your point across. One way to do so is to use literal comparisons. That is, by comparing an unfamiliar thing to a familiar one, one the audience understands, you can clarify the unfamiliar. The literal comparison usually requires finding likenesses in two things that are basically similar in nature. Have you ever eaten fried alligator? What does it taste like? Chicken? Your answer is an example of a literal comparison: two things of like nature (sources of protein) compared in order to make the unfamiliar more familiar.

Another kind of comparison used in description is the figurative comparison. *Figures of speech* usually compare two things of essentially unlike nature. Common figures of speech include some of the following.

Simile. A comparison of two essentially unlike things using words that make the comparison clear ("like," "as," "resembles," "than," and similar words). When you say that a certain child eats like a horse, you are using a simile to indicate a single aspect of the two subjects where the qualities of one make the qualities of the other vivid or interesting by comparison.

Metaphor. A comparison of two essentially unlike things without using words that emphasize the comparison. The metaphor is a more implicit comparison. When we say a person turns beet red or is a mad dog when he is angry, we are using metaphor.

Personification. A comparison of two essentially unlike things in which inanimate objects are given human or animal characteristics, abstractions are given qualities of humans or animals, animals are given human characteristics, and so forth. People who give their cars a name are personifying. If you say your car coughs and dies, you have given it (a machine with internal problems) human characteristics.

Synecdoche (pronounced si-nek'-dekē). A comparison of two unlike things, in this case a part with the whole. If a farmer hires extra help during harvest, he may say he hires four hands. He actually hires four people with eight hands, but the essential aspect of his help is their ability to work with their hands, of course. In class it does not take you long to figure out which students are quick to catch on or which students have come to class well prepared. You may call those students "brains" to indicate their essential characteristics. You do not mean that they sit in the back of the class in a jar of formaldehyde.

Rhetorical Devices. Closely allied with figurative language, these devices are often included in descriptions. They are often examples of verbal irony.

Verbal irony. A discrepancy between what we say and what we mean. You might describe your dorm room as a plush apartment, for example, or your old 2002 Toyota Corolla as your royal coach.

Hyperbole. A deliberate exaggeration for a particular effect. Anyone who lives in Texas understands the basic focus of hyperbole (pronounced hi-per-bo-le, not hyper-bowl—which sounds like a game played between two football teams who have had too much sugar). When we say a mountain of dirty dishes is in the sink, we are using hyperbole. No matter where you park on campus, your car is 7,000 miles from any class you have—truth or hyperbole?

Understatement. A deliberate undercutting or downplaying of importance to create a particular effect. If the rain begins unexpectedly during class, catching you unprepared, and if it rains forty days and forty nights in an hour and a half (hyperbole), and if your car is 7,000 miles from any shelter near a parking lot, and some character wanders past you in a yellow slicker, an umbrella, and hip boots and says, "Damp out, isn't it?" he is understating the situation.

Paradox. An apparent contradiction that proves to be true upon reflection. William Wordsworth's statement that the "Child is father of the Man" seems backward but says something about the relative understanding of the two generations. *All I Really Need to Know I Learned in Kindergarten* would seem to operate upon the same paradox. An oxymoron is a paradox in which the seeming contradiction is contained within a single phrase. The usual examples are "jumbo shrimp" and "sophomore" ("wise fool"). Some more literary references, such as "darkness visible," a "terrible beauty," and "wintry fever" also fit the definition.

Imagery. Obviously you must describe sensory impressions if you are to involve the reader in the point you are trying to make. The five kinds of sensory appeals include visual imagery (appeals to the way things look), tactile imagery (the way things feel), auditory/aural imagery (the way things sound), gustatory imagery (the way things taste), and olfactory imagery (the way things smell). In English there are more words to describe the way things look than to describe any other type of imagery. Usually, the first three kinds of images are used more often in expository writing, but every once in a while, you may be called upon to use all the senses to vivify your writing. While you may start a discussion by saying that something looks good or that it sounds great, you really have not told the audience anything to expand their understanding. You must use specific adjectives to create particular images that evoke corresponding sensations in the audience, to recreate for them the same sensations that you as the writer experienced.

Organization

No descriptive passage exists in a vacuum: it is designed to fit your audience and your purpose. Therefore, most descriptions are used within examples to support whatever point you are making. Descriptions usually support a dominant impression you are trying to convey in your discussion and are organized to present the information in the most clearly logical way for your audience spatially or emphatically. You may choose to arrange according to where things are in space or how they relate to each other (spatial). You may choose, on the other hand, to arrange your description according to the relative importance of your details (emphatic). No matter what the arrangement, the details you select will communicate your point to the reader. In certain circumstances you may want to present an objective description, trying to be as complete and unbiased in your presentation as possible. In other cases, your dominant impression may be subjective. You will want to involve your audience emotionally in your subject. Although the following passage deals with fiction, the same literary devices can be used in expository writing. Consider the following description from Michael McFarland's short story "The False Country."

> The center stripe was the bright line to which the dark world vibrated. It was the flashing middle marker stretching all the way from the horizon of the flat farmland. Far off at its origin was a point that Stephen aimed his car toward. Although it was night, he could see many other dimmer lines—made by the freeway's painted edge, the ditches, the endless fences, even the horizon, and—above the horizon the tree line. They all seemed to begin at this central point and they came toward him at different speeds—sadly, slowly. Finally, reaching him, they slipped by until they were no longer in sight but probably converged at some equidistant point behind. The painted lines were the most dramatic, especially the center one. It constantly started up slowly and crept towards him, gathering speed until it flashed under. Finally it gave itself to the roar of the engine. The car seemed almost to be running on this energy like the toy cars he had played with as a boy. He had pushed them along the floor hard, until the momentum gave them life and they whirred off under their own power.

You will quickly notice the vivid visual and auditory images he creates. Comparison—literal and figurative—and rhetorical devices also contribute to the effect McFarland seeks to convey. At least one comparison appears as he likens the car to "the toy cars he had played with as a boy," and he personifies the lines as "[creeping] towards him," moving toward Stephen "sadly, slowly," examples of alliteration. The fences are called "endless"—a hyperbole, of course. The engine roars, and the lines whir onomatopoeically: the evocative language involves the reader in the description. The dominant impression is subjective. From Stephen's point of view there is much movement, and the lines are the central focus.

Strategic Questions

1. Is my point of view appropriate for my audience? Who are they?
2. What is my purpose? Am I informing or attempting to provide a specific response?
3. Have I created a dominant impression in my description? Is it explicitly stated or implied?
4. Have I made certain the details are concrete and supportive of the dominant impression?
5. Is the essay arranged emphatically, spatially, or chronologically?
6. Have I included more than just sensory impressions?
7. Have I included figurative language? Are the images fresh, not stereotypical?
8. Did I edit carefully, checking for major grammatical and spelling errors?

Activity 6.1

Identify and underline the descriptive devices E. B. White uses in this paragraph from "Once More to the Lake."

One afternoon while we were at that lake a thunderstorm came up. It was like the revival of an old melodrama that I had seen long ago with childish awe. The second-act climax of the drama of the electrical disturbance over a lake in America had not changed in any important respect. This was the big scene, still the big scene. The whole thing was so familiar, the first feeling of oppression and heat and a general air around camp of not wanting to go very far away. In midafternoon (it was all the same) a curious darkening of the sky, and a lull in everything that had made life tick; and then the way the boats suddenly swung the other way at their moorings with the coming of a breeze out of the new quarter, and the premonitory rumble. Then the kettle drum, then the snare, then the bass drum and cymbals, then crackling light against the dark, and the gods grinning and licking their chops in the hills. Afterward the calm, the rain steadily rustling in the calm lake, the return of light and hope and spirits, and the campers running out in joy and relief to go swimming in the rain, their bright cries perpetuating the deathless joke about how they were getting simply drenched, and the children screaming with delight at the new sensation of bathing in the rain, and the joke about getting drenched linking the generations in a strong indestructible chain. And the comedian who waded in carrying an umbrella.

1. To what does he compare the storm? Is the comparison literal or figurative?

2. What images does he use?

3. Which figures of speech are employed?

4. What transitional devices does he use in this paragraph? Why does he repeat "then" in sentence 7?

Activity 6.2

1. Go somewhere on campus. The place may be inside or outside. Make yourself comfortable for a minute, and decide whether the place impresses you favorably or unfavorably. On this sheet, jot down as many specific details, observations, and ideas as you can in ten minutes or so. Focus on your senses—what can you see, touch, taste, hear, or smell.

2. Go somewhere else where you have a good writing surface, space, and quiet. Review your list. Now go through your jottings, and make a specific figure of speech for at least five of them. Create at least five vivid images of at least ten other details. Avoid clichés.

3. Now write your subjective, dominant impression of the place to describe it to your audience.

4. Next, choose specific details, images, and figures of speech to support your dominant impression.

5. Finally, write a paragraph in which you persuade your audience to perceive a place on campus the way you do. Include your dominant impression, specific details, vivid language, logical transitions, and a clincher to emphasize your purpose.

Before you write a description, read the student-written essay "Going Home," by Kathleen Looper under *Student Examples* in the back of the book.

Narration

Description is often used in conjunction with narrative. Every time you tell your friends and family about a particular event in your day, you use narration. Any time you tell a story to answer "What happened?" you use narration. Usually, there is a point to the details you choose to include in your recitation. Your details support a central idea. If the day was horrendous, your details turn into a long whine; if the day was wonderful, your details bolster the effect. A joke, a journal entry, a story, a historical perspective—all require narrative. Narration may be used any number of ways.

- ⊙ As an introductory or concluding technique to gain the reader's interest and create a vivid beginning or ending for the essay

- ⊙ As an essay in itself to explain an event, a process, or to make a point

- ⊙ Throughout an essay to provide personal examples

Elements of Narration

Plot. The sequence of events, called plot in fiction, indicates the order in which events happen. You may want to use chronological order to show how events unfold. Begin with the setting and situation, and proceed to tell the story from first to last. In the process you will pay attention, again, to logical details necessary to fulfill your purpose. Narrative should usually develop causally: an event should logically follow any preceding one. But you may want to present events out of their normal order to emphasize an important effect you are trying to create. Be careful with this kind of development, however. No matter what order you choose, you must describe the beginning, middle, and end to make causal relationships clear. As you present your narrative, you will find that some kind of conflict is intrinsic to your discussion.

Setting. For the most part, setting establishes where and when the events take place. It may be used straightforwardly to emphasize your point, or it may be used ironically. In a narrative the author chooses details that create the illusion of reality for the reader, verisimilitude. Your selection of details helps you make your point and create vivid impressions for the audience. The point of your story will be emphasized by your handling of setting, sequence, and people or characters.

Time. When you describe you are probably more interested in spatial relationships, but in narrative the important relationships are most concerned with time. You will use chronological order most of the time to indicate the beginning, middle, and end of the incident, but as a writer you must decide whether to compress time or to emphasize or de-emphasize certain aspects. Sometimes, you will want to start *in medias res*, in the midst of the action, to vivify the events and put the reader into the moment. No matter which kind of sequence you choose, be particularly careful with verb tenses. In most cases present tense makes sense unless you are referring to incidents that occur in the character's past.

Conflict. Conflict is, of course, a clash of wills, characters, or forces. It can be internal (within you or the central character you are presenting) or external (between two people or forces). Presenting conflict in an extended narrative creates an essential tension necessary to good narrative writing. Unless there is conflict, there really is not much suspense—or interest—generated in the reader.

Dialogue. Another way to make your narrative vivid and immediate is to use dialogue rather than referring to conversations indirectly. Be sure to check your handbook for the proper use of quotation marks and punctuation to allow your characters to speak for themselves.

Character. Characters are the people involved: how you introduce and describe them gives the reader an understanding of your point. They may be described physically or psychologically or both, but the effect is much more vivid if you do not tell the reader how to feel. Instead you need to describe the character in such a way that the reader knows what kind of person he is. Mark Twain once said that it is not enough to tell about an old lady who shows up and is unhappy; "bring her on and let her scream" her head off.

Point of View. While you often use third person ("she," "he") in academic writing, in personal narrative especially, you may be told to use first person ("I") in order to create immediacy and interest. All your choices in any kind of writing are determined by your audience and your particular purpose. Your audience and purpose are essential to the way you present your point. Keep your readers firmly in mind, and present significant details in descriptive language tailored to them.

Organization

Narration, whether used to relate incidents in fiction or sequences in nonfiction, will always move your reader through situations and processes in time. Therefore you must have a clear idea of the progression through time of events that you are going to convey. You might, for example, want to set up a timeline on a sheet of paper with the major events in your sequence placed alongside it. You will also want to be extremely careful with the tenses you use so as not to confuse your reader. While many narratives, such as memoirs, are recalled from the past and require the use of past and past perfect tenses, careful use of the present tense can give immediacy to your narrative. For example, notice the shifts in tense in the following passage from the opening of John Updike's short story, "A&P," which is being retold by Sammy after the event:

> In walks these three girls in nothing but bathing suits. I'm in the third check-out slot, with my back to the door, so I don't see them until they're over by the bread. The one that caught my eye first was the one in the plaid green two-piece. She was a chunky kid, with a good tan and a sweet broad soft-looking can with those two crescents of white just under it, where the sun never seems to hit, at the top of the backs of her legs. I stood there with my hand on a box of HiHo crackers trying to remember if I rang it up or not. I ring it up again and the customer starts giving me hell. She's one of these cash-register-watchers, a witch about fifty with rouge on her cheekbones and no eyebrows, and I know it made her day to trip me up. She'd been watching cash registers forty years and probably never seen a mistake before.

Sammy begins his story *in medias res* and places us in the checkout stand with him as he watches three girls enter the grocery store. The dramatic use of present tense captures our attention, just as the three girls earlier captured his. He then switches to past tense as he describes the girls and his own frozen attention: he cannot remember whether he rang up the crackers or not. He switches again to present tense as he focuses on the old lady in front of him, and then switches to past perfect in describing her probable previous cash-register-watching activity.

In nonfiction narrative, particularly if you are explaining a process, you must pay close attention to your audience and your purpose. How much can you assume your audience knows? How much detail will be needed to convey the process or events? The following paragraph explains—narrates—the operation of Darwinian natural selection in creating the giraffe's long neck. It was published in *Natural History*, the magazine of the American Museum of Natural History in New York City. The magazine is written for nonspecialists interested in science.

> A Darwinian explanation [of the giraffe's long neck] assumes that the neck length has always varied among the individuals in a giraffe population. In the past, the giraffes with the longest necks reached the highest leaves, which were more abundant, and may have held more nutrients than the lower leaves, but were inaccessible to shorter-necked giraffes. Overall, then, the longest-necked animals were the best-fed members of the population. Better nutrition translated into longer or healthier lives, and so longer-necked giraffes produced more offspring than shorter-necked giraffes. With time, differential rates of survival and reproduction

skewed the giraffe population toward animals with elongated necks. The key to the mechanism of Darwinian evolution is natural selection.

Here the authors, Luis and Monika Espinasa, keep their audience firmly in mind. The diction is simple and straightforward, although they assume their audience will know such words and terms as "nutrients" and "differential rates of survival." They stay in the past tense and include such transitions as "In the past," "Overall, then," and "With time" to move the narrative along.

Strategic Questions

1. What is the overall purpose of my narrative? Is it clear? Is the mood appropriate for my purpose?

2. Is the setting included?

3. What is the narrative's conflict? Is the conflict dramatic enough?

4. Does the dialogue enrich my purpose or character portrayal?

5. If I have a flashback or flash-forward, does it highlight the purpose and help create the effect of the overall essay?

6. Do all the characters contribute significantly to the essay's rhetorical situation and purpose?

7. Is the point of view clear and consistent throughout the essay?

8. Are there enough transitional devices to create fluidity in the narrative?

9. Have I avoided stereotypes and clichés?

10. Have I edited carefully, checking for major grammatical and spelling errors?

Activity 6.3

Here is a simple declarative sentence: "The man and his daughter walked through the shopping mall." Fill in the blanks in the sentences below with descriptive words, phrases, and clauses. You will want to consider what the man and his daughter look like (How old are they? What are they wearing? Who are they?), how they are walking (Are they striding? Lolling?), and what that area of the mall looks like (stores, sounds, colors). Are they happy? Upset? Afraid? What will happen at the end of their shopping trip?

1. The _____ man and his _____
   daughter walked through the shopping mall.

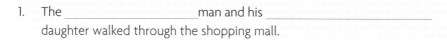

2. The _____ and his _____
    were walking through the shopping mall.

3. The _____ man and _____
    _____ were
    _____ through the _____
    shopping mall _____.

4. _____ the _____ man and
    his _____ daughter were _____ly
    through the shopping mall _____
    and _____.

Activity 6.4

Write a paragraph describing the man and his daughter walking through the mall. Make sure you have a good topic/introductory sentence and a dramatic concluding sentence. Before you write, read the student-written essay "A Seasonal Twist," by Tammy Boggs under *Student Examples* in the back of the book.

Process

We read and follow processes all the time. When we read the directions on how to use the camera on our cell phone, or how to operate a self-service gas pump, we are using process. Process is a habit of mind involving ideas in logical sequences. There is an orderly and efficient way to do almost everything, although nearly everyone thinks his or her way is best. Basically there are two kinds of processes: directional and informational. The directional process explains how to do something so that the reader can duplicate the action suggested, while the informational process explains how a more complicated process is done, but not with the intent of duplication. You do not have to be a miner to understand how strip mining works, nor are you expected to run right out and create a strip mine in your backyard if you read about how the process is done.

Elements of a Process

Process analyses are used in almost anything that requires a step-by-step explanation. When you explain the steps of a chemistry experiment, you are presenting a directional process. You use informational processes every time you explain how Native American lands were colonized, how a bill becomes law, or how the writing process works. When you explain a process, particularly a directional one, you should take several things into consideration.

1. Provide an overview of general principles. Give your reader an understanding of the way you intend to develop your plan.

2. Provide complete details. All the techniques you use in describing anything will, of course, be applicable to describing how a particular process is done.

3. Define any technical terms. Keep your audience in mind, and try to make your explanation clear enough to communicate effectively.

4. Provide reasons for the steps you include. You should tell why it is important to include certain elements of the process as well as explain how to do them.

5. Include negative directions as well as the reasons for doing things a certain way or in a certain order. You must warn the reader in key places about what not to do. Because cyanide is difficult to remove from all kinds of surfaces, including glass, it is probably better not to prepare a beverage in a beaker you usually use for cyanide experiments.

6. Illustrate your process using descriptive techniques. Normally, you will not have diagrams or other visual aids in your writing; therefore, you need to create images to make your process clear.

7. You will have noticed in the course of this discussion that its point of view violates the rules you may have been told about using second person and shifting points of view. Because this book is designed as a set of directions or instructions for the reader, it often uses second person. The purpose and audience determine the point of view you will use in your writing. Sometimes your instructor will insist that you use third person ("one," "he," "she") in order to practice appealing to certain audiences of the type you will write for in many academic settings.

One way to implement the consistent use of third person in a process is to introduce an actor—someone who is logically involved in the process—early in your discussion. If you are describing how to bake bread, the person involved in the process is the baker. When you refer to the baker as the actor in the process, you refer to him or her in the third person. Sometimes you may be asked to use the imperative: a command or request whose implied subject is "you." For example, the directions on the service station gas pump are consistently imperative.

1. Select octane grade; 2. Lift handle; 3. Insert nozzle and pump.

No matter what the assignment requires, you must maintain a consistent point of view. Do not shift from "I" to "you" to "he" and back again. Keep your audience firmly in mind.

Organization

In writing process papers, the same general steps that apply to all writing situations are also important. As you outline, you should group steps logically. You will not put each step in a single short paragraph. The reader should be aware that you have a plan, an outline, but it should not be intrusive. Your outline is the skeleton of your essay; the essay should flesh out that skeleton. Be sure you choose a process that is a suitable length for the paper required, and organize logically, usually chronologically. The thesis statement should indicate the specific groups of steps you will discuss, corresponding to the paragraphs you develop.

Throughout the paper, keep your reader firmly in mind: the audience and the purpose will determine your tone, your techniques, and your direction. Do not condescend to or patronize your audience; explain clearly. In a directional process you may want to use personal narrative, especially in the introduction, to indicate how you became familiar with the process or why you think knowing about this procedure is important or worthwhile. Transitions are particularly important in explaining processes, usually indicating that the steps are chronological for a reason. Generally you will use transitions such as "first," "next," "then," "additionally," and "finally" in addition to any devices you need to make your ideas clearly logical for your reader. You may want to include phrases such as "Be sure to ___ before you try to ___" or "Under no circumstance should you do ___ before doing ___." In your conclusion, you should indicate the results of the procedure—a fluffy soufflé, a law, a well-written essay, an embalmed corpse—and their significance.

Strategic Questions

1. Have I listed all the necessary steps?
2. Is each step explained thoroughly, offering specific, vivid details?
3. Have I defined any terms that might be unfamiliar to the audience?
4. Do the connective words clearly indicate the sequential nature of the process described?
5. Are my sentences varied enough to avoid monotony?
6. Is the purpose clear, either to inform and entertain or to help someone duplicate a step-by-step process?
7. Have I checked for major grammatical and spelling errors?

Activity 6.5

Below are several scrambled steps listing a series of events that make up a process sequence. Unscramble these items, and arrange them in chronological order. Then outline the process, indicating how you would group the events and what you would call each group. Make sure each level is parallel.

_____ 1.   Pour a cup of coffee.

_____ 2.   Rewet hair, and try again.

_____ 3.   Put on shirt and tie after brushing lint off pants.

_____ 4.   Dry off.

_____ 5.   Turn on light while rubbing knot on forehead.

_____ 6.   Start car.

_____ 7.   Brush teeth after changing shirts.

_____ 8.   Arrive at class ten minutes late.

_____ 9.   Find key in sofa.

_____ 10. Dodge vicious squirrel on the way to the car.

_____ 11. Scald yourself in the shower—you forgot to check temperature.

_____ 12. Spill coffee on shirt while putting lint brush away.

_____ 13. Hit "snooze" on clock again.

_____ 14. Fall over tub edge trying to get out of shower.

_____ 15. Get stuck in traffic on FM 1960.

_____ 16. Burn tongue with hot coffee.

_____ 17. Put pants on after putting on socks.

_____ 18. Finish showering.

_____ 19. Drag yourself out of bed.

_____ 20. Turn off lights.

_____ 21. Change tie.

_____ 22. Adjust water temperature.

_____ 23. Put socks on after hair is dried the second time.

_____ 24. Stumble back into the kitchen again with hair still dripping wet.

_____ 25 Fix coffee.

_____ 26. Search frantically for the keys.

_____ 27. Drive 75 mph to make up for lost time changing clothes.

_____ 28. Change shirt.

_____ 29. Having selected your wardrobe, time to dry hair.

_____ 30. Shower after coffee begins to brew.

_____ 31. Lock house.

_____ 32. Drip toothpaste on tie.

_____ 33. Hit snooze on alarm clock.

_____ 34. With tongue still burning from coffee, pick out clothes for the day.

_____ 35. Bump into wall as you move toward the door.

_____ 36. Run over neighbor's cat, but no time to stop now.

_____ 37. Class canceled because professor's favorite cat was run over in the neighbor's driveway.

_____ 38. Back out of driveway.

Activity 6.6

Write a short essay describing your own morning process. Your audience is the other members of your group and your class. Be sure to provide an introduction with a clear thesis statement; also make sure that your essay is not simply a list of actions. Tone is also important. Is your attitude humorous, comic, satiric, serious?

Alternate assignment: Write a short "how-to" process explaining to a new co-worker how to do one action at work. Assume that she will be working with you.

Before writing a process, read the student-written essay "Planting a Vegetable Garden" under *Student Examples* at the back of the book.

Illustration/Example

One of the most commonly used patterns of expository writing is the development of a thesis, idea, or statement by means of illustration/example or exemplification. If, for instance, you wish to tell your audience that, in your opinion, Marvin is not the best choice for the position of Chief Cashier at Citibank, you might proceed to illustrate your opinion with examples of Marvin's behavior. You might provide three examples to illustrate your assertion: (1) Marvin is a chain smoker and lights his cigarettes with $10 bills. (2) Although his salary is now only $100 a week and his parents live in a one-room apartment, Marvin drives a new Lexus and goes on vacations in Bora Bora. (3) Two months ago Marvin returned after another kind of vacation where he was serving ten to twenty years for embezzling $200,000 from the Second Interstate Bank.

Each of these examples serves to show your reader why you do not think highly of Marvin as a bank employee. You have made a statement (Do not make Marvin Chief Cashier) and illustrated your statement with three effective examples of his behavior that should disqualify him from the job. In the exemplification essay, you make a statement and then provide examples to clarify your statement for the audience. The examples should be clear, concrete, appropriate, interesting, and supportive of the thesis statement.

Elements of Example/Illustration

Effective examples have a number of common characteristics.

They are clear. Because the purpose of using examples is to make your general idea clearer to your audience, it should be obvious that the examples must be carefully chosen for their clarity. How clear the example is will depend to some extent on who the readers of the essay are likely to be. If you want to illustrate the economic principle of supply and demand, for instance, you would choose different examples for a professor of business administration than you would for a ninth-grade history textbook. The professor will understand references to gross domestic product, and a good example for her might be a fairly complicated graph showing annual consumption of fuel oil per capita. The ninth grader, however, would probably not find these examples helpful because they would not be clear to him. He would probably benefit more from an illustration based on a sporting goods store and the different price of baseball caps at various times of the year. When you show him that ball caps cost more in January than in July because there were fewer caps available in January, he will begin to see what you mean by "supply and demand." Whenever you choose an example, therefore, you should be sure that it will be clear to your intended audience and that it will make your general statement or thesis clearer to them.

They are concrete. This characteristic is closely allied to clarity because most examples are clearer when they are most concrete. Because of the way most of us think, readers are attracted to and benefit most from particular, specific, detailed examples. In the example already suggested—the illustration of supply and demand by a reference to the price of baseball caps in January—the example will be more effective if you specify "baseball cap" than if you use a more abstract term, such as "wearing apparel." Referring to specific months, such as January and July, to explain why production is lowest, too, will probably be more effective than talking about felicitous and infelicitous manufacturing periods. To illustrate your point, you might even decide to write a short narrative in which Coach Neander complains in a rage to Mr. Strapp, the manager of the sporting goods store (frightening him and causing him to knock down an eight-foot replica of a Dallas Cowboys linebacker display he was putting up), that the caps the coach wants for this team cost $20. The idea is to make the example specific, particular, and concrete because then the thesis will be easier for your audience to understand.

They are appropriate. In order to be effective, to do a good job of illustrating your point, an example should be appropriate; it should be suitable to the idea it illustrates (valid, reasonable) and also to the intended audience (appropriate for their experience, background, and knowledge of the subject). If you wanted to choose an appropriate example of how advertising can sway the consumer and force him to buy something he does not really want or need, you probably would not use the Ford Motor Company's greatest flop, the Edsel, as your example. Such an example would be neither valid nor reasonable because it suggests the opposite of what you want to demonstrate. The Edsel was heavily advertised, but it looked so awful that people refused to buy it.

By the same token, you do not want to choose an example that is so outlandish or exaggerated that it fails to convince your readers because it is not representative. Such an example to demonstrate how advertising can influence the consumer might be "subliminal" advertising. Some years ago there were allegations that advertising messages such as "Buy a Coke" were inserted on single frames of motion pictures. The message would flash on the screen for only a fraction of a second, and the movie patrons would not even be aware they had seen it. They supposedly got thirsty, and Coke sales in the lobby went up. Now, this example might illustrate the power of advertising, and it can be made clear and concrete enough, but it probably is not a good example because it is not appropriate. It is too exceptional and, therefore, unlikely to convince your audience. The charges were never proven, few theaters would have been involved anyway, and it is unlikely that your audience would feel such tactics apply to them. The example, therefore, is not appropriate for your thesis. A more appropriate example could be the number of people, who buy the so-called "miracle drugs" advertised on television and in the newspapers. The drugs are often worthless, but clever advertising succeeds in selling them anyway.

They are vivid and interesting. No example is very useful if the reader does not read it because it is boring. Some of the characteristics already discussed are relevant to interesting examples because an interesting example will probably be clear, appropriate, and (especially) concrete. While some examples are vivid and interesting because of the material presented, almost all examples will benefit from presentation in very specific and descriptive terms.

If for some reason you had to write an essay about "The Best Teacher I Have Known," you would write a more effective and interesting essay if, instead of talking about the "vast knowledge" and "truly wonderful personality" of the teacher, you illustrated your essay with a vividly described example of the time the teacher taught you about propulsion and Newton's laws of motion by having the class build and launch a 29˝ rocket. If you want to write a propaganda leaflet about the awful food in your school cafeteria, do not talk vaguely about inedible food and slime in the ice machine.

Instead, describe in sickening detail the barbecued cockroach nestled in your friend's cheeseburger or the ability of the coffee to etch glass and dissolve your spoon in eighteen seconds. Make your reader participate in the essay to get your point across more quickly and thoroughly than you could with any amount of general verbiage about the teacher's "immense contribution to learning" or the cafeteria's wretched cuisine. Vivid examples can make an essay interesting, exciting, and effective. Dull, generalized examples will put your reader to sleep faster than a rubber hammer.

Organization

The purpose of developing an essay or a paragraph through illustration and example is to make clear the thesis, idea, or subject that you are trying to get across to your readers. You give your audience an illustration in order to explain a more general statement. The examples are samples of the general thesis, giving your readers more specific and concrete illustrations of the idea. The example thus acts as a kind of bridge from you to the readers, making the idea or subject clearer. Suppose you want to convey to your history instructor your idea that the bombings of Afghanistan and war in Iraq did a great deal to heighten the American spirit. This is a general, broad idea, and your audience would like (1) to have it made clearer and more specific for them and easier to understand, and (2) they might like you to give some evidence for your assertion—or at least offer them some reasons to believe that what you say about the incidents and America is true. You can give them both of these things by providing them with good examples. You could, for instance, include in your essay either a single extended example or several examples that will show that what you say is true. In order to demonstrate that the events did enliven the American spirit, you might choose the following examples.

⊙ Historical documents of public polls indicate that over 70 percent of the Americans surveyed felt that the bombings in Afghanistan and the war in Iraq were justifiable.

⊙ Americans generally rallied in support of a military retaliation for the September 11 attacks on New York City and Washington, DC (flag sales, yellow ribbons, fundraisers for victims' families).

⊙ The threat of "weapons of mass destruction" unified the American spirit and a desire to eliminate forces that put national security in peril (military reserve forces called up, billions of dollars appropriated for the war effort, a new cabinet post created).

Your method is thus to illustrate your general statement (that the wars solidified the American spirit) with three examples that make clear to the audience precisely what you mean. You could also have chosen only one of the examples and presented an extended discussion of even greater detail to illustrate your point. Whether an essay is formally called exemplification or not, every composition needs concrete, detailed examples. In either case, the examples clarify your basic point.

These characteristics obviously apply to essays that use illustration and examples as the structural principle, but it is important to note that we use examples in all of our rhetorical patterns, in every kind of expository and persuasive writing. Examine almost any good piece of writing, and you will find examples that are vivid, concrete, clear, interesting, and appropriate. Essays developed by definition, classification, comparison and contrast, process analysis, causal analysis, argumentation, and critical analysis depend on examples to help get their ideas across to their audience. The difference is that an essay developed by illustration uses examples as the structural principle on which it is organized.

Strategic Questions

1. Have I narrowed my subject and sufficiently restricted the focus of my thesis?
2. Have I used three or four examples or fully developed an extended example?
3. Are all examples adequately developed?
4. Are there a sufficient number of specific details to support my generalizations?
5. Do I have an effective conclusion? An interesting title?
6. Have I edited carefully, checking for major grammatical and spelling errors?

Activity 6.7

The following paragraph is taken from a student-written essay titled "Horror Novels as Therapy," by Allison Hinson. Here is her thesis: "In fiction, the horror genre can be recognized by Gothic settings, psychological conflicts, and supernatural events." (The complete essay is in the *Student Examples* section.)

> While Gothic settings can set the mood, psychological horror creates terror in the actual plot. Psychological horror disturbs reality, changing the way we think and act. Horror novels that are based on psychological conflicts create a feeling of terror in the reader because they are plausible. It is conceivable to experience the terror that the young mother and child feel in Stephen King's *Cujo* when they are trapped by the rabid dog. In Anthony Burgess' *A Clockwork Orange* the real horror is not that Alex and his "droogs" are on a rampage in England, but rather that the state forces mind control on him. The psychological conflict in V.C. Andrews' *Flowers in the Attic* is a struggle for power as a mother is slowly brainwashed into giving up her children. Likewise, Robert Louis Stevenson's *Strange Case of Dr. Jekyll and Mr. Hyde* creates horror by bringing attention to the destructive evil inside us all, symbolized by the werewolf. We all possess to some degree the split personalities between what we are and what we know. Thus, it is our identification with these psychological conflicts that make these novels horrifying.

1. Do the examples used actually support the topic sentence, which says horror is created "in the actual plot," and in the next sentence, that such horror "disturbs reality"?
2. Do the examples support the further assertion that they are "plausible" and "conceivable"?
3. Are the details from the novels cited enough to support the writer's generalization?
4. Are three examples enough?
5. Have you read any of these novels? What more contemporary books would you use in writing your own essay?

Activity 6.8

Take one of your favorite activities—playing sports or video games, watching movies, browsing social media, reading—and write a paragraph explaining why you enjoy this activity. Your purpose is to explain to someone who might not like that activity why you enjoy it. Why is it interesting to you? Be sure to support a clear topic sentence with sufficient examples and evocative details.

Definition

We are all curious beings. We begin asking questions in early childhood, and we develop this inquisitive nature throughout our lives. Our curiosity leads us to seek meanings constantly in order to learn or to clarify our understanding. In addition, we are often asked to explain our own ideas or to clarify, through more specific language, something we have said, whether we are having a discussion among friends or responding orally or in writing to an instructor's question. One of the methods of making ourselves more precise is through definition. When someone asks "What do you mean by that?" your answer may be a constructed definition, relating precisely what the specific idea or term means. In putting together that definition, we often have to "translate" what we mean so our audience will understand our meaning better; we literally put our thoughts into other words in order to convey our message in an understandable language. When a definition is precise enough, it enables the audience to distinguish the particular term being defined from other similar terms with which it could be confused. The rhetorical pattern called definition is a convenient method of clarifying or analyzing a word or concept while you examine the term for a broader understanding.

Elements of Definition

There are at least three types of definitions: the informal definition, the formal definition, and the extended definition. Although the first two require little more than a word or perhaps a sentence, the third method of definition may run into a paragraph or even several pages. Definition can be used as a method to introduce your essay, to clarify your terms within other methods of expository writing, or as a means to an end in itself.

Informal Definition (synonym). This definition is usually associated with the speaker's or writer's own explanation of the word with his particular purpose in mind. This is the connotative meaning of the word being defined. It defines the term by offering a synonym, a word that has a meaning similar to that of another word in the same language. The use of a synonym lets the writer clarify his expression by providing a word or term that is more familiar to the audience. For example, if you were asked what you meant by the word "mooncalf," you could simply respond with a synonym such as "idiot" or "imbecile." Remember that a definition requires a common ground between the writer and his audience. This common ground implies that the definition is for a specific person or people involved in the exchange of ideas. For example, if a teenage boy tells his grandfather that his new girlfriend is really hot, his grandfather might suggest that the boy turn down the air conditioning.

Formal Definition. This type of definition is the one most likely to be found in dictionaries and other reference sources. It provides the denotative meaning of the word being defined and is composed of two distinct parts. You must first classify the term to be defined and then distinguish it from other similar terms in the same classification. Note the three steps in the following examples: *A mooncalf is a person who is congenitally foolish or mentally defective. A wife is a woman who is married.* Note that the above two terms—mooncalf and wife—are placed into a broader category or class, limiting the terms to a kind of person or woman, respectively. Then we add the characteristics that distinguish that person or woman from all the other people or women. Not all definitions, however, are this simple. Some are more complex and require even more specific descriptions of the distinguishing traits. The following is a definition of a twentieth-century philosophical movement: *Existentialism is a philosophy that focuses on the uniqueness and isolation of individual experiences in an indifferent universe, regards human existence as unexplainable, and emphasizes man's freedom of choice and responsibility for the consequences of his actions.*

Extended Definition. You will most likely want to use the extended definition method when your definition is as complex as those for existentialism or sexual harassment. This method of definition is what your instructor will most likely expect from you in analyzing some term, phrase, or concept in an essay of several hundred words. Such an examination involves writing an essay on this concept, delving more deeply into its meaning, and citing examples that illustrate the term and the difficulties in defining it. Definition, however, is not just an academic exercise. In the matter of sexual harassment, for instance, much work has gone into arriving at an explicit legal definition, for company policy and civil rights cases before the courts all hinge on how the term is defined. Extended definitions may include one or several methods of development: synonyms, antonyms, formal definitions, narration and description, illustration, comparison or contrast, classification, or causal analysis.

Regardless of which method of development you use to define your term or phrase, you will probably want to use the formal definition for your thesis statement and then develop your essay according to the requirements of that particular rhetorical method. You may wish to define what your term means by negation—that is, by telling your audience what your term does not mean. Dr. Samuel Johnson once defined darkness as the "want of light." If you wish to define the term wife, you may choose to tell your audience that a wife is not a nanny, a maid, or a mistress. While negation is effective in explaining what a term does not mean, it must be accompanied by additional methods of definition. Negation can only help to clarify other statements about what your term does mean.

Regardless of which method you use to write your definition, you should realize in the process that definition is a flexible method of expository writing. It can accommodate you and persuade your audience through almost any format you choose. It helps us to understand the things we see and, sometimes, the things we do not see.

Strategic Questions

1. Have I clearly determined my audience and purpose?
2. Is the organization logical and suitable to the purpose?
3. Did I avoid repeating in the predicate or in the discussion the term I am defining, avoiding a circular definition?
4. Have I avoided vagueness and generalities? Is my definition precise and clear?
5. Have I edited, checking for major grammatical and spelling errors?

Activity 6.9

The following paragraph is taken from a student-written essay titled "Wisdom," by Jennifer Murray. This is her thesis: "However, wisdom is much more than just knowledge gained; it signifies the accumulation of knowledge, the application of learning, and the personification of God's will in the creation of the universe." The complete essay is in the *Student Examples* at the back of the book.

> Just as the accumulation of knowledge is a part of wisdom, so is the application of learning. The ancient Greeks believed that *logos*, or reason and thought, led to *sophia*, or wisdom. These early lovers of wisdom, or philosophers, sought knowledge and attempted to apply it to solving the puzzles of the universe. Further, philosophers such as Aristotle believed that wisdom was necessary to make judgments which coincide with one's understanding of life. This view, also known as "Philosophical Wisdom," is thought to be one of the highest attainable virtues. The Stoics, Greek and Roman philosophers, also had their own ideas about wisdom. To them, not only is wisdom a way of attaining human excellence, it also serves as a way to act according to one's

personal ideals. Attaining wisdom places the philosopher in an enlightened nirvana-like state; however, it occasionally creates conflict for the individual having to deal with a dog-eat-dog existence. In order to release the enlightened man's tortured mind, Stoics, therefore, believed suicide was permissible to relieve the pain of existence. The way to true happiness, Stoics believed, was to want what one gets rather than to try to get what one wants.

Write an essay defining one of your own core values (see Chapter 10 for a list if you need inspiration). Use the student-written essay by Jennifer Murray as a model. Start with a formal definition as your thesis. You can use the dictionary definition or devise one of your own.

Activity 6.10

Provide the missing sections of the following definitions. Remember that each term must be put into its class and then be distinguished from other items of the same class.

1.   A bachelor is _____ who _____.

2.   A sitcom is _____ that _____.

3.   A conspiracy is _____ that _____.

4.   Genius is _____ that _____.

5.   Graffiti is_____ that _____.

6.   Compassion is _____ that _____.

7.   A hypothesis is _____ that _____.

Take one of the above definitions and use it as a thesis. Next, construct THREE topic sentences that would support and develop that thesis. Be precise in your sentences.

I.   _____

_____

_____

II. _____

_____

_____

III. _____

_____

_____

Comparison/Contrast

Although comparison and contrast are seldom used entirely by themselves (often being combined with other rhetorical patterns in the same essay), you have used them yourself while others have used them to make things clear to you. When you were a child, you might have asked your father what a giraffe was. His response might have been something like this: "It is an animal that looks something like a horse, except that it has long legs and a very long neck—much longer than a horse's neck. Its color is much like a leopard's, yellow with black spots, but the giraffe's spots are larger, and he has fewer of them than a leopard has. A giraffe has a black tongue, too—very different from cats and dogs and most other animals." Your father answered your question by comparing and contrasting the giraffe's size, legs, neck, color, and tongue with those of other animals. Because the giraffe is an animal, the best things to compare it with are other animals, members of the same classification. It would be possible to compare the giraffe to a Chevrolet (the giraffe is taller, not a machine, and a different color; it lacks bucket seats and a vinyl roof) or to a telephone pole. (The giraffe is not as tall, can move around better, and does smell better.) However, the comparisons and contrasts possible would not be as useful as the animal comparisons are in giving a child an idea of what a giraffe is. In general, then, we usually compare and contrast things in a group or class defined by our interest, things that have important similarities as well as differences.

Elements of Comparison/Contrast

There are three reasons for developing an essay by comparison and contrast.

To describe or define one item; we do so by relating it to another item with which our reader is familiar. If you wanted to tell your reader how the Texas Senate operates, you might do it by comparing and contrasting the Texas Senate with the United States Senate. You assume that your reader knows something about the US Senate and that he will be able to make the correct associations with the Texas Senate. Obviously, it is important to choose one item with which your reader is already familiar. Comparing the Texas Senate to the United Kingdom's Parliament will not do much good if your reader has no idea how that Parliament operates.

To tell your reader something about both of the subjects by discussing them in relation to some general principle. The general principle should be applicable to both and familiar to the reader. So you might compare and contrast the Texas Senate and the UK's Parliament, your reader being unfamiliar with both, by relating them to principles of democratic government that your reader understands. You might begin by showing that both the Texas Senate and the UK's Parliament use forms of representative government. The people elect representatives to these legislative bodies, and the elected legislators make laws on behalf of the electorate. Here you have compared the Texas Senate and the UK's Parliament in relation to representative government. Because our reader understands how representative government works (the people elect representatives to the legislative body), he now knows something about the Texas Senate and the UK's Parliament.

To compare and contrast several things with which the reader is already familiar in order to help him understand some general principles or ideas with which he is not familiar. If you want your reader to understand what government is, you might compare and contrast American democracy, the UK's parliamentary rule, and the emerging Russian system to show what they have in common. If you want your reader to get an idea of what social science is, you can compare and contrast the academic disciplines of psychology, history, and economics to show what they have in common. In these cases, you would be using comparison and contrast to move from your examples with which the reader is already familiar (American democracy, psychology) to a general description of the classes under which your examples belong (government, social science) about which your reader knows very little or nothing.

Organization

Once you decide to use comparison and contrast, there are two basic ways of organizing your essay. You can present one item fully and then discuss the other, called the block pattern—or you can present a part of one item, then a part of the other, and so on until both are fully demonstrated, which is called the alternating method.

Block Pattern. The first method, sometimes called the block pattern, is usually most appropriate when the elements of comparison and contrast are rather simple, broad, and obvious. The assumption the writer makes when presenting the whole of one subject and then the whole of the other is that a reader will be able to remember the first subject while reading the comparisons and contrasts of the second. Because a complex or extended comparison/contrast would probably be difficult for the reader to remember, we normally use the first method for simple subjects. For example, suppose you want to discuss the differences between two distinct groups of students on your campus. You might set up your contrast in a way similar to Figure 6.1.

Introduction (with thesis statement)

I.   The Science Major

    A. Appearance

    B. Habits and Habitats

    C. Conversations

II. The Liberal Arts Major

    A. Appearance

    B. Habits and Habitats

    C. Conversations

Conclusion

Figure 6.1: Block Pattern Outline

The author of this essay wanted to acquaint the reader with two types of college students. He illustrated one of these types, which he calls "The Science Major," with examples of their appearance, habits/habitats, and conversations. Then, assuming that the reader will be able to remember the description of this type, he compares and contrasts them with another group, which he calls "The Liberal Arts Major." He describes this group, again giving examples of their appearance, habits/habitats, and conversations that point to the differences between the two groups.

Alternating Pattern. In the second basic organizational method, the alternating pattern, the writer structures his essay differently. He discusses one characteristic of the first subject and then a corresponding characteristic of the second subject. He continues alternating the two subjects until the comparison/contrast is complete and both subjects are fully revealed. This pattern is better than the block pattern for long, complex comparison/contrast essays where the subjects are related at a number of points or where the comparisons and contrasts require extensive explanation. The writer decides on the alternating pattern when the block pattern would make it too difficult for the reader to remember the details of the first description while reading the second (Figure 6.2). Notice the structural differences between the two outlines.

Introduction (with thesis statement)

I.   Appearance

    A. The Science Major

    B. The Liberal Arts Major

II. Habits and Habitats
   A. The Science Major
   B. The Liberal Arts Major
III. Conversations
   A. The Science Major
   B. The Liberal Arts Major
Conclusion

Figure 6.2: Alternating Pattern Outline

Strategic Questions

1. Have I used the appropriate pattern of comparison/contrast for my subject, audience, and purpose?

2. Have I included topic sentences that contain references to both items if I chose the alternating pattern?

3. Have I crafted a thesis statement that indicates my purpose (i.e., comparing or contrasting or both), that mentions both items to be discussed, and that makes clear the point I want to show in the essay?

4. Have I used the best order of details for the point I wanted to make?

5. Have I avoided commonplace (cliché) details?

6. Have I edited carefully, checking for major grammatical and spelling errors?

Activity 6.11

Several pairs of items are listed below. Some of the items can be compared, some contrasted. Follow the suggestions of each, and list under the items those bases of comparison you would use in an essay. For example, if you are asked to compare two military leaders of the American Civil War, you might select their origins, educational backgrounds, personalities, and military experiences. You would simply list these four bases of comparison under the items.

1. Compare a computer repairman and a medical surgeon.

   Bases of comparison:

   a. _____

   b. _____

   c. _____

   d. _____

2. Compare a loving relationship with a roller coaster.

    Bases of comparison:

    a. _____

    b. _____

    c. _____

    d. _____

3. Compare a rock concert with a religious service.

    Bases of comparison:

    a. _____

    b. _____

    c. _____

    d. _____

4. Contrast high school students and college students.

    Bases of comparison:

    a. _____

    b. _____

    c. _____

    d. _____

5. Compare or contrast your public self with your private self.

    Bases of comparison:

    a. _____

    b. _____

    c. _____

    d. _____

Now have each member of your group write an appropriate thesis statement for each of the comparisons. Make certain that each thesis has a definite focus and purpose. The focus should contain each of the bases of comparison. Compare and critique the thesis statements.

Activity 6.12

Take one of the thesis statements generated in your group, and write a comparison/contrast essay. Unless you can provide a good rationale for using the block method, use the alternating method of development. Be sure to develop each paragraph with details and clear examples.

Pappadeaux and Joe's Crab Shack

Jona Roy

The following student-written essay is a comparison/contrast between two seafood restaurants. The writer uses the "alternating" method of contrast and clearly states the bases of comparison in the thesis: "the menu, the service, and the overall atmosphere." The two restaurants are then contrasted on each of the above criteria in separate paragraphs. Note the author's use of transitions, such as "on the other hand" and "in contrast," to guide the reader smoothly through the essay.

From a succulent fresh lobster tail to a mouth-watering red snapper filet, everyone loves some type of seafood. Houstonians are lucky; the Gulf of Mexico lies at their back door. Restaurants specializing in seafood are plentiful here. Many Houstonians consider Pappadeaux and Joe's Crab Shack to be the best. Although they both serve wonderful, fresh seafood, the differences in the menu, the service, and the overall atmosphere set them apart from one another.

Pappadeaux offers elegant, elaborate dishes on its menu, while the food described on the menu of Joe's Crab Shack is the sort that tastes best when accompanied by an ice-cold beer and a large plate of french fries. For example, my favorite meal at Pappadeaux consists of a flaky filet of red snapper blackened in hot Cajun spices and smothered in a rich bearnaise sauce. It is then topped with lightly sautéed crawfish tails and mushrooms. Once this concoction touches the tongue, it simply melts. On the other hand, Joe's Crab Shack has been made famous for its barbecued crabs. The cook begins by slowly cooking small Dungeness crabs in a large barbecue pit. Once the crabs have been seared to perfection, the cook tosses them on a large tray, and they are ready for presentation. The waiter then serves these divine crabs with a hammer, a bib, and a roll of paper towels. After pounding on the shell for five minutes, the lucky diner discovers a piece of crab meat which, like the snapper filet, melts in the mouth.

Distinguishing each restaurant further is the service; although it is impeccable at both Pappadeaux and Joe's Crab Shack, the manner in which one is served varies greatly. When dining at the classy Pappadeaux, each patron is greeted by an exquisitely dressed staff. The waitstaff is clad in black slacks, white tuxedo shirts, and classic bow ties, while the hostess dons an elegant dress. The staff greets each diner with the traditional "ma'am" and "sir" and treats her or him with the utmost respect and dignity. In contrast, at the relaxed Joe's Crab Shack the entire staff wears t-shirts and shorts or jeans and treats everyone as if they are life-long friends; greeting patrons with "Hey! How's it going?" is the norm.

The final distinguishing characteristic is each restaurant's atmosphere. The atmosphere at Pappadeaux reminds one of a traditional wedding reception while the atmosphere at Joe's Crab Shack takes one back to an end-of-the-summer beach party. An immaculate white tablecloth adorns each table at Pappadeaux, and large, leafy, green plants dot the interior of the building. Soft, relaxing, classical music is piped through speakers throughout the restaurant. Diners feel compelled to speak in low, hushed tones, making sure not to disrupt the elegant feel of the restaurant. The atmosphere at Joe's Crab Shack conveys an entirely different ambience; lop-sided paintings and photographs cover the walls from top to bottom, and the music blares from every corner. On weekends, management provides live music, and when one of Houston's hometown favorite teams is playing, the game is on one, if not all, of the many televisions. As a finishing touch to this informal setting, old-fashioned beer buckets are placed on each table for use as trash receptacles.

In their menu, service, and atmosphere, Pappadeaux and Joe's Crab Shack could not be more different. The one thing they have in common, other than great service of course, is their amazing, fresh seafood; it is delectable at both.

Classification/Division

Classification and division are forms of analysis used often by most of us even if we do not know the name of the techniques. Although they are methods of expository writing, classification and division are also ways of looking at the world around us. Like illustration and comparison and contrast, classification is a process that involves bringing order out of experience. Like these other methods of expository writing, classification and division are concerned with the general (class) and the relationship to its parts.

Almost all parts fall into a class of some kind, sharing certain characteristics that allow these parts to be classified with a certain group. Thus, a class is determined by a network of significant characteristics shared by all members of the category. If you see a man about 25 years old walking down the street, you will probably pass by him without thinking about him much. Put him into a blue uniform and give him a badge and a gun, and you will both notice him and make judgments about him. (He is a police officer or a cop.) If the man is not dressed in a uniform but is carrying a baby, you think of him as a father and assume that the woman with him is his wife and the mother of the child. In each of these cases you are classifying the man; you are putting him into a category and seeing him as a part of a whole (class). He is a policeman, father, or husband. We are always classifying that which we experience in the world around us, even when we have not the slightest intention of writing an essay of classification.

In the same way, division is a way of thinking about and reacting to our world. We know that things have parts, and we talk about things in terms of those parts. In fact, we often define terms by identifying the parts that make up those terms. A sailboat can be divided into hull, mast, and sails. Social science is made up of history, economics, sociology, geography, and psychology. The government of the United States has three main branches: the executive, legislative, and judicial.

Elements of Classification/Division

The need for care in setting up classifications can be demonstrated by examples of the two kinds of classification used in analysis. The kinds are called simple and complex classifications.

Simple Classification. This form of classification usually involves grouping your subject into two categories. For example, if your purpose is to investigate your experiences with good male teachers, a simple classification merely involves separating the subject "teachers" into good teachers and bad teachers (level one of classification). Step two would be to take the "good teachers" classification and organize it again (level two) into two classes—male and female. If your purpose is to determine how many good male teachers you have had in your academic experience, you pursue only the male classification and abandon the female portion. We call this a simple classification because at each stage or level the analysis primarily consists simply of two opposites to establish two subgroups.

Complex Classification. You most likely will decide to select the complex classification for your composition assignments because this method demands that you delve more deeply into the multiple categories/levels required by your instructor. For instance, if you are expected to consider the full range of your experience with weight lifters in health clubs as student Roberto Loucel does in his essay on page 375, you would choose the complex classification method, beginning with level one. You could, therefore, classify the types of weight lifters one most likely would encounter in health clubs—the annoying socializers, the serious competitive athletes, and the womanizers. Next, if you have chosen the annoying socializers as your focus, you would further classify that group (level two)—the "show-off," the "know-it-all," and the "wanderer." Although this level does not exhaust the types of weight lifters you have experienced, it does include those specific types you wish to discuss in your present analysis (focus). Notice that your analysis in a complex classification is of a much narrower, deeper, more interesting, imaginative, and complex nature than a simple classification.

Organization

When writing a classification essay, make sure that you take the following steps.

Set up a clear basis for the classification, and follow the classification through logically and thoroughly. This means you must be careful to classify your subject distinctly at each level of the analysis. To say that there are three types of bad teachers—the boring, the incomprehensible, and those who drive pickup trucks—is using an indistinct method of classification. Make certain you discuss each category in relation to those elements that link the category to the other categories of the same class, in this case, their methods of instruction. This basis of comparison is used similarly in your comparison and contrast; it is essential in classification as well to make your purpose clear to your audience in examining your categories by classifying them.

Develop your analysis by classification as completely as is necessary for your purpose. Your purpose determines how complete and extensive the classification will be. Your analysis will always be based on some specific interest in the subject being analyzed, and that specific interest must be clearly stated for your reader in the thesis.

Figure 6.3 illustrates the process of complex classification.

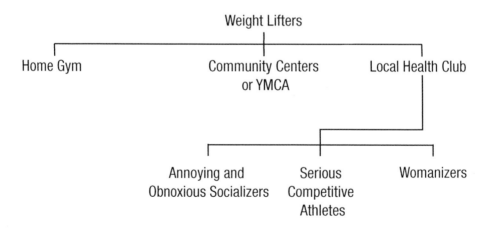

Figure 6.3: Complex Classification Diagram

Develop your classification as completely as is necessary for your purpose in the analysis. Your thesis and your discussion will then include only those types with whom you are personally familiar, although there exist other categories of weight lifters. Just make certain that your reader understands that your classification is limited by your focus/purpose.

Strategic Questions

1. Is the purpose of my classification clear and included in my thesis statement?

2. Is the classification applied to a plural subject (such as different types of pumpers at a gas station, for instance, or teachers), and is the focus on types, categories, or kinds?

3. Is the basis of my classification consistent with my purpose and audience?

4. Is the classification complete, with all relevant categories included?

5. Are the categories arranged in logical or emphatic order?

6. Do the categories overlap? (If an individual member of one category can also be put into another category, as with an incomprehensible teacher who drives a pickup truck, then your categories need rethinking. They must be mutually exclusive and parallel.)

7. Have I edited carefully, checking for major grammatical and spelling errors?

Activity 6.13

Circle the item in each group below that violates the unity of classification, and briefly explain your choice.

Topic: Friends	Topic: Branches of US government
Classes:	**Division:**
Intimate Friends	Legislative
Social Friends	Judicial
Weird Friends	Cabinet
Work Friends	Executive
Topic: Movies	Topic: Students
Classes:	**Classes:**
Adventure	Eager
Romantic	Fashionable
Blockbusters	Tired
Horror	Uninterested
Suspense	
Topic: Schools	Topic: Computer
Classes:	**Division:**
Elementary	Screen
Private	CPU
Secondary	Hard Drive
College	Keyboard
Technical	Laptop

Topic: Trees	Topic: Stores in the Mall
Classes:	**Classes:**
Exotic	Department Stores
Maple	Clothing Stores
Oak	Computer Stores
Pine	Eateries
Birch	Kiosks

Activity 6.14

Write an essay classifying the elements of one of your favorite activities or dividing it into its parts. Be sure it is clearly one or the other. Here are some examples/possibilities. These categories are very broad, so you will need to narrow your topic to a subclass, or even a sub-subclass, before you begin writing. Before writing the essay, read the student-written classification "Weight Lifters," by Roberto Loucel, under *Student Examples* at the back of the book.

Sports	Movies	Food	Dating	Video Games	Online
Football, Soccer, Etc.	Action, Romance, Etc.	Pizza, Hamburgers, Etc.	Perfect, Disaster, Etc.	Shooter, Building, Etc.	Facebook, Snapchat, Etc.
Subclass$_1$	S$_1$	S$_1$	S$_1$	S$_1$	S$_1$
Subclass$_2$	S$_2$	S$_2$	S$_2$	S$_2$	S$_2$
Subclass$_3$	S$_3$	S$_3$	S$_3$	S$_3$	S$_3$

Cause/Effect

Any time we respond to the question "Why?" we are concerned with the causes of an event. For example: Q. Why did you wreck your new car? A. I was responding to a text on my phone and not paying attention when the light turned red. Or, Q. Why did you perform so poorly on the biology final exam? A. I spent all the previous night bailing water out of my bedroom after our subdivision flooded from the heavy rains.

We look for causes when we want to know why something happened. Similarly, when we want to know what happened as a result of the cause or causes, we attempt to determine the effects. When we respond to the questions "What happened then?" or "What would happen if . . . ?" we are looking for effects. Q. What happened because you performed so poorly on the biology final exam? A. I was placed on scholastic probation for a semester. And Q. What will happen if you cannot raise your GPA sufficiently next semester? A. I will be forced to drop out of school and get a job. We are constantly being required to use causal analysis in our attempt to understand events around us.

Elements of Causal Analysis

Causal analysis may be simple or complex. Sometimes a causal analysis simply involves determining the cause or the effect of, say, why your car would not start—dead battery.

However, a more complex analysis might be required when the cause and effect arrangement involves a causal chain. The process requires that the writer begin with either a cause or an effect and then work backward or forward to determine related causes and effects. For example, consider the following scenario. Mr. Strump failed to pay his income tax this year, and the investigating Internal Revenue Service agent discovered that Mr. Strump died on January 1 and thus had no income for the year. Here is an example of a simple causal analysis. The effect (Mr. Strump's not paying taxes) can be traced to a specific cause. (He died on January 1.) A more thorough analysis may be required, however, and thorough analyses can be quite complicated. The IRS agent will probably be satisfied with the reason Mr. Strump paid no income taxes. He died, he had no income, so he paid no tax: case closed. But suppose the agent mentions Mr. Strump's death to Detective Sergeant Wexley of the police department. The sergeant then undertakes a more thorough analysis. Here, Mr. Strump's death becomes the "effect" in question, and the sergeant goes looking for the causes of that death. After a lengthy investigation, the sergeant charges Miss Buxley, Mr. Strump's secretary, with his murder. She was having an affair with Mr. Strump, had sweet-talked him into leaving her six million dollars in his will, was the last person to see him alive, and had a bachelor's degree in chemistry (after an autopsy, it was determined that he was poisoned with a substance that mimicked a heart attack).

As you can see from this example, causality involves two questions: (1) what caused the effect to occur? and (2) under certain conditions, what will be the resulting effect or effects? The first question involves tracing the relationship backward between cause and effect; the second question involves tracing the relationship forward from cause to effect.

Types of Causes

The rules of causation are twofold. (1) Without event A, effect B will not occur, and (2) whenever event A occurs, B will occur later. Several types of causes exist, and the writer must be able to distinguish them in order to sort out the essential events that result in causation. Three types of causes include the following.

Necessary Cause. A necessary cause must be present for an effect to occur; without it the effect cannot happen. For example, in order to have light in your kitchen at home, you must turn on the light switch. The switch mechanism is a necessary cause, but it will not provide light by itself. Electricity must also be present. Event A (switch), in other words, must be present for B (light) to occur.

Contributing Cause. A contributing cause may determine a particular effect, but it cannot determine it alone. For instance, you may make a good grade on an exam if you study your class notes thoroughly; however, other factors come into play as well, such as the quality of your notes, regular attendance in class, and your ability to remember what you reviewed in your notes. Event A (study) may be present for event B (good grade) to occur, but event A does not automatically result in event B. Other factors may also have contributed to your good grade.

Sufficient Cause. A sufficient cause can determine a particular effect by itself, but the effect does not always follow as a result of the cause. For example, a student may fail a course because of poor attendance, but this cause alone does not always lead to failure. A grade average below 60 must be present as well. Event A (poor attendance) can be present for event B (failure), but A does not automatically result in event B.

Causal analysis, then, is concerned with the reasons that things happen. Because of this concern, it is one of the basic techniques of reasoning. When a writer decides to write an essay based on causal analysis, it is very important that he be convincing, for he is discussing something more complex than a light switch. The writer's aim is to demonstrate for the reader why event B (effect) occurred. Why, for example, does high cholesterol cause heart disease? Why did my daughter fail her college courses? In order to do the job convincingly, the writer must make the reader appreciate the logic and thoroughness of the essay. The writer is actually engaged in an intellectual process, and because he is usually appealing to the reader's mind, he must be sure that his analysis is rationally satisfying.

Organization

There are several ways to structure a causal analysis. Because both time and resources are limited, it is often difficult to determine all the causes (or effects) of a complex event. So we might want to concentrate on the most important of a number of causes (or effects) we have identified. For example, if you have ever had to drop a college class, you might list a dozen different reasons for that event: the class started at 7:30; you had to catch a ride with a friend; it was Algebra 101, and you were never good at math; you worked in the afternoon and did not get off until 9:00 p.m.; you were also taking history and English, which required a lot of reading and writing of papers; after a month your friend changed jobs and could no longer take you, which meant you had to scramble to find other ways to school; and last but not least, your mother became sick in the middle of the semester, which meant you had to take her car and drop off your little sister at school at 7:30, making you half an hour late for class for a week. Rather than simply listing all the reasons for dropping the algebra class, you might decide to classify them into transportation problems, lack of time for adequate study, and responsibilities at home, grouping the above causes under their appropriate headings.

Immediate, Intermediate, Remote. Another way is to work logically from the most immediate cause back toward the most basic or remote cause or to start with the basic/remote and work forward to the immediate cause. As an example of the immediate-to-remote sequence, you might discuss today's stagnant wages, blaming them on a slow-growth economy caused by the offshoring of many industrial jobs and the closing of many American factories, which was the result of the implementation of NAFTA (North American Free Trade Agreement) and other free-trade agreements. This analysis would have moved from the immediate level (stagnant wages) through an intermediate level (offshoring of jobs) to a very basic cause (free-trade agreements).

Or you might start with the remote cause and move forward to its logical effect. For example, you start with the 9-11 attacks and move forward to the invasion of Afghanistan and Iraq, which led, in turn, to the destabilization of the Middle East, which led to ISIS.

The Causal Chain. The causal chain works like a series of dominoes aligned in a row. If you knock the first over, the second and the third dominoes will fall in succession, and so on until they have all tumbled. In a causal chain, the remote cause is like the fall of the first domino in the chain, which causes an effect (fall of second domino). This effect becomes the cause of the next effect (fall of third domino). This sequence continues until the immediate cause (the fourth domino) results in the final event (effect) of the chain process. For example, Benjamin Franklin traced the loss of a war (in the eighteenth century) to the failure of a farrier to do his job: "For want of a nail the shoe was lost, for want of a shoe the horse was lost, for want of a horse the rider was lost, for want of a rider the battle was lost, for want of a battle the war was lost." By the way, that is also an example of "the butterfly effect," when small, random events eventually lead to large effects.

When putting together a causal chain analysis, you must remember to observe some very important guidelines. First, because your analysis depends on demonstrating a causal chain, you must make clear to your reader how each cause is directly linked to the other causes included in your essay. For example, after you have discussed one of the causes in the first body paragraph, make certain that you show the connection of your second cause with the one already discussed, whether the second cause is the effect of the first or the cause of the first cause discussed, depending upon whether you began your analysis with the remote or the immediate cause. The same rule applies to the next paragraph. This causal link must be clearly shown in the topic sentence of each paragraph. Otherwise, the chain process will not be apparent to your audience.

Effects. Sometimes a single cause may have multiple effects. For example, what would be the effects on a student who failed a college course? His failure may lead to low self-esteem (effect #1), he may have to forfeit his financial aid (effect #2), and his parents may refuse to pay for any further education (effect #3). Note that these three effects are independent of one another; in other words, one effect does not lead to another. Determining the effects of an event means we are predicting into the future what we assume will happen based on the evidence we have at the present time. We use this method of analysis every day. Before we commit ourselves to a particular act or opt for a specific choice, we often consider the consequences of such an act or choice. In this case, we are speculating about the future results of our decision today. Economic trends and weather predictions are determined by people who are informed enough about certain historical conditions to make educated prognostications regarding the future. You know what the potential effects would be if you failed to succeed in college. Causal analysis is the process that sets this same procedure into a coherent, logical structure. Just like the essay outline shown above that lists the causes for a single effect, the outline traces the multiple effects of a single cause and arranges them in a similar fashion. There are several potential hazards in writing a causal analysis.

1. One such hazard is the *post hoc ergo propter hoc* fallacy. The Latin words mean "after this, therefore because of this" and suggest that because one event follows another event, the first necessarily is the cause of the second. An extreme example might be to say that, as you were driving to class one day, a black cat crossed in front of your car, and soon afterward you were involved in a collision. You then conclude that black cats are omens of bad

luck. This is an example of the post hoc fallacy and is obviously silly, but the writer must beware of asserting that just because something happened first (failure of the final exam) it caused something else (failure of the course) to happen.

2. Another hazard can be avoided if the writer makes sure that his analysis considers all the relevant causes and factors leading up to a certain effect. It may be true that the student's failing the final exam was a cause of his failure of the course, but other causes (poor attendance, poor daily quiz average, sleeping through lectures, assignments usually submitted late if at all, never purchasing the textbook, or having a serious attitude problem, to name a few) may also have to be considered.

3. In order to be convincing, the writer should also offer evidence for his assertions. Simply saying that something was caused by something else is not enough. Because the writer wants his reader's intellectual assent, he must accompany his assertions with proof. If, for example, the writer says that the student's social life was responsible for his failure, then he must give evidence of how it was responsible: that it kept him from studying and that it was more important to him than his academic responsibilities. This third hazard can be avoided if the writer is objective, reasonable, and honest. If it becomes evident to the audience that the writer is condemning the failing student because of his hedonistic, immoral social behavior and his love of heavy metal music and companions with fried brains, then the reader will not be convinced of the validity of the writer's analysis.

Sample Outline: Effect with many causes.

Introduction/thesis—The thesis identifies a single effect (subject) and outlines multiple causes.

I.   Cause #1

II. Cause #2

III. Cause #3

Conclusion (restates effect and three causes)

Sample Outline: Effect with causal chain.

Introduction/thesis—The thesis identifies a single effect (subject) and outlines the causal chain.

I.   Cause #1. Immediate cause of effect.

II. Cause #2. Intermediate cause of effect (and cause of #1)

III. Cause #3. Remote/basic cause of effect (and cause #2)

Conclusion (restates effect and causal chain)

Strategic Questions

1. Is my focus on my purpose? A causal analysis can be primary or supplementary. Its purpose can be to inform, to speculate on possibilities, and/or to persuade. Regardless of the essay's primary purpose, your purpose is, of course, to persuade your audience of the legitimacy of your analysis.

2. Have I proceeded logically? Indicate the complexity of the situation, and look beyond the obvious and superficial. Recognize reasonable probability, and do not overstate. Neither should you settle for simplistic explanations. Determine and differentiate between immediate and remote causes or effects, and provide facts, statistics, details, and/or a personal narrative to explain and exemplify your reasoning.

3. Is my thesis clear? Indicate whether you intend to talk about causes, effects, or both to show your order and development. Make your point clear, and remember who your audience is.

4. Is my organization clear? Some causal analyses are organized chronologically: causes and effects are presented in the order in which they happen, but a strict time sequence can be a problem if the primary causes are buried in the middle of the essay. Your causal analysis should be arranged emphatically with the most significant cause or effect reserved for last.

5. Do I make the relationships between cause and effect clear? While you should qualify what you say, you should be careful not to undercut your own thinking.

6. Have I edited carefully, checking for major grammatical and spelling errors?

Activity 6.15

Discuss the major problems you have faced as a beginning college student. The problems may differ depending on your age, race, gender, and social and family status. Discuss and group these. Next, take what your group determines to be the three most significant problems facing your group as a whole and begin to trace out the causes of those problems. What are the immediate causes, the intermediate causes, and the root or fundamental causes?

For example, finding time to study may be a problem, which may be caused by the number of hours you work, which may be a result of the fact that you have to contribute to household expenses as well as pay for classes, which is a result of your parents' divorce, which itself may have been caused by your father's drinking, which was brought on by his losing his job on an oil rig. Or perhaps making it to class on time is a problem, which is caused by the fact that you must depend on a parent to take you to class. Sometimes the car will not start because it is old. Sometimes you have to stay home with a younger sibling while your parent goes to work. Sometimes your parent oversleeps because he had to work a double shift.

Activity 6.16

Think of something (good or bad) that happened to you recently, and trace the causal chain that resulted in this event. Share with your group and discuss.

What happened recently (event/effect): _____

_____

_____

(immediate cause) _____

_____

_____

(intermediate cause) _____

_____

_____

(intermediate cause) _____

_____

_____

(intermediate cause) _____

_____

_____

(remote/ultimate cause) _____

_____

_____

Activity 6.17

List the reasons that you decided to attend this school. Rank them from least to most important. Next set up an outline for an essay beginning with the thesis: "The three most important reasons I decided to attend this school are…".

Be sure to develop each cause/reason with pertinent examples and details.

Getting Sober

Krystal Holifield

"Getting Sober" is a first-person essay using the cause/effect mode of development. The author uses her own experience as an example of what causes an alcoholic to finally realize she has a problem. Each cause is set in a separate paragraph and clearly labeled—"The first thing," "The second reason," and "But the main reason."

To recognize that they have drinking problems, alcoholics have to be completely miserable and willing to change. When they get to this point, it is called their "bottom." There are "high bottom" and "low bottom" drunks, but it doesn't matter as long as they get sober. There are many different reasons why an alcoholic decides to get sober, but in my own case, I lost my self-esteem, I couldn't control my drinking, and my life became unmanageable.

The first thing that made me think about getting sober was that I lost my self-esteem. I always used to cut myself down in front of people and never knew how to accept compliments—sure signs of low self-esteem. The biggest symptom I had of low self-esteem was that I wasn't comfortable in my own skin or around people unless I was drunk because the only way I could stand myself was when I drank. I also never cared about my appearance, so I wouldn't wear make-up, fix my hair, or bathe regularly. Still, low self-esteem was something I would never have guessed I had—that is, until I thought about killing myself. Then I knew something might be wrong.

The second reason that made me want to get sober was the realization that I couldn't control my drinking. It had become a mental and physical obsession. Since my first drink at the age of twelve I couldn't go a day without a drink, and I could never have just one. By the age of seventeen I was used to drinking a case and a half of beer a day, and for the next two years I lived in a drunken fog. I could not go to school, work, or anywhere else outside my front door without a drink or the promise of one. I finally realized something had to be done when I couldn't get a drink one day and swallowing my own spit made me violently sick. I was forced to drink NyQuil to keep from throwing up because it was the only alcohol in the house.

But the main reason I got sober was that my life became unmanageable. The first thing that made me notice I was out of control was getting kicked out of high school two weeks before graduation. During and after high school I also totaled three cars while driving drunk. In college things didn't get any better. I had a boyfriend who robbed houses, as well as me, so cops came to my house looking for him. Finally I realized that something had to change when I started waking up in places and I didn't know where I was or how I had gotten there.

Getting sober is always the last thing an alcoholic wants to do. Practicing alcoholics usually have low self-esteem, can't control their drinking, and have unmanageable lives, but sobriety always helps remedy these problems. I have been sober for two and a half years, and I could never imagine going back to the way I lived before.

CHAPTER 7
Revising

First, we should get one myth of revision out of the way: revision is not editing. Whereas editing addresses surface-level changes that prepare a text for publication, revision is a deeper consideration of the text that allows us to view the connections between our writing experience and the audience's reading experience.

The word "revision" is literally a *re-vision*, or a *re-seeing*, of our writing—a new vision, a reconsideration of our material for our audience and for ourselves as writers, but within the context, relationships, and changing purpose of our previous work. Do not be surprised when revising if you see your purpose becoming clearer on its own. More than once, through reflective revision, an informative essay has turned into a persuasive campaign; a simple effort at connection becomes a powerful message. Consider the following example of a student's original work, then her revised work.

Original Introduction with Thesis Statement

Single-parent households, domestic violence, health, childcare, and education issues are universal concerns among women across color lines, so why does this counterpublic have to be exclusive to African-American women? Besides the fact that black women are experiencing all these issues on a much larger scale than women of other ethnicities, the answer to that is the exact reason why we face so many of the issues on a much higher scale. Black women are hesitant to share their stories because many times the people who we are to share them with don't have the same social background as we do; therefore, we feel judged. We are less likely to speak up about these issues in public settings because with such negative stereotypes we don't want to be considered angry or bitter. According to rhetorician Dr. Phyllis Ryder, many people don't speak up because the dialect that we use is considered uneducated or improper and therefore our voices are not heard. This is especially true for African-Americans who when speaking plain English are still considered to be speaking African American Vernacular—as if our speech is foreign. Cultural backgrounds of other races might also make it hard to make this type of sphere inclusive. Many women's groups fail to realize the black female life experience suffers levels of oppression and marginalization on a higher degree than by white women. By making the counterpublic exclusive to black women, black women can remove some of the self-doubt they face when entering the public space. The need to silence ourselves for fear of perpetuating stereotypes goes out the window, there is a commonality on levels of oppression, cultural, and life experiences, and women will therefore be more likely to speak up.

Revision

A public sphere is a neutral and inclusive place where strangers can come together to rhetorically exchange information, attitudes, opinions, and concerns. These types of public spheres are rare anyway but are almost nonexistent among African-American women. I am one of the fortunate few who have a group of other women in my life who can relate, empower, and support me. Yet many African-American women do not have such women in their lives, nor do they know where to go to find a group like that. Black women are segregated, marginalized, and oppressed, and because of that most of our voices have been silenced. Several women's groups don't recognize that the experience of a black woman is more oppressive and subjugated than that of women of other races. African-American females everywhere, not just in Houston, need a public sphere—a place where we can discuss issues such as community, health, and economic problems; a place where we can receive relationship and sex counseling, information on childcare, learn how to balance our budgets, and sometimes just provide a listening ear or a firm hug and words of encouragement from people whose experiences are much like our own.

Notice that the revision has taken a new approach to the same topic by addressing a new audience with new information and a new tone.

Resistance to Revision

Emerging writers struggle with revision more than with invention, composition, or editing. There are multiple reasons for this, and each reason needs to be addressed by the writer as a personal challenge. Here are some reasons why some student writers find revision difficult.

Emotional attachment. Writing is hard—we have emphasized that throughout this book. Not only is writing hard, it takes time, involves risk, and exposes us to criticism. So, when we get to a point in our writing when we feel "comfortable" with what we have, we feel relieved and want to stop right there and hit the print button. We are also proud of what we have accomplished thus far and know that revision will expose us to more emotional risk if we tell ourselves that "I need to change something." But it is because we are emotionally attached to our writing that we can use effective revision strategies to further improve our work to make it even more useful to our public audience. Yes, this is risky, but all healthy relationships involve risks.

Time commitment. It is no secret that writers often procrastinate until stress takes over and motivates them to do something just to complete a project. So procrastination is not unique to you, but it is also not very productive. Though some students brag about "knocking out a paper the night before it is due," these projects are rarely insightful, creative, honest, or constructive—they rarely add new knowledge to the student's experience or the world's corpus of knowledge. The simple answer here is to manage your time effectively: start projects early, follow a recursive writing process, seek tutoring early and often, and commit yourself to a writing group where everyone is responsible to each other. In this way, time becomes your ally instead of your enemy.

Writing fatigue. The most rewarding writing takes time. Consider reworking a car engine, preparing for a soccer tournament, or painting a portrait. Eventually our brains just get fatigued with considering the same topic for so many days or weeks. But there are multiple strategies for working against writing fatigue: physical exercise, meditation, conversation with family and friends, or simply doing something different for a while. Play a video game, doodle in your notebook, take a walk, or even work on other intellectual activities, such as reading or solving a chemistry problem. Once your brain changes its attention for a while, you can return to your writing project after a few hours or a few days refreshed. The Buddhist priest Jōkō of Tōtōmi commissioned the original wooden carving of the Great Buddha of Kamakura, which required ten years to complete. Ten years! As the sculptors collaborated, they no doubt exhibited multiple days of mental fatigue and were relieved when they could walk home at the end of a day's work. Yet they persisted. (See next page.)

Fear of failure. Many first-year students have little experience with real revision. As we have said before, writing is hard, and students see revision as just another hard step of writing where they might not succeed. This fear is normal and should be addressed in your reflection journal. We do not want to start over on something we think we have completed, and we do not understand why we need to change the familiar into something unfamiliar—again! Revision can be like moving to a new city or to the other side of your own city. We know that much will remain the same—grocery shops are grocery shops,

traffic lights are traffic lights, parks are parks. But seeing a new city or living on the other side of our own city is a disconcerting experience, at least for a while. We have to awaken our senses in new ways to feel the difference in the old and the new. But with experience comes confidence, and soon these new streets will feel as familiar as our old streets. Just as importantly, we can approach this fear of revision as a common experience of most writers, and an experience that eventually changes from fear to something like excitement. Fear is normal, but once we get busy re-seeing, the work of writing overcomes the fear. Finally, keep in mind what Michael Jordan has said: "I've missed more than 9,000 shots in my career. I've lost almost 300 games. 26 times I've been trusted to take the game-winning shot and missed. I've failed over and over again in my life. And that is why I succeed."

Revision Strategies

At one time, composition scholars argued that revision required a shift from the interior "writer talk" within our own mind to a consideration of the exterior "audience talk" needed for effective communication. That is one way of seeing revision—ensuring that we are really writing *for* the audience as well as for ourselves and not just writing to complete a product. To do this, revision requires control of the thesis and scaffolding of the writing project. As practice, we can consider revision in our work as choices we make as authors. For example, as Catherine Haar and Alice Horning point out in *Revision: History, Theory, and Practice*, revision can mean different things.

Revision as correction. This is what many students do when they are told to revise their papers—they correct the errors in grammar and punctuation; but this is essentially "surface" correction and does not address more fundamental issues, such as clarity and development.

Revision as development and discovery. As authors, our experience of a subject changes as we engage with a topic, as peers read our work and give us feedback, as we see the need for clarification of ideas, and as we see how certain parts of our work need further development. We discover new ideas—and new ways of making ourselves clear.

Revision as rhetorical goal-setting. This type of revision centers on the rhetorical relationship between our audience and us. Depending on our intended audience, the function of our project may change, requiring a different tone or a change in purpose, as we move from an informative essay to a persuasive one.

Revision as assertion of identity. Each of us is complex, with multiple relationships and responsibilities. Revision allows us to emphasize our difference from the accepted modes of being and discourse, thus adding a new voice and new perspective to the collective conversation.

The Purpose of Revision

Remember that writing is always a rhetorical act, and when we use rhetoric of any kind, we consider our situation, purpose, audience, and voice. As you begin to revise, consider these rhetorical questions as you "re-see" your work:

Situation. Every situation calls for a different type of writing.

Academic writing includes description, analysis, classification, and persuasion.

Public writing includes informative projects, service writing, advocacy, and making academic work legible to public audiences.

Personal writing includes reflections, narratives, and blogs.

Purpose. Each situation, in turn, requires a different purpose.

Informative writing is an attempt to enlighten (and entertain) an audience through the use of fact and informed opinion as well as personal experience.

Persuasive writing is the attempt to change the beliefs, attitudes, or behaviors of one's audience.

Expressive writing is often personal and written primarily to explore our own experiences and emotions, though often we may want to share these with others.

Connective writing is a rudimentary form of rhetoric meant solely to maintain personal connections, like asking "¿Qué pasa?" or saying "See you later." We do this through texting and writing emails, for example.

Reflective writing. As we grow and develop mentally and emotionally, we must digest what we have learned formally as well as through personal experience in order to grow. Writing helps us to do that. We can also share that growth in awareness with others. Do not be surprised when revising if you see your purpose becoming clearer on its own.

Audience. Audience is always key whenever our writing is informative or persuasive. Our audience may include these categories.

Instructors, classmates, the campus community

Public organizations, neighborhood groups

Coworkers, bosses

The unseen public on blogs

The relationship with our audience should always be uppermost in our mind; the choices we make can strengthen or weaken that relationship. You may think that we exaggerate when we argue that the writer's relationship with his or her audience is as complex and risky as any interpersonal relationship, but that is the reality of effective writing. Through fiction, poetry, drama, exposition, and persuasion, authors have changed lives and the destinies of nations. You likely will not be asked to write a declaration of independence as Thomas Jefferson was, but neither should you discount the effect your writing can have on your own emotional, intellectual, and social growth or the way it can affect the growth of others. As a central stage of the writing process, revision forces us as writers to consider and reconsider rhetorical relationships of all kinds.

What voice do I present in my writing? (What will the audience think of me because of what I have written?)

How much do I trust my audience? What risks can I take with this text?

What effect do I intend to have on my audience? What do I expect them to learn, feel, or do?

Do I have multiple audiences? How can I address multiple audiences with one text?

What is the rhetorical situation, and how does my text fit into the larger conversation on my topic? How will that conversation change if the situation changes?

Has the text changed me? How am I making and remaking myself through writing?

As we consider our understanding of audience, we should also think about culture—our own culture as well as the culture of our audience. Remember that culture is both *large* and *small*—as large as nations and as small as the family's kitchen table. Understanding culture helps us to understand if we should choose humor or satire, for example. Humor will be embraced by some cultures, whereas satire will offend. Similarly, your own culture may value narrative over linear persuasion. Understanding our own and our audience's cultures—large and small—is a key component of revision.

Activity 7.1

Consider your current project. You have either been assigned, or you have chosen, an audience—perhaps your instructor or your classmates. By making this choice, you have already determined a specific situation and purpose. Identify your audience and explain what choices are appropriate for that audience you made in your invention and structuring. For example, in an academic paper written for your business professor, you might use business jargon and research from business journals, using a cause-and-effect structure to show how to grow a small business.

Next, revise your work for a new audience, such as a neighborhood group. Consider a new structure and a new voice. For example, for a neighborhood cooperative (co-op) you would cut the business jargon and give more examples from mainstream sources, using a general process-analysis structure to show how small businesses strengthen local communities.

Revision for Genre

As we revise, we should also consider what it is that we are writing, including its genre, modality, and medium and how each affects the relationship of the text to the audience and even to ourselves as authors.

Genres are types of presentation (oral, visual, written) that adhere to certain formal conventions and produce certain expectations in their audiences based on culturally recognized symbols. For example, we instinctively know when watching television that a thirty-second public service announcement about municipal transportation is not like an academic lecture about the links between low household incomes and access to nutritious food. The audience knows this difference because of experience and social expectations and "receives" these two genres differently. Genres, each for a different type of public communication, each setting a different expectation in its audience, can be found in college research and writing as well as other, more public, types of writing.

Through understanding genres, we can better understand the purpose of revision—tailoring our writing to meet our audience's expectations. For example, academic genres include these categories.

- ⊙ Expository essays
- ⊙ Literature reviews
- ⊙ Reports

- Case studies
- Business letters
- Abstracts
- Lab reports
- Research essays

We learn the conventions of each type by reading and studying examples in college classes. In addition, public writing also contains many genres, such as these.

- Autobiographies
- Memoirs
- Blogs
- Film reviews
- Reports in community newspapers
- Creative nonfiction pieces

Learning the strategies used in this first semester writing course will allow you to understand how important public writing can be in other situations. For example, while reading alone does not make us better writers, reading as a reflective practice *does* show us other writers' successes and failures with their work. As we practice critical analysis of other texts, we learn strategies to *re-vision* our own work in new ways. Therefore, as you learn to write for college and public use, make it a practice to critically analyze various genres and reflect on these genres in your writing journal.

Thus, critical thinking is part of the *practice* of revision, of seeing how effective writers do what they do. When we critique others' writing, we learn the "moves" writers make. However, we must remember we are seeing a finished project that has already been through the rigorous writing process multiple times—the polished text we see has been *revised* several times before it gets to us. This is why it is helpful to write collaboratively—because writing is usually a social practice. Writing collaboratively gives us that live audience we need to understand how others perceive our writing, as well as providing us examples of how others practice their writing.

Activity 7.2

Consider the multiple disciplines in which you are expected to write: composition, history, business, psychology, nursing, and many others. Identify the audience's writing expectation within one genre in one discipline. For example, your history course may expect you to write a causal analysis of some historic event, such as the Civil War. You will use the writing conventions expected in the history discipline, tracing the influence of slavery and the relationships among socioeconomic classes, political groups, economic swings, religious influences, and whatever else you find relevant to your discussion.

Revise your ideas for a new discipline and a new genre. For example, you could examine the same historic period, but for a sociology class, and use the conventions of sociology for a research proposal to examine how a particular social framework, such as conflict theory, might explain the war.

Revision for Multimodality

As our world has moved into the digital age, effective writing must also consider multimodal forms of communication. This is, in fact, nothing new. Multimodality (using more than one medium to convey a message) today is in every author's hands, including yours. You control the means of your work's publication and its reception by your intended audience. Authors no longer depend solely on black ink on a white sheet of paper to convey their ideas to others. Revising work to employ multiple modes of communication requires us to consider not only the shape of our ideas in the text but also how photography, artistic design, video, sound, and interactive Web spaces can influence our audience's experience and understanding of our ideas. Revising for multimodal communication requires an understanding of visual rhetoric and design. This includes these elements.

Art forms: portraits, street art, posters, still life

Typography: font, font size, emphasis (bold, italic)

Color: choice, coordination of background and foreground

Image: clarity, resolution, appropriateness

Bullets, numbered lists, tables: position, alignment, size

Composition: relationships of all the above as well as to white space

Effective visual rhetoric is a whole academic course in and of itself, but as you react to other texts—print advertisements, billboards, YouTube videos, exposition in textbooks, magazine articles, documentary films, graphic novels—pause to engage the author of these multimodal texts, reflecting on the intended purpose, its efficacy, and your impressions of the rhetorical choices. As we consider revision, and as we consider the visuals used in our writing, we see how the addition, reposition, and deletion of those visuals change our audience's emotional and rational experience.

Sometimes we may want (or may be asked) to change the medium of our message in our revision. We may be expected to present our message through other media, especially software, such as PowerPoint or Prezi. Though revision for these presentation applications is beyond the scope of this chapter, the fundamental rules apply. How do we balance text and visuals appropriately when we consider our rhetorical situation and our audience's expectations?

Activity 7.3

Read the following student paragraph written for an introductory freshman English class. In your group, decide how you might change the paragraph to publish it as a blog, and then as a group rewrite it and share it with the class. Next, decide how you would change it to present it as a speech to your class. Again, rewrite it and share it with the class.

> The first reason video games are an issue is that many video games made today possess content that many people would consider to be obscene. The term obscene covers violence, profanity, and sexual images. Such videogames are usually branded with the M (mature audiences only) rating on the front of the videogame cover. This means that only players seventeen or older should be playing such games. However, many children around the ages of twelve and under are acquiring these video games as gifts or are purchasing the games themselves. Therefore, it can be assumed that the parents are purchasing M-rated games for their children, and that stores are willingly selling these young children M-rated games. As Paul Keegan says in "Violence in Video Games and Other Media Can Cause School Shootings," parents are not following these ratings and stores are not enforcing them, thus allowing young children to view content that is considered obscene (6). Thus, if parents understand and follow the various video game rating labels, and if stores enforce the videogame rating system, then young children will not be as easily able to view mature material.

Revision and Collaborative Writing

Collaboration has become standard practice for modern corporations. Companies such as Google and Microsoft value and promote the synergy that comes from the interaction of their employees in groups. It is a highly valued skill, along with critical thinking and communication. Collaboration can also be very productive in writing. Sharing your ideas and writing with others will help you improve your verbal skills as well as your writing. You will also learn a lot in the process of helping others.

Work with Other Writers in a *Writing Group*. Having a living, breathing, *present* audience experience your text and explain their experience is an immeasurable advantage as you progress as a writer. This is a chance to share your writing experience, as well as your text, with others. Keep your writing journal active with notes, shared experiences, and reflections from these group meetings.

Work in the *Writing Center*. When you use the Writing Center, you are responsible for preparing for the consultation and explaining your purpose and requirements to the tutor. This consultation requires patience and understanding; the writing tutor will be knowledgeable and sincere, but she will not have all the background about you as a writer that your writing group has, for example. If you prepare for your consultation, however, your time with the tutor will be much more productive.

Sign up for a 30- to 45-minute appointment ahead of time, if possible.

Spend 30 to 45 minutes working on your invention assignment before arriving.

Make sure you have all your documents (hard copy or digital) so you do not waste your time.

Bring the writing assignment instructions. Tutors are not responsible for reading anyone's mind or guessing what your project is supposed to accomplish.

Based on the assignment, write down three to five small goals for your consultation time. If you cannot achieve each goal, be prepared to make another appointment to return.

Introduce yourself to your tutor, and discuss your writing strengths and challenges before addressing the specific writing assignment itself.

Take notes about what you discuss with your tutor as well as any other thoughts that come to mind during your discussion. This is still part of invention and becomes a resource for revision.

Work with Your *Writing Instructor.* Most writing instructors are more than happy to discuss whatever writing issues you have, so you can also schedule a meeting or drop by during their scheduled office hours. Your instructor may have experience with hundreds and thousands of student writing projects. Use this time to discuss your own struggle with revision and learn *again* how hard writing is as together you discuss a particular paragraph, sentence, metaphor, or transition that especially troubles you. Together, as you wrestle with re-seeing your work, both of you can better appreciate the real work that writing is.

Reflect on Your *Revision.* Focus on its challenges and successes, its risks and effects. Before, during, and after revision, reflect on the choices you have made and the choices you still can make. Periodically review these reflections to see your progress as a writer. As an exercise, share some of your revision choices with your writing group to test the rhetorical effects on them.

Activity 7.4

With the other members of your group, take the paragraph under Activity 7.3, and turn it into a poster about the dangers of violent video games. Decide what information should go on the poster, what font and point size you should use, what colors, and how the words should be arranged on the page. Design your poster in Word, add pictures or Word art, save it, and then present it to the class. (Review Chapter 12 if necessary.)

Further Revision Strategies

Revision is hard work, but as in all other endeavors, such as music or sports, hard work pays off. In addition to the suggestions above, here are some further revision strategies.

Quiet the inner editor for a while longer. Revision is less about simply satisfying a set of rules than it is about communicating with the audience. (See Chapter 8 for more about editing.)

Challenge your inner voice with your public voice. Consider how your public audience needs to hear a message separate from the message in your head. This is where your writing group becomes so important. Ask each other, "What do you mean by that?" and "Can you show me more examples to clarify this?"

Review the writing instructions, and consider the boundaries of the writing project. What rhetorical risks can you take that will make the project more effective for your situation, purpose, and audience?

Adjust the tone of your project. Can you be humorous, satiric, enthusiastic, ironic, or curious? The way you say something is often as important as what you say.

Identify your project's strengths, and build on these. Write a reflection in your writing journal on the strengths of your writing. Focus on the positive.

Identify your project's weaknesses. Come to understand why these elements are weak, and either strengthen them or delete them.

Restructure by considering an alternative hook and introduction. Revise your thesis to strengthen its relationship with your project, reoutline your work once you finish your composition draft to get the big picture of your project's strengths and direction, and ask whether this structure is the best for your writing purpose.

Provide new and alternative types of evidence for each idea.

Look for logical fallacies in your argument. Eliminate these through discussion with your writing group. (See Appendix 2 for common fallacies.)

Add qualifiers to your claims so that you don't overstate your argument.

Restructure sentences.

Review your conclusion. Instead of a simple summary, revise your conclusion to show your audience what you have learned from your writing experience or how writing has made new meaning in your world.

Check your working thesis statement, and revise it to reflect the topic, discussion points, and assertions that you have actually made in the body and conclusion. Revise that thesis statement as needed.

Read the paper out loud slowly and publicly. Listen to your own voice as you read, and make written notes of ideas as they come to you.

Take a break. Do not try to write for more than an hour at a time, because your brain will exhaust itself. Walk away for a day, then return and practice each of these revision strategies again.

Ultimately, we are responsible for our own writing, and as much as we want to get that coveted grade, we learn by listening to feedback from experienced writers. This does not mean we should always take others' advice, but it is an opportunity to consider multiple options in our revision. We learn first by doing, but we also learn by listening and especially by making mistakes. Revision, fortunately, lets us learn in multiple ways.

A Note on Document Management

You must maintain computer backups of all your revisions, with some way to keep various stages separate, such as HIST1301 Project 3 May 3, then HIST1301 Project 3 May 4. Keep all your writing in the cloud—Google Drive, Microsoft Cloud, your school's network—or on multiple drives. For example, if you have printouts for a sourced paper, then keep everything clearly labeled and in its own folder. One of the most sickening feelings in academic life is losing one's files or breaking one's computer, staring at the ground, wondering whether time machines really exist.

Final Word

You should know that this chapter, as with each chapter of this textbook, has been a collaborative writing project among the authors. For each chapter, a principal author has invented and composed a draft of the chapter's material. Yet for each chapter we have collaborated with each other, seeking feedback, and then revising the chapter for our audience's needs. (That's you.) Even though each of us has years of writing practice and has collectively written tens of thousands of words, we revise our work, repeatedly, because the audience deserves that. So, knowing that we re-vision our work here, you should consider doing the same in your work.

Therefore, instead of seeing revision as a chore, try to see revision as an opportunity to gain a better understanding of your world, your audience, and your own writing process. All help you to mature as a writer. Revision opens multiple pathways for us as writers, and it increases our ability to connect with our audience.

Activity 7.5

Consider your own experiences with revision and your own attitudes toward re-seeing or rewriting your work. Begin with a pro/con chart describing the act of revision.

Why Revise	Why Not Revise

Activity 7.6

Take a paragraph or complete essay you have already written, and share it with your group. Take their suggestions for revision into account, and revise the paper. Next, take this revised paper to the writing lab, and consult with a tutor. After noting down the tutor's suggestions, revise the paper a second time. Finally, make an appointment with your instructor, and take this revision with you. After discussing the paper with your instructor, revise the paper a third time.

Simplicity

William Zinsser

William Zinsser is an American writer, journalist, and teacher. He taught nonfiction writing at Yale for a number of years and has published many books. He lives in New York City. The following is taken from *On Writing Well: The Classic Guide to Writing Nonfiction,* now in its thirtieth anniversary edition (1976).

Zinsser has been writing about writing for a long time, and the following essay has often been reprinted in texts such as this one. In it, Zinsser discusses the most important quality of all good writing: clarity. In revising your own essays, you must constantly question your sentences and word use: What am I trying to say here? Does this sentence make sense? Will the reader understand this reference? As Zinsser points out, the secret to writing clearly is thinking clearly, but the reverse of that statement is also true: writing clearly induces thinking clearly. Zinsser ends with a truism: "Writing is hard work." But, like any other activity you might pursue, writing becomes easier the more you practice it.

Clutter is the disease of American writing. We are a society strangling in unnecessary words, circular constructions, pompous frills and meaningless jargon.

Who can understand the clotted language of everyday American commerce and enterprise: the memo, the corporation report, the business letter, the notice from the bank explaining its latest "simplified" statement? What member of an insurance or medical plan can decipher the brochure explaining his costs and benefits? What father or mother can put together a child's toy from the instructions on the box? Our national tendency is to inflate and thereby sound important. The airline pilot who announces that he is presently anticipating experiencing considerable precipitation wouldn't think of saying that it may rain. The sentence is too simple—there must be something wrong with it.

But the secret of good writing is to strip every sentence to its cleanest components. Every word that serves no function, every long word that could be a short word, every adverb that carries the same meaning that's already in the verb, every passive construction that leaves the reader unsure of who is doing what—these are the thousand and one adulterants that weaken the strength of a sentence. And they usually occur in proportion to education and rank.

During the late 1960s the president of my university wrote a letter to mollify the alumni after a spell of campus unrest. "You are probably aware," he began, "that we have been experiencing very considerable potentially explosive expressions of dissatisfaction on issues only partially related." He meant that the students had been hassling them about different things. I was far more upset by the president's English than by the students' potentially explosive expressions of dissatisfaction. I would have preferred the presidential approach taken by Franklin D. Roosevelt when he tried to convert into English his own government's memos, such as this blackout order of 1942:

> Such preparations shall be made as will completely obscure all
> Federal buildings and non-Federal buildings occupied by the
> Federal government during an air raid for any period of time from
> visibility by reason of internal or external illumination.

> "Tell them," Roosevelt said, "that in buildings where they have to keep the work going to put something across the windows."

Simplify, simplify. Thoreau said it, as we are so often reminded, and no American writer more consistently practiced what he preached. Open *Walden* to any page and you will find a man saying in a plain and orderly way what is on his mind:

> I went to the woods because I wished to live deliberately, to front only
> the essential facts of life, and see if I could not learn what it had to
> teach, and not, when I came to die, discover that I had not lived.

How can the rest of us achieve such enviable freedom from clutter? The answer is to clear our heads of clutter. Clear thinking becomes clear writing: one can't exist without the other. It's impossible for a muddy thinker to write good English. He may get away with it for a paragraph or two, but soon the reader will be lost, and there's no sin so grave, for the reader will not easily be lured back.

Who is this elusive creature, the reader? The reader is someone with an attention span of about 30 seconds—a person assailed by many forces competing for attention. At one time those forces were relatively few: newspapers, magazines, radio, spouse, children, pets. Today they also include a galaxy of electronic devices for receiving entertainment and information—television, VCRs, DVDs, CDs, video games, the Internet, e-mail, cell phones, BlackBerries, iPods—as well as a fitness program, a pool, a lawn and that most potent of competitors, sleep. The man or woman snoozing in a chair with a magazine or a book is a person who was being given too much unnecessary trouble by the writer.

It won't do to say that the reader is too dumb or too lazy to keep pace with the train of thought. If the reader is lost, it's usually because the writer has not been careful enough. This carelessness can take any number of forms. Perhaps a sentence is so excessively cluttered that the reader, hacking through the verbiage, simply doesn't know what it means. Perhaps a sentence has been so shoddily constructed that the reader could read it in any of several ways. Perhaps the writer has switched pronouns in midsentence, or has switched tenses, so the reader loses track of who is talking or when the action took place. Perhaps Sentence B is not a logical sequel to Sentence A; the writer, in whose head the connection is clear, hasn't bothered to provide the missing link. Perhaps the writer has used a word incorrectly by not taking the trouble to look it up.

Faced with such obstacles, readers are remarkably tenacious. They blame themselves—they obviously missed something, and they go back over the mystifying sentence, or over the whole paragraph, piecing it out like an ancient rune, making guesses and moving on. But they won't do that for long. The writer is making them work too hard, and they will look for one who is better at the craft.

Writers must therefore constantly ask: what am I trying to say? Surprisingly often, they don't know. Then they must look at what they have written and ask: have I said it? Is it clear to someone encountering the subject for the first time? If it's not, some fuzz has worked its way into the machinery. The clear writer is someone clearheaded enough to see this stuff for what it is: fuzz.

I don't mean that some people are born clearheaded and are therefore natural writers, whereas others are naturally fuzzy and will never write well. Thinking clearly is a conscious act that writers must force on themselves, just as if they were working on any other project that requires logic: making a shopping list or doing an algebra problem. Good writing doesn't come naturally, though most people seem to think it does. Professional writers are constantly bearded by people who say they'd like to "try a little writing sometime"—meaning when they retire from their real profession, like insurance or real estate, which is hard. Or they say, "I could write a book about that." I doubt it.

Writing is hard work. A clear sentence is no accident. Very few sentences come out right the first time, or even the third time. Remember this in moments of despair. If you find that writing is hard, it's because it *is* hard.

Topics for Writing and Discussion

1. Zinsser says of shoddy writing that "perhaps a sentence is so excessively cluttered that the reader, hacking his way through the verbiage, simply doesn't know what it means. Perhaps a sentence has been so shoddily constructed that the reader could read it in any of several ways." Find two sentences in your own writing (perhaps two redlined by your teacher) that

fit Zinsser's description. Rewrite them, clarifying your ideas, then explain how you did that.

2. Find two sentences in this textbook that you find difficult to read. Copy them, and then explain why they are difficult to understand; next, rewrite them, "simplifying" them.

CHAPTER 8

Editing

As you learned in Chapter 7, revision is the process of "re-visioning," the reshaping of sentences and paragraphs for clarity and cogency. Once you feel confident that you have succeeded in presenting your ideas and accomplished your purpose, the next and final step is editing your draft for correctness, searching closely for grammatical errors, punctuation, and usage. Careful editing, while time-consuming, results in a flowing, polished essay that helps the reader easily follow your ideas. Unfortunately, because students are so pressed for time with deadlines, they often tend to ignore this third phase of the writing process. Yet to skip this very important step is to risk the misreading of your message. For your ideas to be taken seriously by your instructor, or any reader, you must take special care to assure that your project is free of errors that could confuse your ideas or distract your reader.

We recommend that you *not* concern yourself with close editing before you completely finish the revision phase of your drafting. Before you can refine your sentences, you must first feel confident that your final revisions are satisfactory, that they meet your reader's expectations, and that they fulfill the promise you made to your audience regarding your purpose in writing the essay. Even though experienced writers edit throughout the invention and drafting stages, they realize that this last step requires a more intense scrutiny of the essay's mechanics before it is ready for publication. Remember, correctness alone does not guarantee superior writing. It simply means we as writers know we must comply with agreed-upon expectations and standards of correctness if we intend to reach our audience and fulfill our purpose.

While recognizing that conventions of grammar change over time (due today to social media and the internet), we recommend that you observe standard punctuation conventions associated with academic essays and Standard English. As the critic, professor, and novelist John Gardner wrote in *The Art of Fiction: Notes on Craft for Young Writers*: "No one can hope to write well if he has not mastered—absolutely mastered—the rudiments: grammar and syntax, punctuation, diction, sentence variety, paragraph structure, and so forth" (17).

Choosing the conventions of Standard English for specific writing situations (such as blogs, emails, reports, and academic essays) is a rhetorical decision, based on the appropriateness for a given situation and medium. Therefore, we recommend that you, as writer, abide by these rules.

Although every writing difficulty cannot be addressed at the editing stage, certain problem areas should always be covered. These include sentence construction, spelling, word choice, grammar, and punctuation. You know from earlier writing experiences what errors you are most likely to commit, so focus your energy on these. For those problems not included here, consult your handbook.

Proofreading one's own draft can be difficult. Usually by the time we are finished with invention, drafting, and revising, we are either too emotionally attached to what we have written to be objective about it or too sick of it to want to spend one more minute with it. Here are some simple suggestions, however, that might make your task easier. Many successful writers have employed these strategies, but it is up to you to determine which you find most helpful.

Editing for Grammatical Errors

Unless you are writing your first essay, you are already familiar with the types of errors you are likely to make. If you have kept a log or journal of your past grammatical errors (which we strongly recommend), you know what you must check first. These errors range from serious to minor, but each remains important. Correctness is your goal. The following are considered major errors.

Fragments. A sentence fragment is a phrase or dependent clause that lacks a subject, a verb, or sometimes both.

> *Example*: "A city that provides its residents and visitors a plethora of entertainment sources."

> *Revision*: (Add an independent clause to make the sentence a complete thought.) "As a city that provides its residents and visitors a plethora of entertainment sources, Houston offers professional sports, museums, parks, the Livestock Show and Rodeo, and the NASA Johnson Space Center."

If you want to include intentional fragments for emphasis or for effect in your writing, we recommend you use them sparingly (usually only three or four words, such as "In which town?" "But not so wholly," or "Just once!").

Run-On Sentences (also called **Fused Sentences**). A run-on sentence is actually two sentences joined without the proper punctuation or connecting word. There are five options available for correcting this error.

Example: "The Texas A&M alumnus can no longer enjoy the rivalry between his alma mater and the Longhorns the Aggies moved to another conference."

Revision 1: (Create a compound sentence by adding a comma and a coordinating conjunction, such as *for, and, nor, but, or, yet,* or *so.*)

"The Texas A&M alumnus can no longer enjoy the rivalry between his alma mater and the Longhorns, for the Aggies moved to another conference."

Revision 2: (Separate the two clauses with a period, creating two simple sentences.)

"The Texas A&M alumnus can no longer enjoy the rivalry between his alma mater and the Longhorns. The Aggies moved to another conference."

Revision 3: (Restructure the sentence by creating a subordinate clause, resulting in a complex sentence.)

"Since the Aggies moved to another conference, the Texas A&M alumnus can no longer enjoy the rivalry between his alma mater and the Longhorns."

Revision 4: (Add a subordinating conjunction.)

"The Texas A&M alumnus can no longer enjoy the rivalry between his alma mater and the Longhorns since the Aggies moved to another conference."

Revision 5: (Place a semicolon between the two independent clauses.)

"The Texas A&M alumnus can no longer enjoy the rivalry between his alma mater and the Longhorns; the Aggies moved to another conference."

Comma Splices. When two sentences (two independent clauses) are joined with only a comma, the result is a comma splice. The error can be corrected by replacing the comma with a period or a semicolon, or adding a coordinating conjunction to the existing comma.

Example: "I seldom completed my English homework in high school, that's why I make such poor grades in my college English class."

Revision 1: (Combine a coordinating conjunction with the existing comma.)

"I seldom completed my English homework in high school, and that's why I make such poor grades in my college English class."

Revision 2: (Replace the original comma with a period, creating two sentences.)

"I seldom completed my English homework in high school. That's why I make such poor grades in my college English class."

Revision 3: (Replace the original comma with a semicolon.)

"I seldom completed my English homework in high school; that's why I make such poor grades in my college English class."

Other serious grammatical errors:

- ⊙ Subject-verb agreement
- ⊙ Spelling
- ⊙ Pronoun problems (faulty agreement or indefinite reference)
- ⊙ Parallelism
- ⊙ Tense inconsistency
- ⊙ Dangling or misplaced modifiers
- ⊙ General errors in syntax (*Syntax* refers to the structure of a sentence, clause, or phrase. If the reader stumbles over the wording or cannot understand what a sentence says, your essay might contain some serious syntactical errors.)

Less serious grammatical errors (but still distracting):

- ⊙ Misplaced apostrophes
- ⊙ Misused or misplaced commas
- ⊙ Passive voice
- ⊙ Nonstandard capitalization

For these last two groupings, consult your handbook or the Writing Center for identification and corrections of these errors.

Activity 8.1

Take several of the paragraph(s) or essay(s) you have written, and make a list of the grammatical errors that have been marked. Next, go to your handbook, or one of the many websites that discuss these errors, and read the explanation of the problem. If you need further explanation, ask other members of your group or your instructor for help. Finally, do several exercises for each of the problems to check your understanding. Ask your instructor or your writing lab for exercises, or go to the site *Guide to Grammar and Writing* of Capital Community College, which has extensive exercises, or the exercises at *Grammar Bytes!*

Avoiding Wordiness

To communicate ideas clearly, a writer must first have knowledge of the subject, have a specific purpose, know what audience he is writing for, and have a fluent command of words. That is not easy. But like all things, practice is the key to competence. There are many books, both in print and online, that give beginning writers excellent advice on writing clearly. One of the oldest, but one still in many writers' libraries, is *The Elements of Style*, by William Strunk Jr. and E. B. White. Now in its fourth edition, it is a slim paperback with many rules of usage and multiple examples, such as a section that is titled "Omit needless words" that begins with the sentence "Vigorous writing is concise." The early 1918 edition of this work by Strunk is online at the *Bartleby Project* (Columbia University). There are many university writing center sites online that discuss word choice and usage. *Garbl's Writing Center*, for example, has a section on "Style and Usage" with links to many other sites on the Web. The following are a few general rules to help you write clear, concise, and understandable English prose.

Use the Active Voice. Active voice uses fewer words and is more precise than passive voice. In active voice, we place the performer of the action (the subject) first, then the verb, and finally the thing acted upon (the object). *The boy hit the ball.* In passive voice, we reverse this order, placing the object first and the actor in a prepositional phrase last. *The ball was hit by the boy.* Note that the first sentence has five words and the second seven words, though they both say the same thing. While passive voice is necessary in some situations, particularly when the subject or actor is unknown—"When I heard the noise and looked out, my windshield had been shattered"—overuse of the passive voice weakens prose; it usually adds unnecessary words and delays important information until the end of the sentence. Sometimes, in fact, the actor is dropped altogether, and the reader is left to wonder who was responsible for the action. For example, when asked how a vase came to be in pieces on the floor, a child might say, "It was broken," trying to avoid responsibility. Even important people use this dodge to avoid admitting responsibility. For example, when pressed about the Iran-Contra scandal during his tenure as president, Ronald Reagan simply said, "Mistakes were made." (In each of the following pairs of sentences, the first is in passive voice; the second in active.)

> The flowers were grown by a California nursery.

> A California nursery grew the flowers.

> When evaluating the participation level of early registration, it was considered quite successful.

> Early registration was a great success.

> Due to construction in the CE building, the wires were cut.

> CE building workers cut power lines to campus.

Avoid Superfluous Sentence Openers. Every word in a sentence should contribute to advancing the point of your paragraph, so, particularly at the beginning of your sentences, you do not want words that just sit there. For example, the word *there* at the beginning of a sentence can usually be cut without altering the meaning of the sentence.

> There are three ways to produce this effect. They are . . .

> Three ways to produce this effect are . . .

> There are many students who do not listen to their instructors.

> Many students do not listen to their instructors.

> There has been much controversy about women's role in the military.

> Women's role in the military is controversial.

> I think that most students would enjoy working in the computer lab.

> Most students would enjoy working in the computer lab because . . .

Avoid Vague, Abstract Nouns. Cut out vague, woolly, abstract nouns wherever possible, and substitute more specific words. Get rid of such jargon nouns as *case, factor, instance, character, situation, degree, thing, aspect, condition,* and *phase.*

> There are several *factors* that influenced my decision to attend college.

> I decided to attend college because I was broke, living at home, and working at a job I hated.

> The first *instance* of this virus occurred on January 12.

> This virus first occurred on January 12.

> *In the first case,* I got a message telling me I was out of disc space.

> First, I got a message telling me I was out of disc space.

Calvin and Hobbes. Copyright © Bill Waterson

Cut Out Wordy Phrases. Many phrases can be reduced to single words (Table 8.1).

Original Phrase	Revised
As of this date	Today
Prior to	Before
On behalf of	For
Due to	Because
Due to the fact that	Because
At the present time	Now
In this day and age	Today
In a number of cases	Some or Often

Table 8.1: Wordy Phrases

Use Short Words Instead of Multisyllabic Ones. Because modern English is a language with two diverse parents, German and Latin, many times as writers we have a choice between a short Germanic word or a longer Latinate word. Most of the time, the shorter, Germanic word is clearer and more direct. In addition, some people have a tendency to add –*ize* to perfectly respectable words. Avoid that tendency (Table 8.2).

Multisyllabic Word	Revised Shorter Word
Aggregate	Total
Proceed	Go
Demonstrate	Show
Prioritize	Rank
Authorize	Allow
Utilize	Use
Converse	Talk

Table 8.2: Shorter Words

Writing clearly is not easy, but like anything else, it can be learned with a little dedication and practice. While you may never have to, or have the desire to, write a lot, you will always need to communicate your desires, feelings, and opinions. A little knowledge about and practice with words will smooth your passage through the relationships you will build throughout your life and make college, and work, a little easier.

Activity 8.2

Read the following paragraph, and then rewrite it; take out the wordiness, cut the jargon, and revise wordy expressions. Next, add specific detail.

Due to the fact that they are experiencing college for the first time, many students fail to utilize all the aids the college offers. They fail to prioritize their tasks because they lack requisite cognition of the appropriate character of the situation they are in. In this day and age, competing factors impact the student's academic condition. There seem to be many pressures the student must withstand. He usually works, perhaps as much as thirty hours a week. He possibly has to help out at home, in addition, by babysitting younger siblings. It seems to me that all these factors doom him to failure. When he does find time to study, it seems likely that he will be too tired to proceed. He will probably fall into slumber. What does his instructor expect? Can a student work all day and study all night? It seems to me that is impossible.

Editing For Style

Besides editing for grammar and diction, you will also want to check the structure and flow of your sentences, and you should always strive, above all, for clarity. You want your reader to understand you, to get what you are saying. Here are some suggestions on how to achieve that goal.

Combine Sentences. Beginning writers often restrict themselves by limiting their prose to simple sentences because they fear committing errors. However, an endless succession of simple, choppy sentences destroys the flow of words and ideas. Consider combining two, three, or four sentences into a single sentence if all the ideas stated in each are somehow connected. For example, notice the short, choppy, monotonous sentences in the following paragraph.

> The city of Houston offers its residents and visitors a plethora of sources of entertainment for all ages. Its professional sports teams provide year-round entertainment. Its museum district attracts thousands every year. The NASA Johnson Space Center is an international drawing card. The annual Livestock Show and Rodeo brings artists from across the country. Its restaurants are acclaimed for their fine cuisine. Its parks are among the best in the southwest.

Because so many of these supportive sentences repeat beginning words, and because each sentence can be developed further, you might want to combine several of the general classifications of entertainment into one sentence, and then follow it with concrete examples. There are several ways to accomplish this.

- ⊙ Use a series to combine similar ideas: "Houston, a great city for family entertainment, offers professional sports, the NASA Johnson Space Center, the Livestock Show and Rodeo, fine restaurants, art museums, and parks for everyone to enjoy."

- ⊙ Use an introductory phrase or clause to combine your sentences: "Because Houston offers its residents and visitors professional sports, the NASA Johnson Space Center, art museums, the Livestock Show and Rodeo, fine restaurants, and parks, it ranks among the best cities for family entertainment."

- ⊙ Use an appositive to accentuate your major idea. (An appositive is a noun or noun phrase that identifies or adds information to a preceding noun phrase.): "The city of Houston, with its professional sports, museum district, the NASA Johnson Space Center, fine restaurants, parks, and Livestock Show and Rodeo, ranks among the very best sources for family entertainment."

Notice that when these sentences are combined into a single sentence (as a thesis, for example), you can now direct your efforts toward developing the essay, focusing on the specific levels of generality described in Chapter 4.

We are not suggesting that you avoid short sentences altogether. For the sake of emphasis, they can be highly effective. In fact, some professional writers, such as engineers, journalists, and tech writers, employ short sentences almost exclusively. But, in general, strive for a combination of both long and short sentences. Always let your chosen purpose and audience determine your sentence lengths. On the other hand, sometimes a writer mistakenly thinks that the longer the sentence, the more sophisticated it sounds, but it often results in a jumble of words and phrases that do not make sense. Clarity, after all, is the most important goal of expository writing.

Use Action Verbs. Another important component of editing involves examining the verbs you use in your sentences. Remember not to write like you talk. Select verbs that invigorate your sentences, letting your reader more fully understand what you describe. In other words, allow your reader to see what you sense, feel your pain, experience your fear and love, visualize what you see. In addition, avoid static verbs as much as possible (*is, am, has, are*) when a descriptive action verb can create a more vivid image of what you want to convey. For example, consider the following sentences. In the first, replace the static verb with an action verb.

> "He is my old friend."
> "He earned my friendship years ago."
>
> "It was a night to remember."
> "The night produced some of my most cherished memories."

Another method of enriching your sentences involves adding an adverb to your action verb to enliven the statement.

> "He walked into the room."
> "He walked quietly into the room," or
> "He walked stealthily into the room."

The writer must continually ask whether these are the best word choices. For example, one might ask whether the adverb really adds to the descriptive quality of the sentence. For example, what does walking "quietly" look like? The use of the adverb alone does not add any real description to the sentence. For the generic verb "walked," substitute a verb that adds not only action but visual description as well. Here are some examples.

> "He tiptoed into the room." "He casually strolled into the room."
> "He stole into the room." "Being in no hurry, he sauntered into the room."

In these last sentences, changing the verb has compressed action and detail, heightened the reader's interest through word choice, and set up the sentence to develop further the details of the room that will explain his method of movement into the room. (The "What happens next?" comes into play.) Keeping the sentences both active and descriptive allows them to accomplish more and produces a more rhythmic flow to the prose. In addition, avoid sentences that begin "There is," "There are," or "It was." While these constructions are sometimes effective, as a general rule you should consider more specific forms of expression. For example, start your sentence with a strong actor. Rather than beginning with "There are many students who depend on financial aid," let "students" serve as the actor and avoid the passive voice: "Many students depend on financial aid."

Activity 8.3

Study the list of Commonly Confused Words and Phrases in Appendix 3. Next, write the number of the following sentences on your own paper, and then write the correct word from the parenthesis beside each. When you are finished, compare your answers with your group and the class.

1. John's second wife (emigrated, immigrated) to this country in 1978.

2. The (principle, principal) figure in the play delivers an address to the audience.

3. A (carrot, caret, carat) is a proofreader's mark.

4. You may take only five items or (less, fewer) on the trip with you.

5. What (affect, effect) did failing the course have on him?

6. Some students simply will not accept the (consul, counsel, council) I try to give them.

7. Steven Weinberg is an (imminent, eminent) physicist.

8. He (lay, laid) his coat on the floor and then (lay, laid) down on it.

9. (It's, Its) not who you know, but what you know that counts.

10. (Sit, Set) your shoes by the door and (sit, set) down.

Editing Checklist

More than likely, you have participated in several classroom peer reviews. We recommend such reviews throughout the writing process, perhaps, even, for each draft. While these preliminary reviews target thesis, purpose, voice, and audience, and reviews of the second draft focus on paragraph unity, coherence, continuity, and development, a final review should examine correctness, conciseness, and grammar—in short, refinement of your draft.

Before you participate once again in a collaborative peer review, read your draft (or have someone else read it to you) and ask yourself the following questions.

Does my prose sound natural; does it flow smoothly? Do transitional devices function as intended, and do sentences and paragraphs have continuity?

Can I detect any grammatical errors?

Do I use a variety of sentence patterns (compound, complex, simple—short and long)?

Are any words repeated excessively?

Is my word choice satisfactory and appropriate for my audience and purpose?

Does anything seem confusing or awkward?

Do my subjects and verbs agree?

Have I followed the appropriate form of documentation (MLA, APA, Chicago Manual Style, if required)?

Is my manuscript formatted correctly? Did I use the correct font and size of type? Did I space appropriately between the title and the first line of my essay? Did I double-space throughout the essay? Are my pages numbered, and are the margins 1″ on all four sides?

Is my title appropriate for and consistent with the essay's content?

Sample Essay

For the sake of illustration, review the following essay (a second draft), written by student Raymond Perez. For your first reading, do not concern yourself with the editorial remarks in the right margin. What editorial suggestions would you make upon your first reading? List your observations/recommendations. Next, read the essay again, and this time note the editorial remarks. Are your observations similar to those in the right margin?

Klein United Methodist

"The cause of death was not belonging," or that's what I wrote down as my final message. {I didn't know it at the time,∧Klein United Methodist Church (KUMC) was going to be my saving grace.} I was sixteen when I had thought of suicide, but, thankfully, I didn't follow through with any of those thoughts. Back then I was lonely. I didn't feel wanted because I got kicked out of my house in Houston and was sent to live with a parent in Seattle who was absent most of my life. I didn't belong anywhere or to anyone. I felt hopeless. But that is different from what it is today, two years have passed, and now I am a new person. I was once lost, but now I have a place that I can call my own, a community of people on whom I can rely, just as they can rely on me. KUMC became my second chance and gave me a new foundation to rebuild my life and∧help rebuild the lives of others.

The place I found to be my home is located in the heart of Spring, Texas∧on FM 2920 and Kuykendahl Road. Although KUMC isn't the biggest church in town, its massive cross (Figure 1) was at first terrifying to me. I initially felt that the cross would break apart and fall on me. I felt like that because at the time I didn't feel like I deserved to be there—a community that did so much good for others. I don't think now the building matters as much, because it's the people who made up the congregation who would soon become my family.

The congregation is stereotypically white, with a few shades of color mixed in. I have never once felt like I was an outsider because I wasn't white. Yes, at first it was a bit different because in the past I went to churches located in the inner city of Houston. For me, to be one of the few Hispanics going to this church is a good thing—to be an example of diversity.¶However, sometimes I have been treated differently because I am Hispanic. I remember the first time I met the youth leader, Ryan. He was someone out of left field because he was so radical. His teachings weren't just black and white like the Bible. He made us think and use our voice to seek change in our congregation and∧make us want to go out and do good deeds for others. I think what made him different from other leaders was that he wasn't all talk and no action. KUMC isn't like any other church in our area. {The giving nature that each member seems to have is what sets our congregation apart.} The first time I noticed how giving my community is was when I was invited by Bette one Sunday morning to a group called "Love 4 Christ," which meets every second Sunday of each month. The group's task was

Suggested title: "Lost and Found"

but

Move this sentence down to precede the thesis (which is the paragraph's last sentence).

Comma splice: replace comma with a semicolon or a period.

Insert "to" for parallel verb forms.

Because no ZIP code is included, insert comma after "Texas."

No new paragraph.

Begin a new paragraph here.

Insert "to" — parallel verb forms.

Vague—offer more examples to illustrate his radical nature.

to load up our vans with food and items that many of the homeless needed in the nearby Greater Conroe area. I don't think any other church in my area does anything like this. I remember my third time going up to the Salvation Army in Conroe. It was January, and an arctic blast was expected within the next few days. That day we were giving out meals as per usual, but this time we were also handing out jackets and blankets. One lady was overjoyed, and, at that moment, I knew that I was a part of something bigger than myself. {Something that impacts a community of people who needed it.} I didn't expect to see such great kindness from our group who really didn't have to care. I always thought that wealthy people, especially white people, did not care about anyone but themselves, but I was wrong. I am glad that I was wrong.

> Fragment. Delete period after "myself," and insert a comma. Change "something" to lowercase.

I have also noticed our great out reaching this past summer during an event called UMARMY. Figure 2 shows everyone involved during a weeklong period of giving back. We were in Baytown, Texas and our project for that week was to build a wheelchair ramp for an elderly African-American woman whose house had seen better days. She lived in a forgotten part of Baytown, where poverty seemed like the norm. During that week I saw a lot of hesitation within my group because I don't think they have ever truly seen how others could live and do live. However, near the end of that week, I saw personal growth. I saw how upset they were that people lived like that and no one, except groups such as NUMARMY, are going out and helping others improve the quality of their lives. I am so proud to have been a part of a caring project like that. We built a wheelchair ramp for a woman who never even asked for it or expected us or anyone to be there to help her.

> Misspelling—outreaching.

> Insert comma after Texas (no ZIP code provided).

> Change "have" to "had" for tense consistency.

> Insert comma to separate two independent clauses.

> Substitute "is"—SV agreement.

I have faith in our church and in what makes it different. At one point in time women had strong roles in our church. They were leaders in the choir and even gave Sunday sermons in the traditional service. My friend Sydney, who is going to school for ministry in the fall semester, was encouraged to see women with high authority in the church leading the congregation. Sydney expressed to me once that she was excited to see a woman's role expand to being more than just a caretaker or a Sunday school teacher. However, there has been a shift within the last year to a more male-centric church. We recently lost two women who were leaders, and I believe they both showed our congregation that we could learn to move from being a traditional institution to something different and exciting. We have portraits of our present and former leaders in our hallway, and it is refreshing to see something new in the row of portraits. During the shift, I saw a lot of members uncertain of the new leadership and how we would be guided. I am fortunate enough to have witnessed being lead in the right direction. I honestly do sometimes miss the modern element—what I knew when I joined the church about a year ago. Everything seemed so sure and certain, but this year things are starting to be turned around a bit. I never thought that I would be working for the church, but, as luck would have it, I did. While it was only for a brief time, I earned the title of building attendant. One who basically makes sure that the people are who they are supposed to be. If something were to go wrong, I would call the police. Then again nothing has gone wrong (thank God), and I have realized that all I am is a glorified doorman. I realized while opening doors for members during weeknights as they hurried in so that they weren't late for their meeting or practice, that I look away and stare at the ground while I held open the door. I discovered that I am less than them. I have caught myself doing that more than once, and I get angry at myself because I feel like I am less than them because I think all they see is a Mexican holding open a door. They don't seem to care, which should not be the case. I shouldn't feel like that, especially at a church. We're all told from the pulpit to "Love thy neighbor" and to "Treat others how you would want to be treated." I ask myself why I feel the need to do so, to look away. One answer always pops up: they expect that of me—to serve. And I guess they are right because the other Hispanics who are employed by the church do only one of two things, clean or serve.

I talked to a lady named Marisol who cleans when I work at night, and, during the first time we talked, we brought up how as Hispanics we have to prove something. We have not only to prove things to ourselves, but to others so we can gain their approval. While I know we have a place and a right to be here, I never once tried to justify who I am or where I came from since I started attending KUMC. {What Marisol expressed was a bit eye-opening, however; we are played out and classified as servers, but never the ones being served. And it's true, more than ever in KUMC, that people who aren't white are seen as the lesser. I didn't pick up on it at first, but now I have. Working for the church has made

Misspelling ("led")

Fragment—delete the period and insert a comma. Make "One" lowercase.

Problem with paragraph unity. See additional comments following the essay.

it apparent that I am not an equal, but rather a servant, and while that description may seem brash, that is how I perceive it.}

Don't get me wrong, I do love going to the Klein United Methodist Church. It has provided me with a community of people to rely upon in my time of need. When I joined the church, I made a promise to care, lead, and help any member in need and to be there for everyone. It just takes a bit more time and patience to reach out and help when I don't see myself as an equal to everyone else. If I attended a church with people more like me, I am sure that I wouldn't have these feelings, but I don't. Milagro's story is very similar to mine. She dealt with self-harm, too, and we are the only two Hispanics who are young members of the church, but we still feel left out. I chose to attend KUMC and, for the most part, I don't regret it. I pride myself on getting outside my comfort zone, changing my outlook, and flipping the script of what it means to be a Hispanic, particularly a Hispanic in a white community. I think that is what it truly boils down to—an outsider trying to fit in, trying to find a home and a sense of belonging. It's just sad that race is a factor and that I put that pressure on myself. I told myself that I am not good enough because I am not white, that the color of my skin determines my role in the church. I think that is what I have to work on to be a successful member of this community of faith.

> Comma splice. Substitute a period for the comma.

> Beginning with "I chose," let the remainder of the paragraph serve as your conclusion.

Now that you have examined this essay thoroughly, what are your impressions? Is the essay ready for submission to the instructor? While there are considerable problems with (and many merits to) the essay, the main editorial concern is the shift from the positive nature of the thesis/purpose to the misgivings about KUMC and its apparent cultural/ethical bias. To remedy this problem, the writer can either amend his thesis to reflect these misgivings or he can choose to eliminate them entirely and revise the essay to reflect solely on the positive roles the church has played in his life. Regardless of which choice the writer determines to best fulfill his purpose and to maintain thematic unity throughout the essay, he is still faced with the arduous task of revision—an almost never-ending endeavor. No essay is perfect. All we can hope to accomplish is to do our very best to represent our ideas and ourselves in the best way possible. Unfortunately, for many of us, deadlines (those insidious but inevitable boundaries) end our struggle for perfection, resulting in the submission of our essay—both a blessing and a curse.

Activity 8.4

Once you have finished a paper (several drafts, revisions, proofreading), exchange it with several other members of your group. Have them proofread your paper as you proofread theirs. Do not make changes within the paper: simply put a check next to the line or passage you find difficult to read, or where you spot an error in grammar or usage. When each of you is finished, consult on what you have found. If you have unresolved questions, ask your instructor.

Final Word

Students often confuse *editing* with *proofreading*, but the two processes are distinct. You begin editing after you have completed your first, and perhaps second, revision. You go through the steps outlined above: checking for grammar errors, improving sentence structure, further developing points, adding details. The proofreading stage is the final stage of the whole writing process. Ideally, you have finished drafting and editing and have time to put the project aside for a while—at least twenty-four hours if possible. You do this so that when you read through your paper for a final time, you can see it with fresh eyes; you will not be reading what in your mind you *think* you have written. The following are some tried-and-true proofreading techniques.

If you began with a handwritten draft, type it on a computer and print it. Because your own handwriting is so familiar to you, you risk not seeing errors that might be detectable when you convert your draft to print. Always double or triple space your first printed draft, allowing space for you to make corrections and additions.

Always use the spell-check function on your word processor. Be aware, however, that it will not catch usage errors (often including homophones, such as compliment and complement, there and their, too and two, root and route), and it can miss errors completely. Do not rely on this function exclusively for editing.

Delay your editing stage a day or two after completing the revised draft. It will allow you to be more objective when proofreading. You will see the draft in a different light than when you were immersed in its construction.

Read your draft aloud. Read clearly and very slowly. When you detect a problem, underline the section, and then resume reading immediately. You can then address each individually underscored portion later. Repeat this process several times. Record your recitation with your phone, and listen critically to your words as you hear them. You might also enlist a friend and have her read the essay aloud to you—or you read it aloud to her.

If the essay is not your first assignment, you have surely benefited from earlier feedback from your instructor. Proofread this time for any specific errors you have committed before that you recorded in your log or journal or are highlighted in earlier papers in your writing file. Review your former errors, and look now for those specific errors in your current project.

Have a classmate, friend, or family member read your draft, and then ask her for feedback. Another reader can bring a new perspective to the ideas you have offered in the essay and possibly some proofreading skills as well. This method can be particularly beneficial for those writers whose first language is not English. You have most likely shared your early drafts with other readers in the class before you reached the final editing phase. If so, you have already gained insight into content, organization, format, and clarity. Now you might ask your reader to proofread for correctness to determine if any weaknesses or errors remain that demand your attention. Assure your reader once again that you want an honest and critical response. Remember, however, that the act of editing is ultimately your responsibility, not that of your peers or the Writing Center staff.

Finally, a method that will test your patience (and eyesight) is a technique that involves reading the draft backward (i.e., the last sentence first, the next-to-last sentence, second, and so on). This forces you to focus on punctuation and word choice because you are not following the normal flow of ideas in a continuous sequence. You actually read the words and sentences instead of skimming them. Consider each sentence you read fully and independently of the preceding sentence.

Why Humans, Like Ants, Need a Tribe

E. O. Wilson

E. O. Wilson is a preeminent evolutionary biologist who teaches at Harvard University. His primary field is the study of ants, but he has written extensively on a wide range of subjects, including ecology, philosophy, and social issues. His latest book is *Half Earth: Our Planet's Fight for Life* (2016). The following letter is taken from his book *The Creation: An Appeal to Save Life on Earth* (2006).

While E. O. Wilson is an evolutionary biologist who has written many papers for scientific journals, he has also written many articles and books for the general reader. In this essay he takes a specialized subject, the social life of ants, and makes it applicable to ordinary humans. He draws a lesson from ant life and shows how it applies to human life: like ants, we live in tribes. Wilson is able to make his subject clear and interesting, as well as disturbing, because he has kept his general audience in mind. Audience and purpose should always be at the forefront of your own writing as you go through the revising and editing process. What do my readers know and not know, and what is the best way to make clear to them what I am trying to explain?

Have you ever wondered why, in the ongoing presidential campaign, we so strongly hear the pipes calling us to arms? Why the religious among us bristle at any challenge to the creation story they believe? Or even why team sports evoke such intense loyalty, joy, and despair?

The answer is that everyone, no exception, must have a tribe, an alliance with which to jockey for power and territory, to demonize the enemy, to organize rallies and raise flags.

And so it has ever been. In ancient history and prehistory, tribes gave visceral comfort and pride from familiar fellowship, and a way to defend the group enthusiastically against rival groups. It gave people a name in addition to their own and social meaning in a chaotic world. It made the environment less disorienting and dangerous. Human nature has not changed. Modern groups are psychologically equivalent to the tribes of ancient history. As such, these groups are directly descended from the bands of primitive humans and prehumans.

The drive to join is deeply ingrained, a result of a complicated evolution that has led our species to a condition that biologists call *eusociality*. "*Eu-*," of course, is a prefix meaning pleasant or good: euphony is something that sounds wonderful; eugenics is the attempt to improve the gene pool. And the eusocial group contains multiple generations whose members perform altruistic acts, sometimes against their own personal interests, to benefit their group. Eusociality is an outgrowth of a new way of understanding evolution, which blends traditionally popular individual selection (based on individuals competing against each other) with group selection (based on competition among groups). Individual selection tends to favor selfish behavior. Group selection favors altruistic behavior and is responsible for the origin of the most advanced level of social behavior, that attained by ants, bees, termites—and humans.

Among eusocial insects, the impulse to support the group at the expense of the individual is largely instinctual. But to play the game the human way required a complicated mix of closely calibrated altruism, cooperation, competition, domination, reciprocity, defection, and deceit. Humans had to feel empathy for others, to measure the emotions of friend and enemy alike, to judge the intentions of all of them, and to plan a strategy for personal social interactions.

As a result, the human brain became simultaneously highly intelligent and intensely social. It had to build mental scenarios of personal relationships rapidly, both short term and long term. Its memories had to travel far into the past to summon old scenarios and far into the future to imagine the consequences of every relationship. Ruling on the alternative plans of action were the amygdala and other emotion-controlling centers of the brain and autonomic nervous system. Thus was born the human condition, selfish at one time, selfless at another, and the two impulses often conflicted.

Today, the social world of each modern human is not a single tribe but rather a system of interlocking tribes, among which it is often difficult to find a single compass. People savor the company of like-minded friends, and they yearn to be in one of the best—a combat Marine regiment, perhaps, an elite college, the executive committee of a company, a religious sect, a fraternity, a garden club—any collectivity that can be compared favorably with other, competing groups of the same category.

Their thirst for group membership and superiority of their group can be satisfied even with symbolic victory by their warriors in clashes on ritualized battlefields: that is, in sports. Like the cheerful and well-dressed citizens of Washington, D.C., who came out to witness the First Battle of Bull Run during the Civil War, they anticipate the experience with relish. The fans are lifted by seeing the uniforms, symbols, and battle gear of the team, the championship cups and banners on display, the dancing seminude maidens appropriately called cheerleaders. When the Boston Celtics defeated the Los Angeles Lakers for the National Basketball Association championship on a June night in 1984, the mantra was "Celts Supreme!" The social psychologist Roger Brown, who witnessed the aftermath, commented:

> The fans burst out of the Garden and nearby bars, practically break
> dancing in the air, stogies lit, arms uplifted, voices screaming. The hood
> of a car was flattened, about thirty people jubilantly piled aboard, and
> the driver—a fan—smiled happily . . . It did not seem to me that those

fans were just sympathizing or empathizing with their team. They personally were flying high. On that night each fan's self-esteem felt supreme; a social identity did a lot for many personal identities.

Experiments conducted over many years by social psychologists have revealed how swiftly and decisively people divide into groups and then discriminate in favor of the one to which they belong. Even when the experimenters created the groups arbitrarily, prejudice quickly established itself. Whether groups played for pennies or were divided by their preference for some abstract painter over another, the participants always ranked the out-group below the in-group. They judged their "opponents" to be less likable, less fair, less trustworthy, less competent. The prejudices asserted themselves even when the subjects were told the in-groups and out-groups had been chosen arbitrarily.

The tendency to form groups, and then to favor in-group members, has the earmarks of instinct. That may not be intuitive: some could argue that in-group bias is conditioned, not instinctual, that we affiliate with family members and play with neighboring children because we're taught to. But the ease with which we fall into those affiliations points to the likelihood that we are already inclined that way—what psychologists call "prepared learning," the inborn propensity to learn something swiftly and decisively. And indeed, cognitive psychologists have found that newborn infants are most sensitive to the first sounds they hear, to their mother's face, and to the sounds of their native language. Later they look preferentially at persons who previously spoke their native language within their hearing. Similarly, preschool children tend to select native-language speakers as friends.

The elementary drive to form and take deep pleasure from in-group membership easily translates at a higher level into tribalism. People are prone to ethnocentrism. It is an uncomfortable fact that even when given a guilt-free choice, individuals prefer the company of others of the same race, nation, clan, and religion. They trust them more, relax with them better in business and social events, and prefer them more often than not as marriage partners. They are quicker to anger at evidence that an out-group is behaving unfairly or receiving undeserved rewards. And they grow hostile to any out-group encroaching upon the territory or resources of their in-group.

When in experiments black and white Americans were flashed pictures of the other race, their amygdalas, the brain's center of fear and anger, were activated so quickly and subtly that the centers of the brain were unaware of the response. The subject, in effect, could not help himself. When, on the other hand, appropriate contexts were added—say, the approaching African-American was a doctor and the white his patient—two other sites of the brain integrated with the higher learning centers, the cingulate cortex and the dorsolateral preferential cortex, lit up, silencing input through the amygdala. Thus different parts of the brain have evolved by group selection to create groupishness, as well as to mediate this hardwired propensity.

When the amygdala rules the action, however, there is little or no guilt in the pleasure experienced from watching violent sporting events and war films in which the story unwinds to a satisfying destruction of the enemy. The horrors make the fascination. War is the strong life; it is life *in extremis*.

Literature and history are strewn with accounts of what happens at the extreme, as in the following from Judges 12: 5–6 in the Old Testament: the Gileadites captured the fords of the Jordan leading to Ephraim, and whenever a survivor of Ephraim said, "Let me go over," the men of Gilead asked him, "Are you an Ephraimite?" If he replied, "No," they said, "All right, say "'Shibboleth.'?'" If he said "Sibboleth," because he could not pronounce the word correctly, they seized him and killed him at the fords of the Jordan. Forty-two thousand Ephraimites were killed at that time.

Research has shown that tribal aggressiveness goes well back beyond Neolithic times. And there is a good chance that it could be a much older heritage, dating beyond the split 6 million years ago between the lines leading to modern chimpanzees and to humans, respectively.

The patterns of collective violence in which young chimp males engage are remarkably similar to those of young human males. Aside from constantly vying for status, both for themselves and for their gangs, they tend to avoid open mass confrontations with rival troops, instead relying on surprise attacks. The purpose of raids made by the male gangs on neighboring communities is evidently to kill or drive out its members and acquire new territory. The entirety of such conquest under fully natural conditions has been witnessed by John Mitani and his collaborators in Uganda's Kibale National Park. The chimp war, conducted over 10 years, was eerily humanlike. Every 10 to 14 days, patrols of up to 20 males penetrated enemy territory, moving quietly in single file, scanning the terrain from ground to the treetops, and halting cautiously at every surrounding noise. If they encountered a force larger than their own, the invaders broke rank and ran back to their own territory. When they encountered a lone male, however, they pummeled and bit him to death. When a female was encountered, they usually let her go. (This latter tolerance was not a display of gallantry. If she carried an infant, they took it from her and killed and ate it.) Finally, after such constant pressure for so long, the invading gangs simply annexed the enemy territory, adding 22 percent to the land owned by their own community.

Our bloody nature, it can now be argued in the context of modern biology, is ingrained because group-versus-group was a principal driving force that made us what we are. In prehistory, group selection lifted the hominids to heights of solidarity, to genius, to enterprise. And to fear. Each tribe knew with justification that if it was not armed and ready, its very existence was imperiled. Throughout history, the escalation of a large part of technology has had combat as its central purpose. Today, public support is best fired up by appeal to the emotions of deadly combat, over which the amygdala is grandmaster. We find ourselves in the battle to stem an oil spill, the fight to tame inflation, the war against cancer. Wherever there is an enemy, animate or inanimate, there must be a victory.

Any excuse for a real war will do, so long as it is seen as necessary to protect the tribe. The remembrance of past horrors has no effect. It should not be thought that war, often accompanied by genocide, is a cultural artifact of a few societies. Nor has it been an aberration of history, a result of the growing pains of our species' maturation. Wars and genocide have been universal and eternal, respecting no particular time or culture. Overall, big wars have been replaced around the world by small wars of the kind and magnitude more typical of hunter-gatherer and primitively agricultural societies. Civilized societies have tried to eliminate torture, execution, and the murder of civilians, but those fighting little wars do not comply.

Civilization appears to be the ultimate redeeming product of competition between groups. Because of it, we struggle on behalf of good and against evil, and reward generosity, compassion, and altruism while punishing or down-playing selfishness. But if group conflict created the best in us, it also created the deadliest. As humans, this is our greatest, and worst, genetic inheritance.

Topics for Writing and Discussion

1. Wilson makes the point that "modern groups are psychologically equivalent to the tribes of ancient history." Further, he says "the social world of each modern human is not a single tribe but rather a system of interlocking tribes." We are Americans, then Californians—or Texans or Hoosiers; we are Bostonians—or New Yorkers or Houstonians; we are Catholics—or Baptists or Muslims; we identify with different colleges, different sports teams, different ethnic and political groups. We are members of many tribes at once. Write an essay in which you identify the three most important tribes you belong to, ranking them in order of importance and describing what is essential to belonging to each one.

2. There was a long debate in the past century about whether humans were naturally aggressive and warlike or whether at one time we lived peacefully in small groups in an Eden-like nature. Wilson says: "Our bloody nature, it can now be argued in the context of modern biology, is ingrained because group-versus-group was a principal driving force that made us what we are." But Wilson also mentions the concept of *eusociality*, the idea that

humans learned to "perform altruistic acts, sometimes against their own personal interests, to benefit their group." And we have all heard stories of people running into burning buildings to save complete strangers. Based on your own experience, and that of your immediate "tribe," write an essay on which side of our human nature you think predominates. Be sure to give appropriate examples.

CHAPTER 9

Documenting and Formatting

Once you have gone through the process of discovery and invention, and once you have structured and drafted and revised your material, you are ready to assemble it in an appropriate format and present it. Just as there are accepted conventions for using punctuation and word forms in writing, so are there conventions of documenting and formatting. Particularly if you are using information from other sources (see Chapter 2), you will need to present your material in a logical way to be fair both to your sources and to your reader. In addition, pay particular attention to the way you use the following.

- ⊙ Source material
- ⊙ Citations
- ⊙ Publication conventions

Preparing your work for presentation is an important, culminating step in the writing process—even if it is somewhat mechanical in nature by comparison to the earlier, more creative steps. By now, you have already composed your work. Presumably, you are happy with the composition in hand, having revised and edited it until you have achieved the desired level of specificity, accuracy, and development (which is to say, the meaning you intended). Furthermore, you have invested time making sure the conventions of language have been met. Like making sure your necktie is centered or your skirt well-ironed, you have tested your words against the conventions of language to ensure clarity and effectiveness. Applying the proper publication conventions fits perfectly into this analogy. These conventions are formats that further identify you to your chosen audience as a professional. You need not necessarily memorize each convention, but you should know that a format needs to be applied, a "finishing" process that will present your writing as polished—much as dressing in a formal manner might prepare you for work.

Many of the initial stages of the writing process, such as discovering and inventing, were "safe" periods, and so too is the presenting stage. It should not be seen as arduous, but rather a precursor to displaying what you have learned and joining in a great conversation.

Using Source Material

First, discuss the context of your information before using it. For example, include the times and places for your sources if they are relevant to your discussion. For example, if a source comes from the early years of the Zapatista uprising in the 1990s, geography, time, and political context should be provided before you begin using your sources. Otherwise your audience may be lost and confused. Because you want to build trust with your audience, your sources need careful introduction so that your readers can understand why you chose those particular sources.

Paraphrase Versus Direct Quotation

Paraphrasing sources often makes the reading experience, as well as the writing experience, more concise. Paraphrasing is putting a source's ideas in your own words. However, do not simply copy the source, changing one or two of the source's words; that is still plagiarism. Further, you must still identify the source before you paraphrase it. Note the difference in these two paragraphs using the same source—the first as direct quotation, the second as paraphrase.

> Unable to drive their children to school but unwilling to allow them to walk alone to school, many parents oppose the idea of reducing the bus budget simply to save money. School parent Lois Wrigley thinks that at least parents should be given a choice. She said in a newspaper interview, "They should have gave the parents a choice. You can pay for busing or whatever, but there was no choice" (*Houston Chronicle*). Her frustration is evident and is representative of several parents I interviewed who feel parents were not involved in the transportation question.

> Many parents are not able to drive their students to school but won't let them walk by themselves because they are worried about their safety. While some argue that cutting the bus budget is the only way the school is going to save money and keep teachers in the school, these parents think otherwise, claiming that cutting school transportation is not a smart idea. School parent Lois Wrigley showed her frustration in a newspaper interview when she argued that parents should at least have a choice in their children's transportation options (*Houston Chronicle*). Like other parents I interviewed, Wrigley's primary concern is not about the budget, but about the district's lack of engagement with the parents.

The second paragraph reads more smoothly because a paraphrase is used instead of a quotation that did not have essential information in it; it was easily paraphrased, and the reader got the same message.

Quotations, however, are often necessary when a precise statement of the author's ideas is needed, especially if the author's word choice or style is important to your argument. This is especially true in textual or literary analysis, for example. One would hardly paraphrase Lincoln's "Four score and seven years ago" as "It's been eighty-seven years since …" because in this sense the text *is* the message. Make your quotations brief, however. Long quotations detract from your own argument, may confuse your audience, and actually require a heavier responsibility on your part to engage with each idea within the quotation. What you *do not* want to do is create a paragraph of "lists" of quotations. Your purpose is to engage, not to list what others say.

Citing Source Material

Whether you use paraphrase or direct quotation, *always* clearly indicate your source. This gives credit to the original author and establishes your own credibility as a writer. Citation helps your readers find your source readily should they wish to explore it further. *One important suggestion: prepare the list of works cited as you write.* Do not create a separate document for them (see publication conventions below). Simply create a last page of your current document, and add to your list as you go. Too often, inexperienced writers forget to include their list or else forget to include every reference. One proofreading technique when using sources is to place your list of works cited beside your paper and find every source used in your paper, checking to make sure it is properly cited in the list.

Just because you have found a voice that you can engage with and have paraphrased and cited that source, that does not mean your responsibility as a writer is complete. Remember that your writing project is an *engagement* with others. To simply paraphrase, cite, and then leave the conversation is like walking into a living-room conversation, reciting the Gettysburg Address, and then walking out with no explanation for your behavior. As writers, we need to examine our sources and engage with those voices in writing, just as we would with any face-to-face conversation. After using your sources, your power as an author returns, and now you must elaborate and explain why this source is needed in the conversation and your response to it.

Publication Conventions

First, many publication venues do not have specific conventions, but academic venues do, and college courses often require students to use their discipline's conventions. Students often find the conventions of citation more vexing than writing itself. You likely have shared the same feeling as other students, wondering whether some sinister group of academics has in fact conspired to make bibliographic work especially difficult and nitpicky just to cause you frustration. But consider the following.

> Bibliographic work helps you track your own sources for later revision. By maintaining a close record of where you found your information, you have the ability to use these same sources later in new ways in revising your work for new purposes and new audiences.

> Bibliographic work helps your audience engage with you. As your audience follows your own research trail, they can respond to you with more information. This enlarges the sphere of discourse for everyone.

> Bibliographic work is part of entering a specific discipline. Each discipline has its own conventions and expectations, somewhat like a specific culture's dietary rules. These agreed-upon conventions enable information to flow freely among members of the group.

Such rules allow us all to engage in the game as in any sport.

Major Publication Style Manuals

Though the three publication styles mentioned here have thick usage manuals of their own, the fundamental rules are the same. You must always identify authors, titles, publishers, and dates of publication. You will find hard copies of these manuals in your library as well as multiple websites with updated information on each. You will also find various tools, free or for a price, on the internet that claim to automatically set up a list of works cited for you, but by the time you plug in the required data (names, dates, and so on) you might as well go ahead and set up the list yourself. Finally, when you find a source in a database, the database will normally give you its citation in each of these styles. However, many times these citations are not accurate, so you must check them against the appropriate style manuals. The three styles most commonly used in colleges and universities are *The MLA Handbook* (8th ed.), the *Publication Manual of the American Psychological Association* (6th ed.), and *The Chicago Manual of Style* (17th ed.) (Figure 9.1).

Figure 9.1: Major Style Guides

While each of the above style manuals requires you to cite and carefully document the sources you use, each does so in a slightly different way. Before you begin writing your paper, be sure to find out which style your instructor wants you to use. Each is different in the way it handles in-text citations, the list of sources, and the paper's general format. We include here only a brief discussion of their differences. A recent handbook will discuss each in more detail.

In-Text Citations

Modern Language Association (MLA). MLA (8th ed.) states: "Quotations are most effective in research writing when used selectively. Quote only words, phrases, lines, and passages that are particularly apt, and keep all quotations as brief as possible. Your project should be about your own ideas, and quotations should merely help you explain or illustrate them." For quotations of four lines or fewer, include the name of the author, place the quotation in quotation marks, and include the page number of the source in parentheses.

> Example 1: According to Paula LaRocque, "Many writers routinely, and incorrectly, place commas between all adjectives preceding nouns. But we correctly place commas only between adjectives that are equally important and offer similar kinds of information" (30).

> Example 2: Granny Weatherall has a very high opinion of herself. For example, as she is lying in bed she hears Cornelia talking to her husband, and she thinks: "In her day she had kept a better house and got more work done" (81).

However, if a quotation will go over four lines of text, tab in twice from the margin, and do not use quotation marks. Do, however, space before and after it. This is called a block quotation.

Example 3: James Baldwin illustrates his essay in specific, grainy, and shocking detail.

> But the nightmare had not yet really begun. The salesman had been so badly beaten around one eye that it was found necessary to hospitalize him. Perhaps some sense of what it means to live in occupied territory can be suggested by the fact that the police took him to Harlem Hospital themselves—nearly nineteen hours after the beating. For fourteen days, the doctors at Harlem Hospital told him that they could do nothing for his eye, and he was removed to Bellevue Hospital, where for fourteen days, the doctors tried to save the eye. At the end of fourteen days it was clear that the bad eye could not be saved and was endangering the good eye. All that could be done, then, was to take the bad eye out. (1)

American Psychological Association (APA). The APA requires inclusion of the date of the source as well as the author's last name in introductions to sources. At the end of the paraphrase or quotation, put the page number in a parenthesis preceded by a *p*. However, if a quotation will go over forty words, tab in once from the margin and do not use quotation marks. Do, however, space before and after it.

> Example: LaRocque (2009) has pointed out that "Many writers routinely, and incorrectly, place commas between all adjectives preceding nouns. But we correctly place commas only between adjectives that are equally important and offer similar kinds of information" (p. 30).

Chicago Manual of Style. The Chicago Manual requires the introduction of the author in the text followed by a raised note number at the end of the quotation. The actual note itself, containing all the bibliographic data, can be at the bottom of the page or on a separate page following the paper under the heading "Notes." These are called either footnotes or endnotes. If a quotation will go over five lines, tab in once from the margin, single space, and do not use quotation marks. Do, however, space before and after it.

> Example: Paula LaRocque writes in an essay in *The Quill* that "Many writers routinely, and incorrectly, place commas between all adjectives preceding nouns. But we correctly place commas only between adjectives that are equally important and offer similar kinds of information."[1]

Be sure to check your handbook or the internet for the differences in layout and required information between the "Notes" page and the "Bibliography."

Activity 9.1

Read the following passage. Next, using a proper method of introduction and quotation, integrate pertinent information from these paragraphs into several sentences of your own using MLA, APA, or CMS style. (Ask your instructor.)

For thousands of years farmers have used a process of selection and crossbreeding to continually improve the quality of crops. Even in nature, plants and animals selectively breed, thus ensuring the optimum gene pool for future generations. Traditional breeding methods are slow, requiring intensive labor: while trying to get a desirable trait in a bred species, undesirable traits will appear, and breeders must continue the process over and over again until all the undesirables are bred out.

In contrast, organisms acquire one specific gene or a few genes together through genetic modification, without other traits included and within a single generation. However, this technology too is inherently unpredictable, and some scientists believe it can produce potentially dangerous results unless better testing methods are developed.

Sakko, Kerryn. "The Debate over Genetically Modified Foods." *actionbioscience.org.* May 2002.

Activity 9.2

Take each of the following sentences, and rewrite it on your own paper—first as a direct quotation and second using one or more phrases embedded in your own sentence. Use MLA, APA, or CMS style. (Ask your instructor.)

"Since 2000, health care administrative costs have risen from 15% to 30% of the insurance premiums received from customers." Source: Brady Watson. *Failure: How the HealthCare Companies Lost Our Trust.* Viking, 2005. Page 155.

"At the battle of Cajamarca recounted above, 168 Spaniards crushed a Native American army 500 times more numerous, killing thousands of natives while not losing a single Spaniard." Source: Jared Diamond. *Guns, Germs, and Steele: The Fates of Human Societies.* Norton, 1997. Page 35.

Works Cited, References, Bibliography

Modern Language Association (MLA). All sources used in your essay must be included in a Works Cited list at the end of your essay. Entries in the Works Cited list should be arranged alphabetically and double-spaced throughout. Additionally, all lines after the first in each entry should be indented one-half inch (five spaces) or one tab space. MLA lists nine "core elements" for entries in a Works Cited list. (Note the punctuation marks following each.)

- ⊙   Author.
- ⊙   Title of source.
- ⊙   Title of container,
- ⊙   Other contributors,
- ⊙   Version,
- ⊙   Number,
- ⊙   Publisher,
- ⊙   Publication date,
- ⊙   Location.

Below are listed a few of the more common sources you will likely encounter in writing a research paper. If your source is not one of these types, consult the handbook itself (in the library or the Writing Center), or the MLA Style Center (online), or your instructor.

Book

Kolbert, Elizabeth. *The Sixth Extinction: An Unnatural History.* Henry Holt, 2014.

E-Book

Shaw, Marc E., et al. *Girls and the Awkward Politics of Gender, Race, and Privilege.* Lexington Books, 2015. Ebscohost E-book.

Magazine Article: Database

Khimm, Suzy. "In Tragedy's Wake." *New Republic,* vol. 246, no.12, Nov. 2015, pp.13-15. *Academic Search Complete.*

Journal Article: Database

Wolf, Carolyn, and Jamie A. Rosen. "Missing the Mark: Gun Control Is Not the Cure For What Ails the US Mental Health System." *Journal of Criminal Law & Criminology,* vol. 104, no. 4, Fall 2015, pp. 851-78. *Academic Search Complete.*

Newspaper Article: Online

Wilson, Mark D., and Eleanor Dearman. "Body Discovered on University of Texas Campus Sparks Homicide Investigation." *Houston Chronicle* 5 Apr. 2016, www.chron.com/news/local/crime/article/Homicide-in-vestigation-opened-following-discovery-7229338.php.

Website

"Statement on President Obama's Proposed Executive Actions on Gun Control." *NRA-ILA (Institute for Legislative Action),* 5 Jan. 2016, www.nraila.org/articles /20160105/statement-on-president-obamas-pro-posed-executive-actions-on-gun-control.

Note: MLA "recommends the inclusion of URLs in the Works Cited list," but says "if your instructor prefers that you not include them, follow his or her directions." Further, notice that the http:// is omitted. Finally, if an entry in a database or online is assigned a DOI (digital object identifier), cite the DOI instead of the URL.

American Psychological Association (APA). All sources used in your paper must be included on a References page at the end of your paper. They should be arranged alphabetically by the last name of the author, or, if there is no author, by titles (excluding *A, An,* and *The*); further, they are *double-spaced* throughout. In addition, the second and third lines of an entry are indented one-half inch (five spaces) or one tab space. For digital sources, if the source has a DOI (digital object identifier), include it without placing a period at the end of the citation as you would with a Web address. Otherwise include the phrase "Retrieved from" and the URL. The following is a References page with a few of

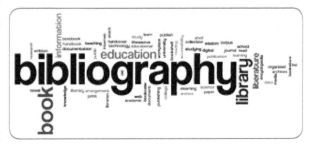

the most common citations—the first to a journal article, the second to a printed book, the third to an online newspaper article, and the fourth to a website. Note the differences between MLA and APA.

References

Frey, R. G. (2005). Pain, vivisection, and the value of life. *Journal of Medical Ethics* 31.4: 202-04. *Academic Search Complete.* doi: 10.1136/jme.2004.008367

Kolbert, E. (2014). *The sixth extinction: an unnatural history.* New York: Henry Holt.

Taylor, A. (2014, November 14). Immigration, Keystone top first day of lame duck. *Houston Chronicle.* Retrieved from http://www.chron.com.

What is a designer baby? (2002). *BIONET.* Retrieved from http://www.bionetonline.org.

The Chicago Manual of Style. All sources used in your paper must be included in a Bibliography at the end of your paper. As with MLA, they should be arranged alphabetically by the last name of the author, or if there is no author, by titles (excluding *A*, *An*, and *The*); further, they are *double-spaced* throughout. In addition, second and third lines of an entry are indented one-half inch (five spaces) or one tab space. Note that the Chicago manual asks for a DOI (a Digital Object Identifier) for database sources and a URL for an open internet source. The following is a Bibliography with a few of the most common citations—the first to a journal article, the second to a printed book, the third to an online newspaper article, and the fourth to a website.

Bibliography

Frey, R. G. "Pain, Vivisection, and the Value of Life." *Journal of Medical Ethics* 31(2005): 202-04. Academic Search Complete. doi: 10.1136/jme.2004.008367.

Kolbert, Elizabeth. *The Sixth Extinction: An Unnatural History.* New York: Henry Holt, 2014.

Taylor, Andrew. "Immigration, Keystone Top First Day of Lame Duck." *Houston Chronicle.* February 13, 2015.

"What is a Designer Baby?" *BIONET.* 2002. http://www.bionetonline.org/english/content/db_cont1.htm.

Activity 9.3

Take the information given in each of the following, and set up a proper list of works cited using MLA, APA, or CMS style. (Ask your instructor.)

Article Title. "Consumer acceptance and labeling of GMOs in food products: a study of fluid milk demand." *Authors.* Kristin Kiesel, David Buschena, Vincent Smith. *Book Title.* Consumer Acceptance of Genetically Modified Food. *Editors.* Robert E. Evenson and Vittorio Santaniello. *Copyright.* 2004. *Publisher.* CABIPub. *Place of Publication.* Wallingford, Oxon, UK. *Article Pagination.* 37-42.

Article Title. "Is GM food the future for Africa?" *Author.* Khadja Sharife. *Magazine Title.* New African. *Date.* January 2009. Pages. 8-13. *Database.* Academic Search Complete.

Article Title. "An Open Mind Wants More: Opinion Strength and the Desire for Genetically Modified Food Labeling Policy." *Authors.* Sonja Radas, Mario F. Teisl, Brian Roe. *Journal Title.* Journal of Consumer Affairs. *Date.* Fall 2008. *Volume and Issue.* 42.3. Pages. 335-61. *Database.* Academic Search Complete.

Article Title. "Frankenfoods will save the world from starvation." *Author.* Melanie Peters. *Newspaper.* The Weekend Argus (South Africa). *Date.* October 5, 2008. *Pages.* 11. *Database.* InfoTrac Newspapers.

Article Title. How Do You Make a Transgenic Plant? *Author.* None Listed. *Website.* Transgenic Crops: An Introduction and Resource Guide. *Date.* March 11, 2004. *Sponsor.* Colorado State University. Date Accessed. March 9, 2009.

Book Title. Issues and Dilemmas of Biotechnology: A Reference Guide. *Author.* Bernice Schacter. *Publisher.* Greenwood Press. *Place of Publication.* Westport, Connecticut. *Copyright Date.* 1999.

Rewrite the following student paragraph and Works Cited page, correcting the problems in quotation and citation using MLA, APA, or CMS style. (Ask your instructor.)

First, animals' rights are violated when they are used in research. Tom Regan, a philosophy professor at North Carolina State University, states: "Animals have a basic moral right to respectful treatment ... This inherent value is not respected when animals are reduced to being mere tools in a scientific experiment" (qtd. in Orlans 26). Animals and people are alike in many ways; they both feel, think, behave, and experience pain. Thus, animals should be treated with the same respect as humans. Yet animals' rights are violated when they are used in research because they are not given a choice. Animals are subjected to tests that are often painful or cause permanent damage or death, and they are never given the option of not participating in the experiment. Regan further says, for example, that "animal [experimentation] is morally wrong no matter how much humans may benefit because the animal's basic right has been infringed. Risks are not morally transferable to those who do not choose to take them" (qtd. in Orlans 26). Animals do not willingly sacrifice themselves for the advancement of human welfare and new technology. Their decisions are made for them because they cannot vocalize their own preferences and choices. When humans decide the fate of animals in research environments, the animals' rights are taken away without any thought of their well-being or the quality of their lives. Therefore, animal experimentation should be stopped because it violates the rights of animals.

Works Cited

Barbara F. Orlans. *In the Name of Science: Issues in Responsible Animal Experimentation.*
New York: Oxford UP, 1993.

Formats

Merriam-Webster's Collegiate Dictionary defines *format* as "the shape, size, and general makeup (as of something printed)." Before you submit your research paper to your instructor for evaluation, be sure you follow precisely any format requirements she has given you.

MLA

⊙ Margins. Allow margins of 1" on top, bottom, and sides.

⊙ Font and type size. Times New Roman, 12.

⊙ Double-space.

⊙ Page numbers. As header in the upper right-hand corner preceded by your last name only. Arabic numerals.

- ⊙ Title Page. Submit a title page only if your instructor requires one or if you are required to submit an outline with your paper. Otherwise, include your name, your instructor's name, the class and section numbers, and the date (all double-spaced) at the top left of your first page.

APA

- ⊙ Margins. Allow margins of 1" on top, bottom, and sides.
- ⊙ Font and type size. Times New Roman, 12.
- ⊙ Double-space.
- ⊙ Page numbers. As header, Title (ALL CAPS) flush left; number flush right. Arabic numerals.
- ⊙ Title Page. "Type your **title** in upper and lowercase letters centered in the upper half of the page. APA recommends that your title be no more than 12 words in length and that it should not contain abbreviations or words that serve no purpose. Your title may take up one or two lines" (Purdue OWL).

- ⊙ Abstract. Your Abstract should be no more than one page and should concisely summarize your paper. Start with your main thesis.

Chicago Manual of Style

- ⊙ Margins. Allow margins of 1" on top, bottom, and sides.
- ⊙ Font and type size. Times New Roman, 12.
- ⊙ Double-space (with the exception of block quotations, which are single-spaced).
- ⊙ Page numbers. As header in the upper right-hand corner. First page, Arabic numerals.
- ⊙ Title page.

Title Pages

For MLA, use a title page only if your instructor requires it, and do not put a number on this page; otherwise put your name, your instructor's name, the class name, and the date on the first page of your text at the top on the left margin.

Final Word

In creating this text, the authors followed the very same process as the one presented in these pages. Although you might think of the last stage, documenting and formatting, as not as important as the earlier stages of inventing, drafting, structuring, and editing, as much time was spent on this very last stage as on the earlier ones. We hope you find the process outlined in this book clear, complete, and useful as you engage in the many writing projects you will undertake in your college career and beyond.

Finally, too often academia chooses to overlook such a close examination of the writing process for the sake of attention to the final "product." Because they are focused on the final product, many instructors (particularly in subjects other than English) often only give their students general instructions, such as the number of pages needed, and then tell them to "go write it," giving them no clear understanding of how to go about writing. In this book, we have tried to remedy this situation. As you begin the process of creating your own works and developing your own new ideas (or new ways of looking at old ideas), we hope you will take pride in your work.

Activity 9.5

Take one of the researched essays you have written, and revise your work with your group. Add at least three additional sources to your writing. Consider your rhetorical purpose before deciding with which voices you will engage. For example, ask these questions.

- Do you want to use a source to support your ideas?

- Do you want a source as a contrast for an idea?

- Do you need a voice to support the context of your project?

With your group, locate resources in your college library catalog and databases and one community source; next, evaluate each source for its rhetorical focus.

- Is it timely?

- Does it address the geography, culture, or heritage of your writing purpose?

- Is it specific enough for your purpose to add to the conversation?

- Do the sources help you ask the right questions or strengthen your proposal?

Is Facebook Making Us Lonely?

Stephen Marche

Stephen Marche is a Canadian-born writer. He has written several books, the latest being *The Hunger of the Wolf: A Novel* (2015). He also writes a monthly column, *A Thousand Words About Our Culture*, for *Esquire* magazine. The following essay was published in *The Atlantic* in May of 2012.

Marche's essay on the effects of Facebook is now several years old. In the years since it was published, however, even more concerns have been raised about the dissemination of "fake" news and conspiracy theories via social media such as Facebook. These media have made it easy for disinformation to spread quickly around the world. They may have been used, for example, to influence the outcome of the 2016 election. That is why clearly identifying and documenting the sources you use is extremely important. Yes, making sure you have reliable sources for the information you use and documenting it correctly is tedious, but not doing so only feeds the misinformation and "bubble" thinking that can lead to disastrous results.

Yvette Vickers, a former *Playboy* playmate and B-movie star, best known for her role in *Attack of the 50 Foot Woman*, would have been 83 last August, but nobody knows exactly how old she was when she died. According to the Los Angeles coroner's report, she lay dead for the better part of a year before a neighbor and fellow actress, a woman named Susan Savage, noticed cobwebs and yellowing letters in her mailbox, reached through a broken window to unlock the door, and pushed her way through the piles of junk mail and mounds of clothing that barricaded the house. Upstairs, she found Vickers's body, mummified, near a heater that was still running. Her computer was on too, its glow permeating the empty space.

The *Los Angeles Times* posted a story headlined "Mummified Body of Former Playboy Playmate Yvette Vickers Found in Her Benedict Canyon Home," which quickly went viral. Within two weeks, by Technorati's count, Vickers's lonesome death was already the subject of 16,057 Facebook posts and 881 tweets. She had long been a horror-movie icon, a symbol of Hollywood's capacity to exploit our most basic fears in the silliest ways; now she was an icon of a new and different kind of horror: our growing fear of loneliness. Certainly she received much more attention in death than she did in the final years of her life. With no children, no religious group, and no immediate social circle of any kind, she had begun, as an elderly woman, to look elsewhere for companionship. Savage later told *Los Angeles* magazine that she had searched Vickers's phone bills for clues about the life that led to such an end. In the months before her grotesque death, Vickers had made calls not to friends or family but to distant fans who had found her through fan conventions and Internet sites.

Vickers's web of connections had grown broader but shallower, as has happened for many of us. We are living in an isolation that would have been unimaginable to our ancestors, and yet we have never been more accessible. Over the past three decades, technology has delivered to us a world in which we need not be out of contact for a fraction of a moment. In 2010, at a cost of $300 million, 800 miles of fiber-optic cable was laid between the Chicago Mercantile Exchange and the New York Stock Exchange to shave three milliseconds off trading times. Yet within this world of instant and absolute communication, unbounded by limits of time or space, we suffer from unprecedented alienation. We have never been more detached from one another, or lonelier. In a world consumed by ever more novel modes of socializing, we have less and less actual society. We live in an accelerating contradiction: the more connected we become, the lonelier we are. We were promised a global village; instead we inhabit the drab cul-de-sacs and endless freeways of a vast suburb of information.

At the forefront of all this unexpectedly lonely interactivity is Facebook, with 845 million users and $3.7 billion in revenue last year. The company hopes to raise $5 billion in an initial public offering later this spring, which will make it by far the largest Internet IPO in history. Some recent estimates put the company's potential value at $100 billion, which would make it larger than the global coffee industry—one addiction preparing to surpass the other. Facebook's scale and reach are hard to comprehend: last summer, Facebook became, by some counts, the first Web site to receive 1 trillion page views in a month. In the last three months of 2011, users generated an average of 2.7 billion "likes" and comments every day. On whatever scale you care to judge Facebook—as a company, as a culture, as a country—it is vast beyond imagination.

Despite its immense popularity, or more likely because of it, Facebook has, from the beginning, been under something of a cloud of suspicion. The depiction of Mark Zuckerberg, in *The Social Network*, as a bastard with symptoms of Asperger's syndrome, was nonsense. But it felt true. It felt true to Facebook, if not to Zuckerberg. The film's most indelible scene, the one that may well have earned it an Oscar, was the final, silent shot of an anomic Zuckerberg sending out a friend request to his ex-girlfriend, then waiting and clicking and waiting and clicking—a moment of superconnected loneliness preserved in amber. We have all been in that scene: transfixed by the glare of a screen, hungering for response.

When you sign up for Google+ and set up your Friends circle, the program specifies that you should include only "your real friends, the ones you feel comfortable sharing private details with." That one little phrase, *Your real friends*—so quaint, so charmingly mothering—perfectly encapsulates the anxieties that social media have produced: the fears that Facebook is interfering with our real friendships, distancing us from each other, making us lonelier; and that social networking might be spreading the very isolation it seemed designed to conquer.

Facebook arrived in the middle of a dramatic increase in the quantity and intensity of human loneliness, a rise that initially made the site's promise of greater connection seem deeply attractive. Americans are more solitary than ever before. In 1950, less than 10 percent of American households contained only one person. By 2010, nearly 27 percent of households had just one person. Solitary living does not guarantee a life of unhappiness, of course. In his recent book about the trend toward living alone, Eric Klinenberg, a sociologist at NYU, writes: "Reams of published research show that it's the quality, not the quantity of social interaction, that best predicts loneliness." True. But before we begin the fantasies of happily eccentric singledom, of divorcées dropping by their knitting circles after work for glasses of Drew Barrymore *pinot grigio,* or recent college graduates with perfectly articulated, Steampunk-themed, 300-square-foot apartments organizing croquet matches with their book clubs, we should recognize that it is not just isolation that is rising sharply. It's loneliness, too. And loneliness makes us miserable.

We know intuitively that loneliness and being alone are not the same thing. Solitude can be lovely. Crowded parties can be agony. We also know, thanks to a growing body of research on the topic, that loneliness is not a matter of external conditions; it is a psychological state. A 2005 analysis of data from a longitudinal study of Dutch twins showed that the tendency toward loneliness has roughly the same genetic component as other psychological problems such as neuroticism or anxiety.

Still, loneliness is slippery, a difficult state to define or diagnose. The best tool yet developed for measuring the condition is the UCLA Loneliness Scale, a series of 20 questions that all begin with this formulation: "How often do you feel ...?" As in: "How often do you feel that you are 'in tune' with the people around you?" And: "How often do you feel that you lack companionship?" Measuring the condition in these terms, various studies have shown loneliness rising drastically over a very short period of recent history. A 2010 AARP survey found that 35 percent of adults older than 45 were chronically lonely, as opposed to 20 percent of a similar group only a decade earlier. According to a major study by a leading scholar of the subject, roughly 20 percent of Americans—about 60 million people—are unhappy with their lives because of loneliness. Across the Western world, physicians and nurses have begun to speak openly of an epidemic of loneliness.

The new studies on loneliness are beginning to yield some surprising preliminary findings about its mechanisms. Almost every factor that one might assume affects loneliness does so only some of the time, and only under certain circumstances. People who are married are less lonely than single people, one journal article suggests, but only if their spouses are confidants. If one's spouse is not a confidant, marriage may not decrease loneliness. A belief in God might help, or it might not, as a 1990 German study comparing levels of religious feeling and levels of loneliness discovered. Active believers who saw God as abstract and helpful rather than as a wrathful, immediate presence were less lonely. "The mere belief in God," the researchers concluded, "was relatively independent of loneliness."

But it is clear that social interaction matters. Loneliness and being alone are not the same thing, but both are on the rise. We meet fewer people. We gather less. And when we gather, our bonds are less meaningful and less easy. The decrease in confidants—that is, in quality social connections—has been dramatic over the past 25 years. In one survey, the mean size of networks of personal confidants decreased from 2.94 people in 1985 to 2.08 in 2004. Similarly, in 1985, only 10 percent of Americans said they had no one with whom to discuss important matters, and 15 percent said they had only one such good friend. By 2004, 25 percent had nobody to talk to, and 20 percent had only one confidant.

In the face of this social disintegration, we have essentially hired an army of replacement confidants, an entire class of professional carers. As Ronald Dworkin pointed out in a 2010 paper for the Hoover Institution, in the late '40s, the United States was home to 2,500 clinical psychologists, 30,000 social workers, and fewer than 500 marriage and family therapists. As of 2010, the country had 77,000 clinical psychologists, 192,000 clinical social workers, 400,000 nonclinical social workers, 50,000 marriage and family therapists, 105,000 mental-health counselors, 220,000 substance-abuse counselors, 17,000 nurse psychotherapists, and 30,000 life coaches. The majority of patients in therapy do not warrant a psychiatric diagnosis. This raft of psychic servants is helping us through what used to be called regular problems. We have outsourced the work of everyday caring.

We need professional carers more and more, because the threat of societal breakdown, once principally a matter of nostalgic lament, has morphed into an issue of public health. Being lonely is extremely bad for your health. If you're lonely, you're more likely to be put in a geriatric home at an earlier age than a similar person who isn't lonely. You're less likely to exercise. You're more likely to be obese. You're less likely to survive a serious operation and more likely to have hormonal imbalances. You are at greater risk of inflammation. Your memory may be worse. You are more likely to be depressed, to sleep badly, and to suffer dementia and general cognitive decline. Loneliness may not have killed Yvette Vickers, but it has been linked to a greater probability of having the kind of heart condition that did kill her.

And yet, despite its deleterious effect on health, loneliness is one of the first things ordinary Americans spend their money achieving. With money, you flee the cramped city to a house in the suburbs or, if you can afford it, a Mc-Mansion in the exurbs, inevitably spending more time in your car. Loneliness is at the American core, a by-product of a long-standing national appetite for independence: The Pilgrims who left Europe willingly abandoned the bonds and strictures of a society that could not accept their right to be different. They did not seek out loneliness, but they accepted it as the price of their autonomy. The cowboys who set off to explore a seemingly endless frontier likewise traded away personal ties in favor of pride and self-respect. The ultimate American icon is the astronaut: Who is more heroic, or more alone? The price of self-determination and self-reliance has often been loneliness. But Americans have always been willing to pay that price.

Today, the one common feature in American secular culture is its celebration of the self that breaks away from the constrictions of the family and the state, and, in its greatest expressions, from all limits entirely. The great American poem is Whitman's "Song of Myself." The great American essay is Emerson's "Self-Reliance." The great American novel is Melville's *Moby-Dick*, the tale of a man on a quest so lonely that it is incomprehensible to those around him. American culture, high and low, is about self-expression and personal authenticity. Franklin Delano Roosevelt called individualism "the great watchword of American life."

Self-invention is only half of the American story, however. The drive for isolation has always been in tension with the impulse to cluster in communities that cling and suffocate. The Pilgrims, while fomenting spiritual rebellion, also enforced ferocious cohesion. The Salem witch trials, in hindsight, read like attempts to impose solidarity—as do the McCarthy hearings. The history of the United States is like the famous parable of the porcupines in the cold, from Schopenhauer's *Studies in Pessimism*—the ones who huddle together for warmth and shuffle away in pain, always separating and congregating.

We are now in the middle of a long period of shuffling away. In his 2000 book *Bowling Alone*, Robert D. Putnam attributed the dramatic post-war decline of social capital—the strength and value of interpersonal networks—to numerous interconnected trends in American life: suburban sprawl, television's dominance over culture, the self-absorption of the Baby Boomers, the disintegration of the traditional family. The trends he observed continued through the prosperity of the aughts, and have only become more pronounced with time: the rate of union membership declined in 2011, again; screen time rose; the Masons and the Elks continued their slide into irrelevance. We are lonely because we want to be lonely. We have made ourselves lonely.

The question of the future is this: Is Facebook part of the separating or part of the congregating; is it a huddling-together for warmth or a shuffling-away in pain?

Well before facebook, digital technology was enabling our tendency for isolation, to an unprecedented degree. Back in the 1990s, scholars started calling the contradiction between an increased opportunity to connect and a lack of human contact the "Internet paradox." A prominent 1998 article on the phenomenon by a team of researchers at Carnegie Mellon showed that increased Internet usage was already coinciding with increased loneliness. Critics of the study pointed out that the two groups that participated in the study—high-school journalism students who were heading to university and socially active members of community-development boards—were statistically likely to become lonelier over time. Which brings us to a more fundamental question: Does the Internet make people lonely, or are lonely people more attracted to the Internet?

The question has intensified in the Facebook era. A recent study out of Australia (where close to half the population is active on Facebook), titled "Who Uses Facebook?," found a complex and sometimes confounding relationship between loneliness and social networking. Facebook users had slightly lower levels of "social loneliness"—the sense of not feeling bonded with friends—but "significantly higher levels of family loneliness"—the sense of not feeling bonded with family. It may be that Facebook encourages more contact with people outside of our household, at the expense of our family relationships—or it may be that people who have unhappy family relationships in the first place seek companionship through other means, including Facebook. The researchers also found that lonely people are inclined to spend more time on Facebook: "One of the most noteworthy findings," they wrote, "was the tendency for neurotic and lonely individuals to spend greater amounts of time on Facebook per day than non-lonely individuals." And they found that neurotics are more likely to prefer to use the wall, while extroverts tend to use chat features in addition to the wall.

Moira Burke, until recently a graduate student at the Human-Computer Institute at Carnegie Mellon, used to run a longitudinal study of 1,200 Facebook users. That study, which is ongoing, is one of the first to step outside the realm of self-selected college students and examine the effects of Facebook on a broader population, over time. She concludes that the effect of Facebook depends on what you bring to it. Just as your mother said: you get out only what you put in. If you use Facebook to communicate directly with other individuals—by using the "like" button, commenting on friends' posts, and so on—it can increase your social capital. Personalized messages, or what Burke calls "composed communication," are more satisfying than "one-click communication"—the lazy click of a like. "People who received composed communication became less lonely, while people who received one-click communication experienced no change in loneliness," Burke tells me. So, you should inform your friend in writing how charming her son looks with Harry Potter cake smeared all over his face, and how interesting her sepia-toned photograph of that tree-framed bit of skyline is, and how cool it is that she's at whatever concert she happens to be at. That's what we all want to hear. Even better than sending a private Facebook message is the semi-public conversation, the kind of back-and-forth in which you half ignore the other people who may be listening in. "People whose friends write to them semi-publicly on Facebook experience decreases in loneliness," Burke says.

On the other hand, non-personalized use of Facebook—scanning your friends' status updates and updating the world on your own activities via your wall, or what Burke calls "passive consumption" and "broadcasting"—correlates to feelings of disconnectedness. It's a lonely business, wandering the labyrinths of our friends' and pseudo-friends' projected identities, trying to figure out what part of ourselves we ought to project, who will listen, and what they will hear. According to Burke, passive consumption of Facebook also correlates to a marginal increase in depression. "If two women each talk to their friends the same amount of time, but one of them spends more time reading about friends on Facebook as well, the one reading tends to grow slightly more depressed," Burke says. Her conclusion suggests that my sometimes unhappy reactions to Facebook may be more universal than I had realized. When I scroll through page after page of my friends' descriptions of how accidentally eloquent their kids are, and how their husbands are endearingly bumbling, and how they're all about to eat a home-cooked meal prepared with fresh local organic produce bought at the farmers' market and then go for a jog and maybe check in at the office because they're so busy getting ready to hop on a plane for a week of luxury dogsledding in Lapland, I do grow slightly more miserable. A lot of other people doing the same thing feel a little bit worse, too.

Still, Burke's research does not support the assertion that Facebook creates loneliness. The people who experience loneliness on Facebook are lonely away from Facebook, too, she points out; on Facebook, as everywhere else, correlation is not causation. The popular kids are popular, and the lonely skulkers skulk alone. Perhaps it says something about me that I think Facebook is primarily a platform for lonely skulking. I mention to Burke the widely reported study, conducted by a Stanford graduate student, that showed how believing that others have strong social networks can lead to feelings of depression. What does Facebook communicate, if not the impression of social bounty? Everybody else looks so happy on Facebook, with so many friends, that our own social networks feel emptier than ever in comparison. Doesn't that *make* people feel lonely? "If people are reading about lives that are much better than theirs, two things can happen," Burke tells me. "They can feel worse about themselves, or they can feel motivated."

Burke will start working at Facebook as a data scientist this year.

John Cacioppo, the director of the Center for Cognitive and Social Neuroscience at the University of Chicago, is the world's leading expert on loneliness. In his landmark book, *Loneliness*, released in 2008, he revealed just how profoundly the epidemic of loneliness is affecting the basic functions of human physiology. He found higher levels of epinephrine, the stress hormone, in the morning urine of lonely people. Loneliness burrows deep: "When we drew blood from our older adults and analyzed their white cells," he writes, "we found that loneliness somehow penetrated the deepest recesses of the cell to alter the way genes were being expressed." Loneliness affects not only the brain, then, but the basic process of DNA transcription. When you are lonely, your whole body is lonely.

To Cacioppo, internet communication allows only ersatz intimacy. "Forming connections with pets or online friends or even God is a noble attempt by an obligatorily gregarious creature to satisfy a compelling need," he writes. "But surrogates can never make up completely for the absence of the real thing." The "real thing" being actual people, in the flesh. When I speak to Cacioppo, he is refreshingly clear on what he sees as Facebook's effect on society. Yes, he allows, some research has suggested that the greater the number of Facebook friends a person has, the less lonely she is. But he argues that the impression this creates can be misleading. "For the most part," he says, "people are bringing their old friends, and feelings of loneliness or connectedness, to Facebook." The idea that a Web site could deliver a more friendly, interconnected world is bogus. The depth of one's social network outside Facebook is what determines the depth of one's social network within Facebook, not the other way around. Using social media doesn't create new social networks; it just transfers established networks from one platform to another. For the most part, Facebook doesn't destroy friendships—but it doesn't create them, either.

In one experiment, Cacioppo looked for a connection between the loneliness of subjects and the relative frequency of their interactions via Facebook, chat rooms, online games, dating sites, and face-to-face contact. The results were unequivocal. "The greater the proportion of face-to-face interactions, the less lonely you are," he says. "The greater the proportion of online interactions, the lonelier you are." Surely, I suggest to Cacioppo, this means that Facebook and the like inevitably make people lonelier. He disagrees. Facebook is merely a tool, he says, and like any tool, its effectiveness will depend on its user. "If you use Facebook to increase face-to-face contact," he says, "it increases social capital." So if social media let you organize a game of football among your friends, that's healthy. If you turn to social media instead of playing football, however, that's unhealthy.

"Facebook can be terrific, if we use it properly," Cacioppo continues. "It's like a car. You can drive it to pick up your friends. Or you can drive alone." But hasn't the car increased loneliness? If cars created the suburbs, surely they also created isolation. "That's because of how we use cars," Cacioppo replies. "How we use these technologies can lead to more integration, rather than more isolation."

The problem, then, is that we invite loneliness, even though it makes us miserable. The history of our use of technology is a history of isolation desired and achieved. When the Great Atlantic and Pacific Tea Company opened its A&P stores, giving Americans self-service access to groceries, customers stopped having relationships with their grocers. When the telephone arrived, people stopped knocking on their neighbors' doors. Social media bring this process to a much wider set of relationships. Researchers at the HP Social Computing Lab who studied the nature of people's connections on Twitter came to a depressing, if not surprising, conclusion: "Most of the links declared within Twitter were meaningless from an interaction point of view." I have to wonder: What other point of view is meaningful?

Loneliness is certainly not something that Facebook or Twitter or any of the lesser forms of social media is doing to us. We are doing it to ourselves. Casting technology as some vague, impersonal spirit of history forcing our actions is a weak excuse. We make decisions about how we use our machines, not the other way around. Every time I shop at my local grocery store, I am faced with a choice. I can buy my groceries from a human being or from a machine. I always, without exception, choose the machine. It's faster and more efficient, I tell myself, but the truth is that I prefer not having to wait with the other customers who are lined up alongside the conveyor belt: the hipster mom who disapproves of my high-carbon-footprint pineapple; the lady who tenses to the point of tears while she waits to see if the gods of the credit-card machine will accept or decline; the old man whose clumsy feebleness requires a patience that I don't possess. Much better to bypass the whole circus and just ring up the groceries myself.

Our omnipresent new technologies lure us toward increasingly superficial connections at exactly the same moment that they make avoiding the mess of human interaction easy. The beauty of Facebook, the source of its power, is that it enables us to be social while sparing us the embarrassing reality of society—the accidental revelations we make at parties, the awkward pauses, the farting and the spilled drinks and the general gaucherie of face-to-face contact. Instead, we have the lovely smoothness of a seemingly social machine. Everything's so simple: status updates, pictures, your wall.

But the price of this smooth sociability is a constant compulsion to assert one's own happiness, one's own fulfillment. Not only must we contend with the social bounty of others; we must foster the appearance of our own social bounty. Being happy all the time, pretending to be happy, actually attempting to be happy—it's exhausting. Last year a team of researchers led by Iris Mauss at the University of Denver published a study looking into "the paradoxical effects of valuing happiness." Most goals in life show a direct correlation between valuation and achievement. Studies have found, for example, that students who value good grades tend to have higher grades than those who don't value them. Happiness is an exception. The study came to a disturbing conclusion:

Valuing happiness is not necessarily linked to greater happiness. In fact, under certain conditions, the opposite is true. Under conditions of low (but not high) life stress, the more people valued happiness, the lower were their hedonic balance, psychological well-being, and life satisfaction, and the higher their depression symptoms.

The more you try to be happy, the less happy you are. Sophocles made roughly the same point.

Facebook, of course, puts the pursuit of happiness front and center in our digital life. Its capacity to redefine our very concepts of identity and personal fulfillment is much more worrisome than the data-mining and privacy practices that have aroused anxieties about the company. Two of the most compelling critics of Facebook—neither of them a Luddite—concentrate on exactly this point. Jaron Lanier, the author of *You Are Not a Gadget*, was one of the inventors of virtual-reality technology. His view of where social media are taking us reads like dystopian science fiction: "I fear that we are beginning to design ourselves to suit digital models of us, and I worry about a leaching of empathy and humanity in that process." Lanier argues that Facebook imprisons us in the business of self-presenting, and this, to his mind, is the site's crucial and fatally unacceptable downside.

Sherry Turkle, a professor of computer culture at MIT who in 1995 published the digital-positive analysis *Life on the Screen*, is much more skeptical about the effects of online society in her 2011 book, *Alone Together*: "These days, insecure in our relationships and anxious about intimacy, we look to technology for ways to be in relationships and protect ourselves from them at the same time." The problem with digital intimacy is that it is ultimately incomplete: "The ties we form through the Internet are not, in the end, the ties that bind. But they are the ties that preoccupy," she writes. "We don't want to intrude on each other, so instead we constantly intrude on each other, but not in 'real time.'"

Lanier and Turkle are right, at least in their diagnoses. Self-presentation on Facebook is continuous, intensely mediated, and possessed of a phony nonchalance that eliminates even the potential for spontaneity. ("Look how casually I threw up these three photos from the party at which I took 300 photos!") Curating the exhibition of the self has become a 24/7 occupation. Perhaps not surprisingly, then, the Australian study "Who Uses Facebook?" found a significant correlation between Facebook use and narcissism: "Facebook users have higher levels of total narcissism, exhibitionism, and leadership than Facebook nonusers," the study's authors wrote. "In fact, it could be argued that Facebook specifically gratifies the narcissistic individual's need to engage in self-promoting and superficial behavior."

Rising narcissism isn't so much a trend as the trend behind all other trends. In preparation for the 2013 edition of its diagnostic manual, the psychiatric profession is currently struggling to update its definition of narcissistic personality disorder. Still, generally speaking, practitioners agree that narcissism manifests in patterns of fantastic grandiosity, craving for attention, and lack of empathy. In a 2008 survey, 35,000 American respondents were asked if they had ever had certain symptoms of narcissistic personality disorder. Among people older than 65, 3 percent reported symptoms. Among people in their 20s, the proportion was nearly 10 percent. Across all age groups, one in 16 Americans has experienced some symptoms of NPD. And loneliness and narcissism are intimately connected: a longitudinal study of Swedish women demonstrated a strong link between levels of narcissism in youth and levels of loneliness in old age. The connection is fundamental. Narcissism is the flip side of loneliness, and either condition is a fighting retreat from the messy reality of other people.

A considerable part of Facebook's appeal stems from its miraculous fusion of distance with intimacy, or the illusion of distance with the illusion of intimacy. Our online communities become engines of self-image, and self-image becomes the engine of community. The real danger with Facebook is not that it allows us to isolate ourselves, but that by mixing our appetite for isolation with our vanity, it threatens to alter the very nature of solitude. The new isolation is not of the kind that Americans once idealized, the lonesomeness of the proudly nonconformist, independent-minded, solitary stoic, or that of the astronaut who blasts into new worlds. Facebook's isolation is a grind. What's truly staggering about Facebook usage is not its volume—750 million photographs uploaded over a single weekend—but the constancy of the performance it demands. More than half its users—and one of every 13 people on Earth is a Facebook user—log on every day. Among 18-to-34-year-olds, nearly half check Facebook minutes after waking up, and 28 percent do so before getting out of bed. The relentlessness is what is so new, so potentially transformative. Facebook never takes a break. We never take a break. Human beings have always created elaborate acts of self-presentation. But not all the time, not every morning, before we even pour a cup of coffee. Yvette Vickers's computer was on when she died.

Nostalgia for the good old days of disconnection would not just be pointless, it would be hypocritical and ungrateful. But the very magic of the new machines, the efficiency and elegance with which they serve us, obscures what isn't being served: everything that matters. What Facebook has revealed about human nature—and this is not a minor revelation—is that a connection is not the same thing as a bond, and that instant and total connection is no salvation, no ticket to a happier, better world or a more liberated version of humanity. Solitude used to be good for self-reflection and self-reinvention. But now we are left thinking about who we are all the time, without ever really thinking about who we are. Facebook denies us a pleasure whose profundity we had underestimated: the chance to forget about ourselves for a while, the chance to disconnect.

Topics for Writing and Discussion

1. Marche uses and mentions a number of sources to support his article on the effects of Facebook. You can find all of them on the internet. For example, find the following references and write a short, annotated bibliography (see Chapter 2) incorporating them: Eric Klinenberg, UCLA Loneliness Scale, a 2010 AARP survey titled Loneliness among Older Adults: A National Survey of Adults 45+, Ronald Dworkin, *Bowling Alone: The Collapse and Revival of the American Community*, Moira Burke, and *Alone Together: Why We Expect More From Technology and Less From Each Other.*

2. Marche also uses some very vague references. Track down the following phrases in his essay.

    ⊙ "a growing body of research"

    ⊙ a "major study by a leading scholar"

    ⊙ "one journal article suggests"

    ⊙ "a 1998 article . . . at Carnegie Mellon"

    ⊙ "a longitudinal study of Swedish women"

    Note the page number and context for each of these references. Do you think that such vague attribution hurts Marche's argument?

3. Take one of the following topics, do some additional research (in library databases or by surveying classmates and friends), and write an essay incorporating information from Marche and your other sources. Be sure to use quotations and citations properly. (See Chapter 9.) Ask your instructor which citation style he or she prefers.

    ⊙ How has social networking changed relationships among college students?

    ⊙ How have family relationships changed because of the influence of social networks?

    ⊙ What are the positive effects of Facebook and other social media?

    ⊙ What are the negative effects of Facebook and other social media?

CHAPTER 10
Analyzing Arguments

In your college classes you will be expected to read and understand essays and chapters from textbooks, but you will also be expected to analyze them and sometimes to argue for or against the position the writer takes. And as citizens of the city, county, state, and nation, you should take an interest in what the city council, the state legislature, and the United States Congress are currently debating. What they decide can directly affect your life. For instance, in Houston there is an ongoing debate about what to do with the aging Astrodome. Should the city spend millions of tax dollars to refurbish it, perhaps by making it into an indoor park, or simply tear it down? Should concealed weapons be allowed everywhere on school campuses in the state? Nationally, what should the country do about immigration: Should we "secure the border" by building a fence across the entire border between Mexico and the United States? What should we do about the estimated 11,000,000 undocumented immigrants currently in the US? Do you really understand the issues? Do you have an opinion about these issues? Could you support your opinion with evidence?

College is the time of life for you to acquire those habits of mind that will allow you to become a fully educated citizen of the world. In order to become that educated adult, you need to acquire certain skills—skills that, over and above those you learn in the job or professional field you are pursuing, will help you to think about and sort through the millions of words and visual images you will encounter during your life. You need to learn to read critically, recognize various types of arguments, write convincing arguments of your own, and analyze the arguments of others.

Analyzing Written Arguments

When reading and responding to arguments, you will necessarily engage in analysis. As you read in Chapter 2, this means reading carefully, annotating, looking up unfamiliar words and allusions, and making sure you understand the essay's claim and the evidence given to support it. In addition to analyzing the cogency of an essay's argument, you might also be asked, or choose, to analyze the way the author appeals to his audience's emotions or how he presents himself as a trustworthy source. Indeed, there are many ways to analyze the importance and impact of a text. For example, Lincoln's *Gettysburg Address* has been analyzed from a number of points of view: its historical context, its political implications at the time, its ethical and emotional appeals, its use of rhetorical tropes, its statement of national beliefs. Whatever you are asked to do, you will need to address a series of questions.

Activity 10.1

Each member should read and annotate the essay "Is Facebook Making Us Lonely?" at the end of Chapter 9. Compare your annotations. Now make a list of all the references to other people and other works, and have group members look them up on the internet. Next, list the evidence Marche uses to support his claim that social media, such as Facebook, are leading to greater loneliness. Discuss and then decide whether the evidence is strong enough to support his claim.

Finding the Claim

Once you have read an essay and annotated it, you need to read it again. (Yes, you have only so much time and your phone is buzzing at you, but a second read will help set the main points of the essay in your mind—and it will be a lot quicker since you can now skim.) While reading, skimming, the essay a second time, see whether you can distinguish the author's claim or claims from any evidence he uses to support those claims. A claim is a sentence that asserts the truth or value of something. Many times people accept the truth of claims simply because they have been told they are true by their parents, religious leaders, or teachers. Or their family or friends believe certain things simply because "everybody believes them." But we know that many things people once believed to be true have later been shown to be false. For example, many years ago people throughout Europe believed that the sun went around the earth. And less than two hundred years ago most people believed that individual species did not change or evolve. (Some still cling to that belief.) However, most of us, most of the time, are unwilling to accept the truth of claims that do not fit into our preconceived view of the world—we demand evidence of the truth of claims, of assertions. For example, some people believe that extraterrestrial beings (aliens) have already visited the earth. Some even claim they have been taken up into alien spacecraft and operated on. Should the rest of us simply believe the truth of these claims? Or should we demand to see evidence that these claims are true?

Not all claims are alike—there are different types of claims. The following are some of the major types.

Factual claims assert something is or is not true, was or was not true, or will or will not be true. For example, if I say that New York City is the largest city in the United States, I am making a factual claim, a claim about reality that can be verified simply by checking the United States Census Bureau's most recent numbers. Or if I say that the Baltimore Ravens will win the Super Bowl next year, I am making a predictive claim about a future event, but we must wait until January for verification of it. Finally, if I say that Socrates lived in fifth-century Athens, I am making a factual claim about the past that can be verified by reading accounts of his life by his contemporaries or by scholars who have studied the period. Therefore, statements of fact can be verified—or falsified—by studying the evidence for or against them.

Value claims are declarative sentences that assert something is good or bad, right or wrong. Some value claims are merely expressions of personal taste, of liking or disliking: "Broccoli tastes bad." "I prefer living in the city to living in the country." "I feel hot." Such claims cannot be disputed. Other value claims are moral or aesthetic judgments: "Stealing is wrong." "A liberal education is better than a technical one." "Andrew Wyeth is a better painter than Jackson Pollock." Such value claims are supported by reference to a code of morality, an accepted ideal, or a set of criteria the one arguing uses as the basis of his claim. The Christian Bible might be the basis for the first claim, the humanist ideal for the second, and standards of realist painting for the third.

Causal claims assert that something is or was the cause of something else. "Smoking is a major cause of cancer" is a causal claim. "Slavery was a major cause of the Civil War" is another.

Definitional claims assert that something is just like, or is exactly the same as, something else. "Keeping animals in cages is just like keeping slaves in shackles" is such a claim. "Abortion is murder" is another.

Deliberative claims assert that something should or should not be done. These are sometimes called claims of policy. "You should quit smoking" is a deliberative claim. "The state of Texas should adopt a law making English its official language" is another deliberative claim.

Looking for Evidence

Next, authors, like good district attorneys, will present different types of evidence to support their claims. Generally, the more evidence there is, the more likely the claim is to be true or the defendant guilty. While there are many types of evidence, and different disciplines have different standards of evidence (there are specific "rules of evidence" in trials, for instance), here are some generally recognized types of evidence.

Facts. According to the National Academy of Sciences, a fact is "an observation that has been repeatedly confirmed and for all practical purposes is accepted as 'true.'" However, what constitutes a "fact" may be open to discussion.

Examples. Examples are used to support generalizations. They give specific instances to illustrate the material, from which inductive generalizations are derived. Examples should be relevant and appropriate; that is, they should directly bear on the issue being discussed, and they should be suitable and fitting, not extreme or unusual.

Authorities. Authorities are experts in various fields. Their work and statements are used as evidence to support claims. An authority may be an expert by virtue of knowledge, skill, experience, training, or education.

Statistics. Numerical data in the form of tables, graphs, or charts are used to support claims. Because contradictory conclusions can be drawn from the same data, special care must be taken in evaluating statistics. Good statistical data are usually presented visually (as charts or tables) as well as numerically; they should also be accompanied by analyses, and the sources of the data should be clearly stated.

Public records. Information drawn from public records, such as the Census Bureau, state agencies, or historical archives, is frequently used as evidence.

Interviews. Personal interviews with people with experience can also be used as evidence, either as examples or as expert testimony.

Personal experience. Relevant personal experience can also be used as evidence, as example or testimony.

Activity 10.2

Assume you are a detective. Based on what you find listed below in a family's garbage can, determine the type of inhabitants in the house. How many people live in the house? What are their approximate ages and interests? Explain your findings/conclusions in a well-structured paragraph, providing sufficient evidence to support your claims/conclusions.

Grocery Receipts	Discarded Mail
Styling gel	College recruitments
Clearasil	Military recruitments
Olay	Alumni magazines from universities
Diet sodas	Stockholder reports
AAA batteries	Paycheck stubs
Jell-O	Ad from MEGA Energy Corp
Gummy bears	McDonald's
Tuna	
Polo cologne	
Decaf coffee	
Lean Cuisine	
Sugar-coated cereal	
Bran flakes	
Donuts	
Case of beer	
Low-cholesterol products	
Ulcer medicine	

Magazines	Canceled Checks
Field & Stream	Dance lessons
Cosmopolitan	The Gap
Rolling Stone	Two County Sheriff's Department Traffic
Better Homes & Gardens	Division citations
TV Guide	Neiman Marcus
Seventeen	Hair salon
Golf Digest	Orthodontist
Country Club Living	Car insurance (three cars)
Vogue	Clinique cosmetics
	Alimony checks to Mrs. X

Distinguishing between Fact, Opinion, and Judgment

Further, when you read an article or an essay, it is important to distinguish between what is a fact, what is merely an opinion, and what is a judgment.

Facts. Facts, as we have seen, assert something is or is not true, was or was not true, or will or will not be true. They can be verified—or falsified—by studying the evidence for or against them. When reading an essay, however, you must distinguish between statements of fact and statements of opinion.

Opinions. Opinions can be merely expressions of personal taste, such as "I hate tomatoes," or "It's hot in here." Such statements cannot be verified, or falsified. People experience things or feel things in different ways. Writers express their opinions all the time. Simply look at the "Letters" section of any newspaper, the comments section at the end of online articles, or Twitter responses. People like to tell you what they think or feel about everything. However, do not confuse such "expressions of opinion" with statements of fact.

Judgments. Judgments are considered expressions of belief about the truth or falsity of certain events or sets of facts. In other words, after studying the details about a certain event or situation, a writer might make a judgment summing up what they all mean or their implications for the future. For example, a jury must "weigh the evidence" presented by the district attorney in a murder trial to determine a defendant's guilt or innocence. Their verdict is a judgment based on their deliberations about the "facts of the case" but in itself is not a fact. Or consider the latest report of the Intergovernmental Panel on Climate Change that says that climate change will have "severe, widespread, and irreversible impacts" on people and our world unless we reduce CO_2 emissions. Again, this is a "considered judgment" by a panel of experts, not a fact. It is, according to S. I. Hayakawa, "a conclusion, summing up a large number of previously observed facts."

Determining Bias

Merriam-Webster's Collegiate Dictionary defines *bias* as "a bent, tendency; an inclination of temperament or outlook, especially a personal and sometimes unreasoned judgment—prejudice." We are all biased in some way. We come to a discussion or conversation with certain attitudes we have inherited from our parents, our family, our religion, and our culture. As the definition implies, sometimes a bias becomes an unreasoned prejudice, which *MW* defines as a "preconceived judgment or opinion; an adverse opinion or leaning formed without just grounds or before sufficient knowledge." Therefore, when we read an article, an essay, or a post online, we should try to determine the bias of the writer. Is the writer striving to be *objective* (without bias), simply reporting what she has found—as in many popular discussions of scientific discoveries—or is the author trying to *persuade* his audience to accept a certain way of looking at a subject—as in an opinion piece in a newspaper? In addition, a good writer knows his audience and will directly appeal to their biases. The words an author uses can be neutral or have positive or negative connotations, and being aware of these words can help you determine the author's bias. In an article for *Scientific American*, "The Believing Brain," Michael Shermer lists six kinds of bias.

- ⊙ Anchoring bias—dependence on a single first principle in making decisions.

- ⊙ Authority bias—dependence on a single authority figure.

- ⊙ Belief bias—acceptance or rejection based on the believability of the conclusions.

- ⊙ Confirmation bias—acceptance only of information that confirms our beliefs.

- ⊙ In-group bias—believing only in those in our group.

- ⊙ Blind spot bias—not seeing the mote (a dust speck) in our own eye.

Therefore, to read critically is to read carefully. You must make an effort to understand a writer's ideas by looking up words and allusions, distinguishing between claims and support, looking for types of evidence, noting the difference between fact, opinion, and judgment, and finding out about the author and any biases he may bring to the conversation. To do less is to be a passive receiver of other people's assertions, to allow others to decide what you believe.

Activity 10.3

Read the following paragraph. Determine whether it is biased, particularly whether it shows one of the six kinds of bias mentioned by Michael Shermer. Next write a short paragraph discussing the bias, supporting your point with brief quotations from the text. Or, show why it is not biased. Discuss what you have learned with your group and the class.

> So, if you want to really hurt me, talk badly about my language. Ethnic identity is twin skin to linguistic identity—I am my language. Until I can take pride in my language, I cannot take pride in myself. Until I can accept as legitimate Chicano Texas Spanish, Tex-Mex, and all the other languages I speak, I cannot accept the legitimacy of myself. Until I am free to write bilingually and to switch codes without having always to translate, while I still have to speak English or Spanish when I would rather speak Spanglish, and as long as I have to accommodate the English speakers rather than having them accommodate me, my tongue will be illegitimate.

Determining Audience, Purpose, Situation, and Tone

If you are asked to write an analysis of an argument, you will need to address a series of questions.

Who is the audience? The intended audience of an essay may be identified by looking at the author's style (his diction and sentence structure), the complexity and type of ideas discussed, the essay's length, its purpose and situation, and the persona adopted by the writer. Where an essay is published, in *Time*, *Field & Stream*, or *Scientific American*, is also a clue to the educational level and interests of the audience. The intended audience is discovered inductively; for example, we might determine that the 5:30 evening news is aimed toward an older, conservative, affluent audience by noting the number of advertisements shown during the half hour for such things as denture cream, investment opportunities, and luxury automobiles.

What is the author's purpose? What does the writer want the reader to understand, to feel, to do? Writers want to change their readers' beliefs or attitudes, make them laugh, make them cry, or make them understand a complex issue. A list of purposes would be very long: to entertain, to per-suade, to explain, to frighten, to teach, to anger, to placate.

What is the situation? All discourse is constrained by the situation in which it appears. Situation, loosely defined, is the context in which a particular text appears or the occasion on which a discourse is delivered. For example, the following are different situations with different contexts: You are required to write a ten-page report on the causes of the American Civil War in a history class. You volunteer to speak to your younger brother's scout troop on *tae kwon do*. You write a letter applying for a summer job at Yellowstone National Park. Each situation or context demands a different response. In analyzing an essay, you should try to determine the situation or context in which the essay was written and the specific constraints such a situation places on what the writer says. Keys to context or situation for published essays include when it was published, in what magazine or journal it was published, and the tone and language employed by the writer.

What is the voice and tone of the author? The writer reveals his personality, attitudes, prejudices, and desires through what he says and the way he says it. Just as there is a narrator who tells a story from a particular point of view, just as there is a "voice" in poetry, so there is a speaker in an essay, a *persona* (in Latin, literally "actor's mask"). A writer may unconsciously reveal the kind of person he is through what he writes. We may determine that he is arrogant, friendly, aloof, narrow-minded, or flippant. More often the writer's purpose, his audience, and the writing situation cause him to assume or adopt a persona. Aristotle says, for example, that when trying to persuade an audience we should present ourselves as honest, open-minded, and knowledgeable, with the *best interests of our audience in mind*. The persona a writer adopts may also reflect his social or cultural role. For example, we expect a priest and a movie critic to write in certain ways, reflecting their different roles and positions in society. Finally, the tone of an essay is closely connected to persona. Writers may adopt tones that are serious, playful, ironic, antagonistic, or passionate, among others. In writing a critical analysis of an essay, you should determine the persona and tone of the writer. Whether consciously or unconsciously revealed, tone is crucial to the total effect a text has on its audience.

Analyzing the Rational Appeal

Aristotle believed that the one quality that set humans apart from the other animals was our ability to reason. Therefore, appealing to other people's reasoning, to what many call "common sense," is a major strategy in most attempts to persuade. If a speaker or writer builds a strong argument, a strong case, for his position, it becomes not only convincing but difficult for others to attack. So it is important to look at the ways people organize and develop arguments. In *An Introduction to Reasoning* (1984), Steven Toulmin presents a simple, practical method for analyzing an argument. He divides his analysis into an attractive scheme of three primary parts—claim, data (grounds), and warrant.

Claim. First find the claim—the conclusion of the argument or the thesis of the essay. Make sure that the claim is a testable claim (that it is possible to support the claim by evidence), and that it is not preposterous or whimsical. Remember that you may base your argument on different types of claims. The grounds used to support the claim will vary depending on the type of claim. For example, the following claim was made by a student in a paper on women in the military: *"Women should not be allowed in ground combat units in the army."*

Grounds. Next look for the data that support that claim, that is, the evidence the writer gives in support of his proposition. For example, the student supported the above claim with the following evidence: *"The fact that a woman can get pregnant may keep her from performing her task, thus rendering the squad ineffective to perform in a combat situation. An example of this situation occurred when I was stationed at Ft. Rucker, Alabama; in my squad there were four men, and each of us was assigned a different task:*

machine gunner, sniper, squad leader, and Dragon gunner. We went on an exercise, and the machine gunner became ill. He was rushed to the hospital, and I had to take over his task. The result of his illness was a catastrophe. When we attacked the enemy we were slower because I had to perform the jobs of two men. Therefore, the squad lost the battle, which not only had an effect on the squad but produced a chain reaction and destroyed the whole company. Thus, if a woman were to be assigned to a combat unit and she became pregnant, it would have a negative influence on the whole company."

Warrant. Third, look for any support that the writer gives to show that the evidence is relevant to the claim. For example, if the writer cites the statement of an authority, does she give the credentials of the authority? Is the authority speaking in his own field of expertise? If a major scientific study is discussed as evidence, are other confirming studies also cited? For example, the student writing on women in combat added the following to the evidence given above: *"More than 1,200 pregnant women were evacuated from the Gulf region during the Gulf War; that is the equivalent of two infantry battalions. If the loss of one man from a squad can cause a company's performance to drop, how much more harm would there be with the loss of two battalions of soldiers? It would have a devastating effect."*

Backing. Fourth, look for information that gives added support to the warrant. For example, our student next added the following sentence to the above warrant: *"The statistics on the number of women evacuated from the Gulf War were released in a report by the Pentagon."*

Rebuttal. Finally, check to see whether the writer has acknowledged counterclaims and arguments; that is, has he mentioned and then refuted claims that contradict his own? Also see whether the writer has explained apparent exceptions to his evidence or mitigated the force of counterclaims in some way. For example, our student included the following in a refutation section: *"Some women argue that many other countries use women in combat roles. This statement is not altogether true. There are very few countries that have women in combat roles. Israel was one of those countries that tried to put women in combat, but they quickly stopped the program because it was a catastrophe. Israel still uses women in its military but does not allow them in combat."*

Using Toulmin's scheme will help you recognize the structure of the argument you are analyzing and the strengths and weaknesses of that argument; however, simply because a writer supplies a warrant and backing for a claim does not mean that his argument is sound or cogent. Be sure to apply the standards of appropriate evidence and reasoning to the argument. Finally, remember that arguments are made to be convincing and that we are inundated daily by the mass media with visual images and hundreds of claims. The only rational stance to adopt in a world such as ours is one based on a respect for truth and an attitude of skepticism. In his essay "Of Cannibals," Michel de Montaigne says, "We should be on our guard against clinging to vulgar opinions and . . . we should judge things by light of reason, and not from common rumor."

Activity 10.4

Identify the claim and the grounds of each of the following arguments, and write them out on a piece of paper.

1. Philosophy is the best subject in which to major because it teaches one to reason, an essential skill for a good life.

2. Cutting wage rates may enable one employer to hire more workers, but cutting the wages of all workers may lead to fewer jobs, not more, because workers would have less to spend on goods.

3. The human mind is not the same thing as the human brain. The human body, including the brain, is a material thing. The human mind is a spiritual thing. Nothing is both a material thing and a spiritual thing.

4. All 70 students who ate dinner at the fraternity house on Friday became ill during the night. None of the students who live at the house but didn't dine there that night became ill, so the illness must have been food poisoning caused by something served for dinner at the house on Friday.

5. The investigation of supernatural phenomena lies outside the realm of science. Therefore, science can neither prove nor disprove the existence of God.

6. But the particular evil of silencing the expression of an opinion is that it is robbing the human race, posterity as well as the existing generation, those who dissent from the opinion still more than those who hold it. If the opinion is right, they are deprived of the opportunity of exchanging error for truth: if wrong, they lose what is almost as great a benefit, the clearer perception and livelier impression of truth, produced by its collision with error.

Logical Fallacies

In addition to using Toulmin's scheme to analyze an argument, be on the lookout for logical fallacies. A fallacy is a faux pas, or misstep, in a chain of reasoning (although fallacies can also be used intentionally to fool the reader or listener). See Appendix 2 for a list of common fallacies.

Activity 10.5

Each of the following statements contains at least one fallacy. Using Appendix 2 as a guide, write out the fallacy or fallacies on a piece of paper. Compare your answers with those of your group and the whole class.

1. Polygraph tests do not provide reliable evidence because their results cannot be trusted.

2. Overcrowded conditions in the inner city have forced people together like rats in a cage. So, like rats, they have turned on one another, fighting and killing. Who can blame them?

3. The city should not take seriously the Director of the Health Department's proposals for increasing the city's health budget. Who can believe a man who has admitted he is a recovering alcoholic and who was recently discovered having an affair with a much-younger intern?

4. We must choose between life and death, between banning this procedure and sanctioning murder. There can be no neutral position on this issue.

5. This college is much like a slaughterhouse; neither the freshmen nor the cattle know what is in store for them. They both get chopped up in the process.

6. According to Savannah Guthrie, interest rates will remain at historic lows for the coming year.

7. We elected Governor Frogmore, and the state has since had record budget deficits. We should not elect him again for another four-year term.

8. More than three-fourths of American universities have required courses on cultural diversity, so our university should also develop and require such a course.

9. Congress should repeal the health care bill. Nearly seventy-five percent of the bill's backers received campaign contributions from the health care industry.

10. This offer will be good for only one more day! Thousands have already taken advantage of this one-time offer. Sign up now; this offer may never be repeated!

Take one of the essays from the *Additional Readings* section of this book, and write an analysis of its rational appeal.

Analyzing the Emotional Appeal

If all people were as dispassionate as Spock or Data on *Star Trek*, then an account of the argument of an essay, of its rational appeal, would be the only analysis we would need to make. Yet while all people may be born with the capacity to reason, reasoning well requires knowledge, training, and practice. However, to echo the French eighteenth-century writer Jean-Jacques Rousseau, we *felt* before we *thought*. Feeling, Rousseau said, is primary; it, not reason, makes us human. Further, as Antonio R. Damasio, Professor of Neuroscience at the University of Southern California, has pointed out, emotions "inform the deployment of logic."

Therefore, when we want to persuade an audience, we often find it necessary to appeal to the personal nature of our topic. People are generally more interested in those matters that touch their hearts than in statistics or logic. The writer of a persuasive argument cannot ignore the fact that much of our identity resides in our emotions and imaginations. If we are to convince readers, we must appeal to their emotions, attempting to ascertain which of our own emotions they will accept or approve. The clever writer can then use certain associations that will elicit the desired emotional response in his audience. For instance, if he is addressing a Christian group, he might associate the idea of human leadership or fellowship with Christ. This reference links the writer's own propositions to what the audience already identifies with and respects. Sometimes a well-placed word or phrase will enhance the emotional appeal of an argument, as when a writer of an essay against pornography mentions "innocent" children. Conversely, astute writers know, because they know the emotional character of their audiences, what not to use in their appeal.

Thus, emotions are powerful forces in humans, and while we might think of some people as "lacking feeling," most people are strongly affected by their emotions. In Book II of *Rhetoric*, on "Emotion," Aristotle lists ten emotions. The first four are positive—calm, friendship, favor, and pity; the next six are negative—anger, fear, shame, indignation, envy, and jealousy. In his 1872 book *The Expression of the Emotions in Man and Animals*, Charles Darwin began the modern discussion of the nature and origin of emotions. More recent investigators have emphasized the neurological basis of emotions and have listed eight main emotions—anger, fear, joy, sadness, acceptance, disgust, surprise, and interest or curiosity. Others have divided emotions into primary and secondary emotions. Robert Plutchik, late professor at the Albert Einstein College of Medicine, lists the eight basic emotions as fear (terror, shock), anger (rage), sorrow (sadness), joy (happiness, glee), disgust, acceptance, anticipation, and surprise. In an article in *American Scientist* in 2001, he gave a three-dimensional "color wheel" model of the emotions (Figure 10.1). From outside in, the opposed emotions on the wheel are as follows.

- ⊙ Pensiveness, sadness, grief—ecstasy, joy, serenity
- ⊙ Boredom, disgust, loathing—admiration, trust, acceptance
- ⊙ Distraction, surprise, amazement—vigilance, anticipation, interest
- ⊙ Annoyance, anger, rage—terror, fear, apprehension

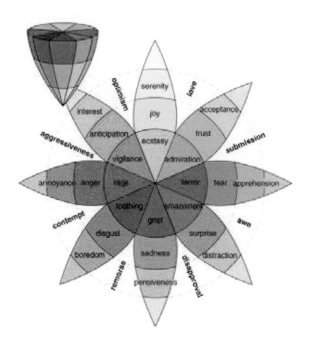

Figure 10.1: **Color Wheel of Emotions**

Further, in an article in *Scientific American*, Michael Shermer states that recent experiments have shown that "the left brain is associated with positive emotions such as love, attachment, bonding and safety." He continues by saying that the emotions help us maintain a balance.

Positive emotions help us build enduring personal resources, such as problem-solving skills, coordination and social resources. Negative emotions, in contrast, help to protect us. Fear causes us to pull back and retreat from risks. Disgust directs us to push out and expel that which is bad for us. Anger leads us to fight back or to signal displeasure at the violation of a social agreement. Jealousy leads us to guard our mates against intruders in pair-bonded relationships.

Finally, while we consider our emotions *natural*, we know that these emotions are conditioned by our culture, our social background, and our individual upbringing. Writers appeal to their particular audience's emotions in order to motivate them to action or to gain their commitment to a belief or a group. For example, writers are well aware that people respond emotionally to words and images that appeal to certain deep-seated human desires, such as love, sex, nourishment, and pleasure. Conversely, people respond emotionally to what they fear: rejection, privation, pain, and death. On the one hand, writers appeal to their audience's sense of comfort, which they derive from belonging to a group, such as a family, city, state, or country, or their affiliation with a certain ethnic or linguistic group, economic class, or political party; on the other hand, writers play on their audience's fear and distrust of things or people who are strange or foreign to them.

The language used in emotional appeals can be direct or subtle. Writers can use words that have an obvious and immediate emotional impact on their audience and that are calculated to provoke a strong and predictable response. For instance, how do you react to the following words: *jerk, extremist, atheist, Bubba, dumb blonde*; or to *peace, patriot, Christian, Muslim, entrepreneur, mother*? For example, note Richard Nixon's use of emotionally charged language in the following paragraph, the conclusion to a famous speech he made on television in September 1952; at the time many people were calling for his resignation as candidate for vice president under Dwight Eisenhower because of allegations of misappropriation of campaign funds.

> But just let me say this last word. Regardless of what happens, I am going to continue this fight. I am going to campaign up and down America until we drive the crooks and the communists and those that defend them out of Washington, and remember, folks, Eisenhower is a great man, and a vote for Eisenhower is a vote for what is good for America.

The words used in this passage depict two contrasting sets of images. The first set creates the image of a man battling against the forces of evil: "I am going to continue this *fight* [. . .] until *we* [Note the shift in person. He is one of us.] drive the *crooks* and the *communists* and *those that defend them* out of *Washington*." Here is the image of a man trying to drive out evil from one of our political holy places, perhaps like Jesus drove the moneychangers out of the temple. The second set of words—"*Eisenhower is a great man*" and "what is *good for America*"—evokes the feelings of pride we have in a renowned military leader and associates those emotions with our feelings of patriotism. These feelings of greatness, goodness, and loyalty to our homeland are linked to the lonely fight against evil conducted by this man on our behalf.

In another example, in 2008, as the war in Iraq entered its sixth year and the number of United States troops rose to over 40,000, President George W. Bush continued to defend the righteousness and necessity of the war. Speaking of those who had given their lives, he said, "One day people will look back at this moment in history and say, 'Thank God there were courageous people willing to serve because they laid the foundation for peace for generations to come.'" Bush here uses the words "God," "courageous," "serve," and "peace" to evoke religious and patriotic emotions. He further intimates that history, "one day," will ultimately be on his side in judging the morality of the war, and that the future "generations to come" will praise those who, under his leadership and command, gave their lives for the benefit of their countrymen. With this statement, President Bush both aligns his policies in Iraq with God, country, and history and implies that those who oppose the war and want to withdraw US forces lack courage, foresight, and backbone.

The emotion of a passage may also arise naturally from the writer's subject and the intensity of the writer's engagement with that subject. For example, few would question the sincerity of the emotion expressed in the following sentences by the Russian writer Leo Tolstoy who, at the peak of his career as a writer, with fame, wealth, an interesting circle of friends, a family—all that a person might desire—suddenly experienced a terrible, gripping sense of the utter futility of life. He wrote of this life-altering experience in *Confession* (here translated by David Patterson).

> If not today, then tomorrow sickness and death will come (indeed, they were already approaching) to everyone, to me, and nothing will remain except the stench and the worms. My deeds, whatever they may be, will be forgotten sooner or later, and I myself will be no more. Why, then, do anything? How can anyone fail to see this

and live? That's what is amazing! It is possible to live only as long as life intoxicates us; once we are sober we cannot help seeing that it is all a delusion, a stupid delusion! Nor is there anything funny or witty about it; it is only cruel and stupid.

The intensity of feeling in this passage arises from the writer's emotional involvement with his subjects—death and the meaning of life. Tolstoy conveys his fear of death and his sense of the utter meaninglessness of life in such phrases as "sickness and death will come," "the stench and the worms," and "I myself will be no more." These words are simple, direct, and unadorned. Tolstoy also employs an everyday image of a drunk versus a sober man to convey his feelings about every man's blindness to the reality of his own death. The emotions we feel when we read such a passage arise directly from the subject and the writer's engagement with it. Tolstoy's primary purpose is to convey his feelings, to make us feel what he himself feels.

In writing an analysis of an essay that focuses on its emotional content, therefore, you will need to look carefully for any emotionally charged words used by the writer, at any images the writer creates through description, and at any figurative language the writer uses. In addition, ask yourself the following questions.

- ⊙ What emotion is the writer trying to make the reader feel?
- ⊙ Is the writer's use of emotion consistent with his purpose?
- ⊙ Is the writer's use of emotion appropriate to the subject, audience, and occasion?
- ⊙ Does the writer's use of emotionally charged language dominate the essay, or is it subordinated to more rational arguments?

Answering these questions will also help you decide what the writer's attitude is toward his material and his audience. For example, is the writer asking the reader to sympathize or be outraged? Is the writer being satiric or ironic?

Finally, what can an analysis of the emotional appeals made in an essay tell us? First, it can clarify a complex argument by helping us separate the emotional appeals from the logical ones. Focusing on the language and metaphors employed by the writer in developing an emotional appeal can help us gain emotional distance, and thus objectivity. Therefore we may begin to notice that the writer gives little solid evidence to support his claims and essentially begs the question he is trying to prove. Or we may find that the emotional language drives home a point supported abundantly by evidence and reason. Second, an analysis of the emotional language and appeals in a speech or an essay can sensitize us to the sometimes-subtle assault on our emotions made in newspapers and magazines, or over television and radio, by politicians, preachers, teachers, and radio talk show hosts (and overwhelmingly in advertisements). Studying the emotional appeals made even in a single essay can help us to understand and to arm ourselves against such assaults. Emotions are very powerful; be wary of allowing yours to be manipulated.

Activity 10.7

Read the following paragraph, and write a short analysis of the author's emotional appeal.

> And even those who do have some knowledge, or those who are disturbed by the reports of cruelty that are occasionally released by animal rights organizations, believe that all animal research is essential to human health and progress in medicine and that the suffering so often involved is a necessary part of the research. This is not true. Sadly, while some research is undertaken with a clearly defined objective that could lead to a medical breakthrough, a good many projects, some of which cause extreme suffering to the animals used, are of absolutely no value to human (or animal) health. Additionally, many experiments simply duplicate previous experiments. Finally, some research is carried out for the sake of gaining knowledge for its own sake. And while this is one of our more sophisticated intellectual abilities, should we be pursuing this goal at the expense of other living beings whom, unfortunately for them, we are able to dominate and control? Is it not an arrogant assumption that we have the right to (for example) cut up, probe, inject, drug, and implant electrodes into animals of all species simply in our attempt to learn more about what makes them tick? Or what effect certain chemicals might have on them?

Analyzing the Ethical Appeal

Besides being rational and emotional creatures, humans also are social creatures who depend on the honesty and reliability of others. Ken J. Rotenberg, Lucy R. Betts, and Pamela Qualter write the following in an article in *Psychology Today*.

> Trusting is the central issue confronting men and women in contemporary society. Close to the heart of Shakespeare's well-known phrase in *Hamlet* ("To be or not to be"), the act of being in the social world depends on a person's decisions to trust or not to trust others almost every moment of every single day. Trust is immensely wide-ranging and spans from trusting the plumber to correctly fix a tap as promised . . . to trusting one's spouse to fulfil his or her promise of fidelity ("To Trust or Not To Trust: That is the Question").

When reading an argument (or listening to a speaker), we are therefore more willing to believe those people who seem knowledgeable, honest, upright, and fair. The ethical appeal is thus, according to Aristotle, the most potent of all the means of persuasion. For writers' arguments to be effective, their ethos must be apparent in their work and realized by their readers. Simply because a writer presents an argument, even with sincerity or emotion mixed in, does not mean that she can expect the reader's assent, or even attention.

However, the way a writer combines the rational and emotional appeals contributes to his ethos in an essay, and although the ethical appeal is not restricted by any given specific rules or qualities, certain components can be discussed. For a writer or speaker to be convincing, he must make apparent to the audience his *good sense*, *goodwill*, and *good moral character*.

Good sense suggests that the writer is capable of making practical decisions and choosing the proper means to achieve an end. It must be apparent to the reader that the writer is confident in his argument and that it is presented in the proper perspective.

Goodwill, the second component, consists in the writer's making clear to his audience that he has nothing but goodwill toward them, that he has their best interests in mind. He must demonstrate that he shares his readers' basic aspirations, and that he shares, too, their sense of decency and honesty. In other words, writer and reader are on the same side.

Good moral character is demonstrated if the writer convinces his audience that he would not deceive them and that he genuinely knows right from wrong. To acquire this trust, the writer must be believable.

How do writers and speakers achieve these goals? First, they show that they know a lot about the subject they are discussing. They may reveal their credentials (their college degrees or their current professions, for example), they may discuss the research they themselves have done or present a wide range of research conducted by others (up-to-date research, of course), or they may provide convincing examples and other support for their generalizations and conclusions. Second, they may show their *thoroughness* by their consideration of all relevant material and points of view that have a bearing on their subject. Finally, they may show their *fairness* by considering opposing points of view and differing interpretations of the facts, by discussing those other positions courteously, and by acknowledging the strengths of those positions where reason demands they should. Ultimately, they want their readers or listeners to believe that they, themselves, are upstanding and credible people who can be believed and who have the welfare of their audience at heart.

Keep in mind that the ethical appeal emerges throughout the essay. It is not something a writer merely inserts in his introduction or between paragraphs. A writer's ethos develops as he makes clear to the reader the possession of all three of the components: the heart is genuine, the intentions good, and the recommendations worthy of the reader's attention.

Writers, like trial lawyers, must convince their audiences to give them fair hearings. While it is a popular cliché that "facts speak for themselves," we should be mature enough to realize that they don't; they must be given a voice and a context by a speaker or a writer, and that voice shapes the way we understand the facts.

Core Values. In addition to expressing good sense, goodwill, and good moral character, writers also express certain basic values. Many of these values, for example the idea of "fair play," have evolutionary roots. For example, Sarah Brosnan and Frans de Waal have studied the concept of fairness among primates, such as capuchin monkeys. (The monkeys became agitated and refused to perform a task if they saw another monkey getting more fruit for performing the same task.) Other values have cultural roots. For example, the American belief in the value of hard work and thriftiness can be traced to our Puritan ancestors in New England. And our values of freedom and individualism go back to the founders of our country, many of whom were steeped in the beliefs of the eighteenth-century Enlightenment and embodied those values in *The Declaration of Independence* and *The Constitution for the United States*. Further, social groups develop certain shared values they believe are important to group cohesiveness and effectiveness. For example, if you work, everyone's being on time every day is crucial to the success of the business, so that value is ingrained in the workers. Many businesses and institutions, such as colleges, develop lists of their "core values." Google "core values" for many examples.

An interesting template of different types of core values is presented in *Argumentation and Critical Decision Making*, now in its 8th edition, by Richard D. Ricke, Malcom O. Sillars, and Tarla Rai Peterson. They identify six basic value systems, and list positive and negative words associated with each.

Puritan-Pioneer-Peasant. The Puritan-Pioneer-Peasant value system is rooted in the idea that people have an obligation to themselves and those around them, in some cases to their God, to work hard at whatever they do. This value system takes on a moral orientation and is what most Americans refer to when they speak of the "pioneer spirit," "Puritan morality," and/or

"Protestant ethic." Some of the words associated with the Puritan-Pioneer-Peasant value system are listed below.

Positives: Activity, work, thrift, morality, dedication, selflessness, virtue, righteousness, duty, dependability, temperance, sobriety, savings, dignity

Negatives: Waste, immorality, dereliction, dissipation, infidelity, theft, vandalism, hunger, poverty, disgrace, vanity

Enlightenment. The Enlightenment value system is rooted in the idea that people find out about the universe through the power of reason. In this system, humans are perceived as basically good and capable of finding answers; people should never be restrained in matters of the mind (i.e., reason must be free); and government is an agreement among individuals to assist society in protecting inalienable rights. Some of the words associated with the Enlightenment value system are as follows.

Positives: Freedom, science, nature, rationality, democracy, fact, liberty, individualism, knowledge, intelligence, reason, natural rights, natural laws, progress.

Negatives: Ignorance, inattention, thoughtlessness, error, indecision, irrationality, dictatorship, fascism, book burning, falsehood, regression

Progressive. The progressive value system is rooted in the idea that progress is inherently good—that progress continually makes things get better. Some of the words associated with the progressive value system are as follows.

Positives: Practicality, efficiency, change, improvement, science, future, modern, progress, evolution

Negatives: Old-fashioned, regressive, impossible, backward

Transcendental. The transcendental value system is rooted in the idea that intuition, as a way of knowing, is a faculty higher than reason (i.e., intuition and emotion transcend reason). In this system, an emphasis exists on humanitarian values, the centrality of love for others, and the importance of feelings. Some of the words associated with the transcendental value system are as follows.

Positives: Humanitarian, individualism, respect, intuition, truth, equality, sympathetic, affection, feeling, love, sensitivity, emotion, personal kindness, compassion, brotherhood, friendship, mysticism

Negatives: Science, reason, mechanical, hate, war, anger, insensitive, coldness, unemotional

Personal Success. The personal success value system is rooted in a highly pragmatic concern for the material happiness of the individual. This value system stresses personal achievement and success. Some of the words associated with the personal success value system are as follows.

> Positives: Career, family, friends, recreation, economic security, identity, health, individualism, affection, respect, enjoyment, dignity, consideration, fair play, personal
>
> Negatives: Dullness, routine, hunger, poverty, disgrace, coercion, disease

Collectivist. The collectivist value system is rooted in the idea of cooperative action and a perceived need to control the excesses of freedom in a mass society. Some of the words associated with the collectivist value system are as follows.

> Positives: Cooperation, joint action, unity, brotherhood, together, social good, order, humanitarian aid and comfort, equality
>
> Negatives: Disorganization, selfishness, personal greed, inequality

Therefore, to analyze the ethical appeal of an argument, we can try to determine what core values the argument expresses. Of course, rarely does an individual express only one of the above value systems; as individuals, we combine many of the above attitudes from different systems depending on our age, our knowledge, and our status.

Activity 10.8

Read either Zora Neale Hurston's "How It Feels to Be Colored Me" or Michael Jernigan's "Living the Dream," and write an analysis of its ethical appeal. What core values does the writer exhibit?

Writing the Analysis

If you are asked to write an "analysis" of an argument, you need to make a plan. First, you need to follow the steps in Chapter 2 under Active Reading (page 19), so that you thoroughly understand the argument presented. Then, to help you decide what to focus on, do the following.

1. First, find the author's thesis (claim). It may be explicitly stated, usually near the beginning of the essay, or it may be implied. If it is implied, then you need to state the claim in your own words.

2. Next, look for any qualifying words throughout the essay, particularly in the thesis. For example, such words as *seems*, *suggests*, and *indicates* weaken the force of a claim or supporting evidence, as do *many*, *might*, *some*, *probably*, and *likely*. More emphatic qualifiers, such as *all*, *every*, *always*, and *impossible* strengthen a claim—but also raise the bar for the evidence needed to prove it.

3. In addition to qualifying words, look for words that are ambiguous, that is, terms that are open to interpretation. For example, *light*, *work*, *right*, *sound*, *hot*, *solid*, *subject*, *average*, *fair*, and *value* all have multiple meanings, depending on context. Further, look for jargon words (such as *factor*, *instance*, and *condition*) that can mean almost anything.

4. Next, list the kinds and amount of evidence the author uses to support his claim. Is the evidence clear? Does he say where the evidence comes from? Review the section above on Toulmin's analysis. If the writer fails to support her claims, or if she uses colorful, emotional language, be sure to note where this occurs.

5. Does the author engage in fallacious reasoning? (See the list of fallacies in Appendix 2.)

6. Does the author consider contradictory claims? If so, does he give evidence to refute them?

7. Does the author exhibit any bias? (See the section on bias above.) In addition, ask yourself what frame of reference, context, or initial assumption the author begins from.

8. What values does the writer exhibit? (See above.)

9. What are the practical implications of the argument? Would the author, or his political party or company, benefit from following his argument/proposal?

10. Now *outline the essay*, focusing on the thesis and the major supports of that thesis (evidence, examples, explanations, extended arguments, causes, effects, and so on). Making this outline will give you a much clearer idea of the structure and scope of the essay.

11. Next, make a decision about what critical approach to take in analyzing your chosen essay. You might want to focus on the writer's use of the rational, emotional, or ethical appeals.

12. Now that you have chosen an approach, read the essay again, listing or otherwise noting examples of the types of support, instances of sound or cogent (or flawed) reasoning, or emotional language you want to emphasize in your essay.

13. Organize the material you have isolated, draw your conclusions, set up a thesis, and write your paper, providing several examples from the essay to support general observations. When you write your introduction, be sure to mention the author's full name and the complete title of the essay you are analyzing.

14. Finally, be sure you give your essay a precise, descriptive title, such as "The Emotional Appeal in Jane Goodall's 'Some Thoughts on the Exploitation of Non-Human Animals.'"

In addition, keep in mind that your reader, while she may be familiar with the text you are analyzing, will not be as familiar with it as you are. (You have just spent a great deal of time working on it.) Therefore, you must guide her through your analysis carefully.

Reminder

1. Be sure that you have an analytical thesis and not a descriptive one. A critical thesis is one that states an *evaluation or judgment* of an essay based on your analysis of it. For example: *In "Some Thoughts on the Exploitation of Non-Human Animals," Jane Goodall mounts a strong emotional appeal by using highly connotative language, vivid figures of speech, and an effective moral analogy.* A descriptive thesis, however, summarizes what the author says and no more: *In "Some Thoughts on the Exploitation of Non-Human Animals," Jane Goodall says that experimenting on animals, even if it benefits humans, is morally wrong.* This thesis will lead the writer merely to summarize what Goodall *says* in her essay; it provides no *analysis* of what she says nor indicates what approach the critical analysis will take.

2. Keep in mind that assertions are not arguments but judgments; they must be supported with details and examples drawn from the essay. For example, if you say that Goodall engages in fallacious reasoning, you must name the fallacies she uses and give examples of them drawn from the text. You must also tie in what the author says to the point you are making. Don't say merely that "Goodall uses emotionally charged words, such as 'concentration camps,' 'suffering,' and 'heartless monsters.'" Instead, for example, say that "Goodall's use of words and phrases such as 'concentration camps,' 'suffering,' and 'heartless monsters' helps to develop her emotional appeal by causing the reader to think of scientists as cruel and inhuman."

3. Never use such phrases as "It is my opinion that . . ." or "I believe that . . . ." A critical analysis is written from a third-person, objective point of view.

4. Do not write about your chosen essay in the past tense; use the historical present: not "Goodall *said*," but "Goodall *says*."

Analyzing Visual Arguments

Many of the strategies used to analyze written or oral arguments can also be used to analyze visual arguments, especially those contained in advertisements, political cartoons, and photographs found in newspapers, promotions, and public service announcements. Because visuals are meant to be interpreted by an audience for one reason or another—to persuade, to sell, to inform, to entertain—we can address them analytically and critically. Because visual messages are different in kind from textual ones (although many visuals contain text), we must use additional tools to analyze them depending on our specific purposes and what types of visuals we are examining. The criteria you use when analyzing a visual include the standard components of context (situation), purpose, audience, and voice/image of the visual's designer/sponsor. In addition, as you read earlier in this chapter, the three appeals—emotional, ethical, and logical—often play a major role in the presentation and effectiveness of a persuasive message. With visual arguments, however, you should also consider the roles played by color, space, layout/design, social/cultural contexts, and the relationship between the visual elements and the message conveyed.

Advertisements

These are the most abundant of these three forms of visual texts. Since their obvious purpose is to sell a concept, idea, or product to a designated audience, specific rhetorical strategies are often used. When examining an advertisement for the purpose of rhetorical analysis, consider the following:

What is being advertised, and for what audience?

What is the sponsor's purpose? Is the purpose to support a claim, sell a product, emphasize a written text?

What general impression do you have of the visual? Is it eye-catching, funny, offbeat?

Does color contribute to the purpose/effect? How does color create the mood of the visual? Do the colors function symbolically or exist more to draw the viewer's attention to an intended focus?

What is the central focal point? Does it immediately attract your attention?

Does the design play a role in the message? For example, does either the background or foreground contribute more or less to the message? Is there an obvious omission of anything one would normally expect in such an ad?

Are people in the ad? Does their ethnic or socioeconomic status play a role in the ad's message? What is their age? Gender? How are these elements related to the overall message?

What emotions are evoked in the ad? How does the ad's text reflect upon the sponsor's image? Is an appeal to reason a part of the text?

Is the written text tied into the overall visual effect? Which is most prominent, the visual or the text?

Can you find additional elements? How do they contribute to the visual?

Photographs

Images highlight what the designer or editor of a story determines to be most important—as our eyes will naturally focus on the picture before engaging the text. Because photographs are frozen moments of time, they help us grasp the immediacy of a situation, whether they accompany a text or stand alone. For example, *National Geographic* magazine is famous for its photographs depicting people and places around the world. In *National Geographic*, it is the full-page pictures that capture our attention. Here, the text supplements the photographs. In other magazines, such as *Scientific American* or *Harper's*, the photographs serve to illustrate the text. So the size and placement of photographs can help us determine the purpose they serve in the overall context of the presentation. In addition, as we look at a photographic image, we can draw inferences about not only what is represented in the image but also what is left out. For example, in a story about protests that led to violence, do the photographs only show people throwing rocks at police and burning cars, or do they only show people being beaten or bleeding on the sidewalk? When examining a photograph for the purpose of rhetorical analysis, consider the following.

What figures appear in the photo? Can you identify their age, ethnicity, social class, profession? Do any of these elements contribute to the visual's meaning?

Do the figures' facial expressions or appearance suggest interpretations consistent with the apparent message of the photo? Does the image express the meaning better than words could?

Does the image suggest what scene preceded the moment captured in the photo? How about what followed?

What seems to be the primary purpose of the message posed by the photo? What specific details lend to the meaning?

Does the photograph have a sponsor? How does the sponsor's relationship to the content itself influence your perception of the photograph?

What is your general impression of the message conveyed by the visual? Does any bias seem apparent in the image? Is there a caption? If so, does it effectively add to or help explain the image?

What is the social or cultural context of the image? How is it linked to the message and/or purpose?

What rhetorical appeals are present in the photo?

Does color contribute to the interpretation of the message?

What is the prevailing tone of the image? Is it consistent with the intended message?

Cartoons

The combination of drawn figures and textual captions sometimes also include what are called speech bubbles or word balloons. They normally appear in the opinion pages of newspapers, in magazines, and on various websites. One of the Pulitzer Prizes (one of fourteen Pulitzer Prizes) given every year is for Editorial Cartooning. As the definition implies, political cartoons can be biased. They take sides on current events, national and international, and present a specific viewpoint—liberal, conservative, Democrat, Republican. Some cartoons, however, such as those in *The New Yorker*, simply present a wry or humorous take on contemporary life. (Simply Google "political cartoons" or "*New Yorker* cartoons," and hit the Images button.) When examining a cartoon for the purpose of rhetorical analysis, consider the following.

What is the general context of the visual?

What current event or events led up to the cartoon?

Where did it appear (The *New York Times, Huffington Post, American Rifleman . . .*)?

Can you identify each character or symbol present in the visual?

Are lines spoken in word balloons? How do the words relate to the overall message of the cartoon?

Is there a caption? What is its tone (satiric, patriotic, ironic, humorous . . .)?

Does the cartoon address a specific political or social event, or is it directed at a specific person or group?

Does the cartoon present a specific position or ideology? For example, would you characterize it as liberal, conservative, probusiness, prolabor, pro-Democrat, pro-Republican . . .)?

Who is the cartoon's intended audience?

Is the cartoonist's message clear? Successful? Partisan?

What does the visual make you feel or think?

What specific details of the cartoon stand out in your mind? How is each related to the message?

All three of these visual genres are arguments and therefore are subject to rhetorical scrutiny and analysis just as is written discourse. So remember to bring your knowledge of rhetoric, with its general elements and appeals, to bear on visual texts as well. You are not limited to the general questions listed above. They are only queries that will allow you to initiate a more fully developed response in time. The answers you derive from these questions will provide the substance for your own argumentative claims in your analysis of the visual. Examining all these details can also help you understand the powerful effect visuals have on all of us.

Analysis of an Advertisement

Examine Figure 10.2, a public service announcement (PSA), looking carefully at all the details.

Figure 10.2: PSA

Now that you have familiarized yourself with the ad, ask yourself the following questions:

What is your immediate reaction to the visual?

What is the dominant image in the visual? The rhetorical situation?

What is its explicit message?

Is there an implied message? What is it?

What text is provided? **Does it complement the visual?**

Does the design play a role in the message? **Does it immediately attract your attention?**

What rhetorical appeals are used in the visual?

The visual evokes horror at what is about to happen—a tragic event. An automobile is about to strike a child because the driver is distracted by his cell phone and the conversation he is having with the adult passenger sitting next to him. The unstated but implied message is that distractions while driving can result in accidents or death.

The main textual message, "THINK OF BOTH SIDES," urges the audience to be as attentive and protective of children outside the automobile as they are with children in the car. An additional cautionary passage at the bottom of the ad reads: "The number of car accidents involving children increases during school holidays. Please be extremely careful." The advertiser/sponsor reiterates that drivers must be especially aware of other children, just as they are protective of their own.

The design of the ad contributes immensely to the message. Note how the focal point—the two children's faces—is the first and most dominant image the audience sees. Being in the center of the frame, with its divided facial depictions and apparent contrast between facial expressions of horror and calm, this focal point sets the mood and tone of the ad. This double image is supported by the caption that states "THINK OF BOTH SIDES," bringing together the written text and the overall visual effect. Note, too, the colors—except for the words "BOTH SIDES" in red letters—are generally muted, which helps direct our focus to the images in the center. The completely faded background is contrasted with the subtle blues and flesh colors in the foreground, again drawing attention to the red letters and two distinct expressions in the center. The adults in the ad appear to be parents whose child is securely placed in his or her own seat in the rear of the car. The parents' distracted focus on each other, a map, and a conversation on a cell phone speak to the potential dangers while driving and failing to observe what is occurring outside the car.

Aside from the obvious emotional appeal for the well-being of our children, the sponsor's ethos is apparent through the general regard for parental awareness and especially the safety of schoolchildren everywhere. The sponsor gains nothing from its ad other than trying to make the world a safer place, which is certainly a demonstration of goodwill. In addition, the implied syllogism—"Distracted drivers kill people; this driver is distracted; therefore, this driver kills people"—suggests support for both the visual and textual messages of the ad.

Additional information can be derived from further examination of the details, but the responses to the questions above should get you started on your path toward a thorough analysis. For example, how does symmetry and contrast play a role in the design? What do the differing facial expressions contribute to the message's impact? And what specific audience is being targeted? Once you have exhausted your question/response process, gather the information you have collected, and begin to group that information into an informal outline for your analysis. For example, your initial outline might look like the following.

Thesis: (Formulate a thesis based on the information you've discovered from the visual.)

I.   Message/purpose of the ad

II. Impressions of the design and effects of the visual

III. Rhetorical appeals used in the ad and their effectiveness

Activity 10.9

Look at the photo below. As a group, decide on answers to the questions listed under "Analyzing Visual Arguments." Next, draw a conclusion about the effectiveness of the ad. Now, individually, write an extended paragraph discussing the ad's effectiveness and appeal.

Letter From Birmingham Jail

Martin Luther King, Jr.

The Reverend Martin Luther King Jr.'s "Letter from Birmingham Jail" is a classic example of argumentative and persuasive writing. It was written in response to a statement by eight clergymen urging the withdrawal of support for the civil rights movement orchestrated by King and other leaders. When you read King's letter, look especially at his use of the ethical, emotional, and logical appeals (both induction and deduction). Also consider the four elements of rhetoric—situation, voice, purpose, and audience. You should discover through your examination of this letter why King is considered one of history's foremost speakers/writers. King's letter is preceded by the statement to which his letter is a reply.

King's letter is famous not only for its message and argument as well as its rational appeal, but also for its rhetoric, its emotional appeal. And strongly woven throughout the text is King's ethical appeal. After all, it is written from jail, where a man working to liberate his people has been unjustly placed. Study this essay, and highlight passages that illustrate King's use of the three appeals. Yes, it is long, but it is well worth the effort.

April 16, 1963
Public Statement By Eight Alabama Clergymen
April 12, 1963

We the undersigned clergymen are among those who, in January, issued "An Appeal for Law and Order and Common Sense," in dealing with racial problems in Alabama. We expressed understanding that honest convictions in racial matters could properly be pursued in the courts, but urged that decisions of those courts should in the meantime be peacefully obeyed.

Since that time there had been some evidence of increased forbearance and a willingness to face facts. Responsible citizens have undertaken to work on various problems which cause racial friction and unrest. In Birmingham, recent public events have given indication that we all have opportunity for a new and constructive and realistic approach to racial problems.

However, we are now confronted by a series of demonstrations by some of our Negro citizens, directed and led in part by outsiders. We recognize the natural impatience of people who feel that their hopes are slow in being realized. But we are convinced that these demonstrations are unwise and untimely.

We agree rather with certain local Negro leadership which has called for honest and open negotiation of racial issues in our area. And we believe this kind of facing of issues can best be accomplished by citizens of our own metropolitan area, white and Negro, meeting with their knowledge and experience of the local situation. All of us need to face that responsibility and find proper channels for its accomplishment.

Just as we formerly pointed out that "hatred and violence have no sanction in our religious and political traditions," we also point out that such actions as incite to hatred and violence, however technically peaceful those actions may be, have not contributed to the resolution of our local problems. We do not believe that these days of new hope are days when extreme measures are justified in Birmingham.

We commend the community as a whole, and the local news media and law enforcement officials in particular, on the calm manner in which these demonstrations have been handled. We urge the public to continue to show restraint should the demonstrations continue, and the law enforcement officials to remain calm and continue to protect our city from violence.

We further strongly urge our own Negro community to withdraw support from these demonstrations, and to unite locally in working peacefully for a better Birmingham. When rights are consistently denied, a cause should be pressed in the courts and in negotiations among local leaders, and not in the streets. We appeal to both our white and Negro citizenry to observe the principles of law and order and common sense.

King's Reply

My Dear Fellow Clergymen:

While confined here in the Birmingham city jail, I came across your recent statement calling my present activities "unwise and untimely." Seldom do I pause to answer criticism of my work and ideas. If I sought to answer all the criticisms that cross my desk, my secretaries would have little time for anything other than such correspondence in the course of the day, and I would have no time for constructive work. But since I feel that you are men of genuine good will and that your criticisms are sincerely set forth, I want to try to answer your statement in what I hope will be patient and reasonable terms.

I think I should indicate why I am here in Birmingham, since you have been influenced by the view which argues against "outsiders coming in." I have the honor of serving as president of the Southern Christian Leadership Conference, an organization operating in every southern state, with headquarters in Atlanta, Georgia. We have some eighty-five affiliated organizations across the South, and one of them is the Alabama Christian Movement for Human Rights. Frequently we share staff, educational and financial resources with our affiliates. Several months ago the affiliate here in Birmingham asked us to be on call to engage in a nonviolent direct action program if such were deemed necessary. We readily consented, and when the hour came we lived up to our promise. So I, along with several members of my staff, am here because I was invited here. I am here because I have organizational ties here.

But more basically, I am in Birmingham because injustice is here. Just as the prophets of the eighth century B.C. left their villages and carried their "thus saith the Lord" far beyond the boundaries of their home towns, and just as the Apostle Paul left his village of Tarsus and carried the gospel of Jesus Christ to the far corners of the Greco Roman world, so am I compelled to carry the gospel of freedom beyond my own home town. Like Paul, I must constantly respond to the Macedonian call for aid.

Moreover, I am cognizant of the interrelatedness of all communities and states. I cannot sit idly by in Atlanta and not be concerned about what happens in Birmingham. Injustice anywhere is a threat to justice everywhere. We are caught in an inescapable network of mutuality, tied in a single garment of destiny. Whatever affects one directly, affects all indirectly. Never again can we afford to live with the narrow, provincial "outside agitator" idea. Anyone who lives inside the United States can never be considered an outsider anywhere within its bounds.

You deplore the demonstrations taking place in Birmingham. But your statement, I am sorry to say, fails to express a similar concern for the conditions that brought about the demonstrations. I am sure that none of you would want to rest content with the superficial kind of social analysis that deals merely with effects and does not grapple with underlying causes. It is unfortunate that demonstrations are taking place in Birmingham, but it is even more unfortunate that the city's white power structure left the Negro community with no alternative.

In any nonviolent campaign there are four basic steps: collection of the facts to determine whether injustices exist; negotiation; self purification; and direct action. We have gone through all these steps in Birmingham. There can be no gainsaying the fact that racial injustice engulfs this community. Birmingham is probably the most thoroughly segregated city in the United States. Its ugly record of brutality is widely known. Negroes have experienced grossly unjust treatment in the courts. There have been more unsolved bombings of Negro homes and churches in Birmingham than in any other city in the nation. These are the hard, brutal facts of the case. On the basis of these conditions, Negro leaders sought to negotiate with the city fathers. But the latter consistently refused to engage in good-faith negotiation.

Then, last September, came the opportunity to talk with leaders of Birmingham's economic community. In the course of the negotiations, certain promises were made by the merchants—for example, to remove the stores' humiliating racial signs. On the basis of these promises, the Reverend Fred Shuttlesworth and the leaders of the Alabama Christian Movement for Human Rights agreed to a moratorium on all demonstrations. As the weeks and months went by, we realized that we were the victims of a broken promise. A few signs, briefly removed, returned; the others remained.

As in so many past experiences, our hopes had been blasted, and the shadow of deep disappointment settled upon us. We had no alternative except to prepare for direct action, whereby we would present our very bodies as a means of laying our case before the conscience of the local and the national community. Mindful of the difficulties involved, we decided to undertake a process of self purification. We began a series of workshops on nonviolence, and we repeatedly asked ourselves: "Are you able to accept blows without retaliating?" "Are you able to endure the ordeal of jail?" We decided to schedule our direct action program for the Easter season, realizing that except for Christmas, this is the main shopping period of the year. Knowing that a strong economic-withdrawal program would be the byproduct of direct action, we felt that this would be the best time to bring pressure to bear on the merchants for the needed change.

Then it occurred to us that Birmingham's mayoral election was coming up in March, and we speedily decided to postpone action until after election day. When we discovered that the Commissioner of Public Safety, Eugene "Bull" Connor, had piled up enough votes to be in the run off, we decided again to postpone action until the day after the run off so that the demonstrations could not be used to cloud the issues. Like many others, we waited to see Mr. Connor defeated, and to this end we endured postponement after postponement. Having aided in this community need, we felt that our direct action program could be delayed no longer.

You may well ask: "Why direct action? Why sit ins, marches and so forth? Isn't negotiation a better path?" You are quite right in calling for negotiation. Indeed, this is the very purpose of direct action. Nonviolent direct action seeks to create such a crisis and foster such a tension that a community which has constantly refused to negotiate is forced to confront the issue. It seeks so to dramatize the issue that it can no longer be ignored. My citing the creation of tension as part of the work of the nonviolent resister may sound rather shocking. But I must confess that I am not afraid of the word "tension." I have earnestly opposed violent tension, but there is a type of constructive, nonviolent tension which is necessary for growth. Just as Socrates felt that it was necessary to create a tension in the mind so that individuals could rise from the bondage of myths and halftruths to the unfettered realm of creative analysis and objective appraisal, so must we see the need for nonviolent gadflies to create the kind of tension in society that will help men rise from the dark depths of prejudice and racism to the majestic heights of understanding and brotherhood.

The purpose of our direct action program is to create a situation so crisis packed that it will inevitably open the door to negotiation. I therefore concur with you in your call for negotiation. Too long has our beloved Southland been bogged down in a tragic effort to live in monologue rather than dialogue.

One of the basic points in your statement is that the action that I and my associates have taken in Birmingham is untimely. Some have asked: "Why didn't you give the new city administration time to act?" The only answer that I can give to this query is that the new Birmingham administration must be prodded about as much as the outgoing one, before it will act. We are sadly mistaken if we feel that the election of Albert Boutwell as mayor will bring the millennium to Birmingham. While Mr. Boutwell is a much more gentle person than Mr. Connor, they are both segregationists, dedicated to maintenance of the status quo. I have hope that Mr. Boutwell will be reasonable enough to see the futility of massive resistance to desegregation. But he will not see this without pressure from devotees of civil rights. My friends, I must say to you that we have not made a single gain in civil rights without determined legal and nonviolent pressure. Lamentably, it is an historical fact that privileged groups seldom give up their privileges voluntarily. Individuals may see the moral light and voluntarily give up their unjust posture; but, as Reinhold Niebuhr has reminded us, groups tend to be more immoral than individuals.

We know through painful experience that freedom is never voluntarily given by the oppressor; it must be demanded by the oppressed. Frankly, I have yet to engage in a direct action campaign that was "well timed" in the view of those who have not suffered unduly from the disease of segregation. For years now I have heard the word "Wait!" It rings in the ear of every Negro with piercing familiarity. This "Wait" has almost always meant "Never." We must come to see, with one of our distinguished jurists, that "justice too long delayed is justice denied."

We have waited for more than 340 years for our constitutional and God-given rights. The nations of Asia and Africa are moving with jetlike speed toward gaining political independence, but we still creep at horse-and-buggy pace toward gaining a cup of coffee at a lunch counter. Perhaps it is easy for those who have never felt the stinging darts of segregation to say, "Wait." But when you have seen vicious mobs lynch your mothers and fathers at will and drown your sisters and brothers at whim; when you have seen hate-filled policemen curse, kick and even kill your black brothers and sisters; when you see the vast majority of your twenty million Negro brothers smothering in an airtight cage of poverty in the midst of an affluent society; when you suddenly find your tongue twisted and your speech stammering as you seek to explain to your six-year-old daughter why she can't go to the public amusement park that has just been advertised on television, and see tears welling up in her eyes when she is told that Funtown is closed to colored children, and see ominous clouds of inferiority beginning to form in her little mental sky, and see her beginning to distort her personality by developing an unconscious bitterness toward white people; when you have to concoct an answer for a five-year-old son who is asking: "Daddy, why do white people treat colored people so mean?"; when you take a cross county drive and find it necessary to sleep night after night in the uncomfortable corners of your automobile because no motel will accept you; when you are humiliated day in and day out by nagging signs reading "white" and "colored"; when your first name becomes "nigger," your middle name becomes "boy" (however old you are) and your last name becomes "John," and your wife and mother are never given the respected title "Mrs."; when you are harried by day and haunted by night by the fact that you are a Negro, living constantly at tiptoe stance, never quite knowing what to expect next, and are plagued with inner fears and outer resentments; when you are forever fighting a degenerating sense of "nobodi-ness"—then you will understand why we find it difficult to wait. There comes a time when the cup of endurance runs over, and men are no longer willing to be plunged into the abyss of despair. I hope, sirs, you can understand our legitimate and unavoidable impatience.

You express a great deal of anxiety over our willingness to break laws. This is certainly a legitimate concern. Since we so diligently urge people to obey the Supreme Court's decision of 1954 outlawing segregation in the public schools, at first glance it may seem rather paradoxical for us consciously to break laws. One may well ask: "How can you advocate breaking some laws and obeying others?" The answer lies in the fact that there are two types of laws: just and unjust. I would be the first to advocate obeying just laws. One has not only a legal but a moral responsibility to obey just laws. Conversely, one has a moral responsibility to disobey unjust laws. I would agree with St. Augustine that "an unjust law is no law at all."

Now, what is the difference between the two? How does one determine whether a law is just or unjust? A just law is a man made code that squares with the moral law or the law of God. An unjust law is a code that is out of harmony with the moral law. To put it in the terms of St. Thomas Aquinas: An unjust law is a human law that is not rooted in eternal law and natural law. Any law that uplifts human personality is just. Any law that degrades human personality is unjust. All segregation statutes are unjust because segregation distorts the soul and damages the personality. It gives the segregator a false sense of superiority and the segregated a false sense of inferiority. Segregation, to use the terminology of the Jewish philosopher Martin Buber, substitutes an "I it" relationship for an "I thou" relationship and ends up relegating persons to the status of things. Hence segregation is not only politically, economically and sociologically unsound, it is morally wrong and sinful. Paul Tillich has said that sin is separation. Is not segregation an existential expression of man's tragic separation, his awful estrangement, his terrible sinfulness? Thus it is that I can urge men to obey the 1954 decision of the Supreme Court, for it is morally right; and I can urge them to disobey segregation ordinances, for they are morally wrong.

Let us consider a more concrete example of just and unjust laws. An unjust law is a code that a numerical or power majority group compels a minority group to obey but does not make binding on itself. This is difference made legal. By the same token, a just law is a code that a majority compels a minority to follow and that it is willing to follow itself. This is sameness made legal.

Let me give another explanation. A law is unjust if it is inflicted on a minority that, as a result of being denied the right to vote, had no part in enacting or devising the law. Who can say that the legislature of Alabama which set up that state's segregation laws was democratically elected? Throughout Alabama all sorts of devious methods are used to prevent Negroes from becoming registered voters, and there are some counties in which, even though Negroes constitute a majority of the population, not a single Negro is registered. Can any law enacted under such circumstances be considered democratically structured?

Sometimes a law is just on its face and unjust in its application. For instance, I have been arrested on a charge of parading without a permit. Now, there is nothing wrong in having an ordinance which requires a permit for a parade. But such an ordinance becomes unjust when it is used to maintain segregation and to deny citizens the First-Amendment privilege of peaceful assembly and protest.

I hope you are able to see the distinction I am trying to point out. In no sense do I advocate evading or defying the law, as would the rabid segregationist. That would lead to anarchy. One who breaks an unjust law must do so openly, lovingly, and with a willingness to accept the penalty. I submit that an individual who breaks a law that conscience tells him is unjust, and who willingly accepts the penalty of imprisonment in order to arouse the conscience of the community over its injustice, is in reality expressing the highest respect for law.

Of course, there is nothing new about this kind of civil disobedience. It was evidenced sublimely in the refusal of Shadrach, Meshach and Abednego to obey the laws of Nebuchadnezzar, on the ground that a higher moral law was at stake. It was practiced superbly by the early Christians, who were willing to face hungry lions and the excruciating pain of chopping blocks rather than submit to certain unjust laws of the Roman Empire. To a degree, academic freedom is a reality today because Socrates practiced civil disobedience. In our own nation, the Boston Tea Party represented a massive act of civil disobedience.

We should never forget that everything Adolf Hitler did in Germany was "legal" and everything the Hungarian freedom fighters did in Hungary was "illegal."

It was "illegal" to aid and comfort a Jew in Hitler's Germany. Even so, I am sure that, had I lived in Germany at the time, I would have aided and comforted my Jewish brothers. If today I lived in a Communist country where certain principles dear to the Christian faith are suppressed, I would openly advocate disobeying that country's antireligious laws.

I must make two honest confessions to you, my Christian and Jewish brothers. First, I must confess that over the past few years I have been gravely disappointed with the white moderate. I have almost reached the regrettable conclusion that the Negro's great stumbling block in his stride toward freedom is not the White Citizen's Counciler or the Ku Klux Klanner, but the white moderate, who is more devoted to "order" than to justice; who prefers a negative peace which is the absence of tension to a positive peace which is the presence of justice; who constantly says: "I agree with you in the goal you seek, but I cannot agree with your methods of direct action"; who paternalistically believes he can set the timetable for another man's freedom; who lives by a mythical concept of time and who constantly advises the Negro to wait for a "more convenient season." Shallow understanding from people of good will is more frustrating than absolute misunderstanding from people of ill will. Lukewarm acceptance is much more bewildering than outright rejection.

I had hoped that the white moderate would understand that law and order exist for the purpose of establishing justice and that when they fail in this purpose they become the dangerously structured dams that block the flow of social progress. I had hoped that the white moderate would understand that the present tension in the South is a necessary phase of the transition from an obnoxious negative peace, in which the Negro passively accepted his unjust plight, to a substantive and positive peace, in which all men will respect the dignity and worth of human personality. Actually, we who engage in nonviolent direct action are not the creators of tension. We merely bring to the surface the hidden tension that is already alive. We bring it out in the open, where it can be seen and dealt with. Like a boil that can never be cured so long as it is covered up but must be opened with all its ugliness to the natural medicines of air and light, injustice must be exposed, with all the tension its exposure creates, to the light of human conscience and the air of national opinion before it can be cured.

In your statement you assert that our actions, even though peaceful, must be condemned because they precipitate violence. But is this a logical assertion? Isn't this like condemning a robbed man because his possession of money precipitated the evil act of robbery? Isn't this like condemning Socrates because his unswerving commitment to truth and his philosophical inquiries precipitated the act by the misguided populace in which they made him drink hemlock? Isn't this like condemning Jesus because his unique God consciousness and never ceasing devotion to God's will precipitated the evil act of crucifixion? We must come to see that, as the federal courts have consistently affirmed, it is wrong to urge an individual to cease his efforts to gain his basic constitutional rights because the quest may precipitate violence. Society must protect the robbed and punish the robber.

I had also hoped that the white moderate would reject the myth concerning time in relation to the struggle for freedom. I have just received a letter from a white brother in Texas. He writes: "All Christians know that the colored people will receive equal rights eventually, but it is possible that you are in too great a religious hurry. It has taken Christianity almost two thousand years to accomplish what it has. The teachings of Christ take time to come to earth." Such an attitude stems from a tragic misconception of time, from the strangely irrational notion that there is something in the very flow of time that will inevitably cure all ills. Actually, time itself is neutral; it can be used either destructively or constructively. More and more I feel that the people of ill will have used time much more effectively than have the people of good will. We will have to repent in this generation not merely for the hateful words and actions of the bad people but for the appalling silence of the good people. Human progress never rolls in on wheels of inevitability; it comes through the tireless efforts of men willing to be co workers with God, and without this hard work, time itself becomes an ally of the forces of social stagnation. We must use time creatively, in the knowledge that the time is always ripe to do right. Now is the time to make real the promise of democracy and transform our pending national elegy into a creative psalm of brotherhood. Now is the time to lift our national policy from the quicksand of racial injustice to the solid rock of human dignity.

You speak of our activity in Birmingham as extreme. At first I was rather disappointed that fellow clergymen would see my nonviolent efforts as those of an extremist. I began thinking about the fact that I stand in the middle of two opposing forces in the Negro community. One is a force of complacency, made up in part of Negroes who, as a result of long years of oppression, are so drained of self respect and a sense of "somebodiness" that they have adjusted to segregation; and in part of a few middle-class Negroes who, because of a degree of academic and economic security and because in some ways they profit by segregation, have become insensitive to the problems of the masses. The other force is one of bitterness and hatred, and it comes perilously close to advocating violence. It is expressed in the various black nationalist groups that are springing up across the nation, the largest and best known being Elijah Muhammad's Muslim movement. Nourished by the Negro's frustration over the continued existence of racial discrimination, this movement is made up of people who have lost faith in America, who have absolutely repudiated Christianity, and who have concluded that the white man is an incorrigible "devil."

I have tried to stand between these two forces, saying that we need emulate neither the "do nothingism" of the complacent nor the hatred and despair of the black nationalist. For there is the more excellent way of love and nonviolent protest. I am grateful to God that, through the influence of the Negro church, the way of nonviolence became an integral part of our struggle.

If this philosophy had not emerged, by now many streets of the South would, I am convinced, be flowing with blood. And I am further convinced that if our white brothers dismiss as "rabble rousers" and "outside agitators" those of us who employ nonviolent direct action, and if they refuse to support our nonviolent efforts, millions of Negroes will, out of frustration and despair, seek solace and security in black nationalist ideologies—a development that would inevitably lead to a frightening racial nightmare.

Oppressed people cannot remain oppressed forever. The yearning for freedom eventually manifests itself, and that is what has happened to the American Negro. Something within has reminded him of his birthright of freedom, and something without has reminded him that it can be gained. Consciously or unconsciously, he has been caught up by the Zeitgeist, and with his black brothers of Africa and his brown and yellow brothers of Asia, South America and the Caribbean, the United States Negro is moving with a sense of great urgency toward the promised land of racial justice. If one recognizes this vital urge that has engulfed the Negro community, one should readily understand why public demonstrations are taking place. The Negro has many pent up resentments and latent frustrations, and he must release them. So let him march; let him make prayer pilgrimages to the city hall; let him go on freedom rides—and try to understand why he must do so. If his repressed emotions are not released in nonviolent ways, they will seek expression through violence; this is not a threat but a fact of history. So I have not said to my people: "Get rid of your discontent." Rather, I have tried to say that this normal and healthy discontent can be channeled into the creative outlet of nonviolent direct action. And now this approach is being termed extremist.

But though I was initially disappointed at being categorized as an extremist, as I continued to think about the matter I gradually gained a measure of satisfaction from the label. Was not Jesus an extremist for love: "Love your enemies, bless them that curse you, do good to them that hate you, and pray for them which despitefully use you, and persecute you." Was not Amos an extremist for justice: "Let justice roll down like waters and righteousness like an ever flowing stream." Was not Paul an extremist for the Christian gospel: "I bear in my body the marks of the Lord Jesus." Was not Martin Luther an extremist: "Here I stand;

I cannot do otherwise, so help me God." And John Bunyan: "I will stay in jail to the end of my days before I make a butchery of my conscience." And Abraham Lincoln: "This nation cannot survive half slave and half free." And Thomas Jefferson: "We hold these truths to be self-evident, that all men are created equal. . . ." So the question is not whether we will be extremists, but what kind of extremists we will be. Will we be extremists for hate or for love? Will we be extremists for the preservation of injustice or for the extension of justice? In that dramatic scene on Calvary's hill three men were crucified. We must never forget that all three were crucified for the same crime—the crime of extremism. Two were extremists for immorality, and thus fell below their environment. The other, Jesus Christ, was an extremist for love, truth and goodness, and thereby rose above his environment. Perhaps the South, the nation and the world are in dire need of creative extremists.

I had hoped that the white moderate would see this need. Perhaps I was too optimistic; perhaps I expected too much. I suppose I should have realized that few members of the oppressor race can understand the deep groans and passionate yearnings of the oppressed race, and still fewer have the vision to see that injustice must be rooted out by strong, persistent and determined action. I am thankful, however, that some of our white brothers in the South have grasped the meaning of this social revolution and committed themselves to it. They are still all too few in quantity, but they are big in quality. Some—such as Ralph McGill, Lillian Smith, Harry Golden, James McBride Dabbs, Ann Braden and Sarah Patton Boyle—have written about our struggle in eloquent and prophetic terms. Others have marched with us down nameless streets of the South. They have languished in filthy, roach infested jails, suffering the abuse and brutality of policemen who view them as "dirty nigger-lovers." Unlike so many of their moderate brothers and sisters, they have recognized the urgency of the moment and sensed the need for powerful "action" antidotes to combat the disease of segregation.

Let me take note of my other major disappointment. I have been so greatly disappointed with the white church and its leadership. Of course, there are some notable exceptions. I am not unmindful of the fact that each of you has taken some significant stands on this issue. I commend you, Reverend Stallings, for your Christian stand on this past Sunday, in welcoming Negroes to your worship service on a nonsegregated basis. I commend the Catholic leaders of this state for integrating Spring Hill College several years ago.

But despite these notable exceptions, I must honestly reiterate that I have been disappointed with the church. I do not say this as one of those negative critics who can always find something wrong with the church. I say this as a minister of the gospel, who loves the church; who was nurtured in its bosom;

who has been sustained by its spiritual blessings and who will remain true to it as long as the cord of life shall lengthen.

When I was suddenly catapulted into the leadership of the bus protest in Montgomery, Alabama, a few years ago, I felt we would be supported by the white church. I felt that the white ministers, priests and rabbis of the South would be among our strongest allies. Instead, some have been outright opponents, refusing to understand the freedom movement and misrepresenting its leaders; all too many others have been more cautious than courageous and have remained silent behind the anesthetizing security of stained glass windows.

In spite of my shattered dreams, I came to Birmingham with the hope that the white religious leadership of this community would see the justice of our cause and, with deep moral concern, would serve as the channel through which our just grievances could reach the power structure. I had hoped that each of you would understand. But again I have been disappointed.

I have heard numerous southern religious leaders admonish their worshipers to comply with a desegregation decision because it is the law, but I have longed to hear white ministers declare: "Follow this decree because integration is morally right and because the Negro is your brother." In the midst of blatant injustices inflicted upon the Negro, I have watched white churchmen stand on the sideline and mouth pious irrelevancies and sanctimonious trivialities. In the midst of a mighty struggle to rid our nation of racial and economic injustice, I have heard many ministers say: "Those are social issues, with which the gospel has no real concern." And I have watched many churches commit themselves to a completely other worldly religion which makes a strange, un-Biblical distinction between body and soul, between the sacred and the secular.

I have traveled the length and breadth of Alabama, Mississippi and all the other southern states. On sweltering summer days and crisp autumn mornings I have looked at the South's beautiful churches with their lofty spires pointing heavenward. I have beheld the impressive outlines of her massive religious education buildings. Over and over I have found myself asking: "What kind of people worship here? Who is their God? Where were their voices when the lips of Governor Barnett dripped with words of interposition and nullification? Where were they when Governor Wallace gave a clarion call for defiance and hatred? Where were their voices of support when bruised and weary Negro men and women decided to rise from the dark dungeons of complacency to the bright hills of creative protest?"

Yes, these questions are still in my mind. In deep disappointment I have wept over the laxity of the church. But be assured that my tears have been tears of love. There can be no deep disappointment where there is not deep love. Yes, I love the church. How could I do otherwise? I am in the rather unique position of being the son, the grandson and the great grandson of preachers. Yes, I see the church as the body of Christ. But, oh! How we have blemished and scarred that body through social neglect and through fear of being nonconformists.

There was a time when the church was very powerful—in the time when the early Christians rejoiced at being deemed worthy to suffer for what they believed. In those days the church was not merely a thermometer that recorded the ideas and principles of popular opinion; it was a thermostat that transformed the mores of society. Whenever the early Christians entered a town, the people in power became disturbed and immediately sought to convict the Christians for being "disturbers of the peace" and "outside agitators." But the Christians pressed on, in the conviction that they were "a colony of heaven," called to obey God rather than man. Small in number, they were big in commitment. They were too God-intoxicated to be "astronomically intimidated." By their effort and example they brought an end to such ancient evils as infanticide and gladiatorial contests.

Things are different now. So often the contemporary church is a weak, ineffectual voice with an uncertain sound. So often it is an arch-defender of the status quo. Far from being disturbed by the presence of the church, the power structure of the average community is consoled by the church's silent—and often even vocal—sanction of things as they are.

But the judgment of God is upon the church as never before. If today's church does not recapture the sacrificial spirit of the early church, it will lose its authenticity, forfeit the loyalty of millions, and be dismissed as an irrelevant social club with no meaning for the twentieth century. Every day I meet young people whose disappointment with the church has turned into outright disgust.

Perhaps I have once again been too optimistic. Is organized religion too inextricably bound to the status quo to save our nation and the world? Perhaps I must turn my faith to the inner spiritual church, the church within the church, as the true ekklesia and the hope of the world. But again I am thankful to God that some noble souls from the ranks of organized religion have broken loose from the paralyzing chains of conformity and joined us as active partners in the struggle for freedom. They have left their secure congregations and walked the streets of Albany, Georgia, with us. They have gone down the highways of the South on tortuous rides for freedom. Yes, they have gone to jail with us. Some have been dismissed from their churches, have lost the support of their bishops and fellow ministers. But they have acted in the faith that right defeated is stronger than evil triumphant. Their witness has been the spiritual salt that has preserved the true meaning of the gospel in these troubled times. They have carved a tunnel of hope through the dark mountain of disappointment.

I hope the church as a whole will meet the challenge of this decisive hour. But even if the church does not come to the aid of justice, I have no despair about the future. I have no fear about the outcome of our struggle in Birmingham, even if our motives are at present misunderstood. We will reach the goal of freedom in Birmingham and all over the nation, because the goal of America is freedom. Abused and scorned though we may be, our destiny is tied up with America's destiny. Before the pilgrims landed at Plymouth, we were here. Before the pen of Jefferson etched the majestic words of the Declaration of Independence across the pages of history, we were here. For more than two centuries our forebears labored in this country without wages; they made cotton king; they built the homes of their masters while suffering gross injustice and shameful humilia-tion—and yet out of a bottomless vitality they continued to thrive and develop. If the inexpressible cruelties of slavery could not stop us, the opposition we now face will surely fail. We will win our freedom because the sacred heritage of our nation and the eternal will of God are embodied in our echoing demands.

Before closing I feel impelled to mention one other point in your statement that has troubled me profoundly. You warmly commended the Birmingham police force for keeping "order" and "preventing violence." I doubt that you would have so warmly commended the police force if you had seen its dogs sinking their teeth into unarmed, nonviolent Negroes. I doubt that you would so quickly commend the policemen if you were to observe their ugly and inhumane treatment of Negroes here in the city jail; if you were to watch them push and curse old Negro women and young Negro girls; if you were to see them slap and kick old Negro men and young boys; if you were to observe them, as they did on two occasions, refuse to give us food because we wanted to sing our grace together. I cannot join you in your praise of the Birmingham police department.

It is true that the police have exercised a degree of discipline in handling the demonstrators. In this sense they have conducted themselves rather "non-violently" in public. But for what purpose? To preserve the evil system of seg-regation. Over the past few years I have consistently preached that nonviolence demands that the means we use must be as pure as the ends we seek. I have tried to make clear that it is wrong to use immoral means to attain moral ends. But now I must affirm that it is just as wrong, or perhaps even more so, to use moral means to preserve immoral ends. Perhaps Mr. Connor and his policemen have been rather nonviolent in public, as was Chief Pritchett in Albany, Georgia, but they have used the moral means of nonviolence to maintain the immoral end of racial injustice. As T. S. Eliot has said: "The last temptation is the greatest treason: To do the right deed for the wrong reason."

I wish you had commended the Negro sit inners and demonstrators of Birmingham for their sublime courage, their willingness to suffer and their amazing discipline in the midst of great provocation. One day the South will recognize its real heroes. They will be the James Merediths, with the noble sense of purpose that enables them to face jeering and hostile mobs, and with the agonizing loneliness that characterizes the life of the pioneer. They will be old, oppressed, battered Negro women, symbolized in a seventy two year old woman in Montgomery, Alabama, who rose up with a sense of dignity and with her people decided not to ride segregated buses, and who responded with ungrammatical profundity to one who inquired about her weariness: "My feets is tired, but my soul is at rest." They will be the young high school and college students, the young ministers of the gospel and a host of their elders, courageously and nonviolently sitting in at lunch counters and willingly going to jail for conscience' sake. One day the South will know that when these disinherited children of God sat down at lunch counters, they were in reality standing up for what is best in the American dream and for the most sacred values in our Judaeo Christian heritage, thereby bringing our nation back to those great wells of democracy which were dug deep by the founding fathers in their formulation of the Constitution and the Declaration of Independence.

Never before have I written so long a letter. I'm afraid it is much too long to take your precious time. I can assure you that it would have been much shorter if I had been writing from a comfortable desk, but what else can one do when he is alone in a narrow jail cell, other than write long letters, think long thoughts and pray long prayers?

If I have said anything in this letter that overstates the truth and indicates an unreasonable impatience, I beg you to forgive me. If I have said anything that understates the truth and indicates my having a patience that allows me to settle for anything less than brotherhood, I beg God to forgive me.

I hope this letter finds you strong in the faith. I also hope that circumstances will soon make it possible for me to meet each of you, not as an integrationist or a civil-rights leader but as a fellow clergyman and a Christian brother. Let us all hope that the dark clouds of racial prejudice will soon pass away and the deep fog of misunderstanding will be lifted from our fear drenched communities, and in some not too distant tomorrow the radiant stars of love and brotherhood will shine over our great nation with all their scintillating beauty.

Yours for the cause of Peace and Brotherhood,

Martin Luther King, Jr.

Topics for Writing and Discussion

1. How is King's letter a conversation? With whom? Why? When?

2. How did King's writing process reflect an inquiry of his world during the civil rights era?

3. How does King develop his credibility and authority as a writer?

4. Study the different sources King uses in the letter to support his argument. How do they connect him to his audience and lend support to the moral authority of his prose?

5. King uses all three of the classical appeals—the rational, emotional, and ethical—in his letter. Focus on one of these appeals (see Chapter 10), and write an analysis of his letter.

6. Focus on one or two paragraphs of King's letter, and write an analysis of King's style (his use of parallel structure, antithesis, and diction, for example).

7. King is justly famous for his advocacy of nonviolent political action. Today people continue his legacy by protesting in the streets against perceived abuses of power by governments and employers. Have you ever engaged in such a protest? Do you think such protests, which are sometimes disruptive of the normal activities of other people, are a legitimate means of our freedom of expression? Why or why not?

Letter to a Southern Baptist Pastor

E. O. Wilson

E. O. Wilson is a preeminent evolutionary biologist who teaches at Harvard University. His primary field is the study of ants, but he has written extensively on a wide range of subjects, including ecology, philosophy, and social issues. His latest book is *Half Earth: Our Planet's Fight for Life* (2016). The following letter is the opening chapter from his book *The Creation: An Appeal to Save Life on Earth* (2006).

Wilson's letter is a clear example of an attempt to "bridge the gap" between himself and who he conceives of as someone who would be completely at odds with what he stands for. It is an example of what is called Rogerian argument, named after the late psychologist Carl Rogers (1902-1987), who pioneered the concept of argument not as winning a debate but as resolving conflict. How does Wilson delineate the differences between himself and the Baptist minister? How does he propose a solution to those differences?

Dear Pastor:

We have not met, yet I feel I know you well enough to call you friend. First of all, we grew up in the same faith. As a boy I too answered the altar call; I went under the water. Although I no longer belong to that faith, I am confident that if we met and spoke privately of our deepest beliefs, it would be in a spirit of mutual respect and good will. I know we share many precepts of moral behavior. Perhaps it also matters that we are both Americans and, insofar as it might still affect civility and good manners, we are both Southerners.

I write to you now for your counsel and help. Of course, in doing so, I see no way to avoid the fundamental differences in our respective worldviews. You are a literalist interpreter of Christian Holy Scripture. You reject the conclusion of science that mankind evolved from lower forms. You believe that each person's soul is immortal, making this planet a way station to a second, eternal life. Salvation is assured those who are redeemed in Christ.

I am a secular humanist. I think existence is what we make of it as individuals. There is no guarantee of life after death, and heaven and hell are what we create for ourselves, on this planet. There is no other home. Humanity originated here by evolution from lower forms over millions of years. And yes, I will speak plain, our ancestors were apelike animals. The human species has adapted physically and mentally to life on Earth and no place else. Ethics is the code of behavior we share on the basis of reason, law, honor, and an inborn sense of decency, even as some ascribe it to God's will.

For you, the glory of an unseen divinity; for me, the glory of the universe revealed at last. For you, the belief in God made flesh to save mankind; for me, the belief in Promethean fire seized to set men free. You have found your final truth; I am still searching. I may be wrong, you may be wrong. We may both be partly right.

Does this difference in worldview separate us in all things? It does not. You and I and every other human being strive for the same imperatives of security, freedom of choice, personal dignity, and a cause to believe in that is larger than ourselves.

Let us see, then, if we can, and you are willing, to meet on the near side of metaphysics in order to deal with the real world we share. I put it this way because you have the power to help solve a great problem about which I care deeply. I hope you have the same concern. I suggest that we set aside our differences in order to save the Creation. The defense of living Nature is a universal value. It doesn't rise from, nor does it promote, any religious or ideological dogma. Rather, it serves without discrimination the interests of all humanity.

Pastor, we need your help. The Creation—living Nature—is in deep trouble. Scientists estimate that if habitat conversion and other destructive human activities continue at their present rates, half the species of plants and animals on Earth could be either gone or at least fated for early extinction by the end of the century. A full quarter will drop to this level during the next half century as a result of climate change alone. The ongoing extinction rate is calculated in the most conservative estimates to be about a hundred times above that prevailing before humans appeared on Earth, and it is expected to rise to at least a thousand times greater or more in the next few decades. If this rise continues unabated, the cost to humanity, in wealth, environmental security, and quality of life, will be catastrophic.

Surely we can agree that each species, however inconspicuous and humble it may seem to us at this moment, is a masterpiece of biology, and well worth saving. Each species possesses a unique combination of genetic traits that fits it more or less precisely to a particular part of the environment. Prudence alone dictates that we act quickly to prevent the extinction of species and, with it, the pauperization of Earth's ecosystems—hence of the Creation.

You may well ask at this point, Why me? Because religion and science are the two most powerful forces in the world today, including especially the United States. If religion and science could be united on the common ground of biological conservation, the problem would soon be solved. If there is any moral precept shared by people of all beliefs, it is that we owe ourselves and future generations a beautiful, rich, and healthful environment.

I am puzzled that so many religious leaders, who spiritually represent a large majority of people around the world, have hesitated to make protection of the Creation an important part of their magisterium. Do they believe that human-centered ethics and preparation for the afterlife are the only things that matter? Even more perplexing is the widespread conviction among Christians that the Second Coming is imminent, and that therefore the condition of the planet is of little consequence. Sixty percent of Americans, according to a 2004 poll, believe that the prophecies of the book of Revelation are accurate. Many of these, numbering in the millions, think the End of Time will occur within the life span of those now living. Jesus will return to Earth, and those redeemed by Christian faith will be transported bodily to heaven, while those left behind will struggle through severe hard times and, when they die, suffer eternal damnation. The condemned will remain in hell, like those already consigned in the generations before them, for a trillion trillion years, enough for the universe to expand to its own, entropic death, time enough for countless universes like it afterward to be born, expand, and likewise die away. And that is just the beginning of how long condemned souls will suffer in hell—all for a mistake they made in choice of religion during the infinitesimally small time they inhabited Earth.

For those who believe this form of Christianity, the fate of ten million other life forms indeed does not matter. This and other similar doctrines are not gospels of hope and compassion. They are gospels of cruelty and despair. They were not born of the heart of Christianity. Pastor, tell me I am wrong!

However you will respond, let me here venture an alternative ethic. The great challenge of the twenty-first century is to raise people everywhere to a decent standard of living while preserving as much of the rest of life as possible. Science has provided this part of the argument for the ethic: the more we learn about the biosphere, the more complex and beautiful it turns out to be. Knowledge of it is a magic well: the more you draw from it, the more there is to draw. Earth, and especially the razor-thin film of life enveloping it, is our home, our wellspring, our physical and much of our spiritual sustenance.

I know that science and environmentalism are linked in the minds of many with evolution, Darwin, and secularism. Let me postpone disentangling all this (I will come back to it later) and stress again: to protect the beauty of Earth and of its prodigious variety of life forms should be a common goal, regardless of differences in our metaphysical beliefs.

To make the point in good gospel manner, let me tell the story of a young man, newly trained for the ministry, and so fixed in his Christian faith that he referred all questions of morality to readings from the Bible. When he visited the cathedral-like Atlantic rainforest of Brazil, he saw the manifest hand of God and in his notebook wrote, "It is not possible to give an adequate idea of the higher feelings of wonder, admiration, and devotion which fill and elevate the mind."

That was Charles Darwin in 1832, early into the voyage of HMS *Beagle*, before he had given any thought to evolution.

And here is Darwin, concluding *On the Origin of Species* in 1859, having first abandoned Christian dogma and then, with his newfound intellectual freedom, formulated the theory of evolution by natural selection: "There is grandeur in this view of life, with its several powers, having been originally breathed into a few forms or into one; and that, whilst this planet has gone cycling on according to the fixed law of gravity, from so simple a beginning endless forms most beautiful and most wonderful have been, and are being, evolved."

Darwin's reverence for life remained the same as he crossed the seismic divide that divided his spiritual life. And so it can be for the divide that today separates scientific humanism from mainstream religion. And separates you and me.

You are well prepared to present the theological and moral arguments for saving the Creation. I am heartened by the movement growing within Christian denominations to support global conservation. The stream of thought has arisen from many sources, from evangelical to unitarian. Today it is but a rivulet. Tomorrow it will be a flood.

I already know much of the religious argument on behalf of the Creation, and would like to learn more. I will now lay before you and others who may wish to hear it the scientific argument. You will not agree with all that I say about the origins of life—science and religion do not easily mix in such matters—but I like to think that in this one life-and-death issue we have a common purpose.

Topics for Writing and Discussion

1. This essay is written as an "open letter" to a group Wilson knows is on the opposite side of the religious/scientific divide in this country. Yet he begins by stating that he, too, was raised as this hypothetical preacher was raised—as a Southern Christian. He is trying to establish common ground between them. His concern is not their differences but how they should both be concerned about nature and the fate of all the other species on earth. Do you think this approach is convincing? Why or why not?

2. Wilson says: "The great challenge of the twenty-first century is to raise people everywhere to a decent standard of living while preserving as much of the rest of life as possible." This is perhaps the major problem facing your and your children's generations. The world population today is over 7 billion, headed to 9 (some say 11) billion by 2050. The effects of human-induced climate change are already being felt, with glaciers melting and

sea levels rising, and so many species are currently going extinct that we are witnessing what some call the sixth mass extinction in earth's history. What can be done about all this? What can you, individually, do? Take any one of these large issues—population increase, climate change, species extinction—do some basic research, and write a paper on what, if anything, people of your generation might do about it. Be sure to avoid plagiarism, and cite your sources.

CHAPTER 11

Writing Arguments

When you read an essay or an argument in English, history, psychology, or any other class, you may be asked to respond to it in writing. No matter what you are specifically asked to do, you must first make an effort to understand the author's meaning and purpose, so you will need to read and annotate the argument. As you read (and reread) the essay, you will begin to form an opinion about it: you will like it, dislike it, perhaps agree with the author's point, or disagree with it—or be totally bored by it. If you are asked simply to react or respond to it, then you must organize your thoughts in some logical fashion and decide on a thesis for your own essay. In other words, you will use the techniques described in the earlier parts of this book to craft your essay.

Another possibility is that you will be asked to "agree or disagree" with the author's thesis or claim in the essay. For example, in the essay "Lifeboat Ethics: The Case Against Helping the Poor," Garrett Hardin argues that rich nations should not provide aid to poor ones because the world's resources are limited, and providing poor people with aid will cause them to have more children, eventually swamping the lifeboat of those living in rich nations. Or, in numerous essays, Peter Singer argues that animals (the nonhuman kind) should be accorded the same status as humans and should be treated as ends in themselves, rather than as "things" to be used for human benefit. In crafting your response, you must decide if you agree with the author's position, if you disagree with it, or if you agree with some points but not others. You must also say *why* you agree or disagree, in effect putting up your own argument. You will need to state clearly the author's thesis and quote from the essay, showing that you understand his argument and mentioning points that you agree with or disagree with. *But you should not attack the author or belittle his argument.* Remember, you are engaging in a rational discussion of a controversial issue. You are joining a conversation.

Traditionally, going back to the rhetoricians of classical Athens, the purpose of an argument is to persuade others to agree with the speaker's or writer's position on an issue. Logic texts emphasize the importance of argument in the discovery of truth. More recently, Carl Rogers has written that the purpose of argument is to help people understand one another "from the other's point of view." In this situation, the point is to find common ground between two positions that are polar opposites, such as the disagreement between those who oppose all abortions and those who think it is a woman's right to choose what happens to her own body.

To construct a persuasive argument, you must determine what your purpose is. Do you intend to persuade by offering a defense or an attack? Because you will be expected to argue your views in an attempt to persuade your reader to see the issues as you do, and, possibly, to act upon the views or recommendations you have prescribed, you must understand and be able to use effectively the rhetorical elements involved in writing persuasive arguments. In addition, the specific audience for your essay determines the approach you take to your argument. Next, with your purpose and audience in mind, you must take a stand on your topic, state a claim that reflects that stand, and finally provide evidence to support that claim.

Finally, if you are asked to write a "research paper" (on a topic suggested by an essay in the readings section of this book, for example), you will not only need to read the headnote and the essay included, but also research the topic further in your library's databases and online.

Whatever you are asked to do, the process involved in writing an argument includes the same elements.

First, read the material. Go through the process of thorough reading, discussed in Chapter 2 under Active Reading (page 19) in order to understand the issues involved before you begin to think about writing a response.

Second, analyze the material. Follow the procedures presented in Chapter 10. Many times students start out with a position on a current issue only to change their minds during the process. Be skeptical, examine the evidence, and look for fallacious reasoning, but don't let your own bias keep you from recognizing a strong argument.

Third, plan your essay. Once you have decided on the point you want to argue, it's time to outline and structure your first draft. Take this draft to a tutor in the Writing Center, and discuss any weaknesses you or the tutor perceive in its grammar, structure, or argument, then do a new draft to strengthen your essay.

Fourth, if you use sources, integrate them into your argument and make sure you cite them correctly. Follow the procedures presented according to the style preferred by your instructor.

Finally, write a final revision. Make whatever changes you think will strengthen your argument; you want it to be as tight and convincing as possible. If time allows, put this final draft aside for a while (a full day is best), and proofread it one last time. Be sure to turn it in when it is due!

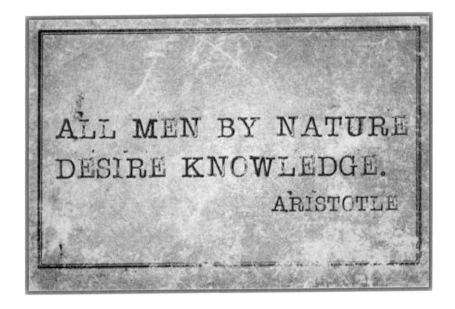

ALL MEN BY NATURE DESIRE KNOWLEDGE.

ARISTOTLE

Determining Your Audience

You must have a clear understanding of your audience. Your audience will shape a great deal of what you say and how you say it and will guide you in determining your particular approach to your topic. First, your language must be appropriate for your readers. It would be unwise to address a group of middle-school readers with complex language and reasoning, just as it would be imprudent to address a group of experts on your topic in a manner that assumes no knowledge on their part. You must always be both clear with and respectful of your audience. In addition, knowing the audience allows you to make certain assumptions in order to select the appropriate and most convincing points to be discussed. It also gives you the ability to anticipate what objections to your ideas your audience will have. Generally, you should assume that your audience is intelligent, informed about your topic, and will not only oppose your position but will likely resist it. By anticipating your audience's opposition, your stand on a given topic will be stronger and more convincing.

While argument begins in conflict, it should, ideally, end in resolution. However, because your topic is controversial, both sides believe they are right, and your opponent will probably have at least one sound argument on his side. Yet even if your readers remain unconvinced that you are right and they are wrong, you can present such a clear and coherent argument that they must admit, at least, the credibility of your position.

Activity 11.1

Read the following paragraphs from the beginning of a short article, and determine the intended audience.

> "What really interests me is whether God had any choice in creating the world."

That's how Albert Einstein, in his characteristically poetic way, asked whether our universe is the only possible universe.

The reference to God is easily misread, as Einstein's question wasn't theological. Instead, Einstein wanted to know whether the laws of physics necessarily yield a unique universe—ours—filled with galaxies, stars, and planets. Or instead, like each year's assortment of new cars on the dealer's lot, could the laws allow for universes with a wide range of different features? And if so, is the majestic reality we've come to know—through powerful telescopes and mammoth particle colliders—the product of some random process, a cosmic roll of the dice that selected our features from a menu of possibilities? Or is there a deeper explanation for why things are the way they are?

Answer the following questions.

1. What is the topic of the essay?
2. How many sentences are in the second paragraph? How many words?
3. Are there any words you would consider difficult or any words anyone in your group needs defining?
4. Does the author use any figures of speech or comparisons?
5. Do you think the paragraph is intended for men? Women? A mixed audience?
6. What sort of magazine or publication do you think this essay appeared in? For example: a peer-reviewed journal, a general science magazine, a general news magazine, a women's magazine?
7. What is the author's purpose? To persuade? Inform? Entertain?
8. Discuss your answers and those of other groups with the class.

Establishing Credibility

First, in any attempt to persuade, we must present ourselves as honest, upright, fair, and knowledgeable. This is what Aristotle called the ethical appeal. The ethical appeal is the most potent of all the means of persuasion. For writers' arguments to be effective, their ethos must be apparent in their work and realized by their readers. Simply because a writer presents an argument does not mean that she can expect the reader's assent or even attention; nor can the mere presence of sincerity bring about the desired assent. To determine the nature of the ethical appeal, one must understand that the writer's words have emotional associations as well as definite meanings. Although the ethical appeal is not restricted by any given specific rules or qualities, certain components can be discussed. For example, three major qualities of the ethical appeal illustrate how writers can reveal their character, their authenticity, through the words they choose.

For a writer or speaker to be convincing, he must make apparent to the audience his *good sense, goodwill,* and *good moral character. Good sense* suggests that the writer is capable of making practical decisions and choosing an acceptable means to achieve an end. It must be apparent to the reader that the writer is confident in his argument, that it is—in fact—correct, and that he views his topic in the proper perspective. Very simply, *goodwill,* the second component, consists in the writer's making clear to his audience that he has nothing but goodwill toward them. He must demonstrate that he shares their good intentions and basic aspirations and that he shares, too, some of their biases and prejudices, if necessary. The third component, *good moral character,* is successfully presented if the writer convinces his audience that he would not deceive them and that he genuinely knows right from wrong. To acquire this trust, the writer must be sincere and believable.

The principles of credibility one practices as a writer of arguments are the same as those one looks to when analyzing arguments. Good writers and speakers must attempt to present themselves as reasonable and trustworthy. They do this, first, by showing that they know a lot about the subject they are discussing. They may reveal their credentials (their college degrees, their current positions in government or at universities, for example), they may discuss the research they themselves have done or discuss a wide range of research conducted by others (up-to-date research, of course), or they may provide convincing examples and other support for their generalizations

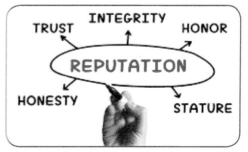

and conclusions. Second, they may show their thoroughness by their consideration of all relevant material and points of view that have a bearing on their subject. Finally, they may show their fairness by considering opposing points of view and differing interpretations of the facts, by discussing those other positions courteously, and by acknowledging the strengths of those positions where reason demands they should. Ultimately, they want their readers or listeners to believe that they, themselves, are upstanding and creditable people who can be believed and who have the welfare of their audience at heart.

Keep in mind that the ethical appeal emerges throughout the essay. It is not something a writer merely inserts in his introduction or between paragraphs. A writer's ethos develops as he or she makes clear to the reader the possession of all three of the components: the heart is genuine, the intentions good, and the recommendations worthy of the reader's attention.

Writers, like trial lawyers, must convince their audience. While it is a popular cliché that "facts speak for themselves," we should be mature enough to realize that they do not; they must be given a voice and a context by a speaker or a writer, and that voice shapes the way we understand the facts.

Activity 11.2

Read the following paragraphs from E. O. Wilson's "Letter to a Southern Baptist Pastor." Underline phrases or statements that show what you think demonstrate the writer's "good sense," "goodwill," and "good moral character." Discuss his ethical appeal with your group and the class.

We have not met, yet I feel I know you well enough to call you friend. First of all, we grew up in the same faith. As a boy I too answered the altar call; I went under the water. Although I no longer belong to that faith, I am confident that if we met and spoke privately of our deepest beliefs, it would be in a spirit of mutual respect and good will. I know we share many precepts of moral behavior. Perhaps it also matters that we are both Americans and, insofar as it might still affect civility and good manners, we are both Southerners. . . .

Let us see, then, if we can, and you are willing, to meet on the near side of metaphysics in order to deal with the real world we share. I put it this way because you have the power to help solve a great problem about which I care deeply. I hope you have the same concern. I suggest that we set aside our differences in order to save the Creation. The defense of living Nature is a universal value. It doesn't rise from, nor does it promote, any religious or ideological dogma. Rather, it serves without discrimination the interests of all humanity.

Defining Terms

Many arguments fail because the writer does not define the terms on which his essay is based. Therefore, make very clear the terms you plan to discuss. State, for example, what you mean by "affirmative action," "sexual harassment," "censorship," "pornography," "aesthetic value," or "redeeming quality." You must define any term your audience, for one reason or another, might misunderstand. Consult a dictionary, or construct your own definition based on your understanding of the term and on the manner in which you discuss the term in your argument.

Sources

Because a crucial element of persuasive argumentation is the evidence you use to support your assertions, you must pay particular attention to the sources of that evidence. Sources include reports in the media, statistics, testimonials, research, and authority. More weight is generally attributed to primary sources than to secondary sources. Primary sources include such things as original documents and eyewitness accounts. Secondary sources are those materials that are based on primary sources. For example, in a political science class you might be asked to write a paper on the freedom of religion in this country. One of your primary sources might be the Constitution itself; your secondary sources might include analyses and interpretations by historians, scholars, and legal experts of what the Constitution means. Secondary sources should be assessed in relation to whatever primary evidence is accessible. You will find that among secondary sources there is usually disagreement, which makes your task of evaluating them more difficult. Sources should be reliable, appropriate, unbiased, authoritative, and depending on your topic, current. For example, check the date of the published source, and see whether there is any material available on the author (Is she a university professor? Has he published other articles on this topic?), and find out who published the material. (Is it a university press, a political organization, a government department?) The more secondary sources you are able to accumulate, the better your chances are at arriving at some general assumptions regarding the validity of the sources you actually use.

Using Reason to Persuade

The rational appeal is one of three methods of persuasion identified by Aristotle. Since his time, it has been discussed, expanded, and analyzed by philosophers, rhetoricians, and scientists. The rational appeal employs logic to convince an audience that the writer's claims are true. In order to employ the rational appeal effectively, however, you must first understand some basic concepts and terms.

First, *logic* can be defined as a method of distinguishing between correct and incorrect reasoning. Because reasoning is represented in arguments, logic is a method for evaluating arguments. An *argument* is an organized discussion of an idea or an issue. It can proceed from a premise or several premises to a conclusion, or it can start with a claim and then give evidence to support that claim. An argument is meant to persuade its readers or listeners that the belief or position held by the arguer is true and valid. Arguments are composed of two types of claims, premises and conclusions. A *premise* is a claim stated by the arguer as evidence for the belief that he is trying to prove. Either the premise will be readily accepted by the audience as being true, or it will be necessary to devise further arguments to show that the premises of the main argument are true. The *conclusion* is the claim expressing the belief that the arguer is trying to persuade the hearer or reader to accept. In a sound argument the conclusion follows logically from the premises. Finally, a sound or cogent argument not only provides evidence that its claims are true—it also makes sure that its conclusions are *validly* drawn from its premises. An argument is valid if its conclusion is properly drawn from its premises—that is, if the established rules of logic have been followed in proceeding from premise to conclusion. To fully grasp the power of logical persuasion, you should consider taking an introductory logic course from the philosophy department. For further information on deductive logic and syllogistic reasoning, look up "Deductive and Inductive Arguments" on the *Internet Encyclopedia of Philosophy* website.

Avoiding Fallacies

A fallacy is a particular kind of defect in an argument caused by unsound or incomplete reasoning. It weakens an argument and makes it vulnerable to attack. There are two kinds of fallacies: Formal fallacies result from not following the rules of formal logic, such as not distributing the middle term in a categorical syllogism. Informal fallacies result from the ambiguity inherent in language, such as when a word is used in two different senses in the same argument, called equivocation. Of the two, the informal fallacies are more regularly employed in everyday argument. After all, normal arguments between people are conducted through language, not mathematical symbols. Therefore, not only should you be familiar with informal fallacies so you can avoid them in your own argumentative essays, you should also be able to identify your opponent's defective arguments, allowing you to refute his claims more easily. See the list of informal fallacies in Appendix 2.

Inventing Arguments

Invention is the process or method writers use to discover arguments. Aristotle divided the process into two parts, finding arguments and devising arguments from scratch. What Aristotle called *nonartistic proofs* are arguments that have already been formulated by others. We call this process *research*. Properly conducted, research will lead to an abundance of information on, and authoritative discussion of, the topic you are writing about. See below for further guidance on finding sources. *Artistic proofs*, according to Aristotle, are arguments you develop on your own; that is, they are arguments you devise through your own ability, your own art, without reference to outside sources. They include the logical appeal, the emotional appeal, and the ethical appeal (discussed in Chapter 10). Finally, Aristotle mentions *topics*, proofs grouped under common headings.

Under *common topics*, for example, Aristotle discusses such genres as definition, comparison-contrast, causal analysis, and the proper use of testimony or authority. You must determine which mode best fits the argument you are making. Under *special topics* for a deliberative discourse (arguments about what we should or should not do to achieve some desired goal), Aristotle points out that an argument can attempt to persuade the reader that a particular solution to a problem is a common good, that it is moral, just, or right. If a writer can do that, readers will more easily offer their assent. In making this kind of an appeal, a writer may refer to the following sensibilities.

- Our religious beliefs (Adultery may be condemned because it is forbidden in the Bible.)
- Our sense of fair play (We may be told that eliminating the capital gains tax will unfairly benefit the very rich, who already pay few taxes.)
- Our belief in law (We may be told that we should not smoke marijuana because it is illegal.)
- Our sense of loyalty to an ideal (It may be argued that political action committees should be severely curtailed because they are inherently undemocratic.)
- Our empathy for fellow humans (All people deserve to have food and shelter.)

Next, one can attempt to persuade readers that a particular solution to a problem will benefit them in some way. Not only may you include that quitting smoking will promote one's health, for example, because health is a common good, but it will also save one money.

In addition to the above—as always when writing—you must pay careful attention to your purpose and audience.

Organizing an Argument

Once you have gathered evidence, you will need to organize your material in a convincing way. In his *Rhetoric,* Aristotle discusses the five parts of the deliberative discourse (a discussion of what we should or should not do to bring about some future goal), only two of which, *invention* and *disposition*, are relevant to the organization of the written essay. Arguments can be organized in many ways. According to Aristotle, there are six parts, or sections, to an argument.

Introduction. In your introduction you need to supply an attention-getting opener to your topic and then a statement of your claim (the stand you intend to take).

Narration. The narration is a discussion of the background of the issue under consideration. Readers, for example, may not know that there is a problem to be solved. The amount of background material you provide depends upon the knowledge of your audience and the complexity of the issue you are dealing with.

Division. In the division you list the arguments you will advance in support of your proposition/claim.

Confirmation. The confirmation is the longest and most important part of your argument. Here you give the evidence to support your proposition/ claim (thesis) arranged in the order you have listed in the division.

Refutation. The refutation is a discussion and rebuttal of your opponents' counterarguments. See below.

Conclusion. In your conclusion make a strong appeal for acceptance of your argument.

In a face-to-face argument, you have the advantage of responding directly to an opponent. In writing, however, you lack this advantage. Therefore, you must depend on refutation when you argue ideas in writing. You can either attack what your opponent has already written or you can anticipate your opponents' arguments. You will show those arguments are, to some degree, wrong, invalid, or fallacious. Methods of refutation include (but are not limited to) pointing out your opponents' weaknesses, such as the following.

⊙ Inappropriate or inaccurate evidence

⊙ Lack of or insufficient evidence

⊙ Questionable authorities

⊙ Faulty premises

- ⊙ Vague or faulty definitions
- ⊙ Errors in deductive logic
- ⊙ Logical fallacies

For the most part, refutation involves undermining an opponent's argument. You might deny that he has proved his claim, refute the truth of his premises, or object to the inferences drawn from the premises. You might say, "I admit the truth of your conclusion, but I challenge its appropriateness in this particular instance because. . ." Let good judgment and common sense rule. Consider your audience and their emotional biases, the occasion, the subject, and your own personality to help you determine the best course of action regarding refutation.

Some instructors prefer (and some situations require) that you refute the opposition before beginning your confirmation. There is reasonable cause for such placement, especially if your opponents' views are shared strongly by your audience. However, if your opponents' arguments are weak, you can afford to delay refutation until the end of your own argument, using your discussion to build a case against your opponents' views. If your audience is hostile to your views, it might work to your advantage, psychologically, to delay your refutation until the end of your argument, to keep the direct attack of your opposition out of sight as long as possible. You need not remind your audience at the outset of your opposition, thus closing their ears to the remainder of what you have to say. By placing the refutation at the end, you may dispose your audience momentarily to hear what you have to say without compounding their hostility. Finally, you can also incorporate refutation wherever it is needed in each paragraph, rather than placing it in a separate section.

Activity 11.3

Read the following paragraph, and then plan and write a refutation of the point(s) made within it.

First, illegal immigrants are, by definition, illegal. When someone commits a crime, he should be punished. In this situation, he should be sent back across the border. Next, even "native born" children of illegals should be sent back since they were conceived by illegal parents. We don't allow thieves and extortionists to keep the money they stole, do we? Further, anyone who hires an illegal (even someone having his lawn mowed by one) should be liable to stiff penalties. Finally, police should be allowed to stop anyone they think is an illegal. Isn't that what police are supposed to do? Stop crimes from being committed?

While this format is the standard method of organizing an inductive essay, it offers you options in the construction of the introductory paragraph and the placement of counterarguments. Consult your instructor for guidelines and preferences.

The following is a sample outline for an inductive argument—one based on a claim or thesis derived from evidence that will be used to support it.

Sample Outline for an Argument Essay

I.   Introduction
    A.   Lead-in to your topic
        1. Startling statistic and/or
        2. Interesting example
    B.   Statement of the generalization you have reached through your research; the proposition or claim you are going to defend in your argument

II. Narration
    A.   Statement of background information to clarify your topic and to illustrate the problem you are dealing with. You might need to include here definitions of terms relevant to your argument.
    B.   Statement listing in one sentence at least three major pieces of evidence (X, Y, and Z) that support your generalization or claim

III. First major piece of supporting evidence (X) as topic sentence
    A.   Subtopic #1 supporting X
        1. Examples
        2. Statistics
        3. Authority
    B.   Subtopic #2 supporting X
        1. Examples
        2. Statistics
        3. Authority

IV and V—Y and Z—follow the pattern of III.

VI. Refutation (optional—see discussion of refutation above)
    A.   Statement of counterargument (alternative conclusion) #1
        1. Evidence #1 to refute or mitigate the force of A
        2. Evidence #2 to refute or mitigate the force of A

    B.   Statement of counterargument (alternative conclusion) #2

         1. Evidence #1 to refute or mitigate the force of B

         2. Evidence #2 to refute or mitigate the force of B

VII.   Conclusion: A strong appeal for acceptance of your generalization and/or a call to action

---

Strategic Questions

1. Have you identified your audience and adopted the appropriate voice for your audience?

2. Is your claim or thesis clear?

3. Is your purpose, or position, on the issues at hand clearly stated?

4. Did you check your premises and reasoning to make sure your argument is sound and valid?

4. Is your argument free of logical fallacies?

5. Is your representation of the facts for your argument honest and accurate?

6. Is your argument supported with adequate and convincing examples?

7. Have you organized your evidence from least to most convincing?

8. Have you accounted for the arguments of the opposition and refuted them either early in the essay, throughout your discussion, or before your conclusion?

9. Are your transitions clear and logical?

10. Does your argument make a significant contribution to your audience's understanding of the point at hand?

Activity 11.4

Take one of the following claims, or one suggested by your instructor, and research and write an argument. These claims are general ones that may be narrowed or altered as long as the resulting claim remains a part of the general issue. Follow proper documentation and formatting procedures. (Use the style preferred by your instructor.) Before writing your essay, read the student-written essay "Violent Video Games=Violent Video Gamers?" by Gelina Breaux in the *Student Examples* section.

1. Drugs [or marijuana] should be legalized.

2. A national tax should be levied on junk food.

3. The state should abolish the death penalty.

4. The sale and distribution of firearms should be severely restricted.

5. Texas should make English its official language.

6. The United States should pass a law creating a process to allow currently illegal residents to become citizens.

7. Genetically engineered foods should be banned.

8. The state should pass a law outlawing the use of cell phones in automobiles.

9. Terminally ill patients who choose to commit suicide should be allowed a doctor's assistance.

10. Affirmative action laws and policies should be abolished.

The Declaration of Independence

Thomas Jefferson and Others

Revered by many Americans, the following hallowed statement is an argument. It starts with an introduction, follows with a narration explaining the philosophical basis of a people's right to choose their own government, states a clear claim detailing the English king's attempts to establish "an absolute Tyranny over these States," follows with a long list of examples to prove the claim, continues with a short refutation, and ends with a strong conclusion.

The *Declaration*, like Lincoln's *Gettysburg Address*, makes ample use of repetition and parallelism. It is a rhetorical set piece meant both to rally the support of the colonists for the revolution as well as the support of great world powers opposed to Great Britain, particularly France. As such, it can still be profitably studied for its use of the emotional and ethical appeals as well as its obvious logical appeal.

IN CONGRESS, JULY 4, 1776

THE UNANIMOUS DECLARATION OF THE

THIRTEEN UNITED STATES OF AMERICA

When in the Course of human events, it becomes necessary for one people to dissolve the political bands which have connected them with another, and to assume among the powers of the earth, the separate and equal station to which the Laws of Nature and of Nature's God entitle them, a decent respect to the opinions of mankind requires that they should declare the causes which impel them to the separation.

We hold these truths to be self-evident, that all men are created equal, that they are endowed by their Creator with certain unalienable Rights, that among these are Life, Liberty and the pursuit of Happiness—That to secure these rights, Governments are instituted among Men, deriving their just powers from the consent of the governed,—That whenever any Form of Government becomes destructive of these ends, it is the Right of the People to alter or to abolish it, and to institute new Government, laying its foundation on such principles and organizing its powers in such form, as to them shall seem most likely to effect their Safety and Happiness. Prudence, indeed, will dictate that Governments long established should not be changed for light and transient causes; and accordingly all experience hath shewn, that mankind are more disposed to suffer, while evils are sufferable, than to right themselves by abolishing the forms to which they are accustomed. But when a long train of abuses and usurpations, pursuing invariably the same Object evinces a design to reduce them under absolute Despotism, it is their right, it is their duty, to throw off such Government, and to provide new Guards for their future security.—Such has been the patient sufferance of these Colonies; and such is now the necessity which constrains them to alter their former Systems of Government. The history of the present King of Great Britain is a history of repeated injuries and usurpations, all having in direct object the establishment of an absolute Tyranny over these States. To prove this, let Facts be submitted to a candid world.

He has refused his Assent to Laws, the most wholesome and necessary for the public good.

He has forbidden his Governors to pass Laws of immediate and pressing importance, unless suspended in their operation till his Assent should be obtained; and when so suspended, he has utterly neglected to attend to them.

He has refused to pass other Laws for the accommodation of large districts of people, unless those people would relinquish the right of Representation in the Legislature, a right inestimable to them and formidable to tyrants only.

He has called together legislative bodies at places unusual, uncomfortable, and distant from the depository of their Public Records, for the sole purpose of fatiguing them into compliance with his measures.

He has dissolved Representative Houses repeatedly, for opposing with manly firmness his invasions on the rights of the people.

He has refused for a long time, after such dissolutions, to cause others to be elected; whereby the Legislative Powers, incapable of Annihilation, have returned to the People at large for their exercise; the State remaining in the mean time exposed to all the dangers of invasion from without, and convulsions within.

He has endeavored to prevent the population of these States; for that purpose obstructing the Laws for Naturalization of Foreigners; refusing to pass others to encourage their migrations hither, and raising the conditions of new Appropriations of Lands.

He has obstructed the Administration of Justice, by refusing his Assent to Laws for establishing Judiciary Powers.

He has made Judges dependent on his Will alone, for the tenure of their offices, and the amount and payment of their salaries.

He has erected a multitude of New Offices, and sent hither swarms of Officers to harass our people, and eat out their substance.

He has kept among us, in times of peace, Standing Armies without the Consent of our legislatures.

He has affected to render the Military independent of and superior to the Civil Power.

He has combined with others to subject us to a jurisdiction foreign to our constitution, and unacknowledged by our laws; giving his Assent to their Acts of pretended Legislation.

For quartering large bodies of armed troops among us.

For protecting them, by a mock Trial, from punishment for any Murders which they should commit on the Inhabitants of these States.

For cutting off our Trade with all parts of the world.

For imposing Taxes on us without our Consent.

For depriving us in many cases, of the benefits of Trial by Jury.

For transporting us beyond Seas to be tried for pretended offenses.

For abolishing the free System of English Laws in a neighbouring Province, establishing therein an Arbitrary government, and enlarging its Boundaries so as to render it at once an example and fit instrument for introducing the same absolute rule into these Colonies.

For taking away our Charters, abolishing our most valuable Laws and altering fundamentally the Forms of our Governments.

For suspending our own Legislatures, and declaring themselves invested with power to legislate for us in all cases whatsoever.

He has abdicated Government here, by declaring us out of his Protection and waging War against us.

He has plundered our seas, ravaged our Coasts, burnt our towns, and destroyed the lives of our people.

He is at this time transporting large Armies of foreign Mercenaries to compleat the works of death, desolation and tyranny, already begun with circumstances of Cruelty and Perfidy scarcely paralleled in the most barbarous ages, and totally unworthy the Head of a civilized nation.

He has constrained our fellow Citizens taken Captive on the high Seas to bear Arms against their Country, to become the executioners of their friends and Brethren, or to fall themselves by their Hands.

He has excited domestic insurrections amongst us, and has endeavored to bring on the inhabitants of our frontiers, the merciless Indian Savages, whose known rule of warfare, is an undistinguished destruction of all ages, sexes, and conditions.

In every stage of these Oppressions We have Petitioned for Redress in the most humble terms: Our repeated Petitions have been answered only by repeated injury. A Prince whose character is thus marked by every act which may define a Tyrant, is unfit to be the ruler of a free people.

Nor have We been wanting in attentions to our British brethren. We have warned them from time to time of attempts by their legislature to extend an unwarrantable jurisdiction over us. We have reminded them of the circumstances of our emigration and settlement here. We have appealed to their native justice and magnanimity, and we have conjured them by the ties of our common kindred to disavow these usurpations, which would inevitably interrupt our connections and correspondence. They too have been deaf to the voice of justice and of consanguinity. We must, therefore, acquiesce in the necessity, which denounces our Separation, and hold them, as we hold the rest of mankind, Enemies in War, in Peace Friends.

We, therefore, the Representatives of the United States of America, in General Congress, Assembled, appealing to the Supreme Judge of the world for the rectitude of our intentions, do, in the Name, and by Authority of the good People of these Colonies, solemnly publish and declare, That these United Colonies are, and of Right ought to be Free and Independent States; that they are Absolved from all Allegiance to the British Crown, and that all political connection between them and the State of Great Britain, is and ought to be totally dissolved; and that as Free and Independent States, they have full Power to levy War, conclude Peace, contract Alliances, establish Commerce, and to do all other Acts and Things which Independent States may of right do. And for the support of this Declaration, with a firm reliance on the protection of divine Providence, we mutually pledge to each other our Lives, our Fortunes and our sacred Honor.

Topics for Writing and Discussion

1. As the preeminent founding document of the United States, *The Declaration of Independence* has been held up as a model for other people around the world "yearning to be free." However, its limited scope has also often been pointed out. For example, the famous phrase "all men are created equal" did not include slaves or women. Since that time, in the United States as well as other countries, the struggle to gain equality by all sorts of groups— women, African-Americans, minorities, and the LGBTQ community for example—has been ongoing and continues to this day. Do you think true equality for all people will ever be achieved? Further, given that different people are born with different abilities and talents, what would true equality even mean? Write an essay defining "equality."

2. To see an extreme case of what it might look like if a society demanded complete equality of its people, read Kurt Vonnegut's short story "Harrison Bergeron." (It can be found on the internet.)

3. Read the "Universal Declaration of Human Rights" on the United Nations website. Article 1 says, "All human beings are born free and equal in dignity and rights. They are endowed with reason and conscience and should act towards one another in a spirit of brotherhood." Is this statement (and the document as a whole) an adequate description of human rights? Write an analysis of this document.

CHAPTER 12

Presenting

Writers are often asked to convert their projects into presentation formats. It is commonplace, in academic circles at least, to be expected to share your ideas orally, whether with a class or with a group of fellow scholars, rather than print copies of your composition and wait while your audience reads through it. When speaking publicly, even to a small group of peers, you can organize critical parts of your research to make key points more emphatic. Presentations allow you a closer interaction with your audience, permitting you to modulate your voice and tone. Understandably, if you are unused to the process of presenting, the pressure of speaking publicly might result in a certain amount of stress and trepidation. You may have spent a considerable amount of time preparing your ideas in writing, but transferring what you have written into an oral format might strike you as an arcane practice, a work of magic, reserved solely for the naturally well-spoken.

How does a writer move from an essay to an oral presentation? The process of developing an oral speech is similar to the steps outlined in this book for writing, albeit engineered for a physical (rather than imaginary) audience. The early stages of creation (researching, inventing, and structuring) are fairly universal for conceiving of ideas to develop into projects. The stages that follow (drafting, revising, editing, and formatting), at least as outlined in these pages, are largely geared toward producing your own writing, and they are not as useful for creating presentations.

The structuring stage is the most suitable time to redevelop your ideas into an oral presentation. Outlines are useful when engineering a writing project but also when creating a framework for your talking points. The outline format will change for public speaking—you are no longer concerned as much with the shape and direction of paragraphs—because you will be designing your presentation around your key points (perhaps arrayed in a different order), assisted by visual aids. For argument's sake, let us assume you have already finished your essay and you are returning to the structuring stage to design a presentation of your work. You might consider how the remaining creative process would change (Table 12.1).

Paper		Presentation
Structuring (Essay Outline)	→	Structuring (Speaking Outline)
Drafting the Paper	→	Developing Visual Aids
Revising the Paper	→	Rehearsing
Formatting the Paper	→	Presenting

Table 12.1: Creative Process for Paper Versus Presentation

Structuring for Presentation

Much like preparing for a paper, the structural step is the most crucial step. Deciding how to anchor your audience (with an adequate introduction strategy), and then guiding them through your central points, is often the difference between a cogent presentation and one after which your audience leaves the room confused and uncertain of your topic.

Remembering that you no longer have the luxury of walking your audience through your paper sentence by sentence, you will need to repurpose your central ideas around more conversational strategies before you share them. As with the preparing of a paper, an outline is the functional standard for preparing for a presentation. As such, there are two types of functional outlines: a **keyword, or phrase-only outline**—which you might use to queue the topics you wish to cover in your speech, subordinating necessary details, and supporting facts—and a **sentence outline,** which you might use to rehearse and then perhaps even memorize for your delivery.

Whichever format you decide upon, the following example might serve as an outline frame for a presentation based upon an analysis paper.

    I. Introduction
        A. Attention Grabber/Personal Connection
        B. Research Question (*Primary Inquiry + Significance*)

   II. Key Point 1
        A. Practical Application of Key Point
        B. Supporting Research
        C. Connection to Research Question (*Significance*)

  III. Key Point 2
        A. Practical Application of Key Point
        B. Supporting Research
        C. Connection to Research Question (*Significance*)

IV. Key Point 3
    A. Practical Application of Key Point
    B. Supporting Research
    C. Connection to Research Question (*Significance*)

V. Conclusion
    A. Restatement of Importance (*Not a Summary of Research*)
    B. Forward-looking Statement

Activity 12.1

Take one of the papers you have written, and reformulate it as a presentation outline.

Note that the **introduction** needs to be modified from that of a writing outline. First, you must garner the attention of your audience. The **attention grabber** might be a startling statistic, or it might be a brief narrative explaining your personal interest in your topic. In this regard, it is more appropriate in an oral presentation to insert yourself into the conversation because you are, quite literally, sharing your research with the audience. With an oral presentation, you often will not have the same amount of time as you might with a written project. Your introduction strategy needs to swiftly but adequately *anchor your subject* while also creating a *connection* between you and the audience.

Once you have their attention, you will need to efficiently state your *primary research focus* (the information that might otherwise be found in your thesis statement). Framing this statement **as a question** could be advantageous for several reasons. For one, it is an inclusive strategy that invites the audience to participate in an exploration of your ideas, as it takes them back in time to when you first started your research, and asking your thesis as a question includes them in the discovery process. Secondly, it stimulates their curiosity. Stating your thesis as it might be written, while acceptable, is a fairly conventional approach, and you run the risk of your audience being less drawn in or interested by your ideas.

In the same way a topic sentence functions in a well-structured essay, your **key points** must be stated clearly, and there should be an implication as to their importance. Let your audience know these are key points. (And you might indicate this on your visual aid, should you be using a PowerPoint, in the header of your slides—see below.) A practical or literal discussion of your key point might be needed (what it is, how it applies to your subject). For example, in a speech on how college-age students perceive government social programs, you might have a slide with the header: "Perceptual Differences Among College Students." In discussing this slide, you might lead off by saying: "When looking  at whether college students see the benefit of government programs, there is a divide among them which is highly dependent on their socioeconomic status, ethnicity, and gender." This could serve as a lead-in to bullets that exist on the slide that make specific references to sources, statistics, or other related material. Remember that headers and bullets in presentation slides are meant to be compact, serving as prompts. However, there is an obligation to be more articulate and elaborate with oral information. This step prepares listeners to accept your supporting research and then provides context for why this matters to your overall research question.

A **conclusion** need not be a mechanical summary of what you've covered in your presentation. On the contrary, you should find a way to tie everything together and return to your thesis/main focus. Ending with a forward-looking statement, such as other areas to take the research, or the broader implications for your work, could leave the audience feeling that your presentation is part of a much larger, more important dialogue or issue.

Developing Visual Aids

When presenting your work, you will likely be afforded the opportunity to use visual aids to support your delivery.

The simplest form of visual aid is a physical sample or example. Examples might include a medical device you are discussing, a photograph, cultural relic (i.e., sample dress, flag), a poster, or scientific materials needed to complete a demonstration or experiment. These kinds of physical objects tend to be more of the "show and tell" variety, and they do not require much more forethought than displaying them at the proper time.

More standard but functional visual aids might include PowerPoint presentations (or Prezis) composed beforehand on a computer. However, this method requires you to have access to a computer and a projector to show them to your audience. These types of visual aids are common enough now that you should be familiar with them, as they can make your presentation easier for the audience to follow when done correctly.

Consider these general guidelines when composing a PowerPoint presentation.

- ⊙ Use **nondistracting colors** that are not too bright, disturbing, or difficult to read.

- ⊙ Use a **title slide** with your paper title and your name on it (much as you would provide a title page for an essay).

- ⊙ Attempt to keep text to a minimum, choosing images over print, to complement your speech. (Many prefer to abide by the **3 x 5 rule,** keeping to three lines of text with five words maximum.)

- ⊙ Attempt to keep text to a minimum, choosing images over wordy print, to complement your speech.

- ⊙ Use content (for these slides) that could serve to direct the presentation, so that you can refer to your visual aid if needed, rather than index cards or prepared speeches. (See "Rehearsing" below.)

- ⊙ Use the appropriate format (MLA, APA, Chicago) as outlined in the Formatting section of Chapter 9.

- ⊙ Use **introductory slides** that help direct your audience with necessary overview, key definitions, or critical methodology needed to understand your research.

- ⊙ Use **headers** that align with your key points to assist the audience in knowing when you are switching talking points.

- ⊙ Use **functional images** that drive forward your project (and make sure to credit the image source). Do not include decorative or otherwise functionless images (i.e., smiling babies, cats, or cartoon images, unless they are a necessary component of your research). **Charts and graphs** are often useful for displaying information visually.

- ⊙ Use proper citations for sources (when inserting quotations or statistics).

- ⊙ Use the appropriate **References or Works Cited** page as your last slide(s).

Should you not have access to a computer and projector, it might be necessary to prepare a poster with the needed visuals or even use a whiteboard. You could alternately create a "topic" outline to post on a classroom board to guide your audience through your primary points.

Activity 12.2

Prepare the first three slides of the outline you developed in Activity 12.1 in PowerPoint or Prezi.

Activity 12.3

Discuss and critique the following slide in your group or the class.

Body Paragraphs

Body paragraphs develop a single idea, each one linked to the thesis statement. Body paragraphs should be:

Unified: Everything within the paragraph should relate to the opening, topic sentence.

Coherent: Words and sentences within the paragraph should be tied together with:

   Repetition of key words and terms
   Transitional words and phrases
   Parallel sentence structures

Developed: Sufficient details and examples should be included to "prove" the point made in the topic sentence.

Rehearsing

You do not need to be trained at formal public speaking to succeed in delivering an oral presentation. However, just as the writing process requires you to revise (revisualize) your work to improve the effectiveness of your strategy, oral presentations require you to take your outline of talking points and your visual aid(s) and rehearse with them to make certain your ideas are related in the most cohesive fashion.

There are several tips and strategies you can employ while rehearsing your presentation.

⊙ You do not need to memorize a speech (though this is an accepted strategy); rather, embed key phrases and talking points into your visual aid so you can refer to them when necessary.

- Practice until you have at least retained your introduction, key talking points, and conclusion and you can elaborate upon them naturally.

- Maintain a conversational but knowledgeable tone (semiformal, not casual).

- Practice and consciously attempt to remove unnecessary "uhm"s, "uh"s, and other casual slips.

- Maintain eye contact with your audience, pivoting only to point at something of interest on your visual aid (or relocate yourself if stuck).

- Do not turn your back to your audience.

- Practice, if possible, in front of another person to get used to having an audience.

- Ask a sample audience for feedback, much as you might ask others to comment upon your writing.

- Generally, organize your key points in the same chronological order as your written essay; however, sometimes you might find it useful to reorder them and rehearse them with a different structure to find the most logical and persuasive structure.

Activity 12.4

Take the slides you prepared in Activity 12.2, and present them to your group. Ask for feedback on your presentation.

Formatting and Presenting

When you finish a writing project, you would normally format your text to make sure you are presenting your work in the appropriate convention (MLA, APA, CMS), and you should perform this step when presenting your work for an oral presentation as well. Obviously, formatting pertains primarily to a visual aid, such as a PowerPoint presentation, but it also applies should you have handouts to distribute to your audience.

You should also prepare yourself to deliver your presentation with a similar regard for professionalism. The following are some tips to consider for the day of the actual presentation.

- Dress nicely, professionally, like you would for your job or an interview.

- Introduce yourself to your audience, and state the title of your presentation (unless a moderator introduces you).

- ⊙ Consider printing a copy of your Works Cited or References page (from your actual paper) to present to your audience.

- ⊙ Relax and enjoy yourself—this is one occasion when you are the expert, sharing what you have learned.

Final Word

This final point is worth repeating and is an appropriate note on which to end this chapter. The advantage of preparation, whether in writing (which has been the thrust of this book) or presenting, is that you have created an environment where you may enthusiastically share what you have learned with an eager audience. Ultimately, this is the purpose of effective communication—to join in a conversation within a larger community of writers and thinkers and to share your ideas so they might prosper and grow in the minds of your audience.

Activity 12.5

Write a short critique of one your instructor's class presentations. Discuss what you think was effective, and offer advice on what you found confusing or difficult to understand. You are not critiquing the content here, just the presentation.

Liking Is for Cowards: Go for What Hurts

Jonathan Franzen

Jonathan Franzen is an American novelist and essayist. His novel *The Corrections* (2001) won a National Book Award and was nominated for a Pulitzer Prize. His novel *Freedom* was published in 2010, and his most recent novel, *Purity*, was released in September 2015. He writes for *The New Yorker* magazine, among others. He is well-known for his outspoken views on the state of modern society and modern literature. The following essay was adapted from a commencement speech Franzen delivered on May 21, 2011, at Kenyon College.

Franzen's discussion of the difference between loving something and merely liking it was presented before a graduating class. What marks the discussion as a speech rather than a written essay? (Keep in mind the setting, in an auditorium, before a large crowd.) For example, is the topic of the speech one that would appeal to young people like yourself just graduating from college? What about Franzen's word choice and use of examples? Is he able to connect, via empathy, with his audience? Finally, do you think he has made clear his distinction between liking and loving?

A couple of weeks ago, I replaced my three-year-old BlackBerry Pearl with a much more powerful BlackBerry Bold. Needless to say, I was impressed with how far the technology had advanced in three years. Even when I didn't have anybody to call or text or e-mail, I wanted to keep fondling my new Bold and experiencing the marvelous clarity of its screen, the silky action of its track pad, the shocking speed of its responses, the beguiling elegance of its graphics.

I was, in short, infatuated with my new device. I'd been similarly infatuated with my old device, of course; but over the years the bloom had faded from our relationship. I'd developed trust issues with my Pearl, accountability issues, compatibility issues and even, toward the end, some doubts about my Pearl's very sanity, until I'd finally had to admit to myself that I'd outgrown the relationship.

Do I need to point out that — absent some wild, anthropomorphizing projection in which my old BlackBerry felt sad about the waning of my love for it — our relationship was entirely one-sided? Let me point it out anyway.

Let me further point out how ubiquitously the word "sexy" is used to describe late-model gadgets; and how the extremely cool things that we can do now with these gadgets — like impelling them to action with voice commands, or doing that spreading-the-fingers iPhone thing that makes images get bigger — would have looked, to people a hundred years ago, like a magician's incantations, a magician's hand gestures; and how, when we want to describe an erotic relationship that's working perfectly, we speak, indeed, of magic.

Let me toss out the idea that, as our markets discover and respond to what consumers most want, our technology has become extremely adept at creating products that correspond to our fantasy ideal of an erotic relationship, in which the beloved object asks for nothing and gives everything, instantly, and makes us feel all powerful, and doesn't throw terrible scenes when it's replaced by an even sexier object and is consigned to a drawer.

To speak more generally, the ultimate goal of technology, the telos of techne, is to replace a natural world that's indifferent to our wishes — a world of hurricanes and hardships and breakable hearts, a world of resistance — with a world so responsive to our wishes as to be, effectively, a mere extension of the self.

Let me suggest, finally, that the world of techno-consumerism is therefore troubled by real love, and that it has no choice but to trouble love in turn.

Its first line of defense is to commodify its enemy. You can all supply your own favorite, most nauseating examples of the commodification of love. Mine include the wedding industry, TV ads that feature cute young children or the giving of automobiles as Christmas presents, and the particularly grotesque equation of diamond jewelry with everlasting devotion. The message, in each case, is that if you love somebody you should buy stuff.

A related phenomenon is the transformation, courtesy of Facebook, of the verb "to like" from a state of mind to an action that you perform with your computer mouse, from a feeling to an assertion of consumer choice. And liking, in general, is commercial culture's substitute for loving. The striking thing about all consumer products — and none more so than electronic devices and applications — is that they're designed to be immensely likable. This is, in fact, the definition of a consumer product, in contrast to the product that is simply itself and whose makers aren't fixated on your liking it. (I'm thinking here of jet engines, laboratory equipment, serious art and literature.)

But if you consider this in human terms, and you imagine a person defined by a desperation to be liked, what do you see? You see a person without integrity, without a center. In more pathological cases, you see a narcissist — a person who can't tolerate the tarnishing of his or her self-image that not being liked represents, and who therefore either withdraws from human contact or goes to extreme, integrity-sacrificing lengths to be likable.

If you dedicate your existence to being likable, however, and if you adopt whatever cool persona is necessary to make it happen, it suggests that you've despaired of being loved for who you really are. And if you succeed in manipulating other people into liking you, it will be hard not to feel, at some level, contempt for those people, because they've fallen for your shtick. You may find yourself becoming depressed, or alcoholic, or, if you're Donald Trump, running for president (and then quitting).

Consumer technology products would never do anything this unattractive, because they aren't people. They are, however, great allies and enablers of narcissism. Alongside their built-in eagerness to be liked is a built-in eagerness to reflect well on us. Our lives look a lot more interesting when they're filtered through the sexy Facebook interface. We star in our own movies, we photograph ourselves incessantly, we click the mouse and a machine confirms our sense of mastery.

And, since our technology is really just an extension of ourselves, we don't have to have contempt for its manipulability in the way we might with actual people. It's all one big endless loop. We like the mirror and the mirror likes us. To friend a person is merely to include the person in our private hall of flattering mirrors.

I may be overstating the case, a little bit. Very probably, you're sick to death of hearing social media disrespected by cranky 51-year-olds. My aim here is mainly to set up a contrast between the narcissistic tendencies of technology and the problem of actual love. My friend Alice Sebold likes to talk about "getting down in the pit and loving somebody." She has in mind the dirt that love inevitably splatters on the mirror of our self-regard.

The simple fact of the matter is that trying to be perfectly likable is incompatible with loving relationships. Sooner or later, for example, you're going to find yourself in a hideous, screaming fight, and you'll hear coming out of your mouth things that you yourself don't like at all, things that shatter your self-image as a fair, kind, cool, attractive, in-control, funny, likable person. Something realer than likability has come out in you, and suddenly you're having an actual life.

Suddenly there's a real choice to be made, not a fake consumer choice between a BlackBerry and an iPhone, but a question: Do I love this person? And, for the other person, does this person love me?

There is no such thing as a person whose real self you like every particle of. This is why a world of liking is ultimately a lie. But there is such a thing as a person whose real self you love every particle of. And this is why love is such an existential threat to the techno-consumerist order: it exposes the lie.

This is not to say that love is only about fighting. Love is about bottomless empathy, born out of the heart's revelation that another person is every bit as real as you are. And this is why love, as I understand it, is always specific. Trying to love all of humanity may be a worthy endeavor, but, in a funny way, it keeps the focus on the self, on the self's own moral or spiritual well-being. Whereas, to love a specific person, and to identify with his or her struggles and joys as if they were your own, you have to surrender some of yourself.

The big risk here, of course, is rejection. We can all handle being disliked now and then, because there's such an infinitely big pool of potential likers. But to expose your whole self, not just the likable surface, and to have it rejected, can be catastrophically painful. The prospect of pain generally, the pain of loss, of breakup, of death, is what makes it so tempting to avoid love and stay safely in the world of liking.

And yet pain hurts but it doesn't kill. When you consider the alternative — an anesthetized dream of self-sufficiency, abetted by technology — pain emerges as the natural product and natural indicator of being alive in a resistant world. To go through a life painlessly is to have not lived. Even just to say to yourself, "Oh, I'll get to that love and pain stuff later, maybe in my 30s" is to consign yourself to 10 years of merely taking up space on the planet and burning up its resources. Of being (and I mean this in the most damning sense of the word) a consumer.

When I was in college, and for many years after, I liked the natural world. Didn't love it, but definitely liked it. It can be very pretty, nature. And since I was looking for things to find wrong with the world, I naturally gravitated to environmentalism, because there were certainly plenty of things wrong with the environment. And the more I looked at what was wrong — an exploding world population, exploding levels of resource consumption, rising global temperatures, the trashing of the oceans, the logging of our last old-growth forests — the angrier I became.

Finally, in the mid-1990s, I made a conscious decision to stop worrying about the environment. There was nothing meaningful that I personally could do to save the planet, and I wanted to get on with devoting myself to the things I loved. I still tried to keep my carbon footprint small, but that was as far as I could go without falling back into rage and despair.

BUT then a funny thing happened to me. It's a long story, but basically I fell in love with birds. I did this not without significant resistance, because it's very uncool to be a birdwatcher, because anything that betrays real passion is by definition uncool. But little by little, in spite of myself, I developed this passion, and although one-half of a passion is obsession, the other half is love.

And so, yes, I kept a meticulous list of the birds I'd seen, and, yes, I went to inordinate lengths to see new species. But, no less important, whenever I looked at a bird, any bird, even a pigeon or a robin, I could feel my heart overflow with love. And love, as I've been trying to say today, is where our troubles begin.

Because now, not merely liking nature but loving a specific and vital part of it, I had no choice but to start worrying about the environment again. The news on that front was no better than when I'd decided to quit worrying about it — was considerably worse, in fact — but now those threatened forests and wetlands and oceans weren't just pretty scenes for me to enjoy. They were the home of animals I loved.

And here's where a curious paradox emerged. My anger and pain and despair about the planet were only increased by my concern for wild birds, and yet, as I began to get involved in bird conservation and learned more about the many threats that birds face, it became easier, not harder, to live with my anger and despair and pain.

How does this happen? I think, for one thing, that my love of birds became a portal to an important, less self-centered part of myself that I'd never even known existed. Instead of continuing to drift forward through my life as a global citizen, liking and disliking and withholding my commitment for some later date, I was forced to confront a self that I had to either straight-up accept or flat-out reject.

Which is what love will do to a person. Because the fundamental fact about all of us is that we're alive for a while but will die before long. This fact is the real root cause of all our anger and pain and despair. And you can either run from this fact or, by way of love, you can embrace it.

When you stay in your room and rage or sneer or shrug your shoulders, as I did for many years, the world and its problems are impossibly daunting. But when you go out and put yourself in real relation to real people, or even just real animals, there's a very real danger that you might love some of them.

And who knows what might happen to you then?

Topics for Writing and Discussion

1. Do you agree with Franzen's statement that "our lives look a lot more interesting when they're filtered through the sexy Facebook interface. We star in our own movies, we photograph ourselves incessantly, we click the mouse and a machine confirms our sense of mastery"? Is Facebook merely a means of communication, or is it a means of self-promotion?

2. Franzen distinguishes "liking" something or someone from "loving" the thing or person. Is his point that "to love a specific person, and to identify with his or her struggles and joys as if they were your own, you have to surrender some of yourself" true? Write a short paper in which you distinguish liking from loving another person.

3. Franzen says "to go through a life painlessly is to have not lived." What does he mean by this statement? Write a short paper in which you try to explain this statement by using examples from your own life and the lives of those you know and love.

Additional Readings

How to Tame a Wild Tongue

Gloria E. Anzaldúa

Gloria E. Anzaldúa (1942-2004) was born in the South Texas town of Raymondville. She attended Texas Woman's University and University of Texas—Pan American. In 1972 she received a master's degree in English and education from the University of Texas at Austin. After working on a doctoral degree in comparative literature at UT, she moved to California and began to write. Her most important book is *Borderlands/La Frontera: The New Mestiza* (1987), from which the following essay is taken.

"We're going to have to control your tongue," the dentist says, pulling out all the metal from my mouth. Silver bits plop and tinkle into the basin. My mouth is a motherlode.

The dentist is cleaning out my roots. I get a whiff of the stench when I gasp. "I can't cap that tooth yet, you're still draining," he says.

"We're going to *have* to do something about your tongue," I hear the anger rising in his voice. My tongue keeps pushing out the wads of cotton, pushing back the drills, the long thin needles. "I've never seen anything as strong or as stubborn," he says. And I think, how do you tame a wild tongue, train it to be quiet, how do you bridle and saddle it? How do you make it lie down?

> "Who is to say that robbing a people of its language is less violent than war?"
>
> —Ray Gwyn Smith

I remember being caught speaking Spanish at recess—that was good for three licks on the knuckles with a sharp ruler. I remember being sent to the corner of the classroom for "talking back" to the Anglo teacher when all I was trying to do was tell her how to pronounce my name. "If you want to be American, speak 'American.' If you don't like it, go back to Mexico where you belong."

"I want you to speak English. *Pa' hallar buen trabajo tienes que saber hablar el inglés bien. Qué vale toda lu educación si todavía hablas ingles con un 'accent'*" my mother would say, mortified that I spoke English like a Mexican. At Pan American University, I and all Chicano students were required to take two speech classes. Their purpose: to get rid of our accents.

Attacks on one's form of expression with the intent to censor are a violation of the First Amendment. *El Anglo con cara de inocente nos arrancó la lengua.* Wild tongues can't be tamed, they can only be cut out.

Overcoming the Tradition of Silence

Ahogadas, escupimos el oscuro.
Peleando con nuestra propia sombra
el silencio nos sepulra.

En boca cerrada no entran moscas. "Flies don't enter a closed mouth" is a saying I kept hearing when I was a child. *Ser habladora* was to be a gossip and a liar, to talk too much. *Muchachitas bien criadas,* well-bred girls don't answer back. *Es una falta de respeto* to talk back to one's mother or father. I remember one of the sins I'd recite to the priest in the confession box the few times I went to confession: talking back to my mother, Pa' tras, *repelar. Hocicona, repelona, chismosa,* having a big mouth, questioning, carrying tales are all signs of being *mal criada.* In my culture they are all words that are derogatory if applied to women—I've never heard them applied to men.

The first time I heard two women, a Puerto Rican and a Cuban, say the word *"nosotras,"* I was shocked. I had not known the word existed. Chicanas use *nosotros* whether we're male or female. We are robbed of our female being by the masculine plural. Language is a male discourse.

And our tongues have become
dry the wilderness has
dried out our tongues and
we have forgotten speech.

—Irena Klepfisz

Even our own people, other Spanish speakers *nos quieren poner candados en la boca.* They would hold us back with their bag of *reglas de academia.*

Oyé como ladra: el lenguaje de la frontera
Quien tiene boca se equivoca.

—Mexican saying

"*Pocho,* cultural traitor, you're speaking the oppressor's language by speaking English, you're ruining the Spanish language," I have been accused by various Latinos and Latinas. Chicano Spanish is considered by the purist and by most Latinos deficient, a mutilation of Spanish.

But Chicano Spanish is a border tongue which developed naturally. Change, *evolución, enriquecimiento de palabras nuevas por invención o adopción* have created variants of Chicano Spanish, *un nuevo lenguaje. Un lenguaje que corresponde a un modo de vivir.* Chicano Spanish is not incorrect, it is a living language.

For a people who are neither Spanish nor live in a country in which Spanish is the first language; for a people who live in a country in which English is the

reigning tongue but who are not Anglo; for a people who cannot entirely identify with either standard (formal, Castillian) Spanish nor standard English, what
recourse is left to them but to create their own language? A language which they
can connect their identity to, one capable of communicating the realities and
values true to themselves—a language with terms that are neither *español ni
inglés,* but both. We speak a patois, a forked tongue, a variation of two languages.

Chicano Spanish sprang out of the Chicanos' need to identify ourselves as a
distinct people. We needed a language with which we could communicate with
ourselves, a secret language. For some of us, language is a homeland closer than
the Southwest—for many Chicanos today live in the Midwest and the East. And
because we are a complex, heterogeneous people, we speak many languages.
Some of the languages we speak are:

1.   Standard English
2.   Working class and slang English
3.   Standard Spanish
4.   Standard Mexican Spanish
5.   North Mexican Spanish dialect
6.   Chicano Spanish (Texas, New Mexico, Arizona, and California have regional
     variations)
7.   Tex-Mex
8.   *Pachuco* (called *caló*)

My "home" tongues are the languages I speak with my sister and brothers,
with my friends. They are the last five listed, with 6 and 7 being closest to my
heart. From school, the media, and job situations, I've picked up standard and
working class English. From Mamagrande Locha and from reading Spanish
and Mexican literature, I've picked up Standard Spanish and Standard Mexican
Spanish. From *los recién llegados,* Mexican immigrants, and *braceros,* I learned
the North Mexican dialect. With Mexicans I'll try to speak either Standard
Mexican Spanish or the North Mexican dialect. From my parents and Chicanos
living in the Valley, I picked up Chicano Texas Spanish, and I speak it with my
mom, younger brother (who married a Mexican and who rarely mixes Spanish
with English), aunts, and older relatives.

With Chicanas from *Nuevo México* or *Arizana* I will speak Chicano Spanish
a little, but often they don't understand what I'm saying. With most California
Chicanas I speak entirely in English (unless I forget). When I first moved to San
Francisco, I'd rattle off something in Spanish, unintentionally embarrassing them.
Often it is only with another Chicana *tejana* that I can talk freely.

Words distorted by English are known as anglicisms or *pachismos.* The *pocho*
is an anglicized Mexican or American of Mexican origin who speaks Spanish with

an accent characteristic of North Americans and who distorts and reconstructs the language according to the influence of English. Tex-Mex, or Spanglish, comes most naturally to me. I may switch back and forth from English to Spanish in the same sentence or in the same word. With my sister and my brother Nune and with Chicano *tejano* contemporaries I speak in Tex-Mex.

From kids and people my own age I picked up *Pachuco. Pachuco* (the language of the zoot suiters) is a language of rebellion, both against Standard Spanish and Standard English. It is a secret language. Adults of the culture and outsiders cannot understand it. It is made up of slang words from both English and Spanish. *Ruca* means girl or woman, *vato* means guy or dude, *chale* means no, *simón* means yes, *churro* is sure, talk is *periquiar, pigionear* means petting, *que gacho* means how nerdy, *ponte águila* means watch out, death is called *la pelona.* Through lack of practice and not having others who can speak it, I've lost most of the *Pachuco* tongue.

Chicano Spanish

Chicanos, after 250 years of Spanish/Anglo colonization, have developed significant differences in the Spanish we speak. We collapse two adjacent vowels into a single syllable and sometimes shift the stress in certain words such as *maíz/ maiz, cohete/cuete.* We leave out certain consonants when they appear between vowels: *lado/lao, mojado/mojao.* Chicanos from South Texas pronounce *f* as *j* as in *jue (fue).* Chicanos use "archaisms," words that are no longer in the Spanish language, words that have been evolved out. We say *semos, truje, haiga, ansina,* and *naiden.* We retain the "archaic" *j,* as in *jalar,* that derives from an earlier *h,* (the French *halar* or the Germanic *halon* which was lost to standard Spanish in the 16th century), but which is still found in several regional dialects such as the one spoken in South Texas. (Due to geography, Chicanos from the Valley of South Texas were cut off linguistically from other Spanish speakers. We tend to use words that the Spaniards brought over from Medieval Spain. The majority of the Spanish colonizers in Mexico and the Southwest came from Extremadura— Hernán Cortés was one of them—and Andalucía. Andalucians pronounce *ll* like a *y,* and their *d's* tend to be absorbed by adjacent vowels: *tirado* becomes *tirao.* They brought *el lenguaje popular, dialeclos y regionalismos.)*

Chicanos and other Spanish speakers also shift ll to *y* and z to s. We leave out initial syllables, saying *tar* for *estar, toy* for *estoy, hora* for *ahora (cubanos* and *puertorriqueños* also leave out initial letters of some words). We also leave out the final syllable such as *pa* for *para.* The intervocalic *y,* the *ll* as in *tortilla, ella, botella,* gets replaced by *tortia* or *tortiya, ea, botea.* We add an additional syllable at the beginning of certain words: *atocar* for *tocar, agastar* for *gastar.*

Sometimes we'll say *lavaste las vacijas,* other times *lavates* (substituting the *ates* verb endings for the *aste).*

We use anglicisms, words borrowed from English: *bola* from ball, *carpeta* from carpet, *máchina de lavar* (instead of *lavadora)* from washing machine. Tex-Mex argot, created by adding a Spanish sound at the beginning or end of an English word such as *cookiar* for cook, *watchar* for watch, *parkiar* for park, and *rapiar* for rape, is the result of the pressures on Spanish speakers to adapt to English.

We don't use the word *vosotros/as* or its accompanying verb form. We don't say *claro* (to mean yes), *imagínate,* or *me emociona,* unless we picked up Spanish from Latinas, out of a book, or in a classroom. Other Spanish-speaking groups are going through the same, or similar, development in their Spanish.

Linguistic Terrorism

Deslenguadas. Somas los del espanol deficiente. We are your
linguistic nightmare, your linguistic aberration, your linguistic
mestizaje, the subject of your *burla.* Because we speak with
tongues of fire we are culturally crucified. Racially, culturally, and
linguistically *somos huérfanos*—we speak an orphan Tongue.

Chicanas who grew up speaking Chicano Spanish have internalized the belief that we speak poor Spanish. It is illegitimate, a bastard language. And because we internalize how our language has been used against us by the dominant culture, we use our language differences against each other.

Chicana feminists often skirt around each other with suspicion and hesitation. For the longest time I couldn't figure it out. Then it dawned on me. To be close to another Chicana is like looking into the mirror. We are afraid of what we'll see there. *Pena.* Shame. Low estimation of self. In childhood we are told that our language is wrong. Repeated attacks on our native tongue diminish our sense of self. The attacks continue throughout our lives. Chicanas feel uncomfortable talking in Spanish to Latinas, afraid of their censure. Their language was not outlawed in their countries. They had a whole lifetime of being immersed in their native tongue; generations, centuries in which Spanish was a first language, taught in school, heard on radio and TV, and read in the newspaper.

If a person, Chicana or Latina, has a low estimation of my native tongue, she also has a low estimation of me. Often with *mexicanas y latinas* we'll speak English as a neutral language. Even among Chicanas we tend to speak English at parties or conferences. Yet, at the same time, we're afraid the other will think we're *agringadas* because we don't speak Chicano Spanish. We oppress each other trying to out-Chicano each other, vying to be the "real" Chicanas, to speak like Chicanos. There is no one Chicano language just as there is no one Chicano experience. A monolingual Chicana whose first language is English or Spanish is just as much a Chicana as one who speaks several variants of Spanish. A Chicana from Michigan or Chicago or Detroit is just as much a Chicana as one from the Southwest. Chicano Spanish is as diverse linguistically as it is regionally.

By the end of this century, Spanish speakers will comprise the biggest minority group in the U.S., a country where students in high schools and colleges are encouraged to take French classes because French is considered more "cultured." But for a language to remain alive it must be used. By the end of this century English, and not Spanish, will be the mother tongue of most Chicanos and Latinos.

So, if you want to really hurt me, talk badly about my language. Ethnic identity is twin skin to linguistic identity—I am my language. Until I can take pride in my language, I cannot take pride in myself. Until I can accept as legitimate Chicano Texas Spanish, Tex-Mex, and all the other languages I speak, I cannot accept the legitimacy of myself. Until I am free to write bilingually and to switch codes without having always to translate, while I still have to speak English or Spanish when I would rather speak Spanglish, and as long as I have to accommodate the English speakers rather than having them accommodate me, my tongue will be illegitimate.

I will no longer be made to feel ashamed of existing. I will have my voice: Indian, Spanish, white. I will have my serpent's tongue—my woman's voice, my sexual voice, my poet's voice. I will overcome the tradition of silence.

> My fingers
> move sly against your palm
> Like women everywhere, we speak in code. . . .
>
> —Melanie Kave/Kantrowitz

"Vistas," *corridos, y comida:* My Native Tongue

In the 1960s, I read my first Chicano novel. It was *City* of *Night* by John Rechy, a gay Texan, son of a Scottish father and a Mexican mother. For days I walked around in stunned amazement that a Chicano could write and could get published. When I read *I Am Joaquín* I was surprised to see a bilingual book by a Chicano in print. When I saw poetry written in Tex-Mex for the first time, a feeling of pure joy flashed through me. I felt like we really existed as a people. In 1971, when I started teaching High School English to Chicano students, I tried to supplement the required texts with works by Chicanos, only to be reprimanded and forbidden to do so by the principal. He claimed that I was supposed to teach "American" and English iterature. At the risk of being fired, I swore my students to secrecy and slipped in Chicano short stories, poems, a play. In graduate school, while working toward a PhD, I had to "argue" with one advisor after the other, semester after semester, before I was allowed to make Chicano literature an area of focus.

Even before I read books by Chicanos or Mexicans, it was the Mexican movies I saw at the drive-in—the Thursday night special of $1.00 a carload—that gave me a sense of belonging. *"Vámonos a las vistas,"* my mother would call out and we'd all—grandmother, brothers, sisters, and cousins—squeeze into the car We'd wolf down cheese and bologna white bread sandwiches while watching Pedro Infante in melodramatic tearjerkers like *Nosotros los pobres,* the first "real" Mexican movie (that was not an imitation of European movies). I remember seeing *Cuando los hijos* se *van* and surmising that all Mexican movies played up the love a mother has for her children and what ungrateful sons and daughters suffer when they are not devoted to their mothers. I remember the singing-type "westerns" of Jorge Negrete and Miguel Aceves Mejia. When watching Mexican movies, I felt a sense of homecoming as well as alienation. People who were to amount to something didn't go to Mexican movies, or *bailes,* or tune their radios to *bolero, rancherita,* and *corrido* music.

The whole time I was growing up, there was *norteño* music sometimes called North Mexican border music, or Tex-Mex music, or Chicano music, or *cantina* (bar) music. I grew up listening to *conjuntos,* three-or four-piece bands made up of folk musicians playing guitar, *bajo sexta,* drums, and button accordion, which Chicanos had borrowed from the German immigrants who had come to Central Texas and Mexico to farm and build breweries. In the Rio Grande Valley, Steve Jordan and Little Joe Hernández were popular, and Flaco Jiménez was the accordion king. The rhythms of Tex-Mex music are those of the polka, also adapted from the Germans, who in turn had borrowed the polka from the Czechs and Bohemians.

I remember the hot, sultry evenings when *corridos*—songs of love and death on the Texas-Mexican borderlands—reverberated out of cheap amplifiers from the local *cantinas* and wafted in through my bedroom window.

Corridos first became widely used along the South Texas/Mexican border during the early conflict between Chicanos and Anglos. The *corridos* are usually about Mexican heroes who do valiant deeds against the Anglo oppressors. Pancho Villa's song, *"La cucaracha,"* is the most famous one. *Corridos* of John F. Kennedy and his death are still very popular in the Valley. Older Chicanos remember Lydia Mendoza, one of the great border *corrido* singers who was called *la Gloria de Tejas.* Her *"El tango negro,"* sung during the Great Depression, made her a singer of the people. The ever present *corridos* narrated one hundred years of border history, bringing news of events as well as entertaining. These folk musicians and folk songs are our chief cultural mythmakers, and they made our hard lives seem bearable.

I grew up feeling ambivalent about our music. Country-western and rock-and-roll had more status. In the '50s and '60s, for the slightly educated and *agringado* Chicanos, there existed a sense of shame at being caught listening to our music. Yet I couldn't stop my feet from thumping to the music, could not stop humming the words, nor hide from myself the exhilaration I felt when I heard it.

There are more subtle ways that we internalize identification, especially in the forms of images and emotions. For me food and certain smells are tied to my identity, to my homeland. Woodsmoke curling up to an immense blue sky; woodsmoke perfuming my grandmother's clothes, her skin. The stench of cow manure and the yellow patches on the ground; the crack of a .22 rifle and the reek of cordite. Homemade white cheese sizzling in a pan, melting inside a folded *tortilla*. My sister Hilda's hot, spicy *menudo, chile colorado* making it deep red, pieces of *panza* and hominy floating on top. My brother Carito barbequing *fajitas* in the backyard. Even now and 3,000 miles away, I can see my mother spicing the ground beef, pork, and venison with *chile*. My mouth salivates at the thought of the hot steaming *tamales* I would be eating if I were home.

Si le preguntas a mi mamá, "¿Que eres?"

> "Identity is the essential core of who
> we are as individuals, the conscious
> experience of the self inside."
>
> —Gershen Kaufman

Nosotros los Chicanos straddle the borderlands. On one side of us, we are constantly exposed to the Spanish of the Mexicans, on the other side we hear the Anglos' incessant clamoring so that we forget our language. Among ourselves we don't say *nosotros los americanos, o nosotros los españoles, o nosotros los hispanos*. We say *nosotros los mexicanos* (by *mexicanos* we do not mean citizens of Mexico; we do not mean a national identity, but a racial one). We distinguish between *mexicanos del otro lado* and *mexicanos de este lado.* Deep in our hearts we believe that being Mexican has nothing *to* do with which country one lives in. Being Mexican is a state of soul—not one of mind, not one of citizenship. Neither eagle nor serpent, but both. And like the ocean, neither animal respects borders.

> *Dime con quien andas y te diré quien eres.*
> (Tell me who your friends are and I'll tell you who you are.)
>
> —Mexican saying

Si le preguntas a mi mamá, "¿Oue eres?" te dirá, "Soy mexicana." My brothers and sister say the same. I sometimes will answer *"soy mexicana"* and at others will say *"soy Chicana" o "soy tejana."* But I identified as *"Raza"* before I ever identified as *"mexicana"* or *"Chicana."*

As a culture, we call ourselves Spanish when referring to ourselves as a linguistic group and when copping out. It is then that we forget our predominant Indian genes. We are 70-80 percent Indian. We call ourselves Hispanic or Spanish-American or Latin American or Latin when linking ourselves to other Spanish-speaking peoples of the Western hemisphere and when copping out. We call ourselves Mexican-American to signify we are neither Mexican nor American, but more the noun "American" than the adjective "Mexican" (and when copping out).

Chicanos and other people of color suffer economically for not acculturating. This voluntary (yet forced) alienation makes for psychological conflict, a kind of dual identity—we don't identify with the Anglo-American cultural values and we don't totally identify with the Mexican cultural values. We are a synergy of two cultures with various degrees of Mexicanness or Angloness. I have so internalized the borderland conflict that sometimes I feel like one cancels out the other and we are zero, nothing, no one. *A veces no soy nada ni nadie. Pero hasta cuando no lo soy, lo soy.*

When not copping out, when we know we are more than nothing, we call ourselves Mexican, referring to race and ancestry; *mestizo* when affirming both our Indian and Spanish (but we hardly ever own our Black ancestry); Chicano when referring to a politically aware people born and/or raised in the U.S.; *Raza* when referring to Chicanos; *tejanos* when we are Chicanos from Texas.

Chicanos did not know we were a people until 1965 when Ceasar Chavez and the farmworkers united and *I Am Joaquín* was published and *la Raza Unida* party was formed in Texas. With that recognition, we became a distinct people. Something momentous happened to the Chicano soul—we became aware of our reality and acquired a name and a language (Chicano Spanish) that reflected that reality. Now that we had a name, some of the fragmented pieces began to fall together—who we were, what we were, how we had evolved. We began to get glimpses of what we might eventually become.

Yet the struggle of identities continues, the struggle of borders is our reality still. One day the inner struggle will cease and a true integration take place. In the meantime, *tenémos que hacer lalucha. ¿Quien está protegiendo los ranchos de mi genie? ¿Quien está tratando de cerrar la fisura enlre la india y el blanco en nuestra sangre? El Chicano, si, el Chicano que anda como un ladrón en su propia casa.*

Los Chicanos, how patient we seem, how very patient. There is the quiet of the Indian about us. We know how to survive. When other races have given up their tongue, we've kept ours. We know what it is to live under the hammer blow of the dominant *norteamericano* culture. But more than we count the blows, we count the days the weeks the years the centuries the eons until the white laws and commerce and customs will rot in the deserts they've created, lie bleached. *Humildes* yet proud, *quietos* yet wild, *nosotros los mexicanos Chicanos* will walk by the crumbling ashes as we go about our business. Stubborn, persevering, impenetrable as stone, yet possessing a malleability that renders us unbreakable, we, the *mestizas* and *mestizos,* will remain.

Topics for Writing and Discussion

1. The United States has been called a melting pot, or a salad bowl, because most of us are immigrants, or the sons and daughters (or grandsons and granddaughters) of immigrants from all over the world. In the process of becoming acculturated, of becoming American, we speak other languages as well as English—German, Chinese, Spanish, for example. These native languages enrich American English, adding words and expressions. If you, your parents, or your grandparents speak a language other than English at home, write an essay on how you navigate these different linguistic worlds.

2. Anzaldúa says: "Chicanos and other people of color suffer economically for not acculturating. This voluntary (yet forced) alienation makes for psychological conflict, a kind of dual identity—we don't identify with the Anglo-American cultural values and we don't totally identify with the Mexican cultural values." In some ways, whether bilingual or not, whether first-, second-, or third-generation immigrants, we live with similar "dual identities" because as we grow up we diverge from the values and way of life of our parents. Write a short essay explaining the dual identities you inhabit.

3. There is an ongoing movement to make English the official language of the United States. (See the website *usenglish.org.)* It has a long history as well. (See *English Only* at *pbs.org.*) Do some research on this topic, and write an essay arguing for or against such a proposal. Be sure not to plagiarize and to cite your sources.

A Report from Occupied Territory

James Baldwin

James Baldwin (1924-1987) was an American writer born in Harlem, New York. His novels, plays, and essays explored the experience of African-Americans in the United States through such works as *Go Tell It on the Mountain* (1953), *Notes of a Native Son* (1955), and *The Fire Next Time* (1963). The following essay was published in *The Nation* on July 11, 1966.

On April 17, 1964, in Harlem, New York City, a young salesman, father of two, left a customer's apartment and went into the streets. There was a great commotion in the streets, which, especially since it was a spring day, involved many people, including running, frightened, little boys. They were running from the police. Other people, in windows, left their windows, in terror of the police because the police had their guns out, and were aiming the guns at the roofs. Then the salesman noticed that two of the policemen were beating up a kid: "So I spoke up and asked them, 'why are you beating him like that?' Police jump up and start swinging on me. He put the gun on me and said, 'get over there.' I said, 'what for?' "

An unwise question. Three of the policemen beat up the salesman in the streets. Then they took the young salesman, whose hands had been handcuffed behind his back, along with four others, much younger than the salesman, who were handcuffed in the same way, to the police station. There: "About thirty-five I'd say came into the room, and started beating, punching us in the jaw, in the stomach, in the chest, beating us with a padded club—spit on us, call us niggers, dogs, animals—they call us dogs and animals when I don't see why we are the dogs and animals the way they are beating us. Like they beat me they beat the other kids and the elderly fellow. They throw him almost through one of the radiators. I thought he was dead over there."

"The elderly fellow" was Fecundo Acion, a 47-year-old Puerto Rican seaman, who had also made the mistake of wanting to know why the police were beating up children. An adult eyewitness reports, "Now here come an old man walking out a stoop and asked one cop, 'say, listen, sir, what's going on out here?' The cop turn around and smash him a couple of times in the head." And one of the youngsters said, "He get that just for a question. No reason at all, just for a question."

No one had, as yet, been charged with any crime. But the nightmare had not yet really begun. The salesman had been so badly beaten around one eye that it was found necessary to hospitalize him. Perhaps some sense of what it means to live in occupied territory can be suggested by the fact that the police took him to Harlem Hospital themselves—nearly nineteen hours after the beating. For fourteen days, the doctors at Harlem Hospital told him that they could do nothing for his eye, and he was removed to Bellevue Hospital, where for fourteen days, the doctors tried to save the eye. At the end of fourteen days it was clear that the bad eye could not be saved and was endangering the good eye. All that could be done, then, was to take the bad eye out.

As of my last information, the salesman is on the streets again, with his attaché case, trying to feed his family. He is more visible now because he wears an eye patch; and because he questioned the right of two policemen to beat up one child, he is known as a "cop hater." Therefore, "I have quite a few police look at me now pretty hard. My lawyer he axe (asked) me to keep somebody with me at all times 'cause the police may try to mess with me again."

You will note that there is not a suggestion of any kind of appeal to justice, and no suggestion of any recompense for the grave and gratuitous damage which this man has endured. His tone is simply the tone of one who has miraculously survived—he might have died; as it is, he is merely half blind. You will also note that the patch over his eye has had the effect of making him, more than ever, the target of the police. It is a dishonorable wound, not earned in a foreign jungle but in the domestic one—not that this would make any difference at all to the nevertheless insuperably patriotic policeman—and it proves that he is a "bad nigger." ("Bad niggers," in America, as elsewhere, have always been watched and have usually been killed.) The police, who have certainly done their best to kill him, have also provided themselves with a pretext *derisoire* by filing three criminal charges against him. He is charged with beating up a schoolteacher, upsetting a fruit stand, and assaulting the (armed) police. Furthermore, he did all of these things in the space of a single city block, and simultaneously.

The salesman's name is Frank Stafford. At the time all this happened, he was 31 years old. And all of this happened, all of this and a great deal more, just before the "long, hot summer" of 1964 which, to the astonishment of nearly all New Yorkers and nearly all Americans, to the extremely verbal anguish of *The New York Times*, and to the bewilderment of the rest of the world, eventually erupted into a race riot. It was the killing of a 15-year-old Negro boy by a white policeman which overflowed the unimaginably bitter cup.

As a result of the events of April 17, and of the police performance that day, and because Harlem is policed like occupied territory, six young Negro men, the oldest of whom is 20, are now in prison, facing life sentences for murder. Their names are Wallace Baker, Daniel Hamm, Walter Thomas, Willie Craig, Ronald Felder and Robert Rice. Perhaps their names don't matter. They might be my brothers, they might also be yours. My report is based, in part, on Truman Nelson's *The Torture of Mothers* (The Garrison Press, 15 Olive Street, Newburyport, Mass., with an introduction by Maxwell Geismar). *The Torture of Mothers* is a detailed account of the case which is now known as the case of The Harlem Six. Mr. Nelson is *not*, as I have earlier misled certain people into believing, a white Southern novelist, but a white Northern one. It is a rather melancholy comment, I think, on the Northern intellectual community, and it reveals, rather to my despair, how little I have come to expect of it that I should have been led so irresistibly into this error. In a way, though, I certainly have no wish to blame Mr. Nelson for *my* errors; he is, nevertheless, somewhat himself to blame. His tone makes it clear that he means what he says and he knows what he means. The tone is rare. I have come to expect it only of Southerners—or mainly from Southerners—since Southerners must pay so high a price for their private and their public liberation. But Mr. Nelson actually comes from New England, and is what another age would have called an abolitionist. No Northern liberal would have been capable of it because the Northern liberal considers himself as already saved, whereas the white Southerner has to pay the price for his soul's salvation out of his own anguish and in his own flesh and in the only time he has. Mr. Nelson wrote the book in an attempt to create publicity and public indignation; whatever money the book makes goes into the effort to free The Harlem Six. I think the book is an extraordinary moral achievement, in the great American tradition of Tom Paine and Frederick Douglass, but I will not be so dishonest as to pretend that I am writing a book review. No, I am writing a report, which is also a plea for the recognition of our common humanity. Without this recognition, our common humanity will be proved in unutterable ways. My report is also based on what I myself know, for I was born in Harlem and raised there. Neither I, nor my family, can be said ever really to have left; we are—*perhaps*—no longer as totally at the mercy of the cops and the landlords as once we were. In any case, our roots, our friends, our deepest associations are there, and "there" is only about fifteen blocks away.

This means that I also know, in my own flesh, and know, which is worse, in the scars borne by many of those dearest to me, the thunder and fire of the billy club, the paralyzing shock of spittle in the face, and I know what it is to find oneself blinded, on one's hands and knees, at the bottom of the flight of steps down which one has just been hurled. I know something else: these young men have been in jail for two years now. Even if the attempts being put forth to free them should succeed, what has happened to them in these two years? People are destroyed very easily. Where is the civilization and where, indeed, is the morality which can afford to destroy so many?

There was a game played for some time between certain highly placed people in Washington and myself before the administration changed and the Great Society reached the planning stage. The game went something like this around April or May, that is as the weather began to be warmer, my phone would ring. I would pick it up and find that Washington was on the line.

Washington: What are you doing for lunch—oh, say, tomorrow, Jim?

Jim: Oh—why—I guess I'm free.

Washington: Why don't you take the shuttle down? We'll send a car to the airport. One o'clock all right?

Jim: Sure. I'll be there.

Washington: Good. Be glad to see you.

So there I would be the next day, like a good little soldier, seated (along with other good little soldiers) around a luncheon table in Washington. The first move was not mine to make, but I knew very well why I had been asked to be there.

Finally, someone would say—we would probably have arrived at the salad—"say, Jim, what's going to happen this summer?"

This question, translated, meant: Do you think that any of those unemployed, unemployable Negroes who are going to be on the streets all summer will cause us any trouble? What do you think we should do about it? But, later on, I concluded that I had got the second part of the question wrong, they really meant, what was *I* going to do about it?

Then I would find myself trying patiently to explain that the Negro in America can scarcely yet be considered—for example—as a part of the labor unions—and he is certainly not so considered by the majority of these unions—and that, therefore, he lacks that protection and that incentive. The jobs that Negroes have always held, the lowest jobs, the most menial jobs, are now being destroyed by automation. No remote provision has yet been made to absorb this labor surplus. Furthermore, the Negro's education, North and South, remains, almost totally, a segregated education, which is but another way of saying that he is taught the habits of inferiority every hour of every day that he lives. He will find it very difficult to overcome these habits. Furthermore, every attempt he makes to overcome them will be painfully complicated by the fact that the ways of being, the ways of life of the despised and rejected, nevertheless, contain an incontestable vitality and authority. This is far more than can be said of the middle class which, in any case, and whether it be black or white, does not dare to cease despising him. He may prefer to remain where he is, given such unattractive choices, which means that he either remains in limbo, or finds a way to use the system in order to beat the system. Thus, even when opportunities—my use of this word is here limited to the industrialized, competitive, contemporary North American sense—hitherto closed to Negroes begin, very grudgingly, to open up, few can be found to qualify for them for the reasons sketched above, and also because it demands a very rare person of any color to risk madness and heartbreak in an attempt to achieve the impossible. (I know Negroes who have gone literally mad because they wished to become commercial air-line pilots.) Nor is this the worst.

The children, having seen the spectacular defeat of their fathers—having seen what happens to any bad nigger and, still more, what happens to the good ones—cannot listen to their fathers and certainly will not listen to the society which is responsible for their orphaned condition. What to do in the face of this deep and dangerous estrangement? It seemed to me—I would say, sipping coffee and trying to be calm—that the principle of what had to be done was extremely simple; but before anything could be done, the principle had to be grasped. The principle on which one had to operate was that the government which can force me to pay my taxes and force me to fight in its defense anywhere in the world *does not have the authority* to say that it cannot protect my right to vote or my right to earn a living or my right to live anywhere I choose. Furthermore, no nation, wishing to call itself free, can possibly survive so massive a defection. What to do? Well, there is a real estate lobby in Albany, for example, and this lobby, which was able to rebuild all of New York, downtown, and for money, in less than twenty years, is also responsible for Harlem and the condition of the people there, and the condition of the schools there, and the future of the children there. What to do? Why is it not possible to attack the power of this lobby? Are their profits more important than the health of our children? What to do? Are textbooks printed in order to teach children, or are the contents of these textbooks to be controlled by the Southern oligarchy and the commercial health of publishing houses? What to do? Why are Negroes and Puerto Ricans virtually the only people pushing trucks in the garment center, and what union has the right to trap and victimize Negroes and Puerto Ricans in this way? None of these things (I would say) could possibly be done without the consent, in fact, of the government, and we in Harlem know this even if some of you profess not to know how such a hideous state of affairs came about. If some of these things are not begun—I would say—then, of course, we will be sitting on a powder keg all summer. Of course, the powder keg may blow up; it will be a miracle if it doesn't.

They thanked me. They didn't believe me, as I conclude, since nothing was ever done. The summer was always violent. And, in the spring, the phone began to ring again.

Now, what I have said about Harlem is true of Chicago, Detroit, Washington, Boston, Philadelphia, Los Angeles and San Francisco—is true of every Northern city with a large Negro population. And the police are simply the hired enemies of this population. They are present to keep the Negro in his place and to protect white business interests, and they have no other function. They are, moreover— even in a country which makes the very grave error of equating ignorance with simplicity—quite stunningly ignorant; and, since they know that they are hated, they are always afraid. One cannot possibly arrive at a more surefire formula for cruelty.

This is why those pious calls to "respect the law," always to be heard from prominent citizens each time the ghetto explodes, are so obscene. The law is meant to be my servant and not my master, still less my torturer and my murderer. To respect the law, in the context in which the American Negro finds himself, is simply to surrender his self-respect.

On April 17, some school children overturned a fruit stand in Harlem. This would have been a mere childish prank if the children had been white—had been, that is, the children of that portion of the citizenry for whom the police work and who have the power to control the police. But these children were black, and the police chased them and beat them and took out their guns; and Frank Stafford lost his eye in exactly the same way The Harlem Six lost their liberty—by trying to protect the younger children. Daniel Hamm, for example, tells us that "...we heard children scream. We turned around and walked back to see what happened. I saw this policeman with his gun out and with his billy in his hand. I like put myself in the way to keep him from shooting the kids. Because first of all he was shaking like a leaf and jumping all over the place. And I thought he might shoot one of them."

He was arrested, along with Wallace Baker, carried to the police station, beaten—"six and twelve at a time would beat us. They got so tired beating us they just came in and started spitting on us—they even bring phlegm up and spit on me." This went on all day. In the evening Wallace Baker and Daniel Hamm were taken to Harlem Hospital for X rays and then carried back to the police station, where the beating continued all night. They were eventually released, with the fruit-stand charges pending, in spite of the testimony of the fruit-stand owner. This fruit-stand owner had already told the police that neither Wallace Baker nor Daniel Hamm had ever been at his store and that they certainly had had nothing to do with the fruit-stand incident. But this had no effect on the conduct of the police. The boys had already attracted the attention of the police, long before the fruit-stand riot, and in a perfectly innocent way. They are pigeon fanciers and they keep—kept—pigeons on the roof. But the police are afraid of everything in Harlem and they are especially afraid of the roofs, which they consider to be guerrilla outposts. This means that the citizens of Harlem who, as we have seen, can come to grief at any hour in the streets, and who are not safe at their windows, are forbidden the very air. They are safe only in their houses—or were, until the city passed the No Knock, Stop and Frisk laws, which permit a policeman to enter one's home without knocking and to stop anyone on the streets, at will, at any hour, and search him. Harlem believes, and I certainly agree, that these laws are directed against Negroes. They are certainly not directed against anybody else. One day, "two carloads of detectives come and went up on the roof. They pulled their guns on the kids and searched them and made them all come down and they were going to take them down to the precinct." But the boys put up a verbal fight and refused to go and attracted quite a crowd. "To get these boys to the precinct we would have to shoot them," a policeman said, and "the police seemed like they was embarrassed. Because I don't think they expected the kids to have as much sense as they had in speaking up for themselves." They refused to go to the precinct, "and they didn't," and their exhibition of the spirit of '76 marked them as dangerous. Occupied territory is occupied territory, even though it be found in that New World which the Europeans conquered, and it is axiomatic, in occupied territory, that any act of resistance, even though it be executed by a child, be answered at once, and with the full weight of the occupying forces. Furthermore, since the police, not at all surprisingly, are abysmally incompetent—for neither, in fact, do they have any respect for the law, which is not surprising, either—Harlem and all of New York City is full of unsolved crimes. A crime, as we know, is solved when someone is arrested and convicted. It is not indispensable, but it is useful, to have a confession. If one is carried back and forth from the precinct to the hospital long enough, one is likely to confess to anything.

Therefore, ten days later, following the slaying of Mrs. Margit Sugar in Mr. and Mrs. Sugar's used-clothing store in Harlem, the police returned and took Daniel Hamm away again. This is how his mother tells it. "I think it was three (detectives) come up and they asked are you Danny Hamm? And he says yes and right away—gun right to the head and slapping him up, one gun here and one here—just all the way down the hall—beating him and knocking him around with the gun to his head." The other boys were arrested in the same way, and, again of course, they were beaten, but this arrest was a far greater torture than the first one had been because some of the mothers did not know where the boys were, and the police, who were holding them, refused for many hours to say that they were holding them The mothers did not know of what it was their children were accused until they learned, via television, that the charge was murder. At that time in the state of New York, this charge meant death in the electric chair.

Let us assume that all six boys are guilty as (eventually) charged. Can anyone pretend that the manner of their arrest, or their treatment, bears any resemblance to equal justice under the law? The Police Department has loftily refused to "dignify the charges." But can anyone pretend that they would dare to take this tone if the case involved, say, the sons of Wall Street brokers? I have witnessed and endured the brutality of the police many more times than once—but, of course, I cannot prove it. I cannot prove it because the Police Department investigates itself, quite as though it were answerable only to itself. But it cannot be allowed to be answerable only to itself. It must be made to answer to the community which pays it, and which it is legally sworn to protect, and if American Negroes are not a part of the American community, then all of the American professions are a fraud.

This arrogant autonomy, which is guaranteed the police, not only in New York, *by the most powerful forces in American life*—otherwise, they would not dare to claim it would indeed be unable to claim it—creates a situation which is as close to anarchy as it already, visibly, is close to martial law.

Here is Wallace Baker's mother speaking, describing the night that a police officer came to her house to collect the evidence which he hoped would prove that her son was guilty of murder. The late Mrs. Sugar had run a used clothing store and the policeman was looking for old coats. "Nasty as he was that night in my house. He didn't ring the bell. So I said, have you got a search warrant? He say, no, I don't have no search warrant and I'm going to search anyway. Well, he did. So I said, will you please step out of this room till I get dressed? He wouldn't leave." This collector of evidence against the boys was later arrested on charges of possessing and passing counterfeit money (he pleaded guilty to a misdemeanor, "conspiring" to pass counterfeit money). The officer's home in Hartsdale, N. Y., is valued at $35,000; he owns two cars, one a Cadillac, and when he was arrested, had $1,300 in his pockets. But the families of The Harlem Six do not have enough money for counsel. The court appointed counsel, and refused to allow the boys counsel of their own choice, even though the boys made it clear that they had no confidence in their court-appointed counsel, and even though four leading civil rights lawyers had asked to be allowed to handle the case. The boys were convicted of first-degree murder, and are now ending their childhood and may end their lives in jail.

These things happen, in all our Harlems, every single day. If we ignore this fact, and our common responsibility to change this fact, we are sealing our doom. Here is the boy, Daniel Hamm, speaking—speaking of his country, which has sworn to bring peace and freedom to so many millions. "They don't want us here. They don't want us—period! All they want us to do is work on these penny-ante jobs for them—and that's *it*. And beat our heads in whenever they feel like it. They don't want us on the street 'cause the World's Fair is coming. And they figure that all black people are hoodlums anyway, or bums, with no character of our own. So they put us off the streets, so their friends from Europe, Paris or Vietnam—wherever they come from—can come and see this supposed-to-be great city."

There is a very bitter prescience in what this boy—this "bad nigger"—is saying, and he was not born knowing it. We taught it to him in seventeen years. He is draft age now, and if he were not in jail, would very probably be on his way to Southeast Asia. Many of his contemporaries are there, and the American Government and the American press are extremely proud of them. They are dying there like flies; they are dying in the streets of all our Harlems far more hideously than flies. A member of my family said to me when we learned of the bombing of the four little girls in the Birmingham Sunday school, "Well, they don't need us for work no more. Where are they building the gas ovens?" Many Negroes feel this; there is no way not to feel it. Alas, we know our countrymen, municipalities, judges, politicians, policemen and draft boards very well. There is more than one way to skin a cat, and more than one way to get bad niggers off the streets. No one in Harlem will ever believe that The Harlem Six are guilty—God knows their guilt has certainly not been proved. Harlem knows, though, that they have been abused and possibly destroyed, and Harlem knows why—we have lived with it since our eyes opened on the world. One is in the impossible position of being unable to believe a word one's countrymen say. "I can't believe what you say," the song goes, "because I see what you do"—and one is also under the necessity of escaping the jungle of one's situation into any other jungle whatever. It is the bitterest possible comment on our situation now that the suspicion is alive in so many breasts that America has at last found a way of dealing with the Negro problem. *"They don't want us—period!"* The meek shall inherit the earth, it is said. This presents a very bleak image to those who live in occupied territory. The meek Southeast Asians, those who remain, shall have their free elections, and the meek American Negroes—those who survive—shall enter the Great Society.

Topics for Writing and Discussion

1. This essay details events that happened over 50 years ago during the civil rights struggles of the '60s. It makes reference to a number of people and situations at the time, such as the arrest of the Harlem Six on April 17, 1964. Shortly after the publication of this essay, on July 16, a policeman shot a 15-year-old black youth, which then led to the Harlem riot. Look up all the references in this essay, and write a report on the momentous events that occurred at that time. Be sure to avoid plagiarism and to cite your sources.

2. In the summer of 2014, another young black man, Michael Brown, was killed by a white police officer in Ferguson, Missouri. That also led to several nights of unrest and confrontations between police and demonstrators. Earlier another black man, Eric Garner, was killed by police in New York. These incidents raise the question of whether anything has changed over the past 50 years. What do you think about the current relations between white and black citizens? Have they improved since Baldwin's report?

3. The quest for civil rights and equality is continued today by African-Americans, other minorities, women, and members of the LGBTQ community. If you are a member of one of these groups, have you experienced discrimination, either formally or subtly? Write a report on your experience.

Baseball or Soccer?

David Brooks

David Brooks is a journalist and syndicated columnist for the *New York Times*. He writes and comments on a wide range of cultural and political issues. This editorial was published on July 10, 2014.

Is life more like baseball, or is it more like soccer?

Baseball is a team sport, but it is basically an accumulation of individual activities. Throwing a strike, hitting a line drive or fielding a grounder is primarily an individual achievement. The team that performs the most individual tasks well will probably win the game.

Soccer is not like that. In soccer, almost no task, except the penalty kick and a few others, is intrinsically individual. Soccer, as Simon Critchley pointed out recently in *The New York Review of Books*, is a game about occupying and controlling space. If you get the ball and your teammates have run the right formations, and structured the space around you, you'll have three or four options on where to distribute it. If the defenders have structured their formations to control the space, then you will have no options. Even the act of touching the ball is not primarily defined by the man who is touching it; it is defined by the context created by all the other players.

As Critchley writes, "Soccer is a collective game, a team game, and everyone has to play the part which has been assigned to them, which means they have to understand it spatially, positionally and intelligently and make it effective." Brazil wasn't clobbered by Germany this week because the quality of the individual players was so much worse. They got slaughtered because they did a pathetic job of controlling space. A German player would touch the ball, even close to the Brazilian goal, and he had ample room to make the kill.

Most of us spend our days thinking we are playing baseball, but we are really playing soccer. We think we individually choose what career path to take, whom to socialize with, what views to hold. But, in fact, those decisions are shaped by the networks of people around us more than we dare recognize.

This influence happens through at least three avenues. First there is contagion. People absorb memes, ideas and behaviors from each other the way they catch a cold. As Nicholas Christakis and others have shown, if your friends are obese, you're likely to be obese. If your neighbors play fair, you are likely to play fair. We all live within distinct moral ecologies. The overall environment influences what we think of as normal behavior without being much aware of it.

Then there is the structure of your network. There is by now a vast body of research on how differently people behave depending on the structure of the social networks. People with vast numbers of acquaintances have more job opportunities than people with fewer but deeper friendships. Most organizations have structural holes, gaps between two departments or disciplines. If you happen to be in an undeveloped structural hole where you can link two departments, your career is likely to take off.

Innovation is hugely shaped by the structure of an industry at any moment. Individuals in Silicon Valley are creative now because of the fluid structure of failure and recovery. Broadway was incredibly creative in the 1940s and 1950s because it was a fluid industry in which casual acquaintances ended up collaborating.

Since then, studies show, theater social networks have rigidified, and, even if you collaborate with an ideal partner, you are not as likely to be as creative as you would have been when the global environment was more fertile.

Finally, there is the power of the extended mind. There is also a developed body of research on how much our very consciousness is shaped by the people around us. Let me simplify it with a classic observation: Each close friend you have brings out a version of yourself that you could not bring out on your own. When your close friend dies, you are not only losing the friend, you are losing the version of your personality that he or she elicited. Once we acknowledge that, in life, we are playing soccer, not baseball, a few things become clear. First, awareness of the landscape of reality is the highest form of wisdom. It's not raw computational power that matters most; it's having a sensitive attunement to the widest environment, feeling where the flow of events is going. Genius is in practice perceiving more than the conscious reasoning.

Second, predictive models will be less useful. Baseball is wonderful for sabermetricians. In each at bat there is a limited range of possible outcomes. Activities like soccer are not as easily renderable statistically, because the relevant spatial structures are harder to quantify. Even the estimable statistician Nate Silver of *FiveThirtyEight* gave Brazil a 65 percent chance of beating Germany.

Finally, Critchley notes that soccer is like a 90-minute anxiety dream—one of those frustrating dreams when you're trying to get somewhere but something is always in the way. This is yet another way soccer is like life.

Topics for Writing and Discussion

1. Brooks sees the difference between baseball and soccer—one is based on individual achievement, the other on team cohesion—as a metaphor for life. He says, "We think we individually choose what career path to take, whom to socialize with, what views to hold. But, in fact, those decisions are shaped by the networks of people around us more than we dare recognize." Write a short essay comparing your own life to either baseball or soccer. Is your success so far dependent more on your individual effort or the support and help of others?

2. Contrary to Brooks's view in this essay, American novels and movies are full of stories about the "lone genius" or the individual who makes it to the top in sports, business, art, and so on (and generally through many difficulties) on his own individual effort. These individuals have risen above their backgrounds. These are our "success stories." Are such stories really myth? Are such individuals merely outliers? Do you know of anyone who has essentially made it on his or her own? If so, write a short essay describing how this individual rose above the status or background he or she was born into.

The Cop Mind

David Brooks

David Brooks is a journalist and syndicated columnist for the *New York Times*. He writes and comments on a wide range of cultural and political issues. The following essay was published in *The New York Times* on December 8, 2014.

Like a lot of people in journalism, I began my career, briefly, as a police reporter. As the Michael Brown and Eric Garner cases have unfolded, I've found myself thinking back to those days. Nothing excuses specific acts of police brutality, especially in the Garner case, but not enough attention is being paid to the emotional and psychological challenges of being a cop.

Early on, I learned that there is an amazing variety of police officers, even compared to other professions. Most cops are conscientious, and some, especially among detectives, are brilliant.

They spend much of their time in the chaotic and depressing nether-reaches of society: busting up domestic violence disputes, dealing with drunks and drug addicts, coming upon fatal car crashes, managing conflicts large and small.

They ride an emotional and biochemical roller coaster. They experience moments of intense action and alertness, followed by emotional crashes marked by exhaustion, and isolation. They become hypervigilant. Surrounded by crime all day, some come to perceive that society is more threatening than it really is.

To cope, they emotionally armor up. Many of the cops I was around developed a cynical, dehumanizing and hard-edged sense of humor that was an attempt to insulate themselves from the pain of seeing a dead child or the extinguished life of a young girl they arrived too late to save.

Many of us see cops as relatively invulnerable as they patrol the streets. The cops themselves do not perceive their situation that way. As criminologist George Kelling wrote in City Journal in 1993, "It is a common myth that police officers approach conflicts with a feeling of power—after all, they are armed, they represent the state, they are specially trained and backed by an 'army.' In reality, an officer's gun is almost always a liability . . . because a suspect may grab it in a scuffle. Officers are usually at a disadvantage because they have to intervene in unfamiliar terrain, on someone else's territory. They worry that bystanders might become involved, either by helping somebody the officer has to confront or, after the fact, by second-guessing an officer's conduct."

Even though most situations are not dangerous, danger is always an out-of-the-blue possibility, often in the back of the mind.

In many places, a self-supporting and insular police culture develops: In this culture no one understands police work except fellow officers; the training in the academy is useless; to do the job you've got to bend the rules and understand the law of the jungle; the world is divided into two sorts of people—cops and a—holes.

This is a life of both boredom and stress. Life expectancy for cops is lower than for the general population. Cops suffer disproportionately from peptic ulcers, back disorders and heart disease. In one study, suicide rates were three times higher among cops than among other municipal workers. Other studies have found that somewhere between 7 percent and 19 percent of cops suffer from post-traumatic stress disorder. The effect is especially harsh on those who have been involved in shootings. Two-thirds of the officers who have been involved in shootings suffer moderate or severe emotional problems. Seventy percent leave the police force within seven years of the incident.

Most cops know they walk a dangerous line, between necessary and excessive force. According to a 2000 National Institute of Justice study, more than 90 percent of the police officers surveyed said that it is wrong to respond to verbal abuse with force. Nonetheless, 15 percent of the cops surveyed were aware that officers in their own department sometimes or often did so.

And through the years, departments have worked to humanize the profession. Over all, police use of force is on the decline, along with the crime rate generally. According to the Department of Justice, the number of incidents in which force was used or threatened declined from 664,000 in 2002 to 574,000 in 2008. Community policing has helped bind police forces closer to the citizenry.

A blind spot is race. Only 1 in 20 white officers believe that blacks and other minorities receive unequal treatment from the police. But 57 percent of black officers are convinced the treatment of minorities is unfair.

But at the core of the profession lies the central problem of political philosophy. How does the state preserve order through coercion? When should you use overwhelming force to master lawbreaking? When is it wiser to step back and use patience and understanding to defuse a situation? How do you make this decision instantaneously, when testosterone is flowing, when fear is in the air, when someone is disrespecting you and you feel indignation rising in the gut?

Racist police brutality has to be punished. But respect has to be paid. Police serve by walking that hazardous line where civilization meets disorder.

Topics for Writing and Discussion

1. This essay was written not long after two cases in which black men were killed by white cops. Both gained national headlines and sparked demonstrations around the country. Since then, there has been an ongoing national dialogue about issues involving race and the police. Have you ever been stopped, either on the street or in your car, by a police officer? If so, write a short account of the incident. How were you treated?

2. There have been charges of police brutality for almost as long as there have been police forces. Brooks's article, however, focuses on what individual police officers face on a daily basis. When they are out in public, they have to be on constant alert, their actions are always subject to review, and they regularly deal with situations ordinary citizens would be traumatized by. If you know someone in law enforcement, interview that person about his or her daily routine, and then write an essay about what you have learned. If you do not know a cop, ask a campus security officer for an interview.

The Real Africa

David Brooks

David Brooks is a journalist and syndicated columnist for the *New York Times*. He writes and comments on a wide range of cultural and political issues. The following essay was published in *The New York Times* on May 8, 2014.

In 2005, Binyavanga Wainaina published a brilliantly sarcastic essay in *Granta* called "How to Write About Africa," advising people on how to sound spiritual and compassionate while writing a book about the continent.

"Always use the word 'Africa' or 'Darkness' or 'Safari' in your title," Wainaina advised. "Never have a picture of a well-adjusted African on the cover of your book, or in it, unless that African has won the Nobel Prize. An AK-47, prominent ribs, naked breasts: use these. If you must include an African, make sure you get one in Masai or Zulu or Dogon dress."

Wainaina had other tips: The people in said book should be depicted as hungry, suffering, simple or dead. The children should have distended bellies and flies on their faces. The animals, on the other hand, should be depicted as wise and filled with family values. Elephants are caring and good feminists. So are gorillas. Be sure to show how profoundly you are moved by the continent and its woes, and how much it has penetrated your soul. End with a quote from Nelson Mandela involving rainbows. Because you care.

There's been something similarly distorted to some of the social media reactions to the Boko Haram atrocities over the past week. It's great that the kidnappings and the massacres are finally arousing the world's indignation. But sometimes the implication of the conversation has been this: Africa is this dark and lawless place where monstrous things are bound to happen. Those poor people need our help.

But this is more or less the opposite of the truth. Boko Haram is not the main story in Africa or even in Nigeria. It is a small rear-guard reaction to the main story. The main story in Africa is an impressive surge of growth, urbanization and modernization, which has sparked panic in a few people who don't like these things.

Many countries in sub-Saharan Africa are growing at a phenomenal clip. Nigeria's economy grew by 6.7 percent in 2012. Mozambique's grew by 7.4 percent, Ghana's by 7.9 percent. Economic growth in sub-Saharan Africa as a whole is predicted to reach 5.2 percent this year. Investment funds are starting up by the dozen, finding local entrepreneurs.

In 2011, roughly 60 million African households earned at least $3,000 a year. By next year, more than 100 million households will make that much.

Trade between Africa and the rest of the world has increased by 200 percent since 2000. Since 1996, the poverty rate has fallen by 1 percent per year. Life expectancies are shooting up.

Only about a third of this new wealth is because of commodities. Nations like Ethiopia and Rwanda, which have no oil wealth, are growing phenomenally. The bulk is because of economic reforms, increased productivity, increased urbanization and the fact that in many countries political systems are becoming marginally less dysfunctional. Africa should not be seen as merely the basket case continent where students, mission trips and celebrities can go to do good work. It has become the test case of 21st-century modernity. It is the place where the pace of modernization is fast, and where the forces that resist modernization are mounting a daring reaction.

We are seeing three distinct clashes. They're happening all over the world, but they exist in bold contrast in Africa.

The first is the clash over pluralism. Africa has seen an explosion of cellphone usage. It's seen a rapid expansion of urbanization. In 1980, only 28 percent of Africans lived in cities, but today 40 percent do. This has led to a greater mixing of tribal groupings, religions and a loosening of lifestyle options. The draconian anti-gay laws in Nigeria, Uganda, Burundi and many other countries are one reaction against this cosmopolitan trend. The second is a clash over human development. Over the past decade, secondary school enrollment in Africa has increased by 50 percent. This contributes to an increasing value on intellectual openness, as people seek liberty to furnish their own minds. The Boko Haram terrorists are massacring and kidnapping people—mostly girls—at schools to try to force people to submit to a fantasy version of the past.

The third is the clash over governance. Roughly 80 percent of Africa's workers labor in the informal sector. That's because the formal governmental and regulatory structures are biased toward the connected and the rich, not based on impersonal rule of law. Many Africans are trying to replace old practices with competent governance. They are creating new ways to navigate between the formal and informal sectors.

Too many of our images of Africa are derived from nature documentaries, fund-raising appeals and mission trips. In reality, Africa faces in acute forms the same problems that afflict pretty much every region these days. Most important: Individual and social creativity is zooming ahead. Governing institutions are failing to perform the basic, elementary tasks.

Topics for Writing and Discussion

1. Africa, like many other places, has undergone rapid change in the past 35 years. These changes have enhanced the lives of millions of people but have also disrupted older social patterns and ways of life. Write an essay in which you explain the changes, both good and bad, that have occurred in your own family, neighborhood, or city.

2. In this essay, Brooks challenges the stereotypes of Africa held by many Western people. It thus raises the topic of stereotypes in general. According to *Merriam-Webster's Collegiate Dictionary*, a stereotype is "a standardized mental picture that is held in common by members of a group and that represents an oversimplified opinion, prejudiced attitude, or uncritical judgment." For example, people have many stereotypes of blondes, football players, fraternity members, different racial and ethnic groups, and so on. Write a short paper in which you explain either a stereotype you hold of another place or group of people or how you or a group you belong to has been falsely stereotyped by others.

How it Feels to Be Colored Me

Zora Neale Hurston

Zora Neale Hurston (1891-1960) was an American writer of several novels and numerous short stories. Born in Alabama, when she was quite young her family moved to Eatonville, Florida, which she considered her hometown. After attending Howard University, Hurston received a scholarship to attend Barnard College, which is affiliated with Columbia University in New York City (as the only black student and first black graduate). She received a degree in anthropology in 1928. Later Hurston won a Guggenhiem Fellowship in 1937 to do ethnographic work in Haiti and Jamaica and began writing her best-known novel, *Their Eyes Were Watching God* (1937). After a period in the forties and fifties when her work was discounted partly because she used dialect in her stories, she was rediscovered and promoted in the seventies by African-American writers such as Alice Walker, Toni Morrison, and Maya Angelou. The following essay was first published in the New York magazine *The World Tomorrow* in 1928.

I am colored but I offer nothing in the way of extenuating circumstances except the fact that I am the only Negro in the United States whose grandfather on the mother's side was *not* an Indian chief.

I remember the very day that I became colored. Up to my thirteenth year I lived in the little Negro town of Eatonville, Florida. It is exclusively a colored town. The only white people I knew passed through the town going to or coming from Orlando. The native whites rode dusty horses, the Northern tourists chugged down the sandy village road in automobiles. The town knew the Southerners and never stopped cane chewing when they passed. But the Northerners were something else again. They were peered at cautiously from behind curtains by the timid. The more venturesome would come out on the porch to watch them go past and got just as much pleasure out of the tourists as the tourists got out of the village.

The front porch might seem a daring place for the rest of the town, but it was a gallery seat for me. My favorite place was atop the gatepost. Proscenium box for a born first-nighter. Not only did I enjoy the show, but I didn't mind the actors knowing that I liked it. I usually spoke to them in passing. I'd wave at them and when they returned my salute, I would say something like this: "Howdy-do-well-I-thank-you-where-you-goin'?" Usually automobile or the horse paused at this, and after a queer exchange of compliments, I would probably "go a piece of the way" with them, as we say in farthest Florida. If one of my family happened to come to the front in time to see me, of course negotiations would be rudely broken off. But even so, it is clear that I was the first "welcome-to-our-state" Floridian, and I hope the Miami Chamber of Commerce will please take notice.

During this period, white people differed from colored to me only in that they rode through town and never lived there. They liked to hear me "speak pieces" and sing and wanted to see me dance the parse-me-la[1], and gave me generously of their small silver for doing these things, which seemed strange to me for I wanted to do them so much that I needed bribing to stop, only they didn't know it. The colored people gave no dimes. They deplored any joyful tendencies in me, but I was their Zora nevertheless. I belonged to them, to the nearby hotels, to the county—everybody's Zora.

But changes came in the family when I was thirteen, and I was sent to school in Jacksonville. I left Eatonville, the town of the oleanders, a Zora. When I disembarked from the river-boat at Jacksonville, she was no more. It seemed that I had suffered a sea change. I was not Zora of Orange County any more, I was now a little colored girl. I found it out in certain ways. In my heart as well as in the mirror, I became a fast brown—warranted not to rub nor run.

But I am not tragically colored. There is no great sorrow dammed up in my soul, nor lurking behind my eyes. I do not mind at all. I do not belong to the sobbing school of Negrohood who hold that nature somehow has given them a lowdown dirty deal and whose feelings are all but about it. Even in the helter-skelter skirmish that is my life, I have seen that the world is to the strong regardless of a little pigmentation more or less. No, I do not weep at the world—I am too busy sharpening my oyster knife.

Someone is always at my elbow reminding me that I am the granddaughter of slaves. It fails to register depression with me. Slavery is sixty years in the past. The operation was successful and the patient is doing well, thank you. The terrible struggle that made me an American out of a potential slave said "On the line!" The Reconstruction said "Get set!" and the generation before said "Go!" I am off to a flying start and I must not halt in the stretch to look behind and weep. Slavery is the price I paid for civilization, and the choice was not with me. It is a bully adventure and worth all that I have paid through my ancestors for it. No one on earth ever had a greater chance for glory. The world to be won and nothing to be lost. It is thrilling to think—to know that for any act of mine, I shall get twice as much praise or twice as much blame. It is quite exciting to hold the center of the national stage, with the spectators not knowing whether to laugh or to weep.

The position of my white neighbor is much more difficult. No brown specter pulls up a chair beside me when I sit down to eat. No dark ghost thrusts its leg against mine in bed. The game of keeping what one has is never so exciting as the game of getting.

---

1 "parse-me-la." A dance movement popular with southern African-Americans at the time.

I do not always feel colored. Even now I often achieve the unconscious Zora of Eatonville before the Hegira. I feel most colored when I am thrown against a sharp white background.

For instance at Barnard. "Beside the waters of the Hudson"[2] I feel my race. Among the thousand white persons, I am a dark rock surged upon, overswept by a creamy sea. I am surged upon and overswept, but through it all, I remain myself. When covered by the waters, I am; and the ebb but reveals me again.

Sometimes it is the other way around. A white person is set down in our midst, but the contrast is just as sharp for me. For instance, when I sit in the drafty basement that is The New World Cabaret with a white person, my color comes. We enter chatting about any little nothing that we have in common and are seated by the jazz waiters. In the abrupt way that jazz orchestras have, this one plunges into a number. It loses no time in circumlocutions, but gets right down to business. It constricts the thorax and splits the heart with its tempo and narcotic harmonies. This orchestra grows rambunctious, rears on its hind legs and attacks the tonal veil with primitive fury, rending it, clawing it until it breaks through to the jungle beyond. I follow those heathens—follow them exultingly. I dance wildly inside myself; I yell within, I whoop; I shake my assegai above my head, I hurl it true to the mark yeeeeooww! I am in the jungle and living in the jungle way. My face is painted red and yellow and my body is painted blue. My pulse is throbbing like a war drum. I want to slaughter something—give pain, give death to what, I do not know. But the piece ends. The men of the orchestra wipe their lips and rest their fingers. I creep back slowly to the veneer we call civilization with the last tone and find the white friend sitting motionless in his seat, smoking calmly.

"Good music they have here," he remarks, drumming the table with his fingertips.

Music. The great blobs of purple and red emotion have not touched him. He has only heard what I felt. He is far away and I see him but dimly across the ocean and the continent that have fallen between us. He is so pale with his whiteness then and I am so colored.

At certain times I have no race; I am me. When I set my hat at a certain angle and saunter down Seventh Avenue, Harlem City, feeling as snooty as the lions in front of the Forty-Second Street Library, for instance. So far as my feelings are concerned, Peggy Hopkins Joyce on the Boule Mich[3] with her gorgeous raiment, stately carriage, knees knocking together in a most aristocratic manner,

---

2 "Beside the waters . . ." is a reference to the first line of a Barnard College song.
3 "Peggy Hopkins Joyce on the Boule Mich" is a reference to the American actress, model, and dancer (1893-1957) well-known at the time for her lavish lifestyle. The Boule Mich is the Boulevard Saint-Michel in Paris.

has nothing on me. The cosmic Zora emerges. I belong to no race nor time. I am the eternal feminine with its string of beads.

I have no separate feeling about being an American citizen and colored. I am merely a fragment of the Great Soul that surges within the boundaries. My country, right or wrong.

Sometimes, I feel discriminated against, but it does not make me angry. It merely astonishes me. How can any deny themselves the pleasure of my company? It's beyond me.

But in the main, I feel like a brown bag of miscellany propped against a wall. Against a wall in company with other bags, white, red and yellow. Pour out the contents, and there is discovered a jumble of small things priceless and worthless. A first-water diamond, an empty spool, bits of broken glass, lengths of string, a key to a door long since crumbled away, a rusty knife-blade, old shoes saved for a road that never was and never will be, a nail bent under the weight of things too heavy for any nail, a dried flower or two still a little fragrant. In your hand is the brown bag. On the ground before you is the jumble it held—so much like the jumble in the bags, could they be emptied, that all might be dumped in a single heap and the bags refilled without altering the content of any greatly. A bit of colored glass more or less would not matter. Perhaps that is how the Great Stuffer of Bags filled them in the first place—who knows?

Topics for Writing and Discussion

1. Have you ever been the only representative of one of the groups with which you identify in a room or at work, school, church, etc.? What did you learn from this experience? Write a short essay explaining how you felt in that situation.
2. Based on reading Hurston's essay, how would you define the difference between Hurston's description of her experience in 1928 and your experience as a minority today? How has that experience changed?
3. Write an essay on how it feels to be uniquely you.

Living the Dream

Michael Jernigan

Michael Jernigan was a marine corporal serving in Iraq when he was severely injured by a roadside bomb on August 22, 2004. The following account of his struggles with PTSD was published in *The New York Times* on October 11, 2009.

Greetings again from the Sunshine State.

As I mentioned in my first post I would like to bring some awareness to an issue facing many of us returning war veterans. Post-traumatic stress disorder (P.T.S.D.) is a monster that war veterans have been facing since the beginning of armed conflict. In a nutshell, it is the stress brought on by a traumatic event. I understand that it is more complicated than that, but I would like to keep it as simple as possible for our purposes here.

I am living with P.T.S.D., and I am thriving in some respects and having problems in others. In this and future posts I plan to use myself and my experiences as examples.

Post-traumatic stress can manifest itself in many different ways. It is usually brought on by a trigger mechanism, or what some might call a catalyst. It can be something very minor that can be easily controlled or it can be so large that it has life altering circumstances.

So what do I mean when I say I am both thriving and having problems at the same time? Well, I can tell you that in school I am thriving. I have been back for a couple of years now and continue to pull a 3-plus grade point average every semester. It is in other parts of my life that I am struggling.

My relationship with my wife has been strained because of the way I react to certain things; my relationship with my stepson has suffered as well. I have quick reactions full of emotion that are not checked before they come out. In many cases they are very aggressive and quite counterproductive. I am impatient in numerous situations and become frustrated easily. To top it all off I often have to overcome bouts of anxiety, especially when I am outside my house. I do well in social situations but I find them physically taxing. I have been receiving help with all of these problems and I am improving at a good rate. My wife and I have worked hard to help me overcome a lot of these symptoms.

One of the most common problems facing our war veterans when we return home is drug and alcohol abuse. We turn to these to escape from emotions. I drank heavily when I returned home. I would drink to the point that I would pass out at night. I would do this because I could not sleep. I could not sleep because there were a healthy wave of emotions that I refused to face. What made sleep hard was the P.T.S.D. in conjunction with a traumatic brain injury. When I would finally sleep I had to deal with some strange and horrific dreams.

I would have dreams that most people would be scared by. I was scared, too, especially when I would have the same dream more than once. One of the strangest dreams took place in Iraq. We would be returning from a foot patrol at night. It was as if I were looking through a set of night vision goggles. There were two gates that we would have to come through at our forward operating base (F.O.B.). I can remember gaining access through the first gate but then not being able to enter the inner part of the base until daybreak. Since we could not get back to our hooches we would decide to sleep under the gun line (155-millimeter howitzers), something that would not be done for safety purposes. Just when I would be drifting off to sleep the gun line would open up. It was at that point that I would awake for real. I was never able to go back to sleep after that.

There were dreams that were both strange and violent. In one of them, I was in the spare bedroom of a condominium that I had rented before I enlisted. When I lived there the only thing in this room was my gun cabinet with all of my rifles and shotguns in it. During my dream I was in this room waist deep in stuffed animals. Someone would enter the room (I could never identify the person) and attack me. We would be fighting in this room. At a certain point in the fight I would gain the advantage. I would bend over this individual and bite his throat out. It was always bloody. Just then I would wake up.

One of the hardest dreams to deal with came back many times. It was one of the scariest in my mind. It took place in Iraq as well. I can remember being on patrol in Mahmudiya. That is the town that I was wounded in. I was always on patrol with a group of Marines. At some point in the dream I would become separated from my patrol. Iraq can be a scary place to find yourself alone in. It got worse. I cannot remember how, but I would lose my rifle (a good Marine does not lose his weapon). I would see a small kid scampering off with my rifle and follow him. I was terrified of returning back to base without my rifle. The kid would enter a building and I knew that I would have to follow him into the building. Keep in mind that I am defenseless. When I would enter the building I always encountered hand to hand combat with a few different individuals at one time. I would always defeat those attacking me. I can remember that I also would find a number of weapons that had once belonged to Marines — pistols, rifles and shotguns. To my dismay I would never find my rifle.

I would see the kid again and chase him one more time. I always wound up chasing him into another building and encountering more and more hand to hand combat situations. I would always find more weapons but never mine. I always picked up the weapons that I would find and bring them with me before I gave pursuit to that kid again. This cycle would never end. I would thrash around in my bed until I would wake up hot and sweating. I could never get back to sleep and was quite disturbed by this dream.

While I was in Washington D.C. I started to make significant progress on many different fronts. I found a counselor there named Carey Smith, a disabled veteran from the Vietnam War. He has been through what I have. He began to teach me how to interpret my dreams in a positive way. I know that this can be hard to do. When he first told me I was very hesitant. As he explained it to me I started to understand what he was talking about.

We came to the conclusion that the dreams were my mind's way of reconciling problems I had. They usually dealt with some guilt I had over one thing or another. In many of these situations, I would have no way of making things better, so my brain would do it for me in my sleep. Once I grasped this concept the dreams became much easier to deal with. I would then wake up in the middle of the night and be able to tell myself that there was nothing wrong and return to sleep. It is great. Currently, I am not dealing with any harsh dreams. I use the term "harsh" because I no longer see these dreams as bad but as healthy and productive.

One of the things that I am learning as I am living with P.T.S.D. is that these feelings can be dealt with positively, that these different symptoms do not have to control my life. I am doing my best to live my life and be happy. There is no magic pill that will make things better. By facing the difficult emotions and learning how to positively react to them my life becomes easier. The emotions are still there — they will probably never go away. But when I face them sober and head on I can live my good dreams and not be controlled by the difficult ones.

Topics for Writing and Discussion

1. Jernigan discusses the effects of post-traumatic stress disorder (PTSD). The latest report of the United States Department of Veterans Affairs lists over 375,000 cases of reported PTSD between 2001 and 2014. If you are a veteran, have you experienced symptoms similar to Jernigan's? Or do you know someone who has experienced PTSD? What can civilians, your classmates, do to help? Or should they do anything?

2. Jernigan recounts a recurring dream from his experience in Iraq. While generally not as violent (we hope), at some point, perhaps because of stress, we all experience recurring dreams. Write an essay describing a recurrent dream you have had, and then try to explain what you think caused it.

My Zombie, Myself: Why Modern Life Feels Rather Undead

Chuck Klosterman

Chuck Klosterman is a novelist, nonfiction writer, and essayist who writes for a number of magazines, including the *New York Times Magazine*. The following essay was published in *The New York Times* on December 3, 2010.

Zombies are a value stock. They are wordless and oozing and brain dead, but they're an ever-expanding market with no glass ceiling. Zombies are a target-rich environment, literally and figuratively. The more you fill them with bullets, the more interesting they become. Roughly 5.3 million people watched the first episode of "The Walking Dead" on AMC, a stunning 83 percent more than the 2.9 million who watched the Season 4 premiere of "Mad Men." This means there are at least 2.4 million cable-ready Americans who might prefer watching Christina Hendricks if she were an animated corpse.

Statistically and aesthetically that dissonance seems perverse. But it probably shouldn't. Mainstream interest in zombies has steadily risen over the past 40 years. Zombies are a commodity that has advanced slowly and without major evolution, much like the staggering creatures George Romero popularized in the 1968 film "Night of the Living Dead." What makes that measured amplification curious is the inherent limitations of the zombie itself: You can't add much depth to a creature who can't talk, doesn't think and whose only motive is the consumption of flesh. You can't humanize a zombie, unless you make it less zombie-esque. There are slow zombies, and there are fast zombies— that's pretty much the spectrum of zombie diversity. It's not that zombies are changing to fit the world's condition; it's that the condition of the world seems more like a zombie offensive. Something about zombies is becoming more intriguing to us. And I think I know what that something is.

Zombies are just so easy to kill.

When we think critically about monsters, we tend to classify them as personifications of what we fear. Frankenstein's monster illustrated our trepidation about untethered science; Godzilla was spawned from the fear of the atomic age; werewolves feed into an instinctual panic over predation and man's detachment from nature. Vampires and zombies share an imbedded anxiety about disease. It's easy to project a symbolic relationship between zombies and rabies (or zombies and the pitfalls of consumerism), just as it's easy to project a symbolic relationship between vampirism and AIDS (or vampirism and the loss of purity). From a creative standpoint these fear projections are narrative linchpins; they turn creatures into ideas, and that's the point.

But what if the audience infers an entirely different metaphor?

What if contemporary people are less interested in seeing depictions of their unconscious fears and more attracted to allegories of how their day-to-day existence feels? That would explain why so many people watched that first episode of "The Walking Dead": They knew they would be able to relate to it.

A lot of modern life is exactly like slaughtering zombies.

If there's one thing we all understand about zombie killing, it's that the act is uncomplicated: you blast one in the brain from point-blank range (preferably with a shotgun). That's Step 1. Step 2 is doing the same thing to the next zombie that takes its place. Step 3 is identical to Step 2, and Step 4 isn't any different from Step 3. Repeat this process until (a) you perish, or (b) you run out of zombies. That's really the only viable strategy.

Every zombie war is a war of attrition. It's always a numbers game. And it's more repetitive than complex. In other words, zombie killing is philosophically similar to reading and deleting 400 work e-mails on a Monday morning or filling out paperwork that only generates more paperwork, or following Twitter gossip out of obligation, or performing tedious tasks in which the only true risk is being consumed by the avalanche. The principal downside to any zombie attack is that the zombies will never stop coming; the principal downside to life is that you will never be finished with whatever it is you do.

The Internet reminds us of this every day.

Here's a passage from a youngish writer named Alice Gregory, taken from a recent essay on Gary Shteyngart's dystopic novel "Super Sad True Love Story" in the literary journal *n + 1*: "It's hard not to think 'death drive' every time I go on the Internet," she writes. "Opening Safari is an actively destructive decision. I am asking that consciousness be taken away from me."

Ms. Gregory's self-directed fear is thematically similar to how the zombie brain is described by Max Brooks, author of the fictional oral history "World War Z" and its accompanying self-help manual, "The Zombie Survival Guide": "Imagine a computer programmed to execute one function. This function cannot be paused, modified or erased. No new data can be stored. No new commands can be installed. This computer will perform that one function, over and over, until its power source eventually shuts down."

This is our collective fear projection: that we will be consumed. Zombies are like the Internet and the media and every conversation we don't want to have. All of it comes at us endlessly (and thoughtlessly), and—if we surrender—we will be overtaken and absorbed. Yet this war is manageable, if not necessarily winnable. As long we keep deleting whatever's directly in front of us, we survive. We live to eliminate the zombies of tomorrow. We are able to remain human, at least for the time being. Our enemy is relentless and colossal, but also uncreative and stupid.

Battling zombies is like battling anything . . . or everything.

Because of the "Twilight" series it's easy to manufacture an argument in which zombies are merely replacing vampires as the monster of the moment, a designation that is supposed to matter for metaphorical, nonmonstrous reasons. But that kind of thinking is deceptive. The recent five-year spike in vampire interest is only about the multiplatform success of "Twilight," a brand that isn't about vampirism anyway. It's mostly about nostalgia for teenage chastity, the attractiveness of its film cast and the fact that contemporary fiction consumers tend to prefer long serialized novels that can be read rapidly. But this has still created a domino effect. The 2008 Swedish vampire film "Let the Right One In" was fantastic, but it probably wouldn't have been remade in the United States if "Twilight" had never existed. "The Gates" was an overt attempt by ABC to tap into the housebound, preteen "Twilight" audience; HBO's "True Blood" is a camp reaction to Robert Pattinson's flat earnestness.

The difference with zombies, of course, is that it's possible to like a specific vampire temporarily, which isn't really an option with the undead. Characters like Mr. Pattinson's Edward Cullen in "Twilight" and Anne Rice's Lestat de Lioncourt, and even boring old Count Dracula can be multidimensional and erotic; it's possible to learn who they are and who they once were. Vampire love can be singular. Zombie love, however, is always communal. If you dig zombies, you dig the entire zombie concept. It's never personal. You're interested in what zombies signify, you like the way they move, and you understand what's required to stop them. And this is a reassuring attraction, because those aspects don't really shift. They've become shared archetypal knowledge.

A few days before Halloween I was in upstate New York with three other people, and we somehow ended up at the Barn of Terror, outside a town called Lake Katrine. Entering the barn was mildly disturbing, although probably not as scary as going into an actual abandoned barn that didn't charge $20 and doesn't own its own domain name. Regardless, the best part was when we exited the terror barn and were promptly herded onto a school bus, which took us to a cornfield about a quarter of a mile away. The field was filled with amateur actors, some playing military personnel and others what they called the infected. We were told to run through the moonlit corn maze if we wanted to live; as we ran, armed soldiers yelled contradictory instructions while hissing zombies emerged from the corny darkness. It was designed to be fun, and it was. But just before we immersed ourselves in the corn, one of my companions sardonically critiqued the reality of our predicament.

"I know this is supposed to be scary," he said. "But I'm pretty confident about my ability to deal with a zombie apocalypse. I feel strangely informed about what to do in this kind of scenario."

I could not disagree. At this point who isn't? We all know how this goes: If you awake from a coma, and you don't immediately see a member of the hospital staff, assume a zombie takeover has transpired during your incapacitation. Don't travel at night and keep your drapes closed. Don't let zombies spit on you. If you knock a zombie down, direct a second bullet into its brain stem. But above all, do not assume that the war is over, because it never is. The zombies you kill today will merely be replaced by the zombies of tomorrow. But you can do this, my friend. It's disenchanting, but it's not difficult. Keep your finger on the trigger. Continue the termination. Don't stop believing. Don't stop deleting. Return your voice mails and nod your agreements. This is the zombies' world, and we just live in it. But we can live better.

Topics for Writing and Discussion

1. Klosterman sees the popularity of zombies as a metaphor for the repetitiousness, the routine, of much of modern life. Whether at school or at work, we do the same things over and over again. Just as we finish one task, another one pops up; just as we finish one paper, we have to write another one. Tasks keep coming at us, just like zombies. Write a short essay on your own form of zombie killing. What are the daily zombies you face, and what keeps you at your task of killing them?

2. Klosterman ends with the sentence "But we can live better." What do you think he means by that? Write an essay on what you think could be done at your school, your workplace, or your home to reduce the zombie population.

What ISIS Could Teach the West

Nicholas Kristof

Nicholas Kristof is a syndicated columnist for *The New York Times*. He writes on a variety of topics, including women's rights, race, and global politics. The following essay was published in *The New York Times* on October 1, 2014. At the time of this essay, ISIS (Islamic State in Iraq and Syria), an extremist Muslim fundamentalist group, had taken over large swaths of Syria and Iraq. They killed thousands of people who held different beliefs, broadcast beheadings on YouTube, and established what they called a caliphate under a strict way of life called sharia law. The United States aided Iraqi forces and others attempting to push back ISIS by engaging in an air war against them.

As we fight the Islamic State and other extremists, there's something that President Obama and all of us can learn from them. For, in one sense, the terrorists are fighting smarter than we are.

These extremists use arms to fight their battles in the short term, but, to hold ground in the long run, they also combat Western education and women's empowerment. They know that illiteracy, ignorance and oppression of women create the petri dish in which extremism can flourish.

That's why the Islamic State kidnapped Samira Salih al-Nuaimi, a brave Iraqi woman and human rights lawyer in Mosul, tortured her and publicly executed her last week. That's why the Taliban shot Malala Yousafzai, then 15 years old, after she campaigned for educating girls. And that's why Boko Haram kidnapped hundreds of schoolgirls in northern Nigeria and announced that it would turn them into slaves.

In each case, the extremists recognized a basic truth: Their greatest strategic threat comes not from a drone but from a girl with a book. We need to recognize, and act on, that truth as well.

For similar reasons, the financiers of extremism have invested heavily in fundamentalist indoctrination. They have built Wahhabi madrassas in poor Muslim countries like Pakistan, Niger and Mali, offering free meals, as well as scholarships for the best students to study in the gulf.

Shouldn't we try to compete?

Shouldn't we use weapons in the short run, but try to gain strategic advantage by focusing on education and on empowering women to build stable societies less vulnerable to extremist manipulation?

The United States' airstrikes have slowed the advance of the Islamic State and averted a genocide against the Yazidi population in Iraq, but it's very difficult to win a war from the air. That's why the Taliban still thrives in Afghanistan after 13 years of American air attacks.

Unfortunately, we're not playing the long game, as the extremists are. We are vastly overrelying on the military toolbox and underemploying the education toolbox, the women's empowerment toolbox, the communications toolbox. We're tacticians; alas, the extremists may be better strategists.

It's not a question of resources, because bombs are more expensive than books. The United States military campaign against the Islamic State, which is also known as ISIS and ISIL, will cost at least $2.4 billion a year and perhaps many times that, according to an estimate from the Center for Strategic and Budgetary Assessments in Washington.

In contrast, Obama seems to have dropped his 2008 campaign promise to establish a $2 billion global fund for education. And the United States gives the Global Partnership for Education, a major multilateral effort, less in a year than what we spend weekly in Syria and Iraq.

This is an area where Congress seems more forward-looking than the president because Congress regularly appropriates substantially more for basic education overseas than Obama requests. Bipartisan legislation, the Education for All Act, would elevate the issue; let's hope that Obama gets behind it.

No one is naïve enough to think that education is a panacea. Al Qaeda leaders, including Osama bin Laden and Ayman al-Zawahri, have been university educated. Iraq, Syria and Lebanon were all reasonably well-educated and supportive of gender equality by regional standards, yet all have been torn apart by civil wars.

Still, the historical record of the last half-century is that education tends to nurture a more cosmopolitan middle class and gives people a stake in the system. In Hong Kong today, we're seeing how educated youth often behave. They are demanding democracy, but peacefully.

Girls' education seems to have more impact than boys' education, partly because educated women have markedly fewer children. The result is lower birthrates and less of a youth bulge in the population, which highly correlates to civil conflict.

I support judicious airstrikes in the short term against the Islamic State, but that should be only one part of a policy combating extremism. And a starting point should be to ensure that the three million Syrian refugees mostly in Turkey, Jordan and Lebanon — especially girls — can get schooling. Right now, many are getting none, and one study published last month found that Syria had the worst reversal in educational attainment in recent history, with enrollment rates for Syrian children in Lebanon less than half the level of those in sub-Saharan Africa.

Yet the Unicef request for education funding for Syrians was only 40 percent financed as of mid-August. If we miss this opportunity, those children will be tinder for future wars and extremism, and we'll be stuck dropping bombs for generations to come.

So let's learn from the extremists — and from those brave girls themselves who are willing to risk their lives in order to get an education. They all understand the power of education, and we should, too.

Topics for Writing and Discussion

1. Kristof makes the point that while bombing, in the short run, may slow the advance of such extremist groups, ultimately only education will create the social change we seek in the region. He says "illiteracy, ignorance and oppression of women create the petri dish in which extremism can flourish." He particularly emphasizes the need for education for women. Write an essay in which you describe the attitudes toward women in your own family or ethnic group. Are they valued equally with men? Is the education of women valued as much as that of men?

2. Historically, in the United States education has been the path of upward mobility for immigrant groups. Today, however, because of many trends, such as outsourcing and the use of digital technologies in the workplace, upward mobility has stagnated. The gap between the super rich and everyone else has widened, and student debt has soared to over a trillion dollars, while at the same time, many industries lack skilled workers. This situation has led some to question the value of a college education. What do you think?

When Whites Just Don't Get it: Part 5

Nicholas Kristof

Nicholas Kristof is a syndicated columnist for *The New York Times*. He writes on a variety of topics, including women's rights, race, and global politics. The following essay was published in *The New York Times* on November 29, 2014.

We Americans are a nation divided.

We feud about the fires in Ferguson, Mo., and we can agree only that racial divisions remain raw. So let's borrow a page from South Africa and impanel a Truth and Reconciliation Commission to examine race in America.

The model should be the 9/11 commission or the Warren Commission on President Kennedy's assassination, and it should hold televised hearings and issue a report to help us understand ourselves. Perhaps it could be led by the likes of Presidents Bill Clinton and George W. Bush and Oprah Winfrey.

We as a nation need to grapple with race because the evidence is overwhelming that racial bias remains deeply embedded in American life. Two economists, Joseph Price and Justin Wolfers, found that white N.B.A. referees disproportionally call fouls on black players, while black refs call more fouls on white players. "These biases are sufficiently large that they affect the outcome of an appreciable number of games," Price and Wolfers wrote.

If such racial bias exists among professional referees monitored by huge television audiences, imagine what unfolds when an employer privately weighs whom to hire, or a principal decides whether to expel a disruptive student, or a policeman considers whether to pull over a driver.

This "When Whites Just Don't Get It" series is a call for soul-searching. It's very easy for whites to miss problems that aren't our own; that's a function not of being white but of being human. Three-quarters of whites have only white friends, according to one study, so we are often clueless.

What we whites notice is blacks who have "made it" — including President Obama — so we focus on progress and are oblivious to the daily humiliations that African-Americans endure when treated as second-class citizens.

"In the jewelry store, they lock the case when I walk in," a 23-year-old black man wrote in May 1992. "In the shoe store, they help the white man who walks in after me. In the shopping mall, they follow me."

He described an incident when he was stopped by six police officers who detained him, with guns at the ready, and treated him for 30 minutes as a dangerous suspect.

That young man was future Senator Cory Booker, who had been a senior class president at Stanford University and was a newly selected Rhodes Scholar. Yet our law enforcement system reduced him to a stereotype — so young Booker sat trembling and praying that he wouldn't be shot by the police.

My sense is that part of the problem is well-meaning Americans who disapprove of racism yet inadvertently help perpetuate it. We aren't racists, yet we buttress a system that acts in racist ways. It's "racism without racists," in the words of Eduardo Bonillo-Silva, a Duke University sociologist.

This occurs partly because of deeply embedded stereotypes that trick us, even when we want to be fair. Researchers once showed people sketches of a white man with a knife confronting an unarmed black man in the subway. In one version of the experiment, 59 percent of research subjects later reported that it had been the black man who held the knife.

I don't know what unfolded in Ferguson between Michael Brown, a black teenager, and Darren Wilson, a white police officer. But there is a pattern: a ProPublica investigation found that young black men are shot dead by police at 21 times the rate of young white men.

If you're white, your interactions with police are more likely to have been professional and respectful, leaving you trustful. If you're black, your encounters with cops may leave you dubious and distrustful. That's why a Huffington Post/YouGov poll found that 64 percent of African-Americans believe that Officer Wilson should be punished, while only 22 percent of whites think so.

That's the gulf that an American Truth and Reconciliation Commission might help bridge just a little. In 1922, a Chicago Commission on Race Relations (composed of six whites and six blacks) examined the Chicago race riots of 1919. More recently, President Clinton used an executive order to impanel an advisory board on race that focused on how to nurture "one America."

A new commission could jump-start an overdue national conversation and also recommend evidence-based solutions to boost educational outcomes, improve family cohesion and connect people to jobs.

White Americans may protest that our racial problems are not like South Africa's. No, but the United States incarcerates a higher proportion of blacks than apartheid South Africa did. In America, the black-white wealth gap today is greater than it was in South Africa in 1970 at the peak of apartheid.

Most troubling, America's racial wealth gap, pay gap and college education gap have all widened in the last few decades.

There are no easy solutions. But let's talk.

Topics for Writing and Discussion

1. Do you think Kristof's proposal to set up a national commission composed of prominent black and white leaders to study the problem of race in America is a good one? Why or why not?

2. Kristof gives several examples of how implicit racial bias affects African-Americans on a daily basis. Have you ever directly experienced racial, ethnic, or gender bias in dealing with others? Write a short essay describing what happened and how you felt.

3. Numerous studies have shown that we all have an implicit bias in favor of members of our own ethnic group and against other ethnic groups. (You might want to reread E. O. Wilson's essay, "Why Humans, Like Ants, Need a Tribe" on page 181.) Given that the US, and now the world, is becoming more integrated and more diverse, what can be done to smooth relations between different "tribes"? Write an essay in which you propose some specific ways to smooth over interethnic relations.

Five Myths About *Brown v. Board of Education*

Imani Perry

Imani Perry is a professor in the Center for African American Studies and an associate in the Program for Law and Public Affairs at Princeton University. She received her PhD and JD from Harvard University in 2000 and has written several books, the latest being *More Beautiful and More Terrible: The Embrace and Transcendence of Racial Inequality in the United States* (2011). She also has written numerous essays in cultural and African-American studies. The following article was published in *The Washington Post* on May 16, 2014.

In the 1954 *Brown v. Board of Education* opinion, the Supreme Court declared that state laws requiring segregation in public schools were unconstitutional. But change didn't come easily, nor are schools all that integrated today. Sixty years after Brown, let's examine some myths about the landmark court decision.

1. *Brown v. Board of Education* was only about school segregation.

   It's true that the case concerned segregation in public schools, but its impact went far beyond education. *Brown* overturned the 1896 Supreme Court ruling in *Plessy v. Ferguson*, which declared that segregated train cars did not violate the equal-protection clause of the 14th Amendment. While it wasn't immediately clear, *Brown* would eventually dismantle segregation in all public facilities such as train cars, restaurants, department stores and more. The case emboldened civil rights protesters, who, for the first time in nearly 100 years of struggle and defeat, found the federal courts on their side.

   Before the *Brown* ruling, Jim Crow laws meant that schooling was not only segregated, often it wasn't even available. As historian James Anderson has noted, high schools in many areas were provided only for white children. After *Brown*, some municipalities were forced to provide high school education for African American youth for the first time.

   The case was also the first step in allowing significant numbers of Asians, Latinos, Africans and Caribbean people to immigrate to the United States. The Civil Rights Act, so diligently fought for by African American activists in the decade following *Brown*, led Congress to change racially discriminatory immigration policies. Immigrants could no longer be legally Jim Crowed, either.

2. *Brown v. Board* ended school segregation.

   American schools are as segregated today as they were 40 years ago, largely because of residential segregation and the racial gaps in wealth and employment. In the 1970s, white flight to affluent suburbs weakened the tax base of cities, hitting black migrants to Northern cities hard. Their schools became under-funded and more isolated than in the Southern Jim Crow states they had fled. Today, the Northeast has the most racially homogenous schools; New York state and Washington, D.C., have the most segregated schools—by race and economic status. And since there is no constitutional right to an education, the federal courts cannot mandate that schools get equal funding. Within schools, advanced programs have become forms of segregation. One study found that, as of 2006, African American students were underrepresented by 48 percent in gifted education; Hispanic students are underrepresented by 38 percent.

The courts have interpreted *Brown* to mean that explicit considerations of race are unconstitutional. As a result, efforts to desegregate—such as affirmative action at the college level or plans to create more diverse primary and secondary schools—are generally considered unconstitutional. Therefore, states are hindered when they try to further integrate schools.

3.   School segregation was a problem only for African Americans in the South.

Although the starkest Jim Crow laws were found in the Deep South, school segregation was practiced all across the United States. Oliver and Darlene Brown, the lead plaintiffs in *Brown v. Board,* brought the case in Topeka, Kansas. Two of the other cases joined in the *Brown* litigation were in Delaware and the District. And the first state court case about racial segregation in schools was in Massachusetts: *Sarah C. Roberts v. the City of Boston* (1849). That ruling declared that it was legal for Boston not to admit 5-year-old Sarah Roberts, who was African American, to her all-white neighborhood school. Although Boston officially stopped having separate schools shortly before the Civil War, in the 1970s it was the site of one of the most vicious and violent desegregation battles.

Brown v. Board of Education had a national and multiracial impact. Before the Supreme Court decision, Mexican Americans were segregated in practice, if not by law, in California, Arizona, Texas and Colorado, with the justification that they were native Spanish-speakers. And in several parts of the country, Asian Americans and Native Americans were also segregated.

4.   African Americans were united in their support for school desegregation.

African Americans generally rejoiced over the *Brown* ruling and the other changes it spurred. However, a number of African American critics didn't want school integration to be a priority in the struggle for racial justice. For instance, Zora Neale Hurston argued that fighting for integration suggested that African American schools—notwithstanding their dedicated and trained faculty members and their role as centers of African American life—were inferior. "How much satisfaction can I get from a court order for somebody to associate with me who does not wish me near them?" she wrote in 1955.

W.E.B. Du Bois also had reservations. In a 1935 article, he argued that "a separate Negro school, where children are treated like human beings, trained by teachers of their own race, who know what it means to be black … is infinitely better than making our boys and girls doormats." Many others warned that desegregation would mean the loss of an important black professional class. They were correct: Many black school administrators and teachers lost their jobs in the process of desegregation. And many communities lost control of their schools. Schools remain segregated, but they are no longer the community pillars they once were. In that sense, African Americans sacrificed their most important social institution, outside of the church.

5.   Affirmative action keeps colleges integrated today.

Affirmative action was imagined as a strategy to create integrated industries, professions, colleges and universities. For hundreds of years, people of color had been systematically excluded from institutions and opportunities. In the late 1960s and early '70s, affirmative action started to crack open the door of opportunity. However, since 1977 the Supreme Court has been steadily limiting the policy's scope. At present, only elite private institutions have the resources to create the very narrowly tailored affirmative action policies allowed by the court. The vast majority of public colleges and universities—which have a duty to serve a broad cross-section of the population—are hamstrung in their efforts to equalize educational opportunity.

Topics for Writing and Discussion

1.   Perry writes: "Before the *Brown* ruling, Jim Crow laws meant that schooling was not only segregated, often it wasn't even available." Who was Jim Crow? Use the internet to track down Jim Crow and what some of the Jim Crow laws were, and then write a report on it. Be sure to avoid plagiarism, and cite your sources properly.

2.   Perry says that schools "are no longer the community pillars they once were. In that sense, African Americans sacrificed their most important social institution, outside of the church." Do you think attending an all-white (or mostly all-white) school, or an all-black (or mostly all-black) school would be helpful or harmful to a child growing up?

3.   As Perry points out, *Brown* did not end school segregation. Schools today are perhaps more segregated than they were in the 1970s. There has also been a pushback against affirmative action, particularly on the college level. For example, after being denied admission to the University of Texas in 2008, Abigail Fisher sued the university, claiming reverse discrimination because race is one of the factors used by UT in admitting students who

do not qualify for automatic admission—those in the top seven percent of their high school graduating classes. The case went to the Supreme Court. In July 2014 and June 2016, the court upheld UT's policy. Write an essay on the use of affirmative action at the college level, either defending it or arguing it should be discontinued.

First, Let's Fire All the Teachers!

Diane Ravitch

Diane Ravitch is a professor in the Steinhardt School of Culture, Education, and Human Development at New York University. She has written extensively on education and the history of education. She was an assistant secretary of education under President George H. W. Bush and was appointed to the National Assessment Governing Board by President Bill Clinton. Her latest book is *Reign of Error: The Hoax of the Privatization Movement and the Danger to America's Public Schools* (2013). The following article was published in *Huff Post: Politics* on May 2, 2010, and later updated on August 9, 2012.

Imagine that you are a teacher in a high school in a high-poverty district. Many of your students don't speak English. Some don't attend school regularly because they have to earn money or babysit with their siblings while their parents are looking for work. Some come to school unprepared because they didn't do their homework.

But you are idealistic and dedicated, you work with each of the students, you do your best to teach them reading, writing, science, math, history, whatever your subject. But despite your best efforts, many of your students can't read very well (they are struggling to learn English), and many of them don't graduate. If your school eliminated all its standards, you could easily push up the graduation rate.

About 45 minutes away is another high school in a much better neighborhood. Its statistics are far better than yours. The children are almost all born in the U.S., and their parents are almost all college graduates with good jobs. Their kids don't go to school hungry, they have their own room and their own computer, and they have stellar test scores to boot. Their graduation rate is very impressive, and most of their graduates go to college.

What is to be done about the first school? President George W. Bush signed a law called "No Child Left Behind," which required constant improvement. The Obama administration wants to rename the law but they too reject any excuses for low performance and low graduation rates.

Recently, the school committee of Central Falls, Rhode Island, voted to fire all 93 members of the staff in their low-performing high school. Central Falls is the smallest and poorest city in the state, and it has only one high school. Those fired included 74 classroom teachers, plus the school psychologist, guidance counselors, reading specialists, and administrators.

Secretary of Education Arne Duncan thought this was wonderful; he said the members of the school committee were "showing courage and doing the right thing for kids." The kids apparently didn't agree because many of them came to the committee meeting to defend their teachers.

President Obama thought it was wonderful that every educator at Central Falls High School was fired. At an appearance before the U.S. Chamber of Commerce on March 1, the President applauded the idea of closing the school and getting rid of everyone in it. At the same meeting, President Obama acknowledged Margaret Spellings, who was President George W. Bush's Education Secretary, because she "helped to lead a lot of the improvement that's been taking place and we're building on."

Well, yes, the President is right; his own education reform plans are built right on top of the shaky foundation of President Bush's No Child Left Behind program. The fundamental principle of school reform, in the Age of Bush and Obama, is measure and punish. If students don't get high enough scores, then someone must be punished! If the graduation rate hovers around 50%, then someone must be punished. This is known as "accountability."

President Obama says that Central Falls must close because only 7% of the students are proficient in math, and the graduation rate is only 48%. Sounds bad, right?

But the President has saluted a high school in Providence, Rhode Island, called "The Met" whose scores are no different from the scores at Central Falls High School. At Central Falls, 55% of the kids are classified as "proficient readers," just like 55% at The Met. In math, only 7% of students at Central Falls are proficient in math, but at The Met—which the President lauds—only 4% are proficient in math. Ah, but The Met has one big advantage over Central Falls High Schools: Its graduation rate is 75.6%.

But figure this one out: How can a high school where only 4% of the students are proficient in math and only 55% are proficient readers produce a graduation rate of 75.6%? To this distant observer, it appears that the school with lower graduation standards rates higher in President Obama's eyes.

President Obama has said on several occasions that he wants to see 5,000 low-performing schools closed. So, yes, there will be plenty of teachers and principals looking for new jobs.

The question that neither President Obama nor Secretary Duncan has answered is this: Where will they find 5,000 expert principals to take over the schools that are closed? Where will they find hundreds of thousands of superb teachers to fill the newly vacant positions? Or will everyone play musical chairs to give the illusion of reform?

As it happens, Central Falls High School had seen consistent improvement over the past two years. Only last year, the State Commissioner sent in a team to look at the school and commended its improvements. It noted that the school had been burdened by frequently changing programs and leadership. With more support from the district and the state, this improvement might have continued. Instead, the school was given a death warrant.

Will it be replaced by a better school? Who knows? Will excellent teachers flock to Central Falls to replace their fired colleagues? Or will it be staffed by inexperienced young college graduates who commit to stay at the school for two years? Will non-English-speaking students start speaking English because their teachers were fired? Will children come to school ready to learn because their teachers were fired?

It would be good if our nation's education leaders recognized that teachers are not solely responsible for student test scores. Other influences matter, including the students' effort, the family's encouragement, the effects of popular culture, and the influence of poverty. A blogger called "Mrs. Mimi" wrote the other day that we fire teachers because "we can't fire poverty." Since we can't fire poverty, we can't fire students, and we can't fire families, all that is left is to fire teachers.

This strategy of closing schools and firing the teachers is mean and punitive. And it is ultimately pointless. It solves no problem. It opens up a host of new problems. It satisfies the urge to purge. But it does nothing at all for the students.

Topics for Writing and Discussion

1. "Education reform" has been a national focus since at least the publication in 1983 of *A Nation at Risk* by President Ronald Reagan's National Commission on Excellence in Education. Since then, schools in the United States have undergone waves of various reform measures designed to increase graduation rates at both high schools and colleges and to improve test scores, particularly in math and science. After President George W. Bush promoted the No Child Left Behind Act in 2001, based on a model he had established as governor of Texas, there has been an increasing emphasis on testing and raising standards. Most of the reform measures are a result of the poor showing of American students on tests taken by students from around the world. For example, one of the most prominent is the Programme for International Student Assessment. On this test, first given in 2000, 15-year-old students take a paper test in math, reading, and science literacy. The latest 2015 results (look them up on the internet) place the US nineteenth in science, twentieth in reading, and thirty-first in math. Drawing on your own experience in school, write an essay on what you see as the major problems in American education. What needs to be changed, improved, retained?

2. Another trend is to rank schools by their graduation rates and performance on standardized tests. Lists of schools are published in the newspaper yearly, with schools ranked as superior, acceptable, needing improvement, or unacceptable, for example. Some states are even considering giving

public schools yearly rankings of A, B, C, D, or F. What do you think of these measures? Do you think labeling schools with a letter grade would help or hinder their improvement?

3. Other trends are the establishment of charter schools, schools that receive public money but are independent of the local school system, such as KIPP (Knowledge is Power Program) and YES Prep, and even turning over what are considered failing schools to private companies to run. Most teachers' groups are against such measures, citing poverty and lack of adequate state support for education as the main reasons students do poorly. As Ravitch says, "It would be good if our nation's education leaders recognized that teachers are not solely responsible for student test scores." Drawing on your own knowledge and experience, write an essay on what you think are the main reasons for students' poor test scores.

Mexicans in America

Richard Rodriguez

Richard Rodriguez was born in 1944 in San Francisco, California, the son of Mexican immigrants. He went to a Catholic school, worked at odd jobs, and eventually attended Stanford University. He received a Fulbright fellowship in 1972 and a National Endowment for the Humanities fellowship in 1976. He has written a number of books, including: *Hunger of Memory: The Education of Richard Rodriguez* (1982), *Days of Obligation: An Argument with My Mexican Father* (1992), and *Brown: The Last Discovery of America* (2002). He has also been a commentator for the *PBS NewsHour* and an essayist for a number of magazines. "Mexicans in America" was published in *Cato Unbound: A Journal of Debate* in 2006.

Some years ago, with the publication of my first book, I became notorious in certain American academic quarters for my opposition to bilingual education and my celebration of assimilation—the child's coming to think of himself as belonging within a society of strangers.

I retain my belief in the necessity of a common American culture. But I am lately appalled by voices raised in this country against Mexican migrant workers.

Americans have tended to abrogate to economists the question of the costs and the benefits of illegal immigration. But, surely, beyond how much Betsy Ross is willing to pay for a head of lettuce, there is the question of morality, there is the question of Mexico. How much of Mexico are we willing to take within our borders? I believe the question might better be asked of a theologian, than an economist.

Mexico is a society formed by an incursion into the New World of the Spanish Catholic counter-reformation. America is a society formed by the flight from England of low-church Protestants.

Mexicans are a cynical people, you will find—sweet, but cynical. Their cynicism derives from the notion of Original Sin and the sense that humans fail inevitably. Mexicans are patient with this knowledge, charmingly so in some instances (lard, beer), dangerously so in other instances, as when Mexicans tolerate civic corruption. It is no coincidence that Mexican border towns have become the fiefdoms of drug lords.

Americans are a hypocritical people—nice people, but hypocritical. Americans prefer unknowing. They believe innocence clings to them by election. Americans prefer to ignore the correlation between our need for drugs and the creation of a vast criminal economy that stretches from Afghanistan to Bolivia to Tijuana.

Mexico represents a special annoyance to the United States because of proximity; because Mexico is forthright in reminding America of the corruption of our past. In the 19th century, Americans were illegal immigrants into Mexican territory. The United States stole the Southwest from Mexico because the United States wanted the Southwest, a desire we unrolled with great mumbo-jumbo and called Manifest Destiny. Everything Americans want to say about illegal immigrants today, history can also say about us.

From his minaret in Cambridge, Massachusetts, Samuel P. Huntington, the Albert J. Weatherhead III Professor at Harvard, peers across the brown Charles River and trembles for the future of America. Professor Huntington is most famously a phrase-maker. His famous phrase was the title of his book, *The Clash of Civilizations*—the book that gave the world a simplistic, albeit thrillingly dark, description of an intransigence between the secular West and the Islamist East. September 11th made the professor a prophet.

In his latest book, *Who Are We?*, Huntington describes an America under siege from Latin American immigrants. His America is a kind of little England, a demi-demi Eden with pudding for dessert and "Masterpiece Theatre." Forget the French Revolution; forget the Dutch; forget Spain, obviously; forget the Massachusetts Indians who rescued the Puritans from winter; forget the African slaves who created the wealth of a young nation. According to Professor Huntington, "Anglo-Protestant culture has been central to American identity." There are no ironies in Professor Huntington's America. There are no ironies because there are no dialectical meetings. There can be none. America was settled by the British, and British it should remain.

I suppose I object to Huntington's nativism more as a Roman Catholic than as a Mexican-American. Even so, as a Mexican American I roll my eyes when Huntington credits England with the American work ethic and implies that a darker race is incapable of equal industry.

The American objection raised against illegal Mexican workers—notably from the economist George Borjas; from C. Ray Nagin, the mayor of New Orleans—acknowledges the fierce energy of Mexican laborers, a work ethic that undermines the wages of the native working class, and that is outperforming the native working class.

Another academic, Victor Davis Hanson, distinguishes himself among disgruntled white voices from the nativist bookshelf, because he is a farmer. Hanson has worked alongside Mexican peasants in California. He knows the fury of their labor. Hanson grouses when a drunk Mexican kid runs a car into a ditch on Hanson's property and abandons it there—a scene John Steinbeck would have treated as tragic and comic. Hanson sees just another mess to clean up. He is not wrong. He is ungenerous.

John Steinbeck had a generous heart. In *The Grapes of Wrath* he describes California's moral outrage against the Okies:

Men who had never been hungry saw the eyes of the hungry. Men who
had never wanted anything very much saw the flare of want in the eyes
of the migrants. And the men of the towns and of the soft suburban
country gathered to defend themselves; and they reassured themselves
that they were good and the invaders bad, as a man must do before
he fights. They said, These goddamned Okies are dirty and ignorant.
They're degenerate, sexual maniacs. These goddamned Okies are thieves.
They'll steal anything. They've got no sense of property rights.

Hanson doesn't see beyond his own grievance, nevertheless Hanson sees
clearly enough that America's native born children—the white and the brown
who prowl the mall in Fresno in tank tops and on cells—are incapable of matching
the Mexican's toil because they do not feel the Mexican's desperation.

Without exactly intending to do so, Hanson reminds me that the debate over
illegal immigration will end up less concerned with the virtues of the Mexican
peasant worker than with the worker's Americanized children who rush to take
on all the demerits of America; who are, in fact, American children.

Rather than credit our American work habit to England or to Calvin, we
might better wonder why it is we still describe America only by reference to
Reformation England and Royalist Spain (as I shall proceed to do here). Mexican
Americans have the bad but telling habit of naming gringos "Anglos." So-called
Anglos name Mexican Americans "Hispanics."

Hispanic. In all the video footage I have seen of people crossing illegally from
Mexico, of people arrested, the faces look more Indian than Spanish. Most of
the illegal immigrants from Mexico may be mestizo, racially, but Indian features
predominate. And isn't that curious? The Indians are illegally coming into the
United States. Indians will always wander in the Americas and they should.

One lasting effect of illegal immigration, I believe, is that we will come to see
America within the Americas. *The New York Times* in a feature story (August 4,
2006) describes the sense of dislocation many Americans in Southeastern states
are feeling with the sudden appearance on the landscape of so many immigrants
from Latin America. The black and white landscape of gothic memory is suddenly
rendered unrecognizable. It may not look like what Faulkner described, but I bet
it looks a lot more like what de Tocqueville saw. Brown illegal immigrants with
Indian faces may usher the Georgian and the Virginian to a recognition that
they now live within the New World—an illegal idea—and not in some distant
colony of England.

There attaches to Mexico and to the Mexican in America a legend of illegality.
Any American kid at the black-and-white cowboy movie understood why the
bandit needed to get to the Mexican border. The outlaw would be free in Mexico,
because Mexico is so thoroughly outside the law. In the updated (and eroticized)

cowboy movie, "Brokeback Mountain," Jack Twist takes his homosexual desire to Juarez, where Mexico consoles him in a dark alley.

For a long time, Mexican border towns have ministered to Americans who slipped over a line to relieve themselves of sanctions. Anything we wanted that was illegal on the American side of the line—liquor, gambling, abortion, divorce, whores—Mexico provided. Mexico was discrete; the American zipped up and returned to the daytime virtue of the United States.

For a long time, Americans have been similarly complicit in transactions for illegal labor. Americans were not as honorable as the Mexican madam, however. Every once in a while, an employer would call the cops on his own workers—just before payday. Or, having used Mexican labor for a generation, America would suddenly decide to go clean and deport vast numbers of Mexicans—many thousands in the Depression years—and then we found, with World War II, that we needed Mexico's labor again.

A great deal has changed in America since the government-licensed "bracero program" of the '40s and '50s brought Mexicans to the United States for seasonal labor. By the 1960s, immigration laws no longer discriminated in favor of Europeans. By the 1960s, entire Mexican families followed in the path of the father or the older brother.

The majority opinion in America is that Mexicans illegally in the United States should not be given citizenship. Mexicans broke the law, Americans say, playing the victim. As regards Mexican labor, America plays both victim and siren.

A mood of Protestant Reformation is sweeping the country. The fear of illegal immigrants along America's southern border has increased proportionally as America's support for the war in Iraq has waned. Americans feel a need to cleanse the country of illegality. September 11th makes that dream of cleansing urgent. We went to war in Iraq to play the actor in history rather than the victim. The wounded nation wanted a war movie with screeching skies and exploding earth and apocalyptic diction. But with the passage of years, after the daily news of car bombings, IED's, the growing tally of war dead and maimed, and with images of hateful, ungrateful brown mobs protesting America's presence in their cinderblock neighborhoods, Americans have grown skeptical of our ability to will a democracy onto a landscape we do not understand.

So we resort to our own desert. The anger we lately tapped to hunt the Arab terrorist, we now direct toward the migrant worker. The illegal immigrant becomes bin-Laden's doppelganger. In order to turn our familiar use of the Mexican peasant into a fear of the Mexican peasant we have had to internationalize him. The migrant has illegally crossed an international border, we say.

In the end, this conflation of the cynical and the neurotic, this neurotic blurring of the peasant-worker with the terrorist could have the effect of creating exactly what America says it fears. If we are unable to distinguish the terrorist from the migrant worker, Americans will end up isolating illegal immigrants and their children from the mainstream, encouraging the adults to see themselves as mired in hopeless illegality, and their children to see themselves as off-spring of the undocumented, thus also criminal. And we will have Arabian Nights on a larger scale than those we witnessed last summer in Paris.

We do not acknowledge the trespasser as someone who is seeking to cross an economic border. America spends precious little of its affinity for biblical language and allusion on the plight of the illegal laborer. On Mexican hillsides, the beatitudes are as real and as plentiful as cardboard shanties. The Mexican peasant has the advantage, if you will allow me to call it that, of coming to America from a Catholic culture that honors suffering; that sees suffering as holy, and poverty as blessed, and therefore accords the poor a position (exactly opposite to the middle-class ethos of American Puritanism) over the middle class.

My own eyes tell me that Mexicans are not dishonored by their poverty, nor are they bent and unwilling to meet my glance. They show up for work early, and they stand outside the café on Fillmore Street as patient as cats in the dawn. Yesterday, I saw two young men, waiting in front of a renovated Victorian house, with their tools arranged in buckets. Their tools were hard-won and well-kept and ready. These were ready men.

Since America will not honor the poverty of the Mexican worker in theological terms, we should at least be clear that the Mexican is such a good worker because of the strength of the Mexican family. Mexicans work for each other; that is their reason for working.

On the other hand, I have heard Mexican astonishment at the kindness of strangers in America. *The stranger gave me some money. The stranger gave me a ride in his truck. The stranger gave me some water.* Whereas in Mexico, all such generosity takes place within the family, in America the generosity among strangers is often easier and more common than among relatives, and this amazes the Mexican.

America is a country where children are raised to leave home, and each generation is expected to seek its own way. The great pronoun of the United States is the Protestant pronoun—the "I." America teaches its children independence and the bravery of the solitary path. The burden of life in America is loneliness. Not coincidentally, Mexican women, illegally in the United States, have been hired into the cold heart of America to sit with the young and the old.

The children of Mexican migrant workers, who are two or even three generations into this country, are faced with competing pronouns, and struggle to reconcile them. On the one hand, the Mexican American is expected to live within a family whose emotional architecture draws the child away from the window.

On the other hand, America presents the child with an open door. As long as you understand this grammatical dilemma for the child struggling between the "we" and the "I," any statistic you want—on Mexican American gangs, early marriage rates, suicide attempts, black-brown tensions, high school dropout rates, military heroism—becomes coherent.

I am a generation removed from the Mexican working class. My parents, who were legally here in the United States, were never called, within hearing of their children, a disgraceful burden to America; were never called an affront to their adopted country; were never called a drag on the morale on the United States of America.

I think no other children of poverty hear—on poisonous talk radio, even from the floor of the Congress—what the children of parents illegally in the United States are forced to hear. The contribution of illegal lives is never counted—never—as praise or admiration or courage or virtue of any kind. It is as though America, having benefited from illegal labor, pretends that the transaction was one of middle-class benevolence. Mexicans should be thankful for a month of cheerless eight-hour shifts, standing there waiting for the old lady to get off the commode. The odd thing is that they are thankful!

As I watched the proliferation of mass demonstrations across the country last spring, I noticed nuns and priests; lots of comic sombreros. I saw Mexican flags—a typical, humorous Mexican thing to do, to wrap yourself in the flag of Mexico, in order to insist on your desire to remain in the United States. I noticed families principally, parents and their children.

It was the first time I had seen the children of illegality demanding that the United States show respect for their parents. It was the first time I had seen illegal parents, standing fearlessly in public with their children. I tell you it was a momentous time in the history of the Americas. I hope you saw it.

Topics for Writing and Discussion

1. Rodriguez says that "Mexicans are a cynical people" and that "Americans are a hypocritical people," but he goes on to explain what he means by these phrases. How do you react to these broad characterizations? Can one define a group, whether Mexican, American, or some other, by a single phrase? Write a short essay in which you characterize your own "group" by a single phrase—and then go on to explain that phrase in some detail and with examples.

2. Rodriguez also points out the differing cultural traditions of Mexico and the United States with regard to family. He says "the Mexican American is expected to live within a family." On the other hand, "America is a country where children are raised to leave home." Write an essay in which you explore

the pull in your own life between family and the "open door" to your own future. Which is most important? How do you accommodate both?

3. Rodriguez points out the contradiction in the complaints of many Americans that undocumented immigrants broke the law in coming here in the first place and that they undercut American labor by working for lower wages than American workers. At the time of writing this book, immigration reform and what should be done about undocumented immigrants—and their children who were born here and are thus Americans—is stalled in a contentious congress. Write an essay on what you think should be done about the millions of undocumented immigrants who are currently in the United States.

Poison Apples

Rebecca Solnit

Rebecca Solnit is a writer living in San Francisco. In addition to a number of books, the latest being *The Mother of All Questions* (2017), she writes for several magazines and is a columnist at *Harper's Magazine*. The following essay was published in the "Easy Chair" column of *Harper's* in December 2014.

Thirty years ago, Apple Computer launched a new product with a messianic commercial in which legions of blank-faced, coverall-clad workers march, as if in a trance, through a strange industrial world. They arrive at a bright screen, which they sit in front of in homogeneous rows to watch a Big Brother-like figure announce the triumph of a mind-controlling monoculture. An athlete speeds toward the massive hall. Her sprinting power, her golden skin and bright red shorts, and even her gender stand in contrast to the zombie shuffle of the male figures.

The ad cuts back and forth between this vivid, supercharged woman in color and the bald ghost-workers in black and white. Pursued by faceless police in riot helmets intent on stopping her, she nevertheless finds time to spin her sledgehammer round and round before hurling it at the screen, where it smashes the image of Big Brother. The screen explodes in brightness, like an atomic blast, before the video cuts to a shot of the audience's illuminated faces, their mouths open in shock. Then comes the famous tagline: "On January 24th, Apple Computer will introduce Macintosh. And you'll see why 1984 won't be like '1984.'" It's perhaps Silicon Valley's first announcement that they don't just make tools; they make culture. But what kind of culture?

This minute-long movie was made in an era of considerable anxiety about the future. *Alien* (1979) postulated the usual hostile invaders, with better effects; *Mad Max 2: The Road Warrior* (1981) showed a chaotic world of post-peak-oil car mania; *Blade Runner* (1982) was set in a Los Angeles that was a weird mix of post-human and post-white, two qualities that were regarded with what seemed like equal dismay; and *The Terminator* (1984) worried about smart machines. This little Apple film was made to pep you up about the future, not to scare you, back in the days when the power of computers was puny compared with now, and nuclear threats were huge.

Watching the commercial again, I recall Delmore Schwartz's short story "In Dreams Begin Responsibilities," which takes place in another movie theater, where the dreaming Schwartz watches the courtship of his parents before his birth and stands up in horror to shout, "Don't do it! It's not too late to change your minds, both of you. Nothing good will come of it, only remorse, hatred, scandal, and two children whose characters are monstrous."

The Macintosh was and is a good product, but the corporation that made it is part of a nightmare industry. I want to yell at that liberatory young woman with her sledgehammer: Don't do it! Apple is not different. That industry is going to give rise to innumerable forms of triviality and misogyny, to the concentration of wealth and the dispersal of mental concentration. To suicidal, underpaid Chinese factory workers whose reality must be a lot like that of the shuffling workers in that commercial. If you think a crowd of people staring at one screen is bad, wait until you have created a world in which billions of people stare at their own screens even while walking, driving, eating, in the company of friends and family — all of them eternally elsewhere. Apple's iPhones will make their users trackable at all times unless they take unadvertised measures to disable that feature. They will be part of the rise of the Internet, which will savage privacy, break down journalism as we know it, and create elaborate justifications for never paying artists or writers — an Internet that will be an endless soup of grim porn and mean-spirited chat and rumor and trolling and new ways to buy things we don't need while failing to make the contact we do need.

I'm still not sure why 1984 the year wasn't supposed to be like *1984* the novel. Maybe it took us longer to get to that Orwellian dystopia, but technology smoothed our path. The way that online documents, including news stories, are endlessly revised to cover up errors and reverse opinions, often untraceably, makes much of the Internet a kind of Ministry of Truth. As for Orwell's double-speak, tech-capitalist euphemisms — like "the sharing economy" for outsourced labor and consolidated profits — fit its pattern nicely. Big Hipster Brother is one of my nicknames for Google — Apple's ascendant younger sibling, the corporation that terrifies Europeans with its ambition to be a global information monopoly, the multifaceted Google that is YouTube, Gmail, the Android operating system, the Chrome operating system, Google Groups, and several other powerful threads that make up the fabric of everyday life. Google is also the world's biggest advertising company, watching you on nearly every website you visit.

Maybe Apple's "1984" ad is the beginning of Silicon Valley's fantasy of itself as the solution, not the problem — a dissident rebel, not the rising new Establishment. The fantasy shows itself in the industry's favorite Orwellian word of recent years, "disrupt." The term is so totemic that just a few months ago *Wired* — which for twenty years has preached the gospel of a utopia just one gadget or app away — used variations on "disrupt" eight times in a single paragraph. The article doesn't explain why Uber (which has been banned in several cities for breaking the law and for its lack of accountability) is better than taxis, or why "Twitter disrupting the media industry; Facebook disrupting the communications industry; LinkedIn disrupting the human resources industry" are good things, or even what the nature of that disruption is.

It's often suggested — but not, apparently, true — that the Apple logo, with its bite taken out, is an homage to Alan Turing, the prophetic British computer genius who was born nine years after Orwell and who died by his own hand in 1954. Or perhaps not by his own hand, but by his own apple; he left one, partially eaten and possibly laced with cyanide, at the site of his suicide. Turing had been a hero of the Second World War, a code breaker and technologist of incomparable intelligence. In 1952 he was convicted of homosexuality (or, as it was then known in British law, gross indecency) and punished horribly. When Turing killed himself, hardly anyone but the government had the capacity to spy on individuals, and even their methods were clumsy and limited. Physical devices were needed to wiretap a phone or bug a room or steam open a letter. Communication wasn't inherently leaky the way it is now.

These days, punishing others for private behaviors can be done by any citizen. Tyler Clementi was a talented young violinist and Rutgers student whose roommate, Dharun Ravi, used Skype to spy on him during a tryst with another man in 2010. A few days later, Ravi, who despised Clementi, remotely activated Apple's iChat (since replaced by Messages) while not in their room and organized a community viewing of Clementi's next rendezvous. When Clementi found online evidence of the viewing, he requested a change of housing arrangements. On September 22, 2010, three days after the iChat incident, Clementi jumped off the George Washington Bridge.

On August 31 of this year, news broke that hackers had released nearly two hundred private photographs of celebrities, mostly women, mostly naked, on the website 4chan. The photos immediately spread to sites such as the notoriously misogynistic Reddit. They were sold for Bitcoin, the online currency, and many had been taken from Apple's iCloud storage system.

Posting the pictures turned them into a kind of revenge porn, albeit against people the posters never had sex with and never would. (It says something about the Internet that it has given rise to a hitherto unimagined genre called revenge porn.) It was a way for the hackers to take away women's power and to aggrandize their own.

One of the actors whose images were in the collection was Jennifer Lawrence, who plays Katniss Everdeen, a rebel against the Establishment, in the Hunger Games film trilogy. Like the heroine of the "1984" commercial, Katniss is a powerful athlete; she runs, climbs, fights, and shoots her arrows. She's more than a sledgehammer swinger: she's a latter-day Robin Hood, a female Che Guevara, a catalyst for the resistance against the Big-Brother-meets-elite-decadence society of the Capitol. Katniss is the rare woman allowed full power in our own dystopian media landscape, where women sometimes seem to exist only as subsidiary franchises, pornographic and otherwise, in male lives.

Privacy is part not only of our dignity but also of our power, political and psychological. A technology-government cabal that insists on more and more privacy for its own acts and less and less for ours is part and parcel of a society in which power is rapidly being stolen from citizens and the thieves are increasingly unaccountable. Jennifer Lawrence and the rest lost bodily privacy in a very high-profile incident; quietly, the privacy of your mind and life — your thoughts, communications, purchases, even your Web searches and movements — has been seeping away, thanks to the collusion of tech and communications corporations with a government intent on violating all of us all the time.

Imagine a sci-fi movie that's a mash-up of the nude-photo scandal and *The Hunger Games*. Who would Lawrence's arrows take out? Apple issued a statement, which read, in part:

> After more than 40 hours of investigation, we have discovered that certain celebrity accounts were compromised by a very targeted attack on user names, passwords and security questions, a practice that has become all too common on the Internet. None of the cases we have investigated has resulted from any breach in any of Apple's systems including iCloud® or Find my iPhone.

In other words: The fact that your account got hacked and your personal photos were stolen doesn't mean that our service has flaws.

Weeks later, a website called emmayouarenext.com appeared, targeting former Harry Potter star Emma Watson. She had been in the news for her work as a U.N. goodwill ambassador, particularly for a speech in which she called on men to step up for feminism. The site, which threatened to leak nude photographs of Watson, claimed to have gotten 48 million page views and 7 million Facebook likes and shares. Watson was trying to encourage solidarity about human rights in the world, and anonymous people were trying to reduce her to flesh. The threat turned out to be baseless, issued by marketers who knew how to draw attention to themselves and didn't care how they did it.

By 2013, the world had begun, at long last, to despise Silicon Valley — for its hubris, its narcissism, and the bad faith of much of what it does. It took that long for people to stop subscribing to the industry's propaganda. Midway through last year Edward Snowden supplied us with new reason to loathe these corporations. As Glenn Greenwald puts it in the beginning of his book *No Place to Hide,* "Technology has now enabled a type of ubiquitous surveillance that had previously been the province of only the most imaginative science fiction." While the focus of Snowden's revelations was the National Security Administration's invasions of privacy — whether German chancellor Angela Merkel's or yours — the cooperation of Silicon Valley (notably Google, Facebook, and Apple) was essential to the NSA. A few smaller companies resisted, and one destroyed itself rather than comply, but most of the giants only offered up excuses when they were caught.

The technology is not necessarily the problem; you go back to 1984 — before smartphones and social media, before our computers all talked to one another — and you know it all could have been different. Online culture took shape at the hands of particular individuals and corporations whose goals were not the liberation of all beings or justice or democracy but profit, the consolidation of power, and the deprivation of the rest of us of the power that lies in privacy. It wasn't a rupture with the past but an expansion of what was worst about that past. As the cybersecurity expert and genuine rebel Jacob Appelbaum puts it in Laura Poitras's new film on Snowden, *Citizenfour*: "What we used to call liberty and freedom we now call privacy. And we say, Privacy is dead."

In *The Terminator,* Arnold Schwarzenegger plays a cyborg sent back in time from the age of the machines to annihilate Sarah Connor, the woman who is going to give birth to the leader of a human revolt against the machines. She's a sort of Madonna of the Luddites. When Apple's "1984" commercial aired during the Super Bowl in January 1984, Edward Snowden was a little more than six months old. He was sixteen months old when *The Terminator* came out. This is another thing you can imagine yelling at Apple and the rest of them, with the kind of hindsight that Delmore Schwartz had about his parents: You're going to become part of a state apparatus that demands infinite privacy for itself and endless nakedness for the rest of us; you're going to invade our privacy in countless ways and with it our dignity and freedom and confidence; but a child has been born who will pit himself against you, who will reveal your secrets and help turn the world against you, who will risk his life to stand up for us and against you.

We could tell the story with more depth, and possibly with more *Terminator* parallels, by mentioning Sarah Harrison, who isn't scheduled to give birth to any messiahs, but who might be viewed as the Sarah Connor in our current revolt against the machines and their masters. It was Harrison, a key associate of WikiLeaks, who traveled with Snowden from Hong Kong to Russia and kept him company as he was stranded in the Moscow Airport. It was Harrison who sought asylum for Snowden and has founded the Courage Foundation to support whistle-blowers and leakers like him.

Orwell's *1984* was, of course, like all science fiction, about the time in which it was created; it could have been titled *1948* for its picture of Stalinist Russia and shabby postwar Britain. Apple's movie from the year 1984 was not science fiction so much as propaganda. It was made by Ridley Scott, whose film *Blade Runner,* released only two years earlier, expounded a darker view of the future, set in 2019.

We now live on the cusp of that future, in a world that is wilder in many ways than anything anyone anticipated. Some of the change is good: the transformation of gender roles, the gains in the rights of the hitherto marginalized, and the new distaste for bullying, everyday violence, hierarchy, and authoritarianism are cumulatively astonishing. Even new technologies have valuable uses for medical and scientific research, decentralized media, political organizing, and more. But most of our world is scary. Climate change, as Bill McKibben has pointed out, essentially means that we have landed on a turbulent, inhospitable planet that is unlike in crucial ways the stable, nurturing world in which we evolved. Society has been divided into a desperate majority and an obscene minority that hoards wealth so colossal it's meaningless.

To tell the truth is now a crime. Chelsea Manning is in prison for decades because she told us what our government does, Edward Snowden is in exile in Russia, and Sarah Harrison is in Germany, unwilling to go back to her native Britain.

As Harrison says, "Britain has a Terrorism Act, which has within it a portion called Schedule Seven, which is quite unique. . . . It gives officials the ability to detain people at the border as they go in or out or even transit through the country. And this allows them to question people on no more than a hunch. . . . All the legal advice received is that the likelihood is very strong that I would be Schedule Sevened." If you want to know who will throw the sledgehammer at the screen of a technological dystopia, Sarah Harrison is a good candidate. Because 2014 has turned out quite a bit like *1984.*

Topics for Writing and Discussion

1. This essay includes a number of allusions to people and events of the recent and not-so-recent past, such as George Orwell's 1949 novel, *1984.* If you are unfamiliar with the names, you can easily Google them. Do you think that this instant availability of information and connection provided by the internet and companies such as Apple and Google, outweighs the loss of privacy Solnit accuses these very companies of enabling? Write a short essay supporting your opinion on this issue.

2. Solnit implies that instead of liberating people from oppressive social and political forces, modern technology has instead helped create a vast surveillance state, one very like the one Orwell's novel depicts. Do you personally feel spied upon? Do you see people like Edward Snowden as heroes or traitors?

3. Solnit also implies that technology continues to oppress women. She writes of our "dystopian media landscape, where women sometimes seem to exist only as subsidiary franchises, pornographic and otherwise, in male lives." There have been many reports in the news of "sexts" gone viral, for example. Using your own experience and that of people you know, write an essay exploring the effects of digital technology on women.

4. Solnit admits that some of the change sparked by the digital revolution is good—"the transformation of gender roles, the gains in the rights of the hitherto marginalized, and the new distaste for bullying, everyday violence, hierarchy, and authoritarianism,"—but that most of the world today is "scary." As college students, you will live in and shape the future. Are you optimistic or pessimistic about it? Write an essay explaining how you view the future.

Student Examples

Going Home

Kathleen Looper

My parents' home is located on three-and-a-half acres south of Akron, Ohio. The area used to be a farming community as recently as the early 1950s. The house faces Pickle Road, which is a combination of tar and gravel. The best time for surfacing the road, in the county's opinion anyway, is the middle of summer when the high humidity and the blazing sun keeps the tar the consistency of melted caramel; it continues to ooze up through the gravel long after the workmen have finished. The edges of the road are always more tar than gravel, and it sticks to shoes and feet. Tires fling the hot sticky mess onto the wheel wells and rocker panels of the cars as they hurry by. The aroma that rises from the hot tar is barely noticeable when compared to the smell of burning rubber that pours from the tire factories in town. There was a time when Akron, Ohio, was known as the "Rubber Capital of the World"; those who lived and worked in the area were used to the smell of burning rubber and therefore did not mind the insignificant fragrance of melting tar, which saturated the air on a hot summer day. From the road the house looks like a picture one might find on an old calendar, the kind of picture a mother takes, not framed especially well, but pleasing to the eye. The house is old. My father and his father built it in 1949. Actually, they started in then, and now, decades later, it is still not quite finished. It is red with a large front porch of concrete with four large square wooden pillars. Dad also built the porch himself and believed that everything that is required to stand up must be set in concrete. Once my brother Richard misjudged the driveway and ran into the porch with Dad's van. One of the pillars broke off, flew into the air, and crashed down on the roof of the van. It popped out of its place like a child's broken tooth, leaving the rest of the porch intact. Because the remaining three pillars were also set in cement, Richard would have had to run into each one separately before the roof would have budged. Richard's accident was merely one more inconvenience to Dad; it only presented a new challenge—to reconstruct a pillar that could be anchored somehow in the same spot and reset in cement.

The original garage, now Dad's shop, is attached to the house by a small enclosed breezeway. Everybody had breezeways back in the '50s. I don't know why; it's not as if there was ever a breeze—except during the winter. One Christmas when there were presents for eight to fit around a tree, someone thought it would be a good idea to set up Christmas in the breezeway. "Christmas" meant a live, pine-forest-smelling evergreen, which occupied most of the room, and a cardboard fireplace. We did not have a real fireplace, and Mom thought it would save the woodwork if we could hang our stockings somewhere besides the painted windowsills. It was pretty realistic looking, too, with cardboard logs and a bright cellophane fire, which seemed to flicker when lit from behind with yellow and red electric lights. But, cozy as it may sound, December in Ohio is not the perfect season for relaxing on the breezeway. So, from then on, the live pine and the fake cardboard fireplace were allowed to remain in the house. Dad's shop in the garage is larger than the house, with two front windows like large rectangular eyes staring at the road, as if to watch for customers. The house also has two eyes, two large picture windows through which we could watch the world go by. And those on the outside can look into the rooms behind the windows, like children peering into a dollhouse. The living room and kitchen lie behind these windows. The house was built this way intentionally because Mother wanted to be able to see what was happening outside. The front door sits quietly between them like the nose on our faces: it seems to do nothing but is vital to our existence. The two bedroom dormers upstairs seem to peek over the roof of the porch like raised eyebrows, to indicate approval or disapproval as the house watches all who travel on Pickle Road.

The house and garage sit back from the road, a distance which allowed us to use the front lawn for a baseball diamond. Mom always preferred that we play at home. There were five maple trees my dad dug out of the woods, and he and Grandpa planted them three in a row along the yard and two in a second row right behind them. When one of the trees died in the back row, it left one lone maple tree looking rather out of place. But during our baseball games it was in the perfect place to serve as first base, and the tree directly across from it was third base. We had to improvise for second base with a rock, an old chair cushion from the shop, someone's shirt, or an extra mitt; we grabbed whatever was available at the time and only had a problem if the mitt was needed for play or the owner of the shirt wanted it back. Dad had not envisioned the baseball diamond in his plan for the yard, for if he had, I know he would have planted a tree for second base.

I visited the old home this past summer, the first summer visit in five years, and the house seemed smaller than I remembered. We usually visit at Christmas when it's cold and the snow covers the ground and house with a white blanket and there are no leaves on the trees. But this visit there was no snow to hide the changes. The trees are larger now, and the house seems small. The house used to stand out and the trees were merely ornaments on the lawn, but now the house seems to be slipping into the greenery. Where the house once stood on flat ground, it is now hidden in a jungle of maple trees and weeping willows. The flat spot of dirt that we knew as Home Plate has disappeared and has been replaced by thick green grass that perfectly matches the rest of the yard and is slowly creeping into the gravel and dirt driveway, crowding it out of its due space. The trees on either side of the house used not to make such a thick wall. Where they used to give only the impression of a fence, they now form a barrier heavy enough to make one forget that there are houses on the other side.

A row of pine trees on the right of the house overlooks a bank and separates Dad's home from that of the neighbors on the hill. Mr. and Mrs. Scott have lived there many years now, but it is still the Weavers' place to us. On the left edge of the property, a white crossrail fence separates the grounds from a piece of land Dad sold unwillingly when he needed money to pay my sister's hospital expenses. Weeping willow trees flank the fence from the road to the top of the drive and around to the back of the house. The drive forms a horseshoe around the house, fitting neatly between the two sets of trees. The weeping willows form the left top of the horseshoe down to the road while the maple trees line up across the front yard; then on the right the row of pine trees stand. The trees seem to form a wall around the house, making it look as though it is sinking into a great hole, or maybe that it's the ripe red tomato in a large salad.

The house seems now, many years later, to be sinking out of sight, engulfed in plant life, just barely able to peek out through the trees. I fear I will come home one summer day and the place where the house once stood will have disappeared into the trees and there will be no voices to lead the way. I will go "home again," but there will be nothing there.

A Seasonal Twist

Tammy Boggs

When I was five years old, my grandparents owned a large ranch in Marquez, Texas, about 150 miles north outside of Houston. My parents, aunts, uncles, and other family members usually went up on weekends. We had cows, horses, chickens, and pigs there, as well as a garden for growing different vegetables. That made for quite a bit of work, but it was fun, too. Our favorite time of year was spring because the pastures were alive with color. Bluebonnets, Indian paintbrushes, and other types of beautiful wildflowers grew there and thrived on the seasonal showers.

One spring, my grandfather invited his sister and brother-in-law, who lived in Maryland, to come visit for the weekend. They usually visited us every year, but only in Houston. My great-uncle Will did not really care for the country much, having lived his whole life in the city. But for some reason that year he and my great-aunt Virginia agreed to come to the ranch for the weekend. Because of this, the main house was full, so my parents offered to stay in the bunkhouse. There was no way any of us could have predicted that our choices could have had dangerous consequences because the following morning after we had all arrived, just after breakfast, a tornado swept through, sweeping away our plans for a relaxing weekend with it.

Since they had planned for us to go horseback riding that morning and had even talked Uncle Will into joining us, my dad and uncles had gone down to the stables to saddle the horses. My mon and I had returned to the bunkhouse to change into jeans and grab a few things. We noticed on the walk over that what had begun as a breezy but sunny spring day had changed dramatically since we had walked over to the main house for breakfast. The sky had darkened considerably, and there was a definite threat of rain in the air. I can remember my mother telling me that we should hurry, but I loved picking the wildflowers so much that our progress was slow at first. As the rain started to fall and the wind increased, my mom suddenly grabbed my hand and we began to run. At the time I thought it was so we would not get wet, and I even giggled when she suddenly swept me up in her arms and ran. You see, while my attention had been on the ground, my mother's had been focused on the sky and the clouds that had begun to swirl in a circular pattern a good distance away. I can remember thinking how pretty it was, all the different shades of gray swirling together in the sky above. I started to wiggle in my mother's arms, wanting her to put me down so I could watch, but she yelled at me to stop, and honestly it was not her yelling at me that made me stop; it was the fear in her voice. This was the first clue I had that something was very wrong, because I think it was the first time I had ever seen my mother afraid. We got to the bunkhouse and ran straight for the small bathroom at the front of the house—the one with no windows. We huddled together on the bathroom floor, me in my mother's lap while she said the "Our Father" over and over. Soon I could not really hear the words because the wind was so loud, along with the rain falling heavily overhead on the tin roof. The next sound I could hear, but only faintly, was my dad shouting for us as he came through the door. My mom called out to him, saying that we had to get out of there and back to the main house, and he yelled back that it was too late; we would never make it in time because the tornado was headed straight for us. I can remember wondering briefly what a tornado was exactly, but then a sound of devastation I will never forget seemed to fill the world.

My father grabbed us up and we stepped into the walk-in shower. The shower pipe was on the outside of the wall, he gathered my mother and me into his arms and then held on to the pipe. The wind roared deafeningly, then suddenly a sound like a skill saw laboring through metal roared above the wind and the roof of the house was completely ripped off. Then, in an instant, it was over, and what had once been a house was now rubble with only three of the four main walls still standing.

Luckily for us, it was not a particularly large tornado, nor had it hit the house directly, or else my family and I could have been seriously injured or killed. It had come close enough to cause serious damage, but other than some scratches and bruises and my father's arm being dislocated from holding my mother and me and the pipe, we were safe.

Meanwhile, my grandfather and uncles had taken shelter in the barn, which had been spared along with the main house, and everyone else was safe. But all they could see from their angle was only two standing walls left of the bunkhouse, so they were terrified that something horrible had happened to us. They jumped into the truck and raced over to what was left of the bunkhouse, praying that we were still alive. They managed to help us out of the debris, and I recall vividly my grandfather pulling me up and holding me so close, as if he never wanted to let me go. They got us all out safely, but when we got back to the main house, things were in a bit of an uproar. My grandmother and aunts were arguing with my great uncle, who had his suitcases in hand and was headed for their car. This angered my grandmother because she felt that he should have been a little less concerned with himself, and more concerned about everyone else. Nevertheless, he and my great-aunt were in the car and gone before anyone had the chance even to say goodbye, to which my grandmother said we were probably well rid of them anyway.

My father told me later that the tornado was similar to how life could be in a way because one has to endure the bad and to be able to enjoy the good things in life. What I got out of this experience is that one should always have a healthy respect for the weather, its beauty as well as its destructive power, especially tornadoes. To this day, when the clouds start to gather and the weather appears ominous, I always head indoors to check the Weather Channel to make sure that there is nothing more than a rainstorm on the way.

Planting a Vegetable Garden

There are three major steps in planting a summer vegetable garden. Besides being good exercise, gardening can bring pleasant family activity to the back yard for a nominal investment.

Many a backyard gardener has become addicted after his first harvest. With a little planning and preparation, as is described below, one may enjoy the fruit of his labor for several weeks during the picking season.

The first major step is preparation. As the gardener begins to prepare for his garden, he needs to be aware of the last predicted date for frost in his area. Also, he should consider the types of crops which would likely flourish in his region. Other considerations are the proper spot, in terms of size, for projected yield, location for a minimum of six hours of sunlight daily, and elevation of the plot for purposes of drainage. Once these factors have been decided, he must gather the proper tools and supplies. These may include gloves, a garden hoe, rotary tiller, water hose, prepared commercial fertilizer of a five-ten-five ration, previously composted material, seeds and plants, such as tomatoes to be set, and, perhaps, some bottomless paper cups for use as support collars.

The second major step to vegetable gardening is that of action. First, the soil must be prepared. This is done by tilling the desired area to remove grass and weeds and to loosen the dirt. Once the grass and weeds are loose, they may be manually picked up and discarded. At this time the gardener should add four pounds, per one hundred square feet, of commercially prepared fertilizer of a five-ten-five ration. Also, it is helpful to add three to four inches in depth of composted matter, for richness and moisture retention. Re-tilling this mixture into the soil will insure proper blending. At this stage, the furrows may be formed by using a hoe and burrowing along in the fluffy ground. The excess dirt may be lightly tossed to each side to form the mounds for planting. When shallow trenches are made in the furrows, the seeds may be planted. Three seeds at a time may be sown at specified intervals noted on the envelope in which they were packaged. When the seeds are planted, the trench may be closed up by pinching the soil back in place over the mound. This is when young seedlings are to be set in the remaining garden area, at one foot intervals.

Now that the actual planting is done, the finishing stage remains. One final touch might be to cover weak or spindly seedlings with inverted paper cups, which are bottomless. Also, the gardener should quench this thirsty new crop with the water hose before spraying clean the tiller blades and hoe. The implements may be put away along with the gloves, unused fertilizer, leftover paper cups, remaining seeds, and the recoiled water hose. Of course, any trash generated by the project needs to be discarded at this time.

The original planning and maintaining of a vegetable garden are a lot of work and not very cost effective for the average family's consumption. Most backyard gardens are small and puny in comparison to amber waves of grain. However, the sore back, the callused hands, and the hours of pulling weeds are usually forgotten with the first juicy bite of a "Big Boy" variety tomato picked from the vine only minutes ago.

Horror Novels as Therapy

Allison Hinson

We humans have a coping mechanism for dealing with the world's problems. Instead of going to a therapist we go to a movie or open a book. In the fifties, to help America accept the fear caused by the atom bomb, Hollywood gave us *Them!* and a series of "big bug" movies. To escape the social ills of today, we open a horror novel. Horror is defined as a feeling of extreme fear or dislike, a disgust that makes one shudder. However, people pay for the pleasure of being horrified. In fiction, the horror genre can be recognized by Gothic settings, psychological conflicts, and supernatural events.

Gothic horror draws us into a gloomy setting with the beauty of its prose. One of the best examples is Shirley Jackson's *The Haunting of Hill House:* "[W]alls continued upright, bricks met neatly, floors were firm, and doors were sensibly shut; silence lay steady against the wood and stone of Hill House, and whatever walked there, walked alone." With this beautifully paced opening, Ms. Jackson sets the tone for her frightening tale. In Edgar Allan Poe's "The Cask of Amontillado" we see the cobwebs and feel the nitre seep into our bones as we follow our narrator on his dark journey: "'The nitre!' I said; 'see, it increases. It hangs like moss upon the vaults....The drops of moisture trickle among the bones.'" Similarly, we know that no good will come from Dracula's castle as Bram Stoker weaves his tale around us.

While Gothic settings can set the mood, psychological horror creates terror in the actual plot. Psychological horror disturbs reality, changing the way we think and act. Horror novels that are based on psychological conflicts create a feeling of terror in the reader because they are plausible. It is conceivable to experience the terror that the young mother and child feel in Stephen King's *Cujo* when they are trapped by the rabid dog. In Anthony Burgess' *A Clockwork Orange,* the real horror is not that Alex and his "droogs" are on a rampage in England, but rather that the state forces mind control on him. The psychological conflict in V.C. Andrews' *Flowers in the Attic* is a struggle for power as a mother is slowly brainwashed into giving up her children. Likewise, Robert Louis

Stevenson's *Dr. Jekyll and Mr. Hyde* creates horror by bringing attention to the destructive evil inside us all, symbolized by the werewolf.

We all possess to some degree the split personalities between what we are and what we know. Thus, it is our identification with these psychological conflicts that make these novels horrifying. Supernatural horror, on the other hand, does the opposite of psychological horror; it brings us outside the known laws of nature. Mary Shelley's *Frankenstein* shows us men reaching beyond set boundaries and finding only pain. Certainly the monster was furious at being brought to life and then denied companionship, and the doctor's irresponsibility brought disaster. In Ira Levin's *Rosemary's Baby,* the terror is in the powerlessness Rosemary feels against the supernatural Satanic forces at work within her body. In Stephen King's *Tommyknockers* we find alien ghosts hoping to take over the world by gaining a foothold in a small town in Maine. This story gives us Pandora's box and allows us to open it, spilling forth the horrors that we knew were inside. Supernatural horror scares us because we feel so helpless before such powerful and mysterious forces.

These three components of horror fiction provide the basis of what makes horror fiction so entertaining and cathartic. The human mind can handle only so much horror in daily life. It is better to release this horror by opening a good book than to succumb to it by opening a vein.

Wisdom

Jennifer Murray

If one asks the majority of people what the word wisdom means, most will answer vaguely that it is the knowledge gained during a lifetime. However, wisdom is much more than just knowledge gained; it signifies the accumulation of knowledge, the application of learning, and the personification of God's will in the creation of the universe (according to the *American Heritage Dictionary,* 6th ed.).

The abstract nature of the word wisdom allows for broad interpretation of its context. To limit the vagueness of the definition, many interpret wisdom as the accumulation of knowledge. In Greek mythology, the goddess Athena was known for her wisdom. Additionally, the personification of animals as possessing wisdom also heavily influenced Greek lore. Owls, for example, are synonymous with wisdom; likewise, foxes, with their cunning nature and ability to outsmart their prey, are considered insightful animals. Age plays a prominent part in the accumulation of learning. In many societies the elderly receive top status as preservers of both culture and knowledge, making them wise and respected members of the community. On a different level, teeth are described as being "wise;" however, these teeth actually do not differ from the rest of the secondary molars except for their tardiness.

Just as the accumulation of knowledge is a part of wisdom, so is the application of learning. The ancient Greeks believed that *logos*, or reason and thought, led to *sophia,* or wisdom. These early lovers of wisdom, or philosophers, sought knowledge and attempted to apply it to solving the puzzles of the universe. Further, philosophers such as Aristotle believed that wisdom was necessary to make judgments that coincide with one's understanding of life. This view, also known as "Philosophical Wisdom," is thought to be one of the highest attainable virtues. The Stoics, Greek and Roman philosophers, also had their own ideas about wisdom. To them, not only is wisdom a way of attaining human excellence, it also serves as a way to act according to one's personal ideals. Attaining wisdom places the philosopher in an enlightened nirvana-like state; however, it occasionally creates conflict for the individual having to deal with a dog-eat-dog existence. In order to release the enlightened man's tortured mind, Stoics, therefore, believed suicide was permissible to relieve the pain of existence. The way to true happiness, Stoics believed, was to want what one gets rather than to try to get what one wants.

Finally, wisdom can also explain God's will in the creation of the universe. The idea of a God who created the heavens and the earth invokes images of a wise and powerful being. The term "God-like" creates the idea of a wise person who has attained supreme knowledge. Also, in Roman Catholic and orthodox versions of the Old Testament, the Hebrew King Solomon urges his people to love righteousness and to seek wisdom. Christians may also remember the three wise men from the Orient who follow the North Star to Bethlehem in search of the baby Jesus. Wisdom, long regarded as one of the highest virtues, allows one to understand God as the ultimate holder of wisdom and the one who bestows wisdom upon the person who seeks Him.

The many meanings of the word wisdom should not be ignored. Whether the accumulation of knowledge, the intellectual application of that knowledge, or an explanation of God's creation of the universe, wisdom indicates a person's struggle to attain mankind's highest goal.

Weight Lifters

Roberto Loucel

Entertainment has been an established part of the American culture almost since its founding. The types of entertainment that most Americans enjoy in today's world are going to the movies, going out to eat, and exercising. Different forms of exercise vary from running and playing sports to weight lifting. Those who enjoy weight lifting can choose to do so in the privacy of their home, in a community center like the YMCA, or in a health club. At a health club one can expect to find a wide variety of male club members. These categories include the obnoxious socializers, the serious competitive athletes, and the predatory womanizers. Those who contribute most to the downside of working out at a local health club are the obnoxious, annoying members. Three types of these annoying, obnoxious people found at the weight room are the show-off, the know it-all, and the wanderer; they easily can be identified by their physical appearance, their social behavior, and their attitude.

The first type, the show-off, is known by his flashy appearance, his misan-thropic social skills, and his arrogant attitude. The show-off is a single male in his twenties who drives a European luxury car; he always comes to the gym wearing a tank top to display his deep tan and a pair of black and green spandex shorts. He is heavily built and all his muscles are well defined. But he is a man with poor social skills; he seldom talks to another soul and always works out by himself. He frequently ignores the greetings and good-byes of the health club employees; when he does answer a friendly "Hi, how is it going" or a "See you later," he does so in a deep, blunt, morbid tone of voice. He also likes to emphasize how strong and masculine he is by working out at the very front and center of the weight room, where everyone can see him. He refuses requests for help from others like a cheerleader refusing to go on a date with a pimply, nerdy classmate. Most people who work out at health clubs would be glad to be free of the show-off.

The second type is the know-it-all; he is identified by his commonplace appearance, moderately developed social skills, and commanding attitude. He is strong and well built, but not to the extent of the show-off. He is a married man in his mid-thirties to early forties who wears athletic shorts and a gray, short-sleeve T-shirt with the name of the health club printed on the front. He is not aloof like the show-off; he engages in conversations with his friends and makes small talk with strangers at the gym. Unlike the show-off, he tends to work out with groups of two or three and is not reluctant to ask for the help of others. He can be quite unpleasant because he verbally reprimands others for not doing an exercise in the correct form; he never misses a chance to remind everyone that he is an expert at weight lifting and finds joy and fulfillment in showing others the proper ways to lift weights. Working out in the presence of a know-it-all is a very frustrating experience for most people.

The third type is the wanderer; he is a family man in his late forties who finds coming to a health club a way to escape from his life at home. He wears a white headband, a pair of casual shorts, a white, cotton T-shirt one size too large, and a pair of old sneakers. This guy's strong point is his social skills because he is addicted to socializing. He talks to anyone—the gym employees, the lady on the treadmill, the guy doing squats—because he can't live without hearing himself talk for more than a minute. As one would imagine, he has no work-out routine; therefore, he is overweight and out of shape. His attitude can best be described as free loading because he relies on the help of other people when he is working out. When he asks the guy doing the leg press to spot him on the bench press, he puts in as little effort as possible and makes the spotter do most of the lifting. The wanderer is by far the most dangerous to a regular client's routine because he constantly interrupts it by talking or by asking for help.

In conclusion, the three types of people whom one needs to watch out for are the show-off, the know-it-all, and the wanderer. The show-off breaks one's concentration like a dry twig, the know-it-all lets all the air out of one's confidence, and the wanderer interrupts one's will to work out like a constantly ringing cell phone. One should avoid excessive exposure to any of these three at all costs; otherwise, the routine that one has put so much effort into to perfect, and the body one has worked so arduously to sculpt, will be a distant memory.

Violent Video Games=Violent Video Gamers?

Gelina Breaux

Violent video games have triggered a relentless debate, viewed by adolescent eyes and shackling minds of addicted adults. This controversy was even addressed as early as 2010 by the Supreme Court in the case of *Schwarzenegger vs. Entertainment Merchants Association* when a ban on selling violent video games to minors was overruled (Denny). Some deem that violent video games demoralize our society, while others view them as aggression releasers and an expression of American freedom. However, isn't there an invisible tape recorder in the virginity of a fertile mind? Are manifestations from violent exposure solid evidence that behavioral problems stem precisely from something as innocent as a video game? Parents must be cognizant of these issues and guard their children from adult-rated violence. Studies of violence and its influence on psychological processes point an accusatory finger at violent video games, which in turn has convinced many researchers that violent behavior is one grievous consequence.

The study of violent exposure's effect on the human psyche began undeniably violent, seared into the painful cognition of war torn soldiers. Col. Dave Gossman, writer of *On Combat and On Killing: The Psychological/Cost of Learning to Kill in War and Society,* conducts lectures about the mental stress that soldiers experience. Gossman states:

> Flashbacks are normal, the effect of powerful neuron pathways being created within the brain when a person experiences pain—much like a child touching a hot stove.... Children who are inundated with violent images from TV and video games are already being desensitized to the same acts of killing that leave such an emotional mark on veterans and police. (P. Anderson)

When a soldier or officer is thrust into the adrenaline of combat, Gossman describes how fear and anger inflict increased heart pulsation and limits blood flow to the brain. Brain function and heart rate are correlated in stages from "yellow, red, and black." The stage "black" is when a person stops thinking completely. This violence causes post-traumatic results if soldiers are not psychologically prepared for warfare. Likewise, television viewers have become desensitized to violence. They cannot physically empathize with a television actor's pain; therefore, repetitive exposure creates unconscious acceptance by viewers. According to the National Television Violence Study (NTVS), it has been estimated that preschool children who watch two hours of television a day will be exposed to approximately 10,000 violent images every year. According to their calculations, the average 11-year-old will witness 8,000 murders and 100,000 other violent acts (Miller 18.3). From these data, it is understandable how such imagines can distort a child's impression of violence in our society.

Imagine not only seeing such violence, but executing the brutality through a video game. Envision a child seeing a murder scene through the eyes of the murderer. The history of video games began during the 1970s, but violent video games were not introduced until the 1990s. Game producers realized that violent video games outsold non-violent. Violent fence riders like *Double Dragon* and *Mortal Kombat* became best-sellers. Nintendo and Sega Genesis competed to see which company could achieve the most sales. Sega added more violence while Nintendo toned down their violence. As a result, Sega outsold Nintendo three to one (Anderson, Gentile, and Buckley 5). When Wolfenstein 3D was introduced in 1993, it gave a player a "first-person shooter" point of view. The player can experience killing others, fighting, and being killed. *Doom* introduced more blood and gore; the game allowed players to kill each other as well as monsters. The advancement in technology created more levels of violence. While the original video games processed 350,000 polygons per second, Microsoft's Xbox, which was released in 2001 , had the capability to process 125 million polygons per second (Anderson, Gentile, and Buckley 6). This created an entire new world of graphics, increasing violent content to make the violence more realistic. Interplay productions, a video game company based in California, created the game *Carmeggedon,* which consisted of motorists obliterating pedestrians. The glamorized advertisement stated it was "as easy as killing babies with axes." Another advertisement for *Life of Crime* said that players were now able to "target specific body parts and see the damage done—including exit wounds" (Pollack 16). So the question yet exists—is such violence a direct influence on video garners, so that they will duplicate these heinous acts?

There have been violent acts stimulated precisely from violent video games. This fact provides a haunting recollection to families of 48 murdered women in Seattle. Gary Ridgway was the confessed serial killer; he kidnapped and murdered these women, sexually abused them, urinated on them, cut up their bodies, and then dumped them. In 2003, prosecutors within King County bargained with Ridgway that they would spare him the death penalty if he confessed. His confession mirrored the quotations from the video game scripts (qtd. Haugen 61-62). Opposed to Ridgway's serial killing, eighteen-year-old Devin Moore was a man without a history of violence. On June 7, 2003, he was held at a police station in Fayette, Alabama, under the accusation of car theft. He attacked and killed his arresting officer with the officer's own pistol, shot another officer twice who came to investigate the gun shots, and after Moore ran outside, he shot and killed an emergency dispatcher with five bullets. The violence lasted less than 60 seconds. During the investigation it was discovered that Moore had played the video game *Grand Theft Auto: Vice City* several months before the attack. His families believed the game encouraged the shootings and filed a multi-million-dollar lawsuit in March 2006 against the video game producers (Haugen 7). Scenes from the video game mirrored Moore's crimes. Moore stated himself, "Life is like a video game. Everybody's got to die sometime." After *Grand Theft Auto III* was introduced, two teenagers in Newport, Tennessee, confessed to be influenced by the game's affects after they had shot a .22-caliber rifle at cars on a highway (Haugen 8). While video games may not cause a person to randomly slice women's heads off, or steal vehicles in a shooting spree at a local police station, it may cause him to have a "killing attitude" towards others. Our views of the world are influenced by what we see. After the Supreme Court overturned the ban of selling violent video games in 2010 (in which the court ruled that violent video games are protected under the First Amendment), scientist Shankar Vedantam proved this concept with an explanation of two scientific studies done by (Psychologist Brad Bushman) on college students. The researchers divided them into two groups-those who played violent video games and those who did not. The researchers then showed the students two gory photos. Those who played violent video games were emotionless and unresponsive. The next study was conducted with the students blasting each other with noise. The college students who played violent video games were more aggressive. Dr. Bushman stated, "Playing violent video games probably will not turn your child into a psychopathic killer, but I would want to know how the child treats his or her parents, how he treats his siblings, how much compassion he has."

There has been much opposition to the opinion that violent behavior is stimulated from a violent video game. After a shooting in Littleton, Colorado, which seemed to be correlated with video games, the video game industry went into defensive mode because of opposing accusations. A news conference took place where video game producer Mr. Lowenstein was questioned. He stated, "The evidence does not support a link between playing video games and community mass murder. Video games don't teach people to hate. Video games don't teach people to be Nazis" (Pollack 16). Mr. Lowenstein may be correct when he says that video games may not cause mass murder, but he has failed to see that there is evidence and supporting links between video games and behavior problems. It is easy to agree with their claim for free-speech rights, but parents must be informed of these adversities and stay alert to how their children are developing thoughts and ideas. Violence is easily accessible to children; Mothers Against Violence in America conducted a group study by sending 17 children out to buy adult rated video games; 15 out of 17 stores sold them to children under 12 (qtd. Haugen 64). There are some who believe that violent video games are actually beneficial. Psychologist Melanie Moore stated, "Children need violent entertainment in order to explore the inescapable feelings that they have been taught to deny, and to reintegrate those feelings into a more whole, a more complex, more resilient selfhood" (Haugen 9). It is illogical to perceive that constant exercise of violent stimulations, though in a fantasy world, will not have an adverse effect on a person's violent tendencies in the real world. Feeding on a sensation naturally produces a larger appetite.

As soldiers bear witness of violence's effect on their psychological processes, violent video games are a proven factor to behavioral problems, as told from psychologists and killers' revealing eerie confessions. Although video game producers have a valid point that a violent video game may not influence "mass murder" in our community, they neglect to see that violent video game exposure is a factor in a causal chain of violent tendencies. Unfortunately, video game violence will progress as graphics improve and media violence escalates. Parents must be proactive and take a second look at the fine print of video game ratings before buying their child some potent infection in a gift package. Children must be warned of the dangers of the fantasy world of video games, violent or non-violent. After all, a video gamer creates his or her own life—not the video game.

Works Cited

Anderson, Craig A., Douglas A. Gentile, and Katherine E. Buckley. *Violent Video Game Effects on Children and Adolescents: Theory, Research, and Public Policy.* Oxford UP, 2007.

Anderson, Patrick B. "Speaker Explains the Psychology of Violence." *LaCrosse Tribune* 1 Feb 2012, http://lacrossetribune.com/news/local/speaker-explains-the-psychology-of-violence/article_d3d4e9a6-4c97-11e1-944e-0019bb2963f4.html.

Denny, Dan. "IU Research Links Violent Video Gaming with Brain Changes." *Herald-Times* 5 Dec. 2011, ww.heraldtimesonline.com/.../news.iu-research-links-violent-video-gaming-with-brain.

Haugen, David M. *Is Media Violence a Problem?* Greenhaven, 2006.

Miller, Michael Craig. "Does Violence in the Media Cause Violent Behavior." *Harvard Mental Health Letter* Sept. 2001.

Pollack, Andrew. "Video Game Industry Gathers Under Siege." *The New York Times* 14 May 1999, http://www.nytimes.com/1999/05/14/us/video-game-industry-gathers-under-siege.html.

Vedantam, Shankar. "It's a Duel: How Do Violent Video Games Affect Kids." *Hidden Brain* 7 Jul. 2011, http://www.npr.org/2011/07/07/137660609/its-a-duel-how-do-violent-video-games-affect-kids.

Appendices

APPENDIX 1

A Short Review of Grammar and Punctuation

(See also "Editing for Grammatical Errors," pp. 164-66.)

Readers expect written English prose to be clear and unambiguous, but in writing we often make mistakes that leave the reader in doubt about our intended meaning. Writing clear sentences is not always easy. Unpracticed writers need to pay particular attention to the following sentence problems, which are usually labeled **major errors**.

Sentence Fragments

Sentence fragments are incomplete sentences, expressing only part of an idea. Remember that a sentence must have both a subject and a verb.

Dependent Clause Fragments

Dependent clause fragments are created when a complete sentence is preceded by a subordinating conjunction, making it dependent on another complete sentence.

> He left early. *Although* he had done very little work that day.
> *Because* to express one's own thoughts about today's society is treason. I
>   held my tongue.

Corrections
> Even though he had done very little work that day, he left early.
> Because to express one's own thoughts about today's society is treason, I
>   held my tongue.

Verbal Fragments

Verbal fragments are created when verbals (usually ending in *ing*) are used instead of main verbs.

> I did not watch the game with the others. *Having* seen it earlier.

This better life, *consisting* of a new car, a bigger house, a better job, or, in other words, more money.

Corrections

Having seen the game earlier, I did not watch it with the others.

This better life consists of a new car, a bigger house, a better job, or, in other words, more money.

Comma Splices (Also Called Run-Ons)

Complete sentences (independent clauses) must be separated by complete stops—periods, semicolons, or coordinating conjunctions.

The streets were crowded with people, some were rushing to do their shopping, others were just standing around.

God is the soul born in each of us, the task of finding Him and living His planned way is left to us.

Columbus did not know for sure that the world was round, he just claimed it to be.

Corrections

The streets were crowded with people: some were rushing to do their shopping; others were just standing around.

God is the soul born in each of us, and the task of finding Him and living His planned way is left to us.

Columbus did not know for sure that the world was round. He just claimed it to be.

Fused Sentences (Also Called Run-Ons)

Fused sentences simply run two complete sentences together without any connectives.

People used to go by wagon to the fishing hole we made the 6-mile trip by foot.

Conformation is not the only difference there are others.

Corrections

People used to go by wagon to the fishing hole; we made the 6-mile trip by foot.

Conformation is not the only difference. There are others.

Subject-Verb Agreement

Subjects and their verbs must agree in number, gender, and person. The major problem for most beginning writers occurs in the present tense, pairing a plural verb with a singular subject or a singular verb with a plural subject.

> The unpredictable *episodes* that *engulfs* the sailors cannot be duplicated.
>   *Correction*: *engulf*
> The *scientist argue* that the universe is expanding. *Correction*: *argues*
> My friend and his mother *is* going. *Correction*: *are* going

In some sentences, particularly those beginning with a prepositional phrase, the subject is thrown behind the verb it agrees with.

> Near the house *stand* two gigantic pine *trees*.
> Over the road *lean* majestic live oaks.

Collective nouns (such as class, team, committee, and herd) usually take *singular* verbs because we think of them as units. Consider these examples.

> The *committee is* in agreement on the procedures to be used in the
>   investigation.
> The *class is* meeting in the room on the left.
> *None* of the students *was* prepared for the test.

Exception: Collective nouns may sometimes refer to the *individual members* of the class or group, so the plural verb is required. Consider these examples.

> The *class talk* among themselves while the teacher is writing on the board.
> After practice, the *team go* to their individual classes.

Nouns ending in -s: Some nouns end in -s but are considered to be singular. Others, however, are plural.

> *Measles was* once a common childhood disease.
> *Statistics was* my hardest class in college.
> The *scissors were* lying on the table.
> The *pants belong* to my father.

Compound nouns take plural verbs, but make certain you are referring to two or more things.

> *The dog and the cat are* lying on the floor together.
> The *director and the producer were* both on stage. [two different people]
> The *director and producer was* on stage. [one person]

Exception: Verbs with the compound nouns *either-or* and *neither-nor* agree with the subject that is closest to the verb.

> Either the book or the *videos are* going to be sold.
> Either the videos or the *book is* going to be sold.

Indefinite pronouns (each, everyone, everybody, nobody...) take singular verbs.

> *Anyone* born in the US *is* automatically a citizen of the country.
> *Anybody* who takes the class *is* eligible for the team.

Exception: When indefinite pronouns refer to a noun following them, they are singular or plural depending on the noun they refer to (all, enough, most, some...).

> *Most* people *are* not happy with Congress.
> *All* of the pizza *was* eaten.

Relative pronouns (who, which, that), agree with the noun in the main clause the pronoun refers to.

> Those *students* who do not take the final *are* sure to fail. (*Who* refers to students.)
> The *bicycle* that I just purchased *has* a flat tire. (*That* refers to bicycle.)

Exception: When a prepositional phrase follows a pronoun, the number of the verb in the dependent clause depends on whether individual members of a group or the group itself has been specified. Consider these examples.

> It is *one* of those cars that *was* damaged in the flood. (Pointing to a specific car out of a group)
> It was one of those *cars* that *were* damaged in the flood. (Pointing to the group)

Pronoun-Antecedent Agreement

Many of the same situations that occur with subject-verb agreement also occur with pronoun-antecedent agreement. Pronouns must agree with the nouns they refer to in number, gender, and case.

> Each *student* will do *their* share. *Correction*: *his* share
> A *motel* should have a swimming pool for *their* patrons. *Correction*: *its* patrons
> For example, *someone* interested in the Spanish language would have *their* major field in Spanish. *Correction*: *his* (or *her*) major field.

Compound Subjects: In sentences with *compound subjects*, pronouns that refer back to them are plural, but with *or* and *nor* they agree with the subject that is closest to the verb.

> John and Mary handed in *their* essays at the same time.
> Neither John nor his friends turned in *their* assignments.
> Either John's friends or John himself will get *his* just reward.

Indefinite pronouns (each, everyone, everybody, nobody…) are usually singular and require singular pronouns that refer back to them.

> *Anyone* born in the US is automatically a citizen and must pay *his* taxes.
> *One* of the students on the team lost *his* contact lens.

Some indefinite pronouns, however, can be either singular or plural (all, enough, most, some…).

> *Some* of the food had lost *its* freshness.
> *Some* of the students refused to hand over *their* phones.

When a pronoun refers back to a noun that can be either masculine or feminine, change the noun itself to plural, and use the plural pronoun. Alternatively, use the masculine pronoun if you are male or the feminine pronoun if you are female. Do not use the awkward *he or she*, or the even worse *him/her*.

> A *student* must be in class on time every day if *he or she* hopes to make an "A."
> *Correction*: *Students* must be in class on time every day if *they* hope to make an A.

Be careful of vague or ambiguous pronoun reference.

On *CNN*, *they* said that the new president would round up all illegal aliens in the country.

Correction: CNN reported that the new president would round up all illegal aliens in the country.

If a student works hard, *you* will succeed.

Correction: If a student works hard, *he* will succeed.

Parallel Structure

Within a sentence, balance—or parallel structure—should be used for ideas that are alike.

Coordinating Conjunctions: Whenever there is a *coordinating conjunction*, the same grammatical structure must go on both sides of the conjunction. A coordinating conjunction is like the pivot on a balance beam.

I like *reading* and *jogging.*
He likes to *goof* off and *act* like a fool.
She is *beautiful* but *dull.*
Valery is always *talking* or *texting* on her phone.

Series: Whenever there is a series, the same grammatical structure must be used in each example.

I like *reading, jogging,* and *riding* my bike.
He is a *procrastinator,* a *dilettante,* and a *liar.*

Linking Verbs: Whenever there is a linking verb, which acts like an equal sign, the same grammatical structure must go on both sides of the verb.

The way *to succeed* is *to work* very hard.
The way *to fail* is *to skip* class.
Running to class every day is *ruining* my health.

Word Pairs: When the "not only . . . but also" and the "both . . . and" structures are used, the same grammatical structure must go on both sides.

The students are not only *intelligent,* but they are also *dedicated.*

Both those who *play* the game and those who *watch* must behave.

Dangling and Misplaced Modifiers

A modifier is a word, phrase, or clause, such as an adjective or an adverb, that points to or changes the meaning of another word. For example, in the phrase *red wagon*, the adjective red modifies wagon; in the phrase *the boy running down the street*, the participial phrase "running down the street" modifies "boy." In sentences, modifiers must clearly point to the words modified; otherwise, they become confusing and misleading.

Dangling Modifiers: A modifier is said to "dangle" when it appears to modify a word in a sentence that it obviously cannot.

> *When only seven years old*, my father took me to my first rodeo.
> The mother handed out cookies to the children *in cellophane bags*.

Misplaced Modifiers: Modifiers can also create confusion because of where they are placed in the sentence. Consider the following sentences. Which is the clearest?

> He read the note by the teacher hanging on the door.
> Hanging on the door, he read the note by the teacher.
> He read the teacher's note hanging on the door.

The word *only* is often misleading. Place it next to the word or phrase it modifies. Which of the following sentences is the clearest?

> I will *only* pass if I turn in the late papers.
> I will pass *only* if I turn in the late papers.
> I will pass if I turn in the late papers *only*.

Inconsistent Changes in Person, Number, Tense, Voice, and Mood

Do not randomly shift person, number, tense, voice, or mood within sentences.

> *John* is a typical 5-year-old; *they* seem to enjoy getting dirty.
> I *play* video games every day, but I *worked* all night.
> He *flies* his drone every chance he *got*.
> He *gives* the book to his girlfriend. She *took* it and left.
> The *professor liked* his students, and he *was* also *liked by* them.
> He *told* me, *turn* down the music!

Faulty Complements: Incomplete Verbs

A *complement* is a word that completes a verb. For example, a direct object is a complement or completer. In the sentence "The boy hit the ball," *ball* is the complement. When a linking verb is used (usually a form of the verb "to be"), the complement is a noun or an adjective, called a predicate noun or a predicate adjective. For example, in the sentence "The girl is president of her class," the word *president* is the complement, a predicate noun. In the sentence "The girl is pretty," the word *pretty* is the complement, a predicate adjective.

The word *is* (a form of the word "to be") in these sentences acts like an equal sign. What goes on each side of the equal sign has to match. For example, if I say, "Acting is when one pretends," the two halves are **not** equal; *acting* is a noun, and *when one pretends* is a clause. This is a **faulty complement**. Instead, I can say "Acting is the art of pretending." Here *acting* is equal to *art*. Both are nouns.

Comparisons

So: A faulty comparison occurs when someone uses *so* as an intensive, meaning *very*. For example, if I say, "I was so happy," the reader is left to wonder—so happy that *what*? A *so* implies a *that*: I was so happy that I jumped up and down.

Like: *Like* is a preposition. Use *like* whenever it is followed by a noun or noun phrase.

> He acted like a fool.
> The moon, like a gigantic balloon, loomed over the horizon.
> Students are not like consumers at the mall.
> Teachers are like drill sergeants barking orders.

As: *As* is a coordinating conjunction. Use *as* whenever it is followed by a phrase or a clause (even when we elide or cut out repeated words),

> He acts in class as he would act on stage.
> She is working hard as she should.
> Customs vary in the United States as [they vary] in Vietnam.

Exception: *As* can also be a preposition and an adverb.

> He works as a computer programmer.
> Her face was as red as a cherry.

Who Versus Which Versus That

Who, *which*, and *that* are relative pronouns. As with all pronouns, they must refer back to nouns.

Who refers back to people (or animals that are named).

> People who text while driving should be given a ticket.
> She is the type of person who always says what she thinks.
> Muffin is a cat who spends a lot of time hunting mice.

Which refers back to things and unnamed animals when the clause does **not restrict** the meaning.

> The dog, which was wearing a large, orange collar, began barking loudly.
> The giant oak, which was leaning over the house, was filled with finches.
> She looked at the mountain, which rose majestically behind her backyard.

That refers back to things and animals when the clause **does restrict** the meaning:

> The dog that was wearing a large, orange collar began barking loudly.
> The giant oak that was leaning over the house was filled with finches.
> She looked at the mountain that rose majestically behind her backyard.

Punctuation

Commas

Commas are used as pauses in sentences, not as full stops. Certain places require commas, and there are places (such as between a subject and a verb) where commas disrupt the flow of a sentence.

Always use a comma in the following situations.

1. Before a coordinating conjunction in a compound sentence

   The boy hit the ball, and the first baseman caught it.

2. To separate items in a series

   I like pizza, fried chicken, chocolate cake, and ice cream.

3. To set off nonrestrictive elements, such as appositives

    Donald Trump, President of the United States, said today he would make his first major address to Congress on Thursday.

4. After certain introductory words and after lengthy phrases and clauses

    On the contrary, Chad is a country in Africa.
    Although we consider ourselves a great democracy, some would say that we are, instead, a plutocracy.

Also use a comma in these situations.

> *In dates*: March 4, 2017
> *Between cities and states (and after the state if the sentence continues)*:
>   Houston, Texas, is the largest city in the state.
> *Before most quotations*: Samuel Johnson once said, "What we hope ever to do with ease, we must learn first to do with diligence."

Never use a comma in these situations.

> To separate subjects from verbs—The boy, hit the ball.
> To separate verbs from their complements—The boy hit, the ball.

Stylistic commas: Commas are sometimes placed in a sentence where the writer wants a pause so the reader may fully understand the meaning or the tone of a sentence. Some writers use more commas; some use fewer.

Semicolons

Semicolons are **only** used in a sentence to separate independent clauses; they take the place of a comma and a conjunction. Rhetorically, they tie together two sentences alike in meaning and close in form, whereas a comma and a conjunction tie sentences disparate in meaning and form.

> The last president was a Democrat; the current president is a Republican.

Rarely, semicolons are used to separate a series that contains a subordinate series.

> The problems we encountered in the warehouse included unsanitary conditions, such as dirty bathrooms and break rooms; lax oversight of workers, such as failure to require goggles and gloves, lack of immediate cleanup of spills, and excessive absenteeism; and dangerous and illegal practices,

such as hazing of young workers, harassment of females, and backdating time stamps.

Colons

Colons are **full stops** and emphasize what follows. They set up formal lists and add phrases and dependent clauses to main clauses. Use colons to do the following.

1. Set up and emphasize a formal or lengthy list

   The president's agenda includes: reforming health care, building a wall along our southern border, increasing funding for the military, and winning reelection in four years.

2. Add fragmentary information to a main clause

   One item is not on his agenda: saving the environment.

3. Set up complete sentence quotations

   One political analyst said of the president: "He will push hard for his programs, take what he can get, and then declare victory."

Apostrophes

Apostrophes are used to show possession or omissions of letters or numbers.

1. Place an apostrophe before the s to show singular possession and after the s to show plural possession.

   The student's book was heavily annotated.
   The students' books were heavily annotated.
   I had to drive my mother-in-law's car today.

2. If a word ends in s, such as *lens*, *cactus*, and *class*, place an apostrophe and another s after the word.

   The lens's optics were faulty.
   The cactus's spines pricked my finger.
   The class's outing was spoiled by the rain.

3. With certain common nouns that end in s, however, such as *measles* and *scissors*, and with proper nouns, such as *Jones* and *Texas*, add only an apostrophe.

The scissors' handle was too small for my fingers.
Tom Jones' book on the American Revolution was required reading for the class.
Texas' Hill Country real estate is in great demand.

4.   Apostrophes are used to indicate contractions. A contraction omits letters between a pair of words and combines them. For example, *we are* can become *we're*.

We're all in this together.
She said *she'd* let him take her to the dance.

5.   Apostrophes are used to indicate elisions (omissions) in dates.

I bought the Mustang in *'05*.

6.   Whenever a noun or pronoun is used before a gerund (a verbal usually ending in *ing*), it must be in the possessive case.

Because *John's* jogging had injured his knee, he was forced to stop his
    exercise program for a while.
The student, playing with his phone, ignored the teacher. Because of the
    student's playing with his phone, he was sent to the principal's office.
The *baby's* crying woke up the parents.
He thought the boys' playing with toy guns was inappropriate.
I heard Julie singing. I enjoyed *Julie's* singing.

Quotation Marks

Quotation marks are used to surround all material taken from a source. According to Shakespeare, "Our doubts are traitors, and make us lose the good we oft might win by fearing to attempt."

Commas and periods go **inside** closing quotation marks; colons and semicolons go **outside** quotation marks.

"Ask not what your country can do for you," said Kennedy, "but what you
    can do for your country."
"To be, or not to be"; this is the primal question.

Question marks (and exclamation marks) may go inside quotation marks but **only** if they are part of the quotation.

"Shall I compare thee to a summer's day?" Shakespeare wrote.

Italics

Italics are used in several situations.

1. Words emphasized as *words* are put in italics.

    The word *autotelic* means "having a purpose in and not apart from itself."

2. Foreign words and phrases not adopted into English are also put in italics.

    Weltschmerz is a German word generally translated as "world weariness."
    The message in many Greek plays is to practice *sophrosyne*, or moderation.

Titles

Some titles are put in quotation marks; some are put in italics.

1. Titles of complete works, or those bought and consumed as **wholes**, are put in italics.
    The Canterbury Tales; *The Writing Arc*; *The Complete Poems of Andrew Marvell.*

2. Titles of **parts** of works, such as chapters of books, individual essays, and short poems, are put in quotation marks: "The Wife of Bath's Tale"; "Poison Apples"; "To His Coy Mistress."

Hyphens, Dashes, and Parentheses

A hyphen is used to separate words that are intended to be seen as a unit. For example, there are a number of hyphenated compounds in English: editor-in-chief, merry-go-round, well-being. However, when two or more words are used as a unit before a noun, they are also hyphenated. (The exception to this hyphenation rule is when the compound begins with an adverb, such as *clearly written statement* or *poorly attended event*.)

The *soon-to-be* president spoke to the crowd.
The *happy-but-weeping* bride threw the bouquet over her shoulder.

A dash is longer than a hyphen (- versus —) and is used to set off fragments or complete sentences that a writer wants to emphasize, either as an addition at the end of a sentence or as a comment within the sentence. The words *surrounding* those within the dashes make a complete sentence that can stand alone.

> She smiled and said hello—without stopping or looking at me.
> It is not fair—it is not just—for immigrants to be denied due process.

Parentheses are used to add additional (generally secondary) information to a sentence (like dashes, but this time for more emphatic or specialized purposes). They are also used in some in-text citation styles. For example, in MLA, page numbers and line numbers are enclosed in parentheses. Note that commas and periods *follow the closing parenthesis.*

> The candidate for office wanted to win over the large crowd (as well as donors) with his speech.
> One of the most trenchant sayings I have ever come across was written by W. H. Auden in "September 1, 1939": "Those to whom evil is done / Do evil in return" (ll. 21-22).

Numbers

Numbers are sometimes written out as words and sometimes expressed as numerals.

1. Write out all numbers that can be expressed in one or two words: *three, nineteen, twenty-five.*

2. Place larger numbers in numeric form: *302; 7,050; 1,360,000.*

3. Dates and times of day, with the exception of "noon" and "midnight," are always put in numeric form: *June 6, 1944; 11:15 a.m.*

4. Never begin a sentence with a numeral: Three hundred people showed up for the funeral.

5. If you are using many numbers in your essay—and some are small numbers of one or two words, and others are larger numbers—put all of the numbers in numeric form.

Abbreviations

Abbreviations are shortened forms of longer words. Use standard abbreviations (such as Dr. and Mrs.) only; do not use chat-speak, such as LOL or BRB, in formal prose. Online, you can find lists of *standard abbreviations* used in states, professions, and other situations.

A Brief Review of the Basics

Sentences are composed of words, phrases, and clauses.

Words: Words can be nouns, pronouns, verbs, or modifiers (adjectives, adverbs): *dog, she, play, happy, seemingly.*

Phrases: Phrases are groups of two or more words. There are noun phrases, adjective phrases, adverb phrases, gerund phrases, infinitive phrases, participle phrases, and prepositional phrases.

Clauses are made up of words and phrases that contain at least one verb and one subject (though the subject can be implied, as in one-word commands such as "Go!") There are two types of clauses, independent clauses and dependent clauses.

Independent Clauses

These are **complete sentences** that can stand alone. Independent clauses, or **complete sentences**, can be distinguished according to their *function*, their *form*, and their *rhetorical use.*

Function: Sentences have different functions, called moods, depending on the speaker's intent. The major moods in English are as follows.

Declarative: A declarative sentence makes a statement. *He went to town.*
Imperative: An imperative sentence issues a command. *Go to town!*
Interrogative: An interrogative sentence asks a question. *Are you going to town?*
Exclamatory: An exclamatory sentence expresses emotion. *Oh my God!*
Subjunctive: A subjunctive sentence expresses a hypothetical, or statement contrary to fact. *If I were rich, I would buy a new car. I suggest you arrive on time for class.*

Form: Sentences take different forms depending on the number and placement of the clauses they contain.

Simple: The boy hit the ball.
Compound: The boy hit the ball, and the second baseman caught it.
Complex: The boy, who was wearing the green cap, hit the ball.
Compound/Complex: The boy, who was wearing the green cap, hit the ball, and the second baseman caught it.

Rhetorical Use: Sentences are described as *loose* or *periodic* according to the way subordinating phrases and clauses are arranged. In a loose sentence (the normal workhorse of English prose), the main clause comes first, with dependent clauses following; in a periodic sentence, the dependent clauses come first, with the main clause at the end.

> *Loose*: The indicted senator strode into the room unabashed, smiling broadly, exuding confidence and goodwill.
> *Periodic*: Unabashed, smiling broadly, exuding confidence and goodwill, the indicted senator strode into the room.

Dependent Clauses

These are subordinate clauses—that is, they are subordinate to a main, or independent, clause. *Because I could not stop*, I ran into the back of the car in front of me. There are three types of dependent clauses: noun clauses, adjective clauses, and adverb clauses. Remember that a clause has a subject and a verb.

Noun Clauses, as the name implies, can take the place of a single noun, functioning, for example, as the subject of a sentence, the direct object of a sentence, a predicate noun, or the object of a preposition.

> *That John was richer than his friends* was obvious from the BMW he drove.
> The teacher said *that the students could not enter the classroom after the door was closed.*
> The student's reason for being late was *that he had been pulled over and given a ticket for speeding.*
> We learned nothing except *what he told us.*

Noun clauses are typically introduced by *that* (as the first three examples above), *whether, if,* and the relative pronouns *who, which, what, why,* and *how*.

> I wondered *whether* the teacher would be on time for class today.
> My friend asked me *if* I had bought the textbook.
> The teacher asked *who* had read the assignment.
> I could not decide *which* tie to wear today.
> *What* the president would do about the crisis was debated by the class.
> I never could decide *why* I acted in that way.
> I don't know *how* I could have done what I did.

Adjective Clauses, similarly, take the place of single adjectives within a sentence, modifying nouns or pronouns. Adjective clauses can be introduced by the relative pronouns *who*, *which*, or *that* and the adverbs *where*, *when*, and *why*.

> The girl *who* won the award bowed before the audience.
> The ribbon, *which* was blue with gold trim, was hung proudly around the girl's neck.
> The ribbon *that* I received was black and had no trim.
> The stage *where* the ceremony was performed was small and dark.
> The time *when* it began was not posted.
> I did not know the reason *why* I had come in third.

Adverb Clauses, finally, take the place of single adverbs, modifying verbs, adjectives, or other adverbs. Adverb clauses can be introduced by such subordinating conjunctions as *when*, *before*, *after*, *while*, *as*, *because*, *although*, and *if*.

> *When* he gave me his absurd excuse, I laughed out loud.
> You must pass the first half of this course *before* you enroll in the second half.
> *After* she left, I began to cry.
> *While* on vacation, I visited my brother. (Note that the subject and the verb of the adverb clause are implied but are not actually written into the clause: While *I was* on vacation . . .)
> You cannot do *as* you please in this class.
> She wept *because* she had won.
> *Although* it was raining, I went on my usual morning bike ride.
> *If* you do not work, you will not pass.

See the illustration of independent and dependent clauses in the **schemes of coordination and subordination** on page 404.

Verbals

A verbal is a word that combines the characteristics of a verb with those of a noun or adjective—or it may itself act as a noun or adjective. There are three types of verbals: infinitives, gerunds, and participles.

Infinitives: An infinitive is a phrase that functions as a noun, an adjective, or an adverb but has the characteristics of a verb. It is usually preceded by *to*.

> *To play in the NFL* is my dream.
> She told her child *to play in the street*.
> *To be* is *to do*.

I gave you the money *to pay for lunch.*
The car *to buy* is the one that gets the best gas mileage.

I always play *to win.*
Are you old enough *to vote?*

Infinitives can sometimes even take their own objects.
It is my dream *to learn to play the piano.*
To write poetry is very difficult.

Gerunds: A gerund is a word that functions as a noun but has the characteristics of a verb; for example, it can take an object.

Writing poetry is very difficult.
Watching television dulls the mind.
I like *making pies.*

Participles: A participle is a word that functions as an adjective but has the characteristics of a verb (and ending in *-ing* or *-ed*). Present participles end in *–ing*; past participles end in *–ed.*

Breathing heavily, I ran down the street.
The woman *calling* to you is Theresa.
His *barking* dog roused the neighbors.

The most *dreaded* punishment was *running* laps.
The recently *fired* pistol was in his hand.
The doctor examined her *injured* arm.

Some Grammatical and Linguistic Terms

(Definitions taken from *Webster's New Collegiate Dictionary*, 9th ed.).

Colloquial. Of or relating to conversation: conversational—relating to everyday, ordinary speech

Etymology. The history of a linguistic form [word] shown by tracing its development since its earliest recorded occurrence in the language where it is found

Grammar. The study of the classes of words, their inflections, and their functions and relations in a sentence

Idiom. An expression in the usage of a language that is peculiar to itself either grammatically or in having a meaning that cannot be defined from conjoined meanings of its elements

Inflection. The change of form that words undergo to mark such distinctions as those of case, gender, number, tense, person, mood, or voice

Linguistics. The study of human speech, including the units, nature structure, and modification of language

Parse. To resolve (as a sentence) into component parts of speech and describe them grammatically

Rhetoric. The art of speaking or writing effectively

Semantics. The study of meanings (of words)

Syntax. The order in which words are put together to form phrases, clauses, or sentences

Usage. The way in which words and phrases are actually used in a language community (as in a particular form or sense)

Schemes of Coordination and Subordination

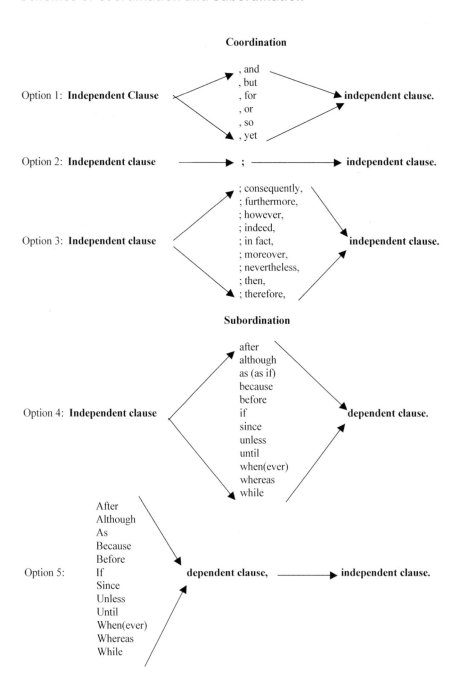

APPENDIX 2

Common Informal Fallacies

A fallacy is a particular kind of defect in an argument caused by unsound or incomplete reasoning. It weakens an argument and makes it vulnerable to attack. However, sometimes writers consciously use such unsound reasoning to bolster their own side of an argument or to deflect criticism away from a weak argument. There are two kinds of fallacies: Formal fallacies result from not following the rules of formal logic, such as not distributing the middle term in a categorical syllogism. Informal fallacies result from the ambiguity inherent in language, such as when a word is used in two different senses in the same argument, called equivocation. Of the two, the informal fallacies are more regularly employed in everyday argument. After all, normal arguments between people are conducted through language, not mathematical symbols. Therefore, not only should you be familiar with informal fallacies so you can avoid them in your own argumentative essays, but you should also be able to identify your opponent's defective arguments, allowing you to refute those claims more easily. The following list includes some of the most common informal fallacies.

Hasty Generalization. An argument that draws a conclusion based on insufficient or inappropriate samplings: "My Chevrolet is a real lemon; therefore, General Motors manufactures inferior automobiles." "Students at State U are rude. Last night the guys in the room next to mine played their stereo at full blast until two in the morning, and as I was on my way to class this morning a bicyclist almost ran me down."

Begging the Question. An argument based on an assumption that has not been proven: "The immoral experimentation on animals for research must be abolished"; "My narrow-minded English instructor seems to have forgotten how difficult it is to be a student."

Circular Reasoning. An argument that goes in a circle, in which one proves the premise by the conclusion and the conclusion by the premise: "The governor would never lie to the public because he is an honest man." "Drugs are harmful because they injure the body." "I believe in God because I believe in the truth of the Bible; I believe in the truth of the Bible because it is the inspired word of God."

Either/or Reasoning. An argument, also called a *false dilemma*, that suggests that only two alternatives exist when more than two actually exist. Valid inferences can be drawn only from alternatives that are exhaustive: "Either he voted Republican or he did not vote Republican" is quite different from "Either he voted Republican or he voted Democratic." People have a tendency to turn difficult issues into simple ones with two sides— black/white, right/ wrong, good/ bad. "If you quit college, you will never succeed in anything you do." "We can recognize that athletes who participate in major sports must be given special consideration at State U, or we can let the university sink into athletic oblivion."

Faulty Analogy. An argument based on a comparison of two things that share few or no common and relevant features. An analogy should be carefully examined to be sure that the things being compared are alike in ways essential to the conclusion being drawn. The fact that they are alike in some ways is not enough. "Since he was a good actor, I'm sure he will make a good president." "Bill, you are a superb computer technician. You seem to have a natural talent for analyzing system problems and remedying them. Surely, then, you should be able to analyze the problems in the rough drafts of your papers and turn them into polished essays."

Argumentum ad Hominem. The Latin phrase means *argument against the man* and names the fallacy of attacking the person rather than his argument. Such an attack may be legitimate when someone presents no argument but his own unsupported testimony. For example, the procedure is frequently used in courts to impeach witnesses who are testifying as experts. If it can be shown that they are not experts or that their testimony cannot be relied on, their trustworthiness as witnesses is seriously challenged. However, if someone presents evidence to support a claim, simply attacking his character is illegitimate. "Mr. Grumpky shouldn't be allowed to serve on the school board; he is a non-Christian." "Of course Senator Sparky voted for the big bailout of Global Mortgage; I hear he's received lots of money from their political action committee."

Argumentum ad Populum. This "appeal to the people" is used particularly by politicians and advertisers. This fallacy ignores the issue at hand to appeal to the in-group loyalties and fears of the audience. Appeals to prejudice and self-interest are also part of this appeal. For example, one might argue that people should be against any form of government regulation of business because America was founded on the principle of freedom from oppression.

Appeal to Ignorance. This argument implies that because no one has proved a particular claim, it must be false; or, because no one has disproved a claim, it must be true. This fallacy usually involves a matter that is either incapable of being proven or has not yet been proven. For example, a frequently heard retort in an argument, say, about the existence of telepathy, is: "Well, you can't prove that it doesn't exist!" This is not a clinching argument, for our inability to disprove a proposition does not establish its truth or falsehood. Keep in mind that the burden of proof rests with the person making a claim.

Tokenism. This fallacy occurs when one makes only a token gesture (does very little of what is required) but then shouts or brags about it as loudly as one can. For example, a company might point to a highly placed executive who is female to show how well they treat and promote women when, in fact, she is the only woman in an executive position in the whole company.

The Straw Man Fallacy. This fallacy occurs when a person misinterprets or distorts an opponent's position to make it easier to attack or when he attacks weaker opponents while ignoring stronger ones. For example, when opponents of gun control characterize those who support some limitations on the ownership and use of weapons as radicals who would do away with hunting and Americans' constitutional right to bear arms, they are attacking a straw man.

Bandwagon fallacy. An argument that claims that something cannot be true (or false) because a majority of people support (or oppose) it. Based on popular opinion, the argument appeals to prejudice and ignores the facts. For example, "It is obvious that any caring parent would not want his/her child attending school where a boy can go into the girls' bathroom."

Slippery Slope. An argument based on an unlikely chain reaction. It consists in objecting to a particular action on the grounds that once an action is taken it will lead inevitably to a similar but less desirable action, which, in turn, will lead to an even less desirable action, and so on. For example, "If we legalize marijuana, the United States will become a nation of addicts and criminals." "If we allow physician-assisted suicide, it will eventually lead to the wholesale killing of the very ill or permanently disabled."

Selective Sampling. Proof offered that contains part of the truth, but not the whole truth. Because not all the facts are stated, the claim can be true and false (misleading?) at the same time (half-truths). For example, "Three out of five dentists surveyed preferred Brand X toothpaste."

Unreliable Testimony. An argument based on an untrustworthy, biased, or unqualified authority. Fame or celebrity does not qualify one as authoritative or expert. For example, "Several of my neighbors support the termination of our school's head coach."

False Cause. An argument that confuses a causal relationship. For example, one might mistake a contributory cause for a sufficient one or assume that because one event occurred before a second event, the first caused the second (an example of the *post hoc, ergo propter hoc* fallacy, a Latin phrase meaning *after this; therefore because of this*.) "Because the city council outlawed firearms, the crime rate has risen." "Research shows that successful people have large vocabularies; therefore, one way to become successful is to develop a large vocabulary."

APPENDIX 3

Commonly Confused Words and Phrases

There are many words in English that sound alike or are spelled alike (called homophones and homographs) but that have different meanings according to context. The following are some of the more common.

Accept, Except: The verb *accept* means "to give an affirmative answer to" or "to receive." The verb *except* means "to exclude"; as a preposition, *except* means "with the exclusion of."

Advice, Advise: Pronounced and spelled differently—*advice* is a noun, and *advise* a verb.

Affect, Effect: *Affect*, meaning "to influence," is a verb only. *Effect* may function as a verb or a noun. The verb *effect* means "to bring about" or "to achieve"; the noun *effect* means "the result."

Allusion, Illusion: An *allusion* is a reference to something, for example a Biblical allusion; an *illusion* is something that is not as it seems, such as a mirage.

Already, All Ready: *Already* means "before or by the time specified." *All ready* means "completely prepared."

Alright, All Right: *Alright* is an unacceptable spelling of *all right*.

Among, Between: *Among* always implies more than two, a group; *between* literally implies only two.

Amount, Number: *Amount* refers to quantity and *number* to things that can be counted.

Bare, Bear: *Bare* (adj.) means naked, unadorned; *bare* (verb) means to strip or uncover; a *bear* (noun) is an animal, and *bear* (verb) means to carry or produce.

Capital, Capitol: *Capital* refers to the chief city of a state or country; *capitol* refers to the specific building where a legislature meets.

Carat, Caret, Carrot: A *carat* is a unit of weight for precious stones; a *caret* is a proofreading symbol (^); a *carrot* is a vegetable.

Complement, Compliment: A *complement* is something that completes (as a predicate adjective); a *compliment* is an expression of praise.

Conscience, Conscious: Do not confuse *conscience*, the noun, with *conscious*, the adjective.

Council, Counsel, Consul: A *council* is an assembly, like a city council (councilor); *counsel* (noun, verb) refers to advice (counselor); a *consul* is a foreign service officer.

Data, Criteria, Phenomena: Plurals of *datum, criterion, phenomenon*.

Differ From, Differ With: *Differ from* means "to stand apart because of unlikeness." *Differ with* means "to disagree."

Emigrate, Immigrate: *Emigrate* means "to leave a place of abode for residence in another country." *Immigrate* means "to come for permanent residence into a country of which one is not a native."

Eminent, Imminent: *Eminent*, means outstanding, prominent; *imminent* means about to occur or impending.

Farther, Further: *Farther* refers to physical distance and *further* to degree. Paris is *farther* away than New York; the *further* you progress in math, the more difficult the problems become.

Fewer, Less: *Less* refers to value, degree, or amount; *fewer* refers to number, to the countable.

Hanged, Hung: *Hanged* is used in referring to executions, *hung* to objects.

Imply, Infer: The writer or speaker *implies*; the reader or listener *infers*. *Imply* means "to suggest without stating"; *Infer* means "to reach a conclusion based upon evidence."

Incredible, Incredulous: *Incredible* means "too extraordinary to admit of belief." *Incredulous* means "inclined not to believe."

Ingenious, Ingenuous: *Ingenious* means "clever, resourceful," as "an ingenious device." *Ingenuous* means "open, frank, artless," as "ingenuous actions."

Its, It's: *Its* is a possessive pronoun; *it's* is a contraction of it is.

Lay, Lie: *Lay* is a transitive verb meaning to put or place something. It always takes an object. Its principal parts are *lay, laid, laid. Lie* is intransitive and means to recline or to remain. Its principal parts are *lie, lay, lain.*

Lose, Loose: *Lose* means "to cease having." *Loose* (verb) means "to set free."

Moral, Morale: The noun *moral* means "lesson, maxim"; the adjective *moral* means "pertaining to right conduct, ethical." *Morale*, a noun, refers to "a cheerful, confident state of mind."

Passed, Past: *Passed* is the past tense and past participle of *pass* (They *passed* by yesterday). *Past* is an adjective, adverb, and preposition (In the *past*); a *pastime* is a spare time activity.

Plain, Plane: *Plain* means unadorned, simple, or easily understood; a *plane* is an aircraft, a carpenter's tool, or a flat surface.

Principal, Principle: Distinguish between *principal*, an adjective or noun meaning "chief" or "official," and the noun *principle*, meaning "fundamental truth."

Quote, Quotation: *Quote* is a verb; *quotation* is a noun. Do not use *quote* as a shortened form of *quotation*. I found the *quotation* (not *quote*) on page two of the document.

Right, Wright, Write: *Right* means morally, legally, properly; a *wright* is a maker, such as a playwright; to *write* is a verb meaning to inscribe with letters.

Set, Sit: *Set* is a transitive verb meaning to put or place; its parts are *set, set, set. Sit* is an intransitive verb meaning to be seated; its parts are *sit, sat, sat.* However, a hen *sets*, concrete *sets*, and the sun *sets*.

Sight, Site, Cite: *Sight* refers to vision, *site* refers to a physical area of reference, and *cite* refers to a quotation.

There, Their, They're: *There* is an adverb or an expletive; *their* is a possessive pronoun; *they're* is a contraction for *they are*.

To, Too, Two: Distinguish the preposition *to* ("to the store") from the adverb *too* ("too cold") and the numeral *two* ("two apples").

APPENDIX 4

Common Roots and Affixes from Greek and Latin

Many words in English, particularly in the sciences, are built from Greek and Latin. The word *democracy*, for example, is made up of two Greek roots, *demos* (meaning "the people," because the Athenian populace was divided into *demes*, and *cracy,* meaning "power" or "rule"). If you know some of the more common of these roots and affixes (prefixes and suffixes), you will not only know the basic meaning of the word, but you will be able to guess the meaning of new words you encounter that are based on these roots. There are a number of sites on the internet with more complete lists. The following are some of the more common ones.

a, an (Gk. un, not, without)	asexual, amoral, anarchy
ante (L. before, in front of)	antebellum, antecedent, anteroom
anthrop (Gk. human being)	anthropology, philanthropy, misanthropy
arch, archy (Gk. rule)	anarchy, monarchy, oligarch
aut, auto (Gk. same, self)	automobile, autonomous, automatic
bi, bio, bios (Gk. life)	biology, biography, autobiography
biblio (Gk. book)	bibliography, bibliophile, Bible
chron (Gk. time)	chronology, chronic, synchronize
cide (L. to kill)	insecticide, suicide, homicide
circum (L. around, about)	circumference, circumlocution, circumspect
co, col, com, con (L. with, together)	concurrent, condense, cohabit

cosmos (Gk. universe)	cosmic, cosmopolitan, cosmonaut
cracy (Gk. strength, power, rule)	democracy, aristocracy, meritocracy
cred (L. belief)	credit, incredible, credence
dis (L. apart, not, exclude, opposite)	disagreeable, disable, disaster
e (L. not, absent, out, away, thoroughly)	eradicate, evaporate, evident
ethno (Gk. race, nation)	ethnocentric, ethnic, ethnography
eu (Gk. good)	eulogize, euphemism, euphoria
ex (L. from, out of)	expatriate, extort, exhaust
gamy (Gk. marriage)	exogamy, bigamy, monogamy
ge, geo (Gk. earth)	geography, geology, geometry
graph, grapho, graphy (Gk. write, writing)	phonograph, monograph, biography
gymn, gymno (Gk. naked, bare)	gymnasium, gymnosophist, gymnosperm
gyne, gyneco (Gk. woman)	gynecology, gynecocracy, misogyny
gyr, gyro (Gk. ring, circle)	gyrate, gyre, gyroscope
heter, hetero (Gk. different)	heterosexual, heterodox, heterogeneous
hom, homo (Gk. same, similar)	homogeneous, homosexual, homonym
hydr, hydro (Gk. water)	hydrophobia, hydrofoil, hydroelectric
hyper (Gk. above, beyond, super)	hyperbole, hyperactive, hypersensitive
idio (Gk. own, peculiar)	idiom, idiosyncrasy, ideology
inter (L. between, among)	interstellar, international, internecine
intra (L. within, during, between)	intramural, intrastate, intravenous
intro (L. inside, into, within)	introvert, introduce, introspection
logy (Gk. word, science)	analogy, mythology, biology

marine (L. sea)	submarine, marina, maritime
meter (Gk. measure)	thermometer, barometer, pentameter
micr, micro (Gk. small, short)	microscope, microcosm, micrometer
mis, miso (Gk. hatred)	misanthropist, misogynist, misogamy
mon, mono (Gk. alone, single)	monogamy, monologue, monosyllabic
multi (L. many, much)	multiple, multinational, multifarious
ne, neo (Gk. new, recent)	neologism, neon, neoclassicism
onym (Gk. name, word)	synonym, antonym, acronym
orth, ortho (Gk. straight, right, true)	orthodontist, orthography, orthodox
pan (Gk. all, completely)	panacea, panorama, pantheism
path, patho, pathy (Gk. suffering, emotion)	apathy, empathy, pathos
ped (L. foot)	biped, pedal, pedestrian
per (L. through, thoroughly)	perambulate, perception, percolate
peri (Gk. around, about, near)	periscope, perigee, periphery
phil, philo (Gk. loving, lover)	philosopher, philanthropist, Anglophile
phobe, phobia (Gk. fear)	hydrophobia, agoraphobia, claustrophobia
phone (Gk. sound)	telephone, phonology, homophone
phot, photo (Gk. light)	photograph, photosynthesis, photoelectric
pod (Gk. foot)	podium, pseudopodium, podiatry
poly (Gk. many)	polygamy, polyglot, polygon
pre (L. before, in front of)	prefix, preface, premarital
pro (L. before, in front of)	protract, protest, pro-American
prot, proto (Gk. before, primary)	protocol, protagonist, prototype

pseud, pseudo (Gk. false, sham)	pseudonym, pseudopod, pseudepigraphy
psyche (Gk. mind)	psychology, psychedelic, psychic
scope, scopy (Gk. viewing, observation)	microscope, telescope, horoscope
sophia (Gk. wisdom)	sophist, philosopher, sophomore
sub (L. under, beneath)	submarine, substitute, subsume
syn (Gk. with, together)	synchronize, synonym, synthesis
tel, tele (Gk. far, distant)	telephone, television, telegraph
therm, thermo (Gk. heat)	thermometer, thermal, thermodynamics
trans (L. across, beyond, through)	transcribe, transfer, transient

Works Cited

Akers, R. L. "Family Social Control." *Sociology, UKEssays,* 1998.

American Association of College and Research Libraries. *Common Ground at the Nexus of Information Literacy and Scholarly Communication.* 2013.

Anzaldúa, Gloria E. "How to Tame a Wild Tongue." *Borderlands/La Frontera: The New Mestiza.* Aunt Lute, 1987.

Baldwin, James. "A Report from Occupied Territory." *The Nation,* 11 July 1966.

Barber, Zachary. "Mutating Standards: Racial Representation in Comic Books." Student Essay.

Boggs, Tammy. "A Seasonal Twist." Student Essay.

Born, Debbie. "Rings to Ruin." Student Essay.

Brooks, David. "Baseball or Soccer?" *The New York Times,* 10 July 2014.

---. "The Cop Mind." *The New York Times,* 8 Dec. 2014.

---. "The Real Africa." *The New York Times,* 8 May 2014.

Burke, Kenneth. *The Philosophy of Literary Form.* 3rd. ed., U of California P, 1941.

Cedillo, Pete. " Lessons from the Military." Student Essay.

Chatfield, Tom. "I Type, Therefore I Am." *Aeon,* 27 May 2013.

Corder, Jim. W. *Rhetoric: A Text-Reader on Language and Its Uses.* Random House, 1965.

Council of Writing Program Administrators. *Framework for Success in Postsecondary Writing.* 2011.

Dillard, Annie. "This Is The Life." *Harper's Magazine,* June 2002, pp. 13-15.

"Distracted Driving: Think of Both Sides." Public Service Announcement. *Red Pepper.* Ekaterinburg, Russia, "That'll Make You Stop and Think." *Boredpanda.com.*

Franzen, Jonathan. "Liking Is for Cowards: Go for What Hurts." *The New York Times*, 28 May 2011.

Frey, R. G. "Pain, Vivisection, and the Value of Life." *Journal of Medical Ethics*, vol. 31, 2005, pp. 202-04. *Academic Search Complete.*

Gardner, John. *The Art of Fiction: Notes on Craft for Young Writers.* Knopf, 1983.

Gonzales, Andrés. " A New Life." Student Essay.

Haar, Catherine. *Revision: History, Theory, and Practice.* Parlor, 2006.

Hinson, Allison. "Horror Novels as Therapy." Student Essay.

Holifield, Krystal. "Getting Sober." Student Essay.

"Honda Helps Make the World a Little Safer—Safely." Honda Advertisement. Honda.

Hurston, Zora Neale. "How it Feels to Be Colored Me." 1928.

Jefferson, Thomas et al. *The Declaration of Independence.* 4 July 1776.

Jernigan, Michael. "Living the Dream." *The New York Times*, 11 Oct. 2009.

Johnson, Teddi Dineley. "Pedestrians: Take the Steps to Stay Safe." *The Nation's Health, American Public Health Association,* Apr. 2011.

Kenneally, Joyce. Student Essay.

King, Jr., Martin Luther. "Letter From Birmingham Jail." *Why We Can't Wait.* Harper, 1964, pp. 85-110.

Klinkenborg, Verlyn. "Our Vanishing Night." *National Geographic,* Nov. 2008.

Klosterman, Chuck. "My Zombie, Myself: Why Modern Life Feels Rather Undead." *The New York Times*, 3 Dec. 2010.

Kolbert, Elizabeth. *The Sixth Extinction: An Unnatural History.* Holt, 2014.

Kristof, Nicholas. "What ISIS Could Teach the West." *The New York Times*, 1 Oct. 2014.

---. "When Whites Just Don't Get It: Part 5." *The New York Times*, 29 Nov. 2014.

Lamott, Anne. "Shitty First Drafts." *Bird by Bird: Some Instructions on Writing and Life*. Pantheon, 1994.

LaRoque, Paula. "Use Comma Sense When Constructing Stories." *The Quill*, vol. 96. no. 2, 2008, p. 30.

Looper, Kathleen. "Going Home." Student Essay.

Loucel, Roberto. "Weight Lifters." Student Essay.

Marche, Stephen. "Is Facebook Making Us Lonely?" *The Atlantic*, May 2012, pp. 60-69.

Murry, Jennifer. "Wisdom." Student Essay.

Ogle, Donna. *K-W-L Chart*. 1986.

Perry, Imani. "Five Myths About Brown v. Board of Education." *The Washington Post*, 16 May 2014.

"Planting a Vegetable Garden." Student Essay.

Ravitch, Diane. "First, Let's Fire All the Teachers!" *Huff Post: Politics*, 8 Sept. 2012.

Riecke, Richard D., Malcom O. Sillars, and Tarla Rai Peterson. *Argumentation and Critical Decision Making*. 8th. ed., Pearson, 2013.

Rodriguez, Richard. "Mexicans in America." *Cato Unbound: A Journal of Debate*, 14 Aug. 2006.

Rogers, Carl. "Communication: Its Blocking and Its Facilitation." *Northwestern University Information*, vol. 20, no. 25, 1952, pp. 9-15.

Roy, Jona. "Pappadeaux and Joe's Crab Shack." Student Essay.

Solnit, Rebecca. "Poison Apples." *Harper's Magazine*, Dec. 2014, pp. 5-7.

Stavans, Ilan. *Spanglish: The Making of a New American Language*. HarperCollins, 2003.

Strunk, Jr., William, and E. B. White. *The Elements of Style*. 3rd ed., Macmillan, 1979.

Taylor, Andrew. "Immigration, Keystone Top First Day of Lame Duck." *PBS NewsHour,* 13 Nov. 2014.

Tyler, Alec. "Consequences of an Act." Student Essay.

Watterson, Bill. "Calvin and Hobbes." Comic strip, *Houston Chronicle,* 11 Feb. 1993.

Weissmann, Jordan. "The Decline of the American Book Lover." *The Atlantic,* 21 Jan. 2014.

Wilson, E. O. "Letter to a Southern Baptist Pastor." *The Creation: An Appeal To Save Life on Earth.* Norton, 2006.

---. "Why Humans, Like Ants, Need A Tribe." *Newsweek,* 2 April 2012.

"What is a Designer Baby?" *BIONET.* 2002.

Wong, Kate. "Neandertal Minds." *Scientific American,* Feb. 2015, pp. 36-43.

Zinsser, William. "Simplicity." *On Writing Well.* Harper, 1998.

Copyright Acknowledgments

Perry, Imani. "Five Myths About *Brown v. Board of Education*" from The Washington Post, May 16, 2014. Used with permission of the author. All rights reserved.

Ravitch, Diane. "First, Let's Fire All the Teachers" from *The Huffington Post*, Sept. 8, 2012. All rights reserved.

Rodriguez, Richard. "Mexicans in America" originally appeared in *Cato Unbound*, August 14, 2006. Copyright © 2006 by Richard Rodriguez. Reprinted by permission of Georges Borchardt, Inc., on behalf of the author.

Solnit, Rebecca. "Poison Apples" from *Harper's Magazine*. Copyright © 2014 by *Harper's Magazine*. All rights reserved. Reproduced from the December 2014 issue by special permission.

Wilson, E.O. "Letter to a Southern Baptist Pastor: Salutation" from *The Creation: An Appeal to Save Life on Earth*. Copyright © 2006 by Edward O. Wilson. Reprinted with permission of W.W. Norton. All rights reserved.

Wilson, E.O. "Why Humans, Like Ants, Need a Tribe" from *Newsweek*, April 2, 2012. Reprinted with permission. All rights reserved.

Zinsser, William. "Simplicity" from *On Writing Well*, Seventh (30th Anniversary) Edition, published by HarperCollins. Copyright © 1976, 1980, 1985, 1988, 1990, 1994, 1998, 2001, 2006 by William K. Zinsser. Reprinted by permission of the William K. Zinsser Trust.

Index